P9-CQK-066

MIGHT NATURE BE CANADIAN?

Might Nature Be Canadian?

Essays on Mutual Accommodation

WILLIAM A. MACDONALD

Published for the School for the
Study of Canada at Trent University
by McGill-Queen's University Press
Montreal & Kingston • London • Chicago

© William A. Macdonald 2020

ISBN 978-0-2280-0145-4 (cloth)
ISBN 978-0-2280-0146-1 (ePDF)
ISBN 978-0-2280-0147-8 (ePUB)

Legal deposit first quarter 2020
Bibliothèque nationale du Québec

Printed in Canada on acid-free paper

This publication is one of the outcomes of the Canadian Narrative Project hosted at Trent University by the School for the Study of Canada. The Canadian Narrative Project was designed to promote a broad and dynamic conversation of the shared and separate stories of the Canadian narrative and Canada's collective efforts at mutual accommodation. While the School for the Study of Canada facilitates the Canadian Narrative Project, the views expressed in this publication remain those of the author alone.

Funded by the   Financé par le
Government   gouvernement
of Canada   du Canada

  Canada Council   Conseil des arts
                      for the Arts   du Canada

We acknowledge the support of the Canada Council for the Arts.
Nous remercions le Conseil des arts du Canada de son soutien.

Library and Archives Canada Cataloguing in Publication

Title: Might nature be Canadian? : essays on mutual accommodation /
William A. Macdonald.
Other titles: Essays. Selections.
Names: Macdonald, William A. (William Atwood), author.
Description: Published for the School for the Study of Canada at
  Trent University. | Includes bibliographical references and index.
Identifiers: Canadiana (print) 20190205504 | Canadiana (ebook) 201902056 1x
  | ISBN 9780228001454 (cloth) | ISBN 9780228001461 (ePDF) | ISBN
  9780228001478 (ePUB)
Subjects: LCSH: Canada—Civilization—21st century. | LCSH: Globalization—Canada.
Classification: LCC FC95.5.M33 2020 | DDC 971—dc23

This book was typeset in 11/14 Sabon.

To Molly Anne – my wonder girl,
who has made possible everything I have achieved.

Contents

Foreword

As the twenty-first century ends its first two decades, the opaqueness of our future has never been thicker. An outbreak of fresh front lines of conflict, some military, many social, makes for a confusing time. That is why *Might Nature Be Canadian?* arrives at an important juncture as we seek the support necessary to help guide debate.

This book is about solutions to problems. Many of the problems are known already. Rather than list the familiar, let's simply describe them as powerful forces representing a truly global transition. In particular, this book comes to our aid as we ponder the question of what our future is to be.

I first met Bill Macdonald in 2014 when he asked me to lunch. "I have met every editor of *The Globe and Mail* since Dic Doyle (editor 1963–78)," he said, "and I want to meet you." I was just weeks on the job and was interested in hearing from a man with perspective.

My host turned out to be a man in a hurry – determined, focused, and a little unsure. Mr Macdonald knew enough to know what he didn't know, but after nine decades, he knows a lot. We could not foresee the changes then that are today part of the everyday lexicon – Brexit and Wexit, Prime Minister Trudeau II and his minority government, President Trump. We were more successful in foreseeing challenges brought on by interdependent trade relationships and a growing wave of nationalist fervour on many continents.

Assessing how we got here, and cogently arguing where we are headed, has become an increasingly rare quality. Analyzing what Canada can do about it is rarer still.

I was impressed with the thoughtfulness of what I heard and offered Mr Macdonald space in *The Globe and Mail* to further his arguments and to increase the intellectual capital the newspaper was putting into the market place. The book you are reading follows from his series of essays in the newspaper.

The greatest advantage of this book is the offer of fresh paths. How do we take the opportunities, including the natural bounty of Canada, and ensure a responsible future? How do we create national policy when the global trade routes and movement of humanity are so interconnected? The book's strength comes not from answers when they are found but from the tough questions that are asked.

Mr Macdonald has a no-nonsense approach. Neither hectoring nor omniscient, the book offers a confident assessment rooted in the lessons of history. Does history have anything to teach us? For those content to sweep our past away, this book will be an unsatisfying read. Mr Macdonald's conviction that history repeats, and that consideration of future challenges must confront past experiences, is refreshing. This analysis includes truth and reconciliation. It seeks an economy that represents something more than simple shareholder value. It provides clues about where we may make mistakes in our future and how best to reduce the errors. That is at times unfashionable thinking, but it is surely correct to argue on the thin line of our personal experiences that our young country is a place for ideas, a place of welcome, and a place with a bright future, all based on the principle of mutual accommodation.

Optimism is not in vogue these days, but it takes only a brief trip outside our borders to return to the realization of just what advantages we enjoy. Mr Macdonald writes that the story of humanity is about journeys – about how life itself is a form of migration in space and time. But the challenges at home are growing. "Most of us are not fear-driven refugees," he writes. "Yet many people who are physically safe in Canada still feel unsafe because of the multiple changes going on around them. They feel that Canada is somehow leaving them behind."

So for a country with such natural advantages, the biggest question Mr Macdonald poses is what we are going to use those advantages for. This book is something of a quest that offers a vision, not along party political lines, but for finding solid policy ground – one that will stand the test of time by putting humanity first amid competing economic and at times dangerous political pressures.

David Walmsley
Editor-in-Chief, *The Globe and Mail*
Toronto

———————

It is an honour and a privilege to be asked to open the conversation that William A. Macdonald, or Mr Macdonald as we call him, has invited Canadians to join with this timely and forceful book. He is what we would consider one of the great Elders of Canada. As a twenty-seventh generation Hereditary Chief from the Ahousaht First Nation, and as a member of an Indigenous family of Nuu-chah-nulth, Blackfoot, and Mohawk lineages, we can confirm that "Elder" in our cultural understanding and tradition refers to a village person of great experience and acquired intergenerational wisdom whose counsel is sought and respected by the community. Canada is one such village, and for many decades Mr Macdonald has applied both the wisdom of those who have come before him and his own lived experience and teachings. What gives great mark to his Elder status is that he has also valued and listened to the teachings and wisdom of those who are unlike him in order to make a contribution to the country that he loves.

In this book, Mr Macdonald has taken the best of what we know to be true of him in our friendship and brought it to his "friends" in Canada, including inviting those who may be wrestling with the construct of what Canada means to them. In our Nuu-chah-nulth language, he has done the important work of the leadership principle of "Tlowa-ee-stulth," which means the gentle pushing up against and "showing" a governance system and governing ideologies so that we may together reflect on what Canada means to us, how we experience Canada, and how we find a path forward that allows for the important

"seeing of one another." Mr Macdonald has the ability to inspire and
spark the curiosity in each of us in a loving way so that we can look
at problems together and imagine the true magic and possibility that
is before us. We would say that he captures in this conversation about
Canada the essence of "Ha-mat-tsup," which roughly translates as to
"show" or "surface" that which is not necessarily first seen. He has
done this in a way that compels us to have difficult conversations, so
that as individuals, as communities, as regions, and as Canada we can
"Ho-peet-stulth" (help one another), "Up-hai-stulth" (be kind to one
another), and "Ha-hope-stulth" (teach one another).

It wasn't until we as a couple left the world of politics five years
ago that we had a sense of connection with the country – a connection we had sought for many years. As activists, we had been
engaged in a struggle for Indigenous people and their rights, against
injustices, and that had led to a perceived and real disconnect from
Canada. This period of our lives preceded what we now understand
as Reconciliation, which has become a mainstay in the political language of our country. We, as a couple and as individuals, have found
ourselves in the same situation that Mr Macdonald wisely encourages Canada to embrace: to pursue self-discovery.

As we investigate and discuss Canada, we find that its story is both
tragic and heroic, a multiplicity of tales that weave together to create
an integrated and cohesive historical narrative that forms the back-
bone of today's expression of governance. As with any couple who
strive for a future together, we Canadians begin by being curious to
understand the lens of each other. Then we start to look through the
windows into the past and into the present, and we see what it was
that those who forged the first Indigenous-settler treaties saw 150
years ago – our shared humanity. We understand our inescapable
connection as feeling and thinking human beings, and accept that
our shared purpose and responsibility is one of forging a relationship
built on mutual understanding. We find gratitude in what we learn
about and see in one another, to the point where we simply cannot
imagine a life alone, without the other. We work every day to find
the good in each other, to hold onto it with care, even as we respect
healthy boundaries. We live our lives in the belief that we can make
one another great and good. We do so, first, by taking the time to
listen, to gain understanding and resist the urge of trying to fix one

another. We try to get closer and develop an affection, even to find love for one another – "Ya?ak stuthl" in our language. In this, as with any couple, we feel hope and optimism for our children and for generations to come.

As my grandmother said to me in 2008, when Prime Minister Harper offered an apology for the damage done through the tragedy of the residential school era, "They are just beginning to see us." In similar vein, Mr Macdonald, we are grateful for this book, and we see you. "Kleco Kleco" – deepest thanks.

Shawn Ah-up-wa-eek Atleo
Former National Chief of the Assembly of First Nations

Heather Atleo
Co-founder with her husband of the
Atleo Centre for Compassionate Leadership
Squamish, BC

Preface

The essays in this volume seek to advance a single and simple theme
– that mankind has found four better ways of going about things:
freedom, science-based technologies and processes, mutual accommodation, and compassion. These methods are best when they are
balanced and go hand in hand. Freedom and science have been dominant in the West since the Renaissance. This emphasis has led to two
results. It has brought the accumulated post-Renaissance achievements into today's first global moment in history. It has also provoked populism and the current rise of centrifugal forces within and
between countries. Mutual accommodation is urgently needed if the
outcome is to be bearable and a new Dark Age avoided.

I discovered Alfred North Whitehead at a bookstore near McGill
University when I was a student there in the years 1945–48. As a
professor at the University of Cambridge, Whitehead had been a
philosopher of mathematics and then of science. After he moved to
Harvard University in 1923, he became a philosopher of everything.
Recently, I have begun to wonder if two of Whitehead's ideas are
now coming together in Canada. First, civilization (Canada) is the
triumph of persuasion over force.* Second, quantum particles can be
in more than one place at the same time.† If true, that would mean

---

* Alfred North Whitehead, "From Force to Persuasion," *Adventures of Ideas*
(1933), chap. 5.
† Alfred North Whitehead, "The Quantum Theory," *Science and the Modern World*
(1925), chap. 8.

nature can be simultaneously both inflexible (what I call "either/or") and inclusive or accommodating (what I call "both/and"). Is it possible, then, that nature at its heart may be Canadian?

These two ideas caught my attention about seventy-five years ago. Recently, I told David Cameron, the dean of arts and science at the University of Toronto, that I thought I would begin the Preface to this book (largely *Globe and Mail* essays, with updates) with the question, "Might nature be Canadian?" He responded, "Not the first sentence of the preface, but the title of the book." And so it is.

Robert Wright, the American biologist who wrote *Nonzero: The Logic of Human Destiny* (1999), says: "The arrow of human history begins with the biology of human nature. That arrow ... points toward larger quantities of nonzero-sumness. As history progresses, human beings find themselves playing nonzero-sum games with more and more other human beings. Interdependence expands, and social complexity grows in scope and depth." It sounds not unlike Canada's path so far.

The world has changed enormously since I wrote my early *Globe and Mail* essays. First came Brexit, then President Donald Trump, who has been withdrawing the United States from global responsibilities while President Xi Jinping has proclaimed himself president of China for life and is fast building his boat, rail, and road links to Europe through the Middle East. In the midst of a lot of bad non-Canadian news, Canada has two strong stories – the new path forward on the Indigenous people front; and Toronto as it becomes one of the great global cities of the next fifty years.

Here is my view of where Canada stands right now. We have come for the first time in history to a moment of huge (potentially overwhelming) global transition, which began when the West moved on from the Middle Ages to the Renaissance. Freedom and science have overwhelmed mutual accommodation and compassion. The relative weakness of the latter two has resulted in the dangerous centrifugal imbalances that have emerged in the Western world of the early twenty-first century. The West has many key strengths, but it needs to make better use of them. It needs more mutual accommodation to do so.

A better balance of the four better ways of going about things has become urgent, if the world of the future is to be bearable. Otherwise, the world will be dominated again by force and violence, and the achievements of civilization we have seen since the end of the Middle Ages will recede or disappear. In the intertwined world we now live in, boundaries are still needed, just as they are in families between parents and children. But the old tribal, ethnic, religious, and national boundaries are not by themselves enough to make either our identities or our physical selves safe.

Two big changes are going on in Canada within the vast transformational forces that are impacting the whole world right now. First, Canada is emerging as a different kind of great country for a different kind of world. Second, Canada has always been dependent on others – first, the United Kingdom, and then the United States. Today it remains simultaneously intertwined with the rest of the world, yet it has never been more on its own. During the last year it has found itself almost entirely alone opposite an aggressive United States, China, and Saudi Arabia. Trends of the last two decades have seen ever greater divergence between Canada and the United States. This gap will keep getting larger, unless and until the United States can make a big dramatic pivot toward more mutual accommodation and inclusiveness.

Canada has fallen short of what its economy needs for almost fourteen years, after the twenty very good years of increasing economic and financial discipline under Prime Ministers Brian Mulroney and Jean Chrétien. Neither of its two good news stories – improving the relationship with the Indigenous people and Toronto – will be easy or assured. Still, they are happening after a long sixty-year period (commencing in 1960 with the Quiet Revolution in Quebec) in which Canada successfully confronted and overcame strong existential and identity threats – threats that Europe and the United States are themselves now beginning to face and which they may or may not overcome.

If the rest of the world goes badly wrong (which it may), things will also get very hard for Canada, despite its vast array of unmatched strengths. Canada came together to confront a United States in existential political turmoil and convinced of its "manifest destiny" on the North American continent. It has often had to stand up to the United States and has always found a way to do so. Now it also has to do the same opposite an overreaching President Xi Jinping in China.

The way forward for Canada, Toronto, and Indigenous relations will take place within increasingly challenging global and domestic conditions whose outcomes are extremely uncertain. Global economic stresses intensified in the 1980s as Ronald Reagan launched the United States on an economy-wide debt spree that included not only government but the business and household sectors as well. The economic and financial overreach that started with Reagan was followed more than two decades later by the overreach of China's global economic surge in 2005. Together, they created the worldwide global and domestic economic, financial, and political imbalances that led, first, to the post–Lehman crises and now the populism and centrifugal forces in the West – Brexit, followed by the election of Donald Trump and resurgent nationalism in Europe. Under Trump, the United States is again headed into high levels of debt, largely limited so far to the US federal government. China is now encountering the contradictory stresses of trying to live in one country and one world with two systems.

The convergence of the forces of freedom and science is leading to a moment of huge transformation similar, perhaps, to the birth of the Renaissance six centuries ago. This scale of current change creates unavoidable risks for everyone. There are, however, two counterforces to extreme bad outcomes: stronger and broader global economic underpinnings; and an intertwined world where half of the population is now middle class with a big stake in outcomes.

Canada is arguably the best place to be today, despite its current pressing challenges of competitiveness and living within its means. Canada's net country and household-sector debt are not yet improving enough, despite recent apparently strong Canadian economic numbers (that may not be quite as lastingly strong as they look). The recent slightly lower Canadian consumption is likely the result of an expected Bank of Canada path of keeping interest rates higher than in a United States that has started to lower its interest rates, reinforced by ongoing anxiety about the future of the Canadian economy – an anxiety partly driven by Trump's presidency.

Canada's mutual accommodation ways are desperately needed by the world – most urgently by the United States, China, and the European Union. It would be in Canada's own interest to play whatever international role it can. Our history with compassion and mutual accommodation can balance the power of freedom and science/technology that have become dominant in the West and could yet destroy our civilization. To survive, it is essential that those nations normally attached to force at home and abroad discover that mutual accommodation is the better way for countries to settle their differences and live together peacefully (and competitively) on the same planet.

The immediate economic challenges may be more likely to flow not from today's trade wars but from new financial and/or economic crises in 2020–22 and battles over technology. These crises will probably be difficult to overcome because of the current US federal debt surge and an excessive and over-long US monetary stimulus. Belatedly, the US monetary stimulus finally appeared to be on a reduction path led by the Federal Reserve (though stalled right now), but it has yet to reach positive net interest rates (after inflation). So far, it has been normalizing, not tightening, rates. The rising trade protectionism is increasingly detrimental for both the global economy and global peace. The looming struggles between China and the West/United States will be more and more over global leadership in the technologies of the future. A better-balanced global economy is needed for a bearable outcome for everyone.

The world needs the United States and China to see that the way forward is a twofold task. Their first task is to work together for a reshaped stable global economic and geopolitical order that reflects the technology, globalization, and related societal changes now underway. Their second task is to compete against each other within that order for whatever ascendancy they choose to seek. It is vital for the whole world (including for the superpowers themselves) that their rivalry take place within a fundamentally stable, fair, and balanced order. Otherwise, there will be no winners – only losers (a repeat – or even worse – of the 1914–45 era).

The West/United States retains substantial advantages over China in terms of military prowess, technology, freedom, and alliances. These advantages are weakening in the post-Trump, post-Brexit world. Their decline is due more to what each of the United States and Europe are doing to themselves than to increasing Chinese strengths. Those strengths are large and real, but they are also limited. The astute Nomura Group chief economist, Richard Koo, has recently drawn attention to the Chinese need to avoid the middle-income trap, where the success that comes with higher incomes also brings higher costs – and those costs in turn send production to lower-cost countries. Until now, China's rise has been on its own terms, but that has changed. China is currently in overreach, at the same moment that the Trump United States is in both overreach and underreach – partly the result of its disruptive withdrawal from its economic, financial, and geopolitical overreach of the previous twenty years. In addition to the middle-income trap confronting China, the country, because of its demographic imbalance, also faces a surplus drop in its share of global exports by 2040.

Will it be China or the United States that finally gets its reach closer to the demands of reality? Or will they get there more or less at the same time? Or will they both fail? China overdid it in 2005, with its huge global export surge. It was foreseeable that this surge, unless moderated, would affect US politics negatively for longer-term Chinese interests. During my visit to China in 2010, I predicted this outcome in both Shanghai and Beijing. I also said, at an earlier 2009 post–Lehman Brothers symposium in Toronto, that there was a real risk that the post-war inclusive global economic and financial order would not be sustainable, in part because China's export surge was bad for both the United States and China.

In the years before President Xi Jinping and President Trump came to power, China was primarily seen by most countries in the West as a market opportunity and a low-cost supplier. Now, China is increasingly regarded as using its growing economic clout coercively and going too far in stealing Western technology. A US/China mutual accommodation – what the world most needs – looked doable before Trump and Xi, but now it seems less achievable. It is not impossible, however. The rising economic imbalances that led to the post–Lehman crises – excessive demand in the United States and insufficient demand in China, along with Germany and Japan continuing to have excessive current account surpluses – persist as the current economic expansion moves toward its end.

Both China and the United States face huge challenges in domestic economic management and in related domestic political evolution and stability. China is becoming more aggressive (and less governance reform and rule of law oriented) on the domestic politics front, while the United States is more domestically and globally politically divisive. China has understood better than the West that it needs a social contract on which its domestic political stability rests. This contract in turn requires a stable global economic order, as well as for China to overcome the middle-income trap and minimize its demographic aging challenges. The United States already faces an identity challenge. It could also face a potential existential political challenge in its unresolved gender/patriarchy issues (pollster Michael Adams says that only 23 percent of Canadians think men should dominate the family, but 50 percent of Americans hold that belief; one hundred years ago, the percentage in both countries was 95 percent). The US patriarchy challenge could conceivably become today's equivalent of the existential US race/slavery/Civil War challenge in the nineteenth century. China has no such existential or identity problems. It must, however, find a political way of dealing with its vastly changed post-Mao political and economic world at home. Both of the United States and China require a minimum level of global economic and political stability to address their domestic political challenges successfully. Neither has either one right now.

The recent important book by Graham Allison, a Kennedy School professor at Harvard, titled *Destined for War: Can America and China Escape Thucydides's Trap* (2017), investigates the failure of the established power, Sparta, to cope with the rising power of Athens. Two huge differences between today's world and the worlds in which Athens (in the fifth century BC) and Germany (1914–45) were new rising powers provide grounds for hope. First, the United States, despite its Trump-inflicted self-harm, is on the whole still relatively stronger than China, though that advantage cannot be guaranteed forever. It should, however, last long enough for the United States to recover the real sources of its greater strengths. Second, the world is simply too intertwined for either the United States or China to separate from it. As Quebec premier Robert Bourassa told a small group privately some thirty years ago at the height of Canada's Quebec separatism crisis, "Even if Quebec voted to separate, it could not do so, because we are too intertwined." Accepting the reality of "intertwined" is the path forward for both China and the United States.

Whichever one of them accepts that reality in practice will do best over both the short and the long haul.

As never before in its history, Canada will have to fit its own challenges into those much bigger ones facing the rest of the world. No country will prove big enough or strong enough to avoid doing the same to varying degrees. The idea of sovereignty free of the necessities of accommodation with others is a dangerous fantasy – the Brexit and Trump delusions. The post-1945 world that emerged from the multiple horrors of the 1914–45 era introduced new ideas, visions, and projects. They led to a much more prosperous and peaceful era. You cannot fight something with nothing. The world and Canada once again need new visions, ideas, and projects, but the time for finding them is rapidly shortening. As many countries as possible need to act decisively and quickly. Unfortunately, in human history, foresight is rarely forthcoming when it is needed. Too often, it takes ultimately unbearable horror stories to force the new ways forward – as after the 1914–45 years and after the pre-1815 Napoleonic era.

The great task of the post-2019 world is to find a less costly way forward to a better world. Great power dominance that works only for the great powers should no longer be conceivable to even the most super of superpowers. Trump disagrees. So may Xi. But it is not clear yet where the United States and China will come out. Right now, China is into the kind of overreach that brought the collapse of the Soviet Union and threatens today's politically dysfunctional Trump America. China seems to understand that it cannot go alone and that it needs the rest of the world. But does it fully understand what it will have to do to continue the amazing economic achievements it has made since 1978? It made the right decision to choose the economy over politics forty years ago, but, as in baseball, it will need more than one pitch to keep winning. China is no exception to that rule, nor is the United States. Both countries face big choices they are not yet ready for.

The centrifugal forces now besetting the West are looking for a new direction and momentum. The news from China is that it too has the same needs. The West found a post-1945 path forward that worked, as did China after 1980. Each one is now weakening and coming up against strong counterforces. The West is withdrawing from leadership of an inclusive global order, while in China, President

Xi, speaking on the fortieth anniversary of Deng Xiaoping's great initiative that unshackled the economy, failed to signal his support for ongoing reform. Instead, he doubled down on the importance of continuing political leadership by the Communist Party – something that has meant, under Xi, a steady retreat from the reforms that have transformed China. History has shown that separating economics from politics has never worked well for any long period of time. It is unlikely that increased Communist control of business in China will work, without more legally protected democracy and freedom. China and the United States each have to make the huge strategic decision that they will need each other for as far ahead as they can see, and then do what it takes.

My personal and professional life has been dominated by three different kinds of power: love (family); persuasion (mutual accommodation); and force (state-enforced law and strong economic players). More than seventy years as an adult has taught me that the best outcomes result from the mutual accommodation of all three forms of power. There are many forms of separateness and connectedness in the world. Each is strengthened, and all do best, when they can be mutually accommodated. The biggest personal mutual accommodation is of the self with others. Erik Erickson wrote that being adult is asserting oneself in ways that enhance the ability of others to assert themselves. Jesus told his followers to love others like oneself. The mutual accommodation of others and oneself is the biggest and most rewarding mutual accommodation of all.

My life has been blessed by my family of origin and by my wife, Molly Anne, and our children and grandchildren. We have also each been blessed by being born and living our adult lives in Canada. Our youngest son married a Chinese-Canadian young woman born to two mainland Chinese parent immigrants to New Brunswick. In her remarks at the post-wedding dinner, Molly Anne spoke: "Bill and I are both Wasps. We thought all our children would marry Wasps. Only one has. Now, our youngest child is marrying a woman from the great civilization of China. We think we are the better for it." She got a standing ovation.

The majority of essays in this volume were published originally in the *Globe and Mail* between 2015 and 2018. In the time since they appeared, the world has changed completely – with the election of President Donald Trump in the United States, the life appointment of President Xi Jiping in China, the results of the Brexit referendum in Britain, the increasing influence in the world of President Vladimir Putin in Russia, Kim Jong-un in North Korea, and other dictatorial leaders, and the general weakening of the liberal global system of agreements and trade. So far as Canada is concerned, neither the world nor our particular neighbourhood is as good as it appeared to be in mid-2015. As we prepare for the future, it is imperative that we re-evaluate our position, stand more on our own, and make certain we look after our own politics, society, and economy. To update my original essays to mid-2019, I have added introductions to each chapter and, in addition, written several new essays on topics of current concern.

Acknowledgments

In preparing this book for publication, I have been helped by many people, and I would like to take this opportunity to thank them. They are, in alphabetical order: Peter Andersen, Heather Atleo, Shawn Atleo, Kendall Behnish, David Cameron, Ramsay Cook, John Crow, Wendy Dobson, John English, Daniel Gagnier, Susan Golets, Nestor Golets, William Humphries, William Innes, Richard Koo, David Macdonald, Dougal Macdonald, Alex Macdonald, Tiff Macklem, Peter Mansbridge, Pamela McGregor, David Mulroney, Julia O'Sullivan, Terry O'Sullivan, John Parisella, Rosemary Shipton, Dr Edward Shorter, Suzanne Stewart, Dr Charlotte Stuart, Harry Swain, Richard Vipond, David Walmsley, Jean Wittenberg, and Martin Wolf.

MIGHT NATURE BE CANADIAN?

PART ONE

On Mutual Accommodation

What Is Mutual Accommodation?

INTRODUCTION

Mutual accommodation is about co-operation, compromise, and inclusion. It helps to get things done by making room for others, though some pressure or force might be needed along the way. It strengthens, not weakens, identities. In an ideal world, everyone would be a winner. Mutual accommodation makes that outcome more possible. Throughout its history, Canada has exhibited a stronger drive toward mutual accommodation than any other country – an approach that has allowed its increasingly diverse citizens to live together peacefully and successfully, even as they retain their own culture, language, and religion. The United States has the opposite drive – to division – a characteristic that, under the present government, is becoming ever more powerful.

In the current troubled times, the world must adopt its own forms of mutual accommodation models in order to avoid the violence, hatred, and economic disruptions of the 1914–45 period. Family therapists say that sometimes we must fight, because fighting is the strongest form of communication, but if we are going to fight, we must know when to stop and how to negotiate (a high bar few can reach). Canada is simultaneously a huge story (because of the high relevance today of its mutual accommodation ways) and a small story (its population equalled only .005 percent of the world population in 2017).

Little England started to spread freedom around the world five centuries ago. Little Canada needs to spread mutual accommodation today. Great leaders and great countries make many mistakes, even

big ones, but they get the most important things right. The United
States is a great country now at risk of getting some great things
wrong. It made a huge historic pivot in 1945. It must make another
such pivot now. Will it be up to it? Mutual accommodation is the
only way forward if the United States is to remain a great country,
though it will long remain important.

The world is "both/and" (flexible) and "either/or" (inflexible). It
is best when necessary either/or-ness can be accommodated within a
larger both/and-ness. It is not zero-sum – it is non-zero sum, which is
the way of nature.

I. THE NATURE OF MUTUAL ACCOMMODATION*

Charles Darwin's ideas about evolution and the survival of the fittest
portray a world that is competitive, one divided into winners and
losers. On this basis, co-operation and accommodation are for losers
– as US President Donald Trump, the champion of unbridled competition, might put it.

But they are not. The simple words "mutual accommodation" seem
to resonate as a way of going about big things in a much better way.
They also reflect the broadly shared way in which Canadians have
made their country work – not always, but more often than not. As
the world grapples with social upheaval and economic turmoil, it is
time to look at the concept more closely.

The simplest way of thinking about mutual accommodation is that
it helps to get things done by making room for others. It is often
about compromise, and always requires an understanding of what
each side needs. Inclusion is the key driver. Mutual accommodation
may be about shared purposes, values, interests, and beliefs; it may
simply make room for different approaches; or it may just make a
particular goal possible. Each objective may be very hard to achieve
– indeed, impossibly hard at times. Although mutual accommodation
is big and its reach inexhaustible, it does not always work, and force
may be needed along the way.

* Published as "Time to Reconsider the Nature of Life, Liberty, and the Pursuit of
Happiness," *Globe and Mail*, August 29, 2015.

Mutual Accommodation Today

The big challenges facing mutual accommodation traditionally involve clashes over nationality, race, ethnicity, religion, language, territory, status, resources, and money – and how best to overcome them. In the early twenty-first century we are seeing the resurgence of some of these clashes with potentially dangerous intensity, as well as the addition of new challenges posed by population growth and the use and abuse of the planet. At some point, and in many different ways, these dual challenges are likely to bring enormous pressures on our ability to achieve mutual accommodation.

Doing well most of the time is not enough. Throughout history there have been admirable examples of the achievement of mutual accommodation. In terms of individual countries, Canada is probably the standout. As Ken Dryden, the hockey great who became a federal Cabinet minister, put it, Canada has become a "do what it takes" country. However, to continue to succeed, we need to understand not only our mutual accommodation triumphs but our failures, too.

In 1859 the English political philosopher John Stuart Mill published his famous 50,000-word essay *On Liberty*, and the same year Darwin's *On the Origin of Species* appeared, describing evolution as the product of "the struggle for life." But just as liberty was no more important an idea in Mill's day than mutual accommodation is for our times, US journalist Robert Wright has quite a different interpretation of Darwin's thinking.

In his book *Nonzero: The Logic of Human Destiny* (1999), Wright argues that biological and cultural evolution are shaped and directed primarily by what he calls "nonzero-sumness" – a term used in game theory to describe co-operative games in which both sides win (two sums rather than the zero-sum conclusion in competitive games). Although he accepts the idea of natural selection, he argues that throughout human history we have evolved to states of increasing complexity – and greater rewards for complexity. This evolution has been more adaptable and inclusive (both/and) than rigid and exclusive (either/or) – but always involves both. We have reached the stage where we need to move beyond winners and losers to inclusion and collaboration.

The deepest, broadest mutual accommodation would be a world where there is room for everyone to be a winner – if they so choose. This goal may forever be beyond humanity's reach, but grasping for it would transform the world. If the success of some groups or countries over a full life cycle did not blunt the potential for success of others, then all the winners could participate in a world of progress and accomplishment akin to the mature stage in human development described by the German-American psychoanalyst Erik Erikson.

Shared and Separate Stories

Some people see separate stories as a source of Canadian strength – and they are. The co-existence of many separate stories is one form of mutual accommodation. Non-inclusive societies like only one story. But shared stories can also be advantageous.

Separate stories are stronger if there is a real shared story (not one constructed for political or self-serving purposes) that includes all members of the population. Mutual accommodation is about opening up possibilities, not narrowing them. Canada's shared mutual accommodation story excludes no particular separate story, but it can change the historical and conceptual contexts in which these separate stories are perceived. Or, as the Austrian psychotherapist Alfred Adler put it, what happens is important, but how it is perceived can have even more important consequences. We must pay attention to perception.

The separateness of things is more than the breakup or disruption of their everyday connectedness, and the connectedness of things always reconnects what is separate. I have observed this dynamic at the heart of everything that happens and use it to figure out what is really going on. It has never let me down, and it applies to how separate and shared stories relate.

Successes and Failures

A world of two sums (win/win) that add up to a more than one zero sum (win/lose) moves beyond the political compromises that have made Canada possible. It leads to a more inclusive Canada that affects everyday life and cultural attitudes. Canadians today are more familiar than ever with the need for political compromise. We are not likely to see any major political party push for a divisive program based on its own narrow-base prejudices, as the Conservatives did with conscription during the First World War. It took the party sixty-five years to recover in Quebec. Mackenzie King learned that lesson as prime minister, and he went on to become the great consolidator of Sir Wilfrid Laurier's political vision of public purpose through compromise. A solid majority of Canadians like inclusion – witness the fact that Canada is one of few Western countries without serious divisions over immigration.

Throughout our history, political leaders devoted to mutual accommodation, along with their followers, have made Canada a coast-to-coast-to-coast country, despite the pressures of an expansionist United States and the challenges of French-English and Catholic-Protestant divisions. Without war or even much violence, Canada became a country – and stayed together. It overcame the same kind of national and religious differences that most countries find very hard to manage.

Canada's mutual accommodation challenges between 1867 and 1945 were primarily political. They revolved around French and English, Quebec and the rest of the country, language and schools – all deep, fundamental issues that were settled through compromise. The arrival of waves of immigrants from all over the world in the twentieth century moved Canada beyond these issues. Since 1945, Canada has used political compromise and inclusion to consolidate two great strategic and structural achievements: embracing the differences we find in our society, and handling the Quebec separatist threat to the nation's future.

Canada has also had its failures, most enduring in its relations with the First Nations (and which I believe are about to improve). Other episodes include the racism that excluded a shipload of Sikhs from landing in British Columbia in 1914; the anti-Semitism that kept out Jews who had escaped the Nazis in 1939; the internment of Japanese-Canadians during the Second World War and the confiscation of their property; and the confinement of Doukhobor children in the 1950s so they could be forced to go to school. As everywhere in the world, there has also been some violence in individual labour disputes. The positive news is that, apart from the unfinished business with First

Nations, these sorts of regressions have not occurred during the last
half-century in Canada. Over all, the magnitude of our achievement
outweighs the shortfalls.

Canada and the World

We engage in many voluntary acts of mutual accommodation every
day, such as letting people with disabilities go first in line. These acts
are easy. Even letting one's spouse have her or his way is not really
that hard most of the time. However, the kind of lasting mutual
accommodation that involves political compromise, compassion,
freedom, and the law can be hard, at least at the start.

Canada's mutual accommodation has focused on the big, hard-
to-manage divisions within societies and between countries. Before
1867 there was the *Quebec Act of 1774* and the Lafontaine-Baldwin
partnership in 1848. Then followed Confederation itself (in a form
flexible enough to centralize for war, counter economic catastrophe, and return to a more decentralized world as times changed),
a French-Catholic prime minister (Laurier) only twenty-nine years
later, and getting through two divisive world wars. More recently
there has been the Charter of Rights and Freedoms, with its notwithstanding clause – which was forced on Pierre Trudeau by the
provinces but went on to save the country by allowing Quebec to
pass Bill 101 and protect the French language. A similar clause in the
US Constitution would negate the right-wing claim that the courts
are overriding elected representatives. In Canada, however, the courts
can be overruled if politicians think the electorate is ready to see the
Charter overridden. The asymmetric elements in national medicare
and the Canada Pension Plan are also ways of accounting for differences among provinces.

The pursuit of public purpose through compromise is harder for
Americans for two main reasons. First, public purpose runs against
the grain of many Americans, although they have still managed to
achieve a lot of it at the federal level (too much for some). Second,
the fact that the country got started with one war and was preserved
with another has put force in the driver's seat in a way that has never
happened in Canada. Still, the United States has also had its own
great mutual accommodation moments:

- crafting the Constitution, with representation by population winning for the presidency and the House of Representatives, and equality of the states winning for the Senate;
- leading the great post-1945 achievement based on broadening the inclusive order in the world, containing what cannot be included, and acting collectively;
- expanding civil rights, as the US political system responded to a mostly non-violent movement.

The key mutual accommodation challenges in the United States are unresolved racist attitudes, equal race-related rights protection, and the current divisive turmoil of its politics. No other country, however, has ever had so many separate and diverse sources of initiating action. Also, the United States probably has more individuals capable of being leaders in mutual accommodation than any other country. Unfortunately, a broad swath of public opinion does not yet accept the necessity of compromise and flexibility.

In the aftermath of Europe's near suicide – two wars and the Holocaust – the rise of the European Union represents another great achievement in mutual accommodation. There is still a lot of unfinished business, however, particularly in the economically strained Eurozone. Europe may well be in the early uncertain stages of its own existential crisis. But Germany's decision to accept 800,000 or more refugees is remarkable by the standards of all history.

The big challenge today is a crowded world – there are too many people, too many ideas, too much change, and too much carbon to continue with the present order. We must move to a system of broader mutual accommodation in order to build the foundation for a better world of wider prosperity – where more people will live in peace and safety. Over the last two centuries Canada has been able to find its way to mutual accommodation, in part because it developed in a place and at a time that had none of these problems of overcrowding. Its physical space was huge for its sparse population, change was slow, and new ideas had the time to take hold.

Nowhere in the world today is there anything like the usable physical space Canadians and Americans had during their formative years. It is imperative we find ways to create more safe, socio-cultural space where individuals and groups can find, and be, themselves. Confident self-responsibility is the surest path to workable mutual accommodation – and much else.

Neitzsche's will to power was based on his stated rejection of compassion and mutual accommodation (he used those two words). The will to power – the opposite to mutual accommodation – underlay the European hell of the first half of the twentieth century. Power to contain – and in rare cases, to win – is crucial. The power to impose, no matter the purpose, is what the twenty-first century cannot accommodate.

2. CANADA'S MUTUAL ACCOMMODATION STORY*

In his Charles R. Bronfman lecture in 2000, Ken Dryden, the great Canadiens goaltender, compared national games in the United States and Canada. Football, he said, more so than baseball, requires central control – the opposite of hockey. In hockey, once the puck is dropped, there is chaos. The only choice players have is to do what it takes. The example of Canada's game has helped to shape Canada.

The Canadian story has always been different from the American – one of evolution, not revolution; persuasion rather than force; and compromise over winning. Its initial English and French connections were gradually weakened, not ruptured. In contrast, the United States was formed and preserved by force. Both the American break from Britain in 1775–83 and the split between North and South in 1861–65 were sudden and violent. Canadian history, in contrast, has always been more political than military.

Since Canada began as a nation – Quebec in 1608 and then Confederation in 1867 – it has had three big achievements. First, despite its difficult geography and challenging history, with its French/English split and proximity to the United States, it has survived, not just as a nation but with one province, Quebec, distinctive in language and religion. Second, Canada has consolidated its territory from the Atlantic to the Pacific and north to the Arctic. Finally, despite divisions of nationality, culture, language, religion, and class, it has developed a political and socio-cultural outlook that works. Its

* Published in the *Globe and Mail*, May 21, 2018.

one big failure has been with the Indigenous people, although that is now beginning to be addressed.

One simple idea captures the Canadian story: use words, not force; make railways, not war. It is a story driven by persuasion. Alfred North Whitehead, the great philosopher from Cambridge and Harvard universities, said civilization is the triumph of persuasion over force. One could say Canada is also the triumph of persuasion over force. Today, Western civilization itself is at risk – only the spread of mutual accommodation can save it. There is no other acceptable civilization on hand to replace it.

Canada's defining narrative began early, with reliance by European traders and settlers on the Indigenous people in a difficult geography. From the beginning, it has put practical considerations ahead of nationalism, ethnic difference, religion, class and ideology – the sources of division in post-Renaissance Europe. Over the years, Canada has extended this tradition of mutual shaping and accommodation. It has not been entirely free of violence, but its primary markers have been a vision of where it wants to be and the reality of what works on the ground. The combination of stability, balance, trusted institutions, asymmetry, and accommodation alongside simultaneous equal and special treatment for its citizens has made Canada's mutual accommodation ways possible.

Canadians have exhibited a stronger drive toward mutual accommodation than any other country. As a result, Canada has become a different kind of great country for a different kind of world, and is prepared to enter the next stage of world history. Mutual accommodation is not the answer for every problem, but for the next decades, its presence or absence will shape the world. The more it spreads, the better the world will be. If it fails, the outcome could be worse than in the 1914–45 period.

Canadian federalism's way of governing diversity could provide a stable global path forward beyond nationalism and the nation state. The United States, China, and Russia are nuclear-powered, inflexible, force-based nation states with powerful nationalisms. Their effective reach has shrunk. The West must believe in itself but stop thinking that its ways of doing things will suit every country. China must learn the dangers of overreach and underreach from the mistakes of Western powers – most recently, the United States.

Canada has mostly done what it takes for diverse people to live successfully together. It has found that the more one accommodates the strengths of other individuals, groups, or countries, the stronger one becomes. The United States, in contrast, focuses on ideology too much. Ideology divides and excludes too much reality – a bad way forward in today's world. It would do well to heed Canada's mutual accommodation ways, where no one size fits all, every outcome is custom made, and you do what it takes to make things work.

The American psychotherapist Erik Erickson said that being an adult was asserting oneself in ways that help others to assert themselves – a tough kind of mutual accommodation. The world needs more adult leaders and followers. The Canada miracle is that it has often had enough of both. The Canadian mystery is why?

3. MUTUAL ACCOMMODATION: AN IDEA WHOSE TIME HAS COME*

The world has never had more people, more diversity, or less-robust borders – it has never been more connected, yet disconnected. These trends will continue – the result of six centuries of freedom and technology that have weakened previous sources of Western cohesion. The need for mutual accommodation is urgent if we are to live in a bearable world.

Mutual accommodation is not a path to eliminate power and force, but rather a way for humans to better manage them both. It makes room for others. It is often about compromise and always requires understanding of what every player requires. Inclusion is key. Mutual accommodation may be about shared purposes, values, interests, and beliefs, or it may simply make a goal doable. Despite its inexhaustible reach, it does not always work. Force is sometimes needed, though applying force requires knowing how far to go and when to stop.

Mutual accommodation demands careful listening and speaking, and the belief that a shared and meaningful order lies at the heart of

* Published as "Missing in Action: Mutual Accommodation," *Globe and Mail,* May 16, 2018.

things. Geography creates problems in communication, while abrupt breaks from history can lead to even bigger breaks. The US Civil War lasted just four years, but its divided aftermath persists to this day. Force can bring lasting political turmoil, while persuasion can take longer. Its results, however, last longer, too.

In the twentieth century there were two great mutual accommodations on the world stage: the non-violent resistance movements led by Mahatma Gandhi, Martin Luther King Jr., and Nelson Mandela; and the US-led broadening of the inclusive global order after 1945, which contained those countries and forces that were not yet ready for inclusion. The world has become too intertwined for power and force to hold sway alone. Mutual accommodation is difficult and, to succeed, it needs support from free markets, a robust media, fearless universities, institutions that deliver the rule of law, and democratic governance that delivers.

Honda Motor Company was founded in 1959 and produced its first automobile in 1970. It never bought into the Ronald Reagan/ Margaret Thatcher mantra of "shareholder value" as the primary driver of business. Rather, it looked at all stakeholders – suppliers, consumers, workers, and communities – not just investors, in its business decisions. That is mutual accommodation, Honda-style. When Honda decided to establish a plant in Brazil, the government wanted it to be in the Amazon Valley – a location where none of the workforce in the assembly plant could read an operator's manual. Honda found a way around that, without diminishing any standards. It achieved the best kind of win-win mutual accommodation. Back in Japan, Honda built an assembly plant in Kyushu; 70 percent of the employees hired had physical disabilities. This inclusiveness shaped the plant from day one and was not just an add-on.

Ray Dalio, the author of *Principles: Life and Work* (2017), is the founder and co-chairman of Bridgewater Associates – one of the world's largest and best-performing hedge funds (with about US$160 billion in assets under management). His tenets of radical transparency, believability weighting, and idea meritocracy, integrated into algorithms, have created a recipe for highly successful decision-making about investments. Markets are largely effective but imperfect instruments for mutual accommodation. In Mr Dalio's system, algorithms provide the basic financial-market data for specific investments. A specialized group of people then apply their well-disciplined thinking to each case, resulting in the best investment decisions. In a tough world, this method provides a hard-nosed successful mutual accommodation way to invest.

2

The Need for Strong Institutions, Leaders, and Policies

INTRODUCTION

The greatest threat to our Western democracies comes not from totalitarian states but from within – from the accelerating centrifugal forces of populism in our own countries. Together, the 2016 US elections and Brexit – the British decision to leave the European Union – threaten the West with political turmoil. To restore equilibrium following the catastrophe of September 11, 2001, the financial collapse of 2008, and the disaffection of all those citizens who feel left behind by governments and society, we desperately need new visions, ideas, and projects, and a reshaped, inclusive world order.

Before we can achieve this goal, we will require leaders and followers as well as institutions that can be trusted. All our institutions are experiencing trust deficits. They are often justified, but we need institutions we can minimally trust. Erich Fromm, the Frankfurt-born psychologist, said that the rise of Hitler was made possible by a flight from freedom. Americans too often regard freedom as the absence of restraints. Fromm saw that aspect, but he also realized that freedom needs to be constrained by our shared humanity and what others need. The only freedom that is worthwhile needs to be limited, but more by ourselves than others. Mutual accommodation is one of the best sources of needed limits. It constitutes an accepted blend of inner and outer restraint.

The whole world, not just the West, has been increasingly driven by two powerful forces: liberty and science. The rigid either/or forces have steadily overbalanced the flexible both/and capacities for compassion and mutual accommodation. Both forces originate in the West and have moved on to the rest of the world. This lack of balance has become the central challenge of the twenty-first century.

In *The Clash of Civilizations and the Remaking of World Order* (1996), Samuel P. Huntington argued that the West faced a conflict between Western and other cultural and religious identities. Not so: the greater threat to the West is from within. If Western values and civilization are to endure, the West must first diagnose the nature of that threat. The West still has huge strengths, but if so-called populism further weakens them, the fight to preserve our freedoms will be lost. What replaces them will not be better.

The 2016 US election and the British decision to leave the European Union are the symptoms of a much bigger moment in world history. Both represent and propel the rising centrifugal forces in the world. They remind us of two grave past events: the US Civil War (1861–65) and the fateful Munich appeasement – "peace in our time" – of Germany's strongman, Adolf Hitler, in 1938. Together, the US election and Brexit threaten the West with renewed political turmoil.

A New Moment in History

I have found the idea of a new moment in history quite useful. Eras come to an end when the strong momentum that has overridden everything in their wake weakens while, simultaneously, the counterforces they provoke gain strength. When the tumultuous Napoleonic era ended in Europe in 1815, it was followed by a long period of mostly rising peace and prosperity. It ended when an emerging and aggressive Germany could not be accommodated in a wider global order – something that hardly existed at the time.

The following period of 1914–45 was marked by the horror story of two world wars, a global depression, the Holocaust, and the near suicide of Europe. A relatively golden period of increasing peace and

Published as "Calm, Compassion, and Common Sense Will Help Forge a Way Forward," *Globe and Mail*, January 13, 2017.

prosperity followed until the turn of the century. Then two calamitous events broke the magic: the September 11, 2001, attack on the World Trade Center in New York and the 2008 collapse of Lehman Brothers. These major challenges are now playing out in intensifying centrifugal forces within the West and the return of expansionist forces in Russia, Iran, and China (perhaps somewhat less so in China, which better understands its economic dependence on the rest of the world).

The Centrifugal Forces of Populism

There is a backlash against too much and too fast integration. So-called elites, who believed in and profited from the broad values of inclusiveness, failed to account for their impact on those who could not keep up with the pace of change. Brexit supporters and Donald Trump capitalized on the fallout. Most of the suggested solutions so far stand to make things worse, not better.

The elites understood that the world is complex but failed to see that integration would only increase complexity and make outcomes even less manageable for more people. Nor did they see its unfairness. The Brexiters and Mr Trump correctly saw the need for a very big shakeup. The European Union and the Washington/Wall Street establishment need reshaping, not destruction. Will the arsonists who are trying to burn them down be able to do the reshaping? Not much they have said so far suggests they can – or even that they comprehend the complexity of our world.

Things could get a lot worse before they get better – and that might not be during our children's or even our grandchildren's lives. It depends on what we start to do now. We have the strengths, but do we have the will?

The Challenge for the West

Two developments would change prospects for the better: strong, visionary leadership and a reshaped, inclusive global order. First, able leaders and a sufficient number of followers are needed to contain and then reshape the dangerous centrifugal forces within Europe and the United States. Second, a change of heart toward an inclusive global order is needed from Russia and China.

The West will become more vulnerable to hostile outside forces unless the centrifugal forces within can be contained. The only current leader who might take on her share of the task is Angela Merkel, whose party lost so many seats in the 2017 election that she was forced into a shaky coalition. She is threatened on multiple fronts – primarily from the refugee challenge in Europe, reinforced by the continent's pervasive economic insecurity, for which Germany bears a lot of responsibility. The US economy has more favourable prospects. But how long will they last? The country is undergoing its worst political turmoil in 150 years.

On the world stage, Russia and Iran stand against most actions to strengthen the postwar inclusive global order or to work for its constructive reshaping. It is difficult to see needed change from either, but that could end. Although pro-democracy forces in Europe have been weakened, they do not yet face authoritarian takeovers in either France or Germany. The situation is different today from that in 1938. The West is much stronger; authoritarian powers are weaker than Germany and Japan were at that time; but the United States is no longer the powerful "good guy" available to help – rather, it's becoming part of the problem.

The Path to a Better Balance

Two quite different but related ideas help clarify the urgent need for better fundamental balance. First, the great philosopher Alfred North Whitehead suggested two seemingly contradictory ideas: narrowness is the basis of all achievement, and the universe is vast. The challenge of all life is to mutually accommodate the narrowness needed for achievements and the vision to understand the vastness and complexity of our world. Unfortunately, the West has too often concentrated on the narrowness at the expense of the vastness.

The second idea came from a CEO friend. He said that all good leaders require four strong characteristics (producer, administrator, integrator, and entrepreneur), but no one has more than two. When you choose an executive with a particular two, you must make sure that the No. 2 executive has the other two – yet another example of how pervasive the need for mutual accommodation has become.

Four Ways of Doings Things in a Better Fashion

The four broad ways humans have found to go about things in a better way are freedom, science, mutual accommodation, and compassion. The West's problem is that its driving force since the Renaissance in the early 1400s has been liberty and science. The power of that narrowness and what it has achieved is enormous.

Now, the rise in centrifugal forces needs to be balanced by a greater capacity for mutual accommodation and compassion. Countries are like leaders. If they tend to be strong in two areas, they may not be able to find ways within themselves to achieve a better balance and will need other countries to assist.

Countries strong in the capacity for mutual accommodation are scarce, but Canada is one of them. This ability gives Canada a potentially important role to play in global affairs.

What We Can Learn from Japan and the New Testament

On my first visit to Japan, in 1975, I bought the only serious book about the nature of Japan I have ever seen written by a Japanese author – *Japanese Society* by Chie Nakane (1970). It gave me a new way of comparing societies and countries. Nakane argues that societies are shaped by the relative dominance of vertical and horizontal forces and institutions. She sees Japan as deeply vertical.

Adopting her perspective, I rate the United States as deeply horizontal. This diagnosis means that strong horizontal forces, such as freedom and markets, are less influential in Japan; while strong vertical forces based on relationships, mutual obligations, and consensus are much stronger in that country. It comes down to a preference in the United States for rights and freedom, in contrast to the preference in Japan for relationships and consensus. Arguably, relationships in the United States are too weak, while rights in Japan could be stronger.

Some years ago I used this comparison, along with two quotes from the New Testament, to explain to a group of CEOs that people want to be treated both as equals and as special. In the Bible, Jesus is quoted as saying that the rain (nature) falls on the just and the unjust alike (equal treatment), while also saying the very hairs of your head are numbered (each person is special).

To my surprise, all seven executives agreed. In their experience, everyone in their companies wanted to be both equal and special. The threat to Western institutions and values today is that their driving forces have been too horizontal and impersonal. They have not been sufficiently balanced by the vertical and the personal. One result is the populism and growing unmanageability we now face.

A Need for Magical Thinking

The best approach to a post-Brexit, post-Trump world is to be calm and creative. We need calm to face the combined internal and external challenges that could bring the end of Western civilization – losing its values while gaining nothing comparable to replace them.

We also need to be creative to overcome the limits of the post-Brexit, post-Trump world. Four years ago the clever Las Vegas magician Jeff McBride said yes to my assertion that "magic would not be magic if it really was magic." He added that limits can only be overcome by creativity – which is where magic comes from. Calm and common sense seem the best ways forward most of the time. Big, deep, broad crises also call for creativity. If you get the diagnosis right, you greatly improve the chances of getting the cure right.

The West's crisis comes from the deep sources of its increasingly unmanageable imbalances over six centuries. The world's challenge now – not just the West's – is to maintain and improve the strength of freedom and science, and to use creativity to match them with the needed limits that flow from mutual accommodation and compassion. That is the only way for Western values to survive. And there are no other competitive values on offer.

If you doubt that science, freedom, and compassion can come together, look at what Médecins Sans Frontières has accomplished. Consider how much more this humanitarian organization could do if there was more mutual accommodation. Freedom, science, compassion, and mutual accommodation are all beneficial in their own ways. Together, they provide the cumulative strengths the whole world needs.

I have been a modest and passionate Methodist all my life. However, I am deeply grateful that Pope Francis, the only religious leader (indeed, the only leader of any kind) able to speak to the whole world, is not a man of rules, doctrines, or hierarchy but of compassion. The Pope's compassion and Canada's mutual accommodation are what the world most urgently needs. Together, they are the antidote to a kind of politics that, while recognizing the needs of some of the marginalized and left-out groups, also exploits and aggravates them.

Liberal democracy is in peril. The rule of law and a political system that make governing possible are key to the future of both Canada and the West. What we took for granted after 1945 is now under threat – this time from within. As Pogo famously said, "We have met the enemy and he is us."

3

Vibrant Middle Classes and Five Essential Institutions: Rule of Law, Democratic Governance, Free Markets, Robust Media, Fearless Universities

Possibly the most fundamental outcome of the economic and technological changes toward the end of the twentieth century was the shift from a producer-dominant world of scarcity to a consumer-dominant world of declining scarcity. In previous human history, all the key societal and political fights took place inside the producer-dominant world of scarcity. In the post-scarcity world, the ultimate fights have been less around scarcity outcomes and more about other issues. We live in a fundamentally new world in which what the consumer wants is becoming bigger than what producers want. That is why union power, socialism, and class division are becoming less important. The emergence of a consumer-dominant world has been matched by the rise of a global middle class and the global intertwinedness of economies. The ever-growing strengths of this global middle class and intertwinedness have enabled us so far to preserve enough of the post-war inclusive global liberal order.

The middle class matters for two big societal reasons: it drives demand in the global economy; and it is far more demanding of governments. The middle class is key to preserving the global liberal order because it has by far the biggest stakes in the outcome. That has recently played out in Hong Kong, with the middle class fighting against a strong Beijing effort to legalize its hostage-taking – a very encouraging development that may yet end in heartbreak.

The world is changing for better and for worse at its fastest rate in history. These changes have been making it both more stable and less stable. Never before has it been both more separate or more connected. It has also never been more intertwined. And its top-down vertical structures are becoming more difficult to make work. More horizontal (the uncaring world of nature, technology, and markets) and less vertical (the caring world of the individual and society) looks like the irreversible path of the future. A majority of people in Western countries have joined the middle class over the last 150 years. Brookings reported in September 2018 "a global tipping point – that half the world is now middle class or wealthier."

The central importance of a strong and growing middle class is not just that it includes (hopefully) most of the voters or that it is intrinsically better for everybody. Rather, the key fact is that this middle class is increasing in a world where vast change is weakening traditional institutions. The declining trust in these institutions, if not addressed in a timely manner, can accelerate and become mutually reinforcing. This decline may falter if and when the pace and scale of change diminishes. For the moment, the never-more-connected/disconnected world we now live in has resulted in diminished societal and personal stability. Hierarchy is also in decline and is not likely to change – ever. There is too much complexity and fast-moving change going on. This instability could prove a stumbling block for China and other authoritarian and top-down countries. It will also prove a challenge for every kind of top-down institution.

Change needs stability. Stability needs change. How do we accommodate both? That is one of the very big questions the West now faces. Societies that are not small and tribal need mutually trusted institutions to sustain themselves. Part of the answer is to refocus on the five key institutions on which our liberal order rests: the rule of law; democratic governance; free markets; robust media; and fearless universities. We need to make sure they are trustworthy and that they help bring everybody minimum good outcomes.

The rule of law underpins everything. Without it, none of the other four institutions are safe. Indeed, each needs the other to remain secure. So far, free markets and democratic governance procedures have remained largely safe. Right now, the greatest threat comes from attacks on the media as "fake" and from tweets that have not been independently tested for accuracy and balance. Demagogues always depend on a disillusioned electorate that loses its desire for and ability to distinguish what is factual from what is fictitious and/or deliberately deceitful. This guardianship used to be the job of editors and journalists. It still is in the public media, but Western citizens will have to get smarter on their own behalf.

Free markets and democratic governance are sophisticated forms of mutual accommodation – not always perfectly achieved but impossible to achieve in any other way. The inability or unwillingness to compromise is a rising threat to US democracy. A sense that one is being unfairly left out is another big threat to sustaining democratic governance. The West needs a post-Thatcher/Reagan world (see Chapter 22). Canada's governance system is arguably the best in the world. It has been through existential and identity crises and has so far come out the other side. Unlike the United States, its voters are driven by moderation. This quality has, by and large, seen Canada over the decades get more or less what it really wants politically and avoid what it really does not want. It has the same two parties it started with in 1867, though, over the years there have been many narrow regional and ideological parties that have been part of making the system deliver and that have disappeared when no longer needed.

Right now, Canada's rule of law (see Chapter 6) and democratic governance (see Chapter 5) is still working. The United States is less fortunate. It has a president who attacks a robust free press and the country's judges. Fortunately, so far, it still seems to have a basic majority of people rooting for freedom under the law, democratic governance, and a robust media. It is, however, seeing rising extremism in both the Republican and the Democratic parties. Societally, it is increasingly divided, and its divisiveness is more about who is "white" or not. The "white" fear they are the past; the non-white increasingly feel they are the future. Most non-white feel better about their futures, as they head toward becoming a majority in the country. The 2020 US election will be huge on multiple fronts. Who the Democrats choose will be key. Trump has been a large, pervasive, self-centred, and exhausting presence. The extreme left of the Democratic Party are offering extreme disruptive policy change as the way forward. It is usually best to offer a contrast to a big, divisive disruption. Whether the Democrats will or can offer real change that contrasts positively with Trump-style disruption and divisiveness remains to be seen.

The fifth key institution is fearless universities able to be attended by all who want to benefit from them. In Canada, the required fearlessness is threatened on two fronts. First, in a consumer-dominant world, universities cannot afford to let groups from the producer side block reforms that make their programs more responsive to what students will need to learn for the future. The resistance to this much-needed leader-driven change often comes primarily from unionized staff. Second, the inflexible (either/or) approach of some students who automatically oppose principled people such as Marie Henein (the exceptional criminal lawyer who defends the rule of law and, on that basis, represented Jian Ghomeshi) and noisily protest whenever she tries to speak. They want to prevent their fellow students from hearing what these speakers have to say. This dogmatism fundamentally undermines what a university is all about. The United States has an added third challenge – extremely high student debt. All Canadian universities need public funding. If universities cannot stand up to self-interested employees who block needed reform or to fearful students who are afraid of free speech, the basis of publicly funded financial support will be undermined.

PART TWO

Canada's Mutual Accommodation

4

Mutual Accommodation
Is Part of Canada's DNA

INTRODUCTION

Throughout its history, Canada has exhibited a stronger drive toward mutual accommodation than any other country. It has mostly put what works ahead of nationalism, ethnic difference, religion, class, and ideology, thereby avoiding war and violent conflict. Canada has been blessed by voters and leaders who learn from what works and fails – alongside governing leaders who have combined vision, practical boldness, and an ability to work and get along with a wide range of diverse people. It has one big failure (and many smaller ones): its relationship with the Indigenous people is its biggest piece of unfinished mutual accommodation business. The good news is that this issue is on the path to becoming better, long and painful as the past will continue to be, as both the Indigenous and the non-Indigenous try to move forward.

The United States is different. The dominance of its freedom, science, and technology strengths enabled it to lead the first global trade and inclusive world order for over six decades following 1945. But the world has changed in the early years of the twenty-first century. The United States now needs a huge new pivot beyond its historic strengths and toward mutual accommodation. Is it up to that? This question will be the major issue of the next few decades. The United States will continue to count, no matter what it does. But can it become helpful again within more realistic limits? It overreached under Ronald Reagan and George W. Bush; and now with Donald

Trump, it is both underreaching and overreaching – and worse. Despite its multiple huge strengths, the United States still lacks the essential characteristic needed to thrive in this new era – ever more mutual accommodation.

Canada, under Stephen Harper, strengthened its national unity on the Quebec, Western Canada, and Indigenous people fronts. Fortunately, the country has so far not been burdened with the negative anti-immigrant sentiments that have been rising in the G7 nations. Now, to preserve and advance these gains, it is up to Justin Trudeau or his successor to reset the economy on a more viable longer-term path and to face the third key challenge for all Canadian prime ministers – its relationship with the United States. Trudeau has failed to reset the Canadian economy on a more viable path but has done about as well with the Trump-led United States as any leader could. The high stakes ahead will require Canada to extend its proven abilities in mutual accommodation to the world stage, but at a time when the world simultaneously needs it more than ever while becoming increasingly less open to it.

Canadians have yet to grasp the reality – evident at the time of the 2015 election – that Canada's economy could be headed for the rocks unless the new government embarked on an effective policy course correction. Unfortunately, that correction is still nowhere in sight. Canada's 2015 rocks were self-made: living beyond our means and falling behind on competitiveness. Today the Canadian economy is facing other intensifying challenges from outside Canada – populism in Europe (including Brexit), protectionism in the United States under Trump, and friction with China. One result of these centrifugal forces is the rising threat of trade wars at a time when the United States and global economic expansions are reaching their end. The 1930s witnessed what happens when too much debt leads to depression or near-depression and is combined with trade protectionism. The result – the Great Depression and the horrors of the Second World War.

Justin Trudeau and the federal Liberals have been doing as well as they can on the US and national unity fronts. They know that, in the case of the Trans-Mountain Pipeline, no single issue, no matter how important, can ever be allowed to prevail over what national unity requires. On many other issues, the Liberals are proving to certain key groups to be less inclusive than expected – to men in general;

to those over fifty; to those with different visions from them on single issues who do not want to be financially punished for it; and to those who create and build businesses and wealth. This Liberal political narrowness, alongside a US neighbour that does not know its way forward or what it has become, is where things stand in 2019. If the United States cannot move beyond the limitations of Trump and were to re-elect him in 2020, a second presidential election victory will make him almost totally uncontainable. In the new world in the midst of multiple Trump traumas, the United States primarily depends on trade with Canada and Mexico. China, in turn, depends more on trade and also on many more countries than does the United States.

1. THE MAGIC OF THE CANADIAN IDEAL*

Two ideas: Canada is magic, and that magic has conjured up one of history's truly transformational ways in which to do things better.

All creativity involves overcoming limits. Canada's magic results from the way it has overcome the limits of geography and history in its relations first with its mother countries, France and Britain, and then with its powerful southern neighbour, the United States. These stories create our magic. In the current challenging times for Canada and the world, we need to understand them and use them to our advantage.

At the dawn of the twenty-first century, we began a new moment in history. Good moments are often followed by bad stretches, and the Western world had enjoyed nearly six positive decades since the end of the Second World War in 1945. That period ended suddenly on September 11, 2001. In the years since we have faced the post-2008 economic and financial crises, the geopolitical challenges of Vladimir Putin's Russia, and Islamic State terrorism in the Middle East. The post-war inclusive global order led by the United States is, under President Donald Trump, rapidly becoming less global and less inclusive.

Canada is still an unknown country – it has a shared story, but few people know and understand what that story is. It is high time

---

* Published in the *Globe and Mail*, June 13, 2015.

Canadians had a national conversation about this magic story and learned how to use it for the benefit of its citizens and the world.

Throughout their history, Canadians have exhibited a stronger drive toward mutual accommodation than any other country – especially in comparison with the United States, which is currently paralyzed by political and social divisions. Mutual accommodation – the shared Canadian story – is crucial today not only in Canada but globally.

Here are some fundamental ideas to spark the national conversation. When considered together, they put Canada and mutual accommodation at the centre of the next stage in world history.

The troubled global order, the weak global economy, and the challenge of fostering economic growth in Canada while returning to live within our means will require resilience and adaptability. To help us along the way, usable history will become very important – the shared and individual stories that bind us together as a nation.

Canada's story is not marked by dramatic events, but the strength of our separate stories makes a powerful shared narrative. After 150 years of consolidating our coast-to-coast-to-coast country since Confederation, Canada has reached a point where its stories mutually reinforce one another. All through its challenging history, Canada has found it necessary to put what works ahead of nationalism, ethnic difference, religion, class, and ideology.

Canada's shared narrative is defined by its achievements in mutual accommodation and its socio-cultural bent. Canada has got one of the great governance lessons of history right – the necessity of mutual accommodation for a good and decent life. Accomplishing this goal makes Canada not just a good country but a great country.

Great countries (like great leaders) make many mistakes, including big ones, but they get the most important things right. The most significant piece of unfinished mutual accommodation in Canada is its relationship with the First Nations.

Three Clear Examples

Historically, the choices made by leaders and followers have entrenched the Canadian narrative of mutual accommodation. Three of the major stories focus on Louis-Hippolyte LaFontaine and Robert Baldwin in 1848; the election and re-election of Sir Wilfrid Laurier from 1896 to

1908; and the role played by Sir Arthur Currie and his Canadian Army during the First World War in the defeat of Germany. Some historians consider Currie the Allies' greatest general from that conflict.

The vision of LaFontaine and Baldwin manifested itself in 1848. They led the only reform movement in the Western world during that tumultuous year which ended as a responsible government and never lost its democracy. In this case, the francophone Catholic LaFontaine in Lower Canada needed the strength of the anglophone Protestant Baldwin from Upper Canada to overcome the anti-reform position of the Quebec clergy. Baldwin, in turn, needed the strength of LaFontaine to combat the anti-reform power of the Family Compact.

Both these leaders were able to work together successfully at a time when differences of religion and nationality were intense. When LaFontaine lost his Quebec seat, and Baldwin lost his in Ontario, each ran successfully in the other's province, despite these deep divisions. This accommodation showed, two decades before Confederation, that a shared public purpose pursued through compromise could trump nationality and religion with Canadian voters.

The idea of restraint is also a striking element in this story. LaFontaine stood down the anti-reform mob in Montreal by asserting that reform would prevail without recourse to violence – a century before Mahatma Gandhi championed non-violence in India, Nelson Mandela in South Africa, and Martin Luther King in the United States.

As for Laurier, his vision was political – to achieve peace, prosperity, and public purpose through compromise and accommodation. He said that the twentieth century would belong to Canada – and in many ways that proved true in the relative quality of life available in Canada to ordinary people. It became true primarily because Canada followed the Laurier vision of public achievements through compromise and restraint. The very election of Laurier, a francophone Catholic from Quebec, as prime minister only thirty years after Confederation is but one example.

This approach was so powerful and suited to Canada that it kept the federal Liberal Party in office three out of every four years over the following century. The less flexible (instinctively either/or, win/lose) Canadian leaders have been either restrained in their actual behaviour or, along with their party, made to pay the price of not being restrained. The federal Liberal Party is still paying a price, three decades later, for Pierre Trudeau's unilateralism and his initial lack of restraint on both the Constitution and the National Energy Program. The Conservative Party similarly paid a six-decade price in Quebec for Robert Borden's inability to find the conscription compromise needed in the First World War.

Leaders with the right followers, and followers with the right leaders, can do great things. Both came together for Canada in the final years of that war – a coming-of-age moment for the country. At Vimy Ridge in April 1917, Currie first led his Canadian Corps to victory – making it the only army on the Western Front to capture a fortified ridge. During the Hundred Days offensive from August to November 1918, the Corps outflanked the Germans, leading to their only real defeats in the war at the Drocourt-Quéant Line and the Canal du Nord – both key to ending the conflict.

In advance of Vimy Ridge, Currie decided to make his battle plan (but not the date) available to every soldier. As the battle unfolded, he wanted them all to understand what was going on and be able, if needed, to operate without direction. No other country was socio-culturally flexible enough to do that. Even today, few chief executives would take that kind of risk.

Together these strong and proud visions have made Canada a great country, and the choices that made these achievements possible have made it a magic country – a nation able to overcome its limitations through creative solutions. But much remains to be done in bringing the First Nations into full participation in our unique mutual accommodation story. The words "cultural genocide" used by Chief Justice Beverley McLachlin in her lecture in Toronto in May 2015 drew headlines, as did the recommendations of the Truth and Reconciliation Commission of Canada that same year. This report will take its place alongside others that have shaped our history – the Durham, Rowell-Sirois, and Bilingualism and Biculturalism reports – all of them milestones in mutual accommodation.

Resource development and education are the urgent issues for First Nations. Canada has lost much of the past decade in economic development because the federal and Alberta governments, along with natural-resource industries, ignored the opportunity they had to work with First Nations. As for Ottawa's stalled Education Bill, the best way forward is to move beyond politics by making the program optional. That would enable those Aboriginal communities anxious to educate their young people to do so.

Four Ways to Be Better

Since the Middle Ages, the Western world has tried to make things better in four powerful ways: through freedom, science, compassion, and mutual accommodation.

Freedom and science (which includes education and technology) represent the power of the inflexible either/or and have been the dominant drivers. Compassion and mutual accommodation – the power of the flexible both/and – have been much less influential. Amid all the global tensions today, it is crucial that these four basic qualities act more in unison. Otherwise, the future will become hellish again, as it was from 1914 to 1945.

Journalist Martin Wolf wrote in the *Financial Times* that "we are doomed to co-operate." That does not mean, of course, that we will. Zbigniew Brzezinski, a US national security adviser when Jimmy Carter was president, believed that mutual accommodation is the only way forward for both China and the United States. He may be right, but only time will tell.

On the foreign-policy front, Canada should be working the com promise side, doing the independent thinking about the world and what is going on, and seeking the relationships that could make it a useful player. No other country is better positioned to be helpful in a world that desperately needs creativity in overcoming limits.

Canada is not a mistake-free zone. Canadians have work to do, but little sense of what it entails right now, let alone for the future. For example, since the 2008 financial crisis, they have been suffering from moral smugness and economic complacency. Canada has run annual current account deficits of some $55 billion – money borrowed to sustain consumption, not to build Canada or enhance its ability to create lasting jobs. The current account deficit is already starting to rise again because of the oil-price collapse, despite a lower Canadian dollar and a stronger US economy.

The federal government faces a Canadian economy that demands a major set of structural and macro-economic policy shifts. The oil collapse is a huge shock to an economy that has been living on credit while its growth and supply-side competitiveness have declined. Still, Canada's medium and longer-term prospects continue to look strong. What happens in the short term seems more problematic.

If Canada is to address the current economic challenges, it is essential for the government to rein in excess consumer demand, run federal deficits a bit longer to finance public infrastructure and pro-capital-creation tax policies, and focus on a stronger supply-side performance.

I have three suggestions to get us back on track. First, we must once again learn to live within our means. Second, we must urgently address mutual accommodation with the First Nations. And third, we must immediately focus our foreign policy on long-term and strategic goals in our interest. Only then will we be ready for the transformational changes that are sure to come.

Canada's mutual accommodation drive gives us hope. No other single idea, if taken on board globally, could do more to change the world in a positive way in the decades ahead.

2. HOW CANADA'S EIGHT LEADERS OF SPECIAL VISION GUIDED THE WAY*

Great countries get the leaders they need just when they need them the most. Exactly why that happens is both a mystery and a miracle. If it keeps happening, as it has so far for Canada, the result is a kind of magic – the magic of creatively overcoming challenges and limits that look almost impossible.

In its relatively short history, Canada has had eight leaders of special vision, not all of them chosen at the ballot box.

Six Governing Visionaries

What can we learn from the personalities and events that shaped the way we do things in our country? Canada's defining narrative began early, with the reliance, amid a difficult geography, of European traders

---

* Published in the *Globe and Mail*, July 7, 2015.

and settlers on Aboriginal people. Over the centuries, the nation that has emerged has continued – in fact, extended – this tradition of mutual shaping and accommodation. Canada has not been entirely free of violence, but its primary markers have been a blend of vision and of what works on the ground. In this way, it has been a great country unlike any other in history.

Canada's three greatest visionary leaders – Samuel de Champlain, John A. Macdonald, and Wilfrid Laurier – each combined vision, practical boldness, and an ability to work and get along with a wide range of diverse people. Two other politicians, Robert Baldwin and Louis-Hippolyte LaFontaine, showed that political and social reform could be achieved by non-violent means. William Lyon Mackenzie King, Canada's longest-serving prime minister, was the skillful consolidator of their achievements. Consolidation can be as vital as initiation, although it requires a different type of vision, boldness, and patience.

Today all these leaders would recognize that many of their visions are embedded in the fabric of modern Canada.

Champlain wanted a new kind of society – one in which Aboriginals and Europeans could live together in amity and with mutual respect. Individualism underlies the American dream – the right to "life, liberty and the pursuit of happiness" for every citizen that is reflected in the Declaration of Independence and the Constitution. The Canadian dream comes from someone remembered as an explorer but who arrived here as a soldier personally familiar with the horrors of war.

Champlain had many dreams – among them the colonization of New France, which he succeeded in doing, and finding a passage to China, which did not exist. The greatest of his dreams focused on humanity and peace. In North America, Champlain became a political leader and statesman who, through his ability to get along with different people, was able to convert his dreams into reality.

Canada's dream includes individual desires for freedom, material advance, and happiness, just as America's includes wishes for a better, fairer, and more equal and open society. But the initial aspirations of these two countries were and remain distinct. "And that," as US poet Robert Frost put it in another context, "has made all the difference."

Macdonald's vision was national – for a transcontinental country in the northern half of North America. This country had to accommodate people of French and English heritage, of Catholic and Protestant faith. It had to be ready to stand up to the United States and to build a sound economy. Macdonald remains the country's greatest builder, striving for a nation of "one people, great in territory, great in enterprise, great in credit, great in capital." He got three big things right: Confederation, a transcontinental railway, and containment of American expansionism. He also got English-French politics mostly right, although the execution of Louis Riel aggravated the political challenges from western Canada and francophone Quebec. Finally, when the country needed a looser federation than Macdonald sought, his Confederation allowed it.

Macdonald found, in his partnership with George-Étienne Cartier, a way forward on the Quebec political front that others followed. His model has endured for more than 150 years. And he recognized how fundamental mutual respect was to mutual accommodation: "Treat them as a nation, and they will act as a free people generally do – generously," he said of French-speaking Canadians. "Call them a faction and they become factious."

In a private letter just before the inauguration of what he called "the confederate government" on July 1, 1867, Macdonald described what he felt had been achieved: "By the exercise of common sense and a limited amount of the patriotism which goes by the name of self-interest, I have no doubt the Union will be good for the Country's weal." And so it has turned out.

Confederation was a first. No previous colonials had written their own constitution. It set in motion a coast-to-coast-to-coast country that has survived and thrived. Canada also has emerged as one of the better places to live and, because of its achievements in mutual accommodation, one of history's truly remarkable countries. And because of the potential importance of this idea to the world right now, Canada has vastly more runway ahead than it has used so far.

The visions of its founders have shaped Canadian society in ways that have been mutually reinforcing. Champlain's desire for a diverse and peaceable society remains a dominant, if not yet fully realized ideal. For example, much remains to be done in mutual accommodation with the First Nations and, currently, in finding ways to cope with anxieties about extreme Muslim groups, fed in part by a fearful US neighbour and its hyped-up media.

The belief of Baldwin and LaFontaine in reform through non-violent means has become the Canadian way. Macdonald's vision has led to the quality of life that Canadians enjoy, while Laurier's political model of accommodation has, for the most part, been followed. Together these visions have made Canada – a country of unexpected magic.

Two Cultural Visionaries

Mutual accommodation involves two fundamentals: an effective two-way communication and a belief that a shared and meaningful order exists at the heart of things. Geography creates one kind of communication problem – it helps to explain why western Canadians feel alienated from Ottawa and Toronto, and why midwestern Americans disdain Washington and New York. But breaking away from history can result in much bigger and deeper communication challenges than holding on to it. The US Civil War lasted for just four years but the aftermath still persists, contributing to our neighbour's current political turmoil.

Canada did have its own historical break with its two mother countries, but it was not abrupt. Rather, its English and French connections have remained, though they have gradually become less relevant over the years. The American rupture between North and South was sudden, violent, and destructive, followed by subsequent not always happy reconnections. Canada's recent existential crisis concerning Quebec was peaceful and lasted for decades. These differences have produced distinctive communication, institutional, and socio-cultural results in both countries.

It's no accident, perhaps, that Canada's two greatest non-political visionaries in the mid-twentieth century, Northrop Frye and Marshall McLuhan, both addressed communication issues. Each came partly out of the University of Toronto, an intellectual environment that had been greatly influenced by Harold Innis, a pioneering theorist in economics, communications, and the media.

Like Innis, Frye and McLuhan had a Canadian, as distinct from an American, sense of the fundamental shared order at the heart of things. Between them they captured better than anyone else the nature of the transformational communication and identity changes of the post-1945 era. McLuhan grasped the scale and scope of the incipient revolution of modern communications technology, along with some of its socio-cultural implications. For him, the medium was the message, and, because the technology was global, the world had become a global village. Frye grasped the reality that culture is fundamental and that all culture is local in expression. Although culture is shaped by the medium, it is not the medium. For Frye, culture and nationality come from a shared order, and all literature has the same anatomy. The global village is also a globe of villages.

The successful or unsuccessful reconciliation of the global village with the globe of villages is what the next decades in the world will largely be about. For Frye, the world of the imagination (inner) is the only place of unlimited individual freedom, unlike the physical (outer) world of limits and possibilities. The shared structure of all imaginative literature is what makes us human.

The Americans, more than any other society, have a never-ending drive for outer freedom in search of new possibilities with the fewest possible limits. Frye argued that free individual responses, rather than manipulated responses, would produce genuine and sustainable human cohesion. He saw the media as too often a world of manipulated mass response, leaving less space for individual reflective response – and, I would add, for real mutual accommodation that lasts.

The US media may be a particular problem for Canadian culture. But as Frye famously said, the problem was even greater for American culture. Culture for Frye was not simply high culture: it was the characteristic response of individuals and groups to what they find before them. While Canadians seem to lean toward "underlying unity and order," many Americans prefer the "struggle between good and evil until the final moment of victory or judgment."

What a Difference a Border Makes

Alarmingly, the drive toward irresolvable divisions (the endless struggle between good and evil) produces a world of slippery slopes and apocalyptic dangers. It makes democratic politics and mutual accommodation much more difficult to achieve. Today, there is more internal political turmoil in the United States than at any time since the

Civil War. In an era of terrorism, it is important for Canadians, living next to a fearful country, to keep their cool and hang on to mutual accommodation as the best way to go – even when it does not work quickly or well and even when it fails.

Canada used its first 150 years to consolidate the initially thin coast-to-coast thread that made the country improbable into one that was strong and viable. It withstood the centrifugal forces within and the external expansionist instincts of the United States from without. It survived the global convulsions of two world wars and a great depression. Now, as it is tries to cope with the world's latest challenges, it has the "usable history" – proven tactics for getting through difficult situations – that it needs to move forward. Canada must now use it or lose it.

Not surprisingly, narratives have emerged from the many challenges, successes, and failures in this vast country, home to diverse peoples from many parts of the world. These stories, however, have rarely been national stories. More commonly they are regional and local stories of everyday life – from First Nations, the Québécois, western Canada, the North, immigrants, and francophone Canadians outside Quebec. Only Ontario, particularly since 1945, has consistently regarded Canada in a more national way. Now, as Ontario finds itself in a Canada that no longer works all that well for its economy, this outlook may also change. What is certain is that many more shared and separate stories will emerge from what Canada and the rest of the world are experiencing right now.

Canada's glue is still its unknown shared narrative. Its future lies in a return to the boldness that created Canada in 1864–67. Canada enters this new era with an exceptional range of strengths. Paradoxically, these same strengths will make Canada more vulnerable than ever to those who want what it possesses. They may also make Canadians more anxious. Our best defence will be twofold: to articulate our stories in order to understand who we are and what we stand for; and to discuss what Canada should do to seize the opportunities and minimize the risks that accompany good fortune. We could well now be entering a second Sir John A. Macdonald moment of huge challenge in our history – one that will again call for boldness in pursuit of the improbable.

3. TO BE A GLOBAL ROLE MODEL, CANADA MUST REALIZE WHAT SETS IT APART*

Use words, not force. Make railways, not war. These overly simple ideas capture the Canadian national story – one that differs from those of most other countries.

Canada's story has increasingly been driven by persuasion. The American story has more often been shaped by war and violence: the Revolutionary War, Civil War, Indian wars, Mexican wars, lynching, and the almost 400 million guns in private hands. These differences in how to go about things and how to make a good society are huge. They come from the fact that the histories of the two countries are dissimilar, as are the choices each has made along the way. Over the years the differences have been the source of both strength and weakness.

The United States has been great when it comes to freedom as well as science and technology – the most transformative forces for doing things in a better way since the Renaissance. There is still more to do, but science and freedom now face limits because the United States lacks mutual accommodation – the key to a satisfactory way forward.

So, while the United States remains unmatched, it is now less indispensable because so much is inherently beyond its reach. The world today is different and needs a different kind of country, which means Canada's special task is to help advance mutual accommodation outside as well as within its borders.

Since its beginnings – first Quebec in 1608 and then Confederation in 1867 – Canada has had three very big achievements. First, it has survived – not just as a nation but as one that includes the distinctive province of Quebec. Second, it made itself a coast-to-coast-to-coast nation. Finally, despite its divisions of nationality, culture, language, religion, and class, it has developed a political and socio-cultural outlook that works.

All these achievements have been based on mutual accommodation. Today's Canada is the product of its capacity for mutual accommodation and a belief in an underlying shared order. How well

---

* Published in the *Globe and Mail*, June 22, 2015.

is this historical fact understood in 2017, our 150th anniversary of Confederation?

Seven Key Ideas

The Canadian Narrative Project is a collaboration with Bill Innes, who has spent his career in the global oil industry in Canada, Europe, Japan, and the United States. He and I are not historian wannabes who think we have a better grasp of Canadian history than others. The purpose of the project is very simple: to get Canadians talking about whether Canada has a shared story; whether that story is indeed mutual accommodation, and whether understanding that story will strengthen us for the future.

At the heart of the project is the notion that, in many ways, Canada is still the *unknown country* that inspired the famous 1942 book with that title written by Bruce Hutchison, the late journalist and political commentator.

That idea is one of seven that shape the notion of Canada as the product of mutual accommodation. The second is the concept of *usable history*, which stems from a piece in the *New Yorker* by US historian William Pfaff soon after the collapse of the Soviet Union. Newly emerged Russia's problem, he said, was that it had no usable history – which comes from what has worked to get a country through something hard in its past. Interestingly, after the 9/11 terror attacks, Mayor Rudy Giuliani found New York's usable history in what Londoners did during the Second World War to endure the Blitz.

Third, the central idea that *shared stories* are the stuff of usable history – a vital source of strength or of weakness – comes from many diverse places.

The four remaining ideas are more original and therefore may be less familiar. Although Canadians instinctively understand the term *mutual accommodation* as a practical way to go about much of their business, the idea has not been expressed previously in two simple words. Amid everything that is going on in the world today, it becomes ever more central, not only for Canada but for other nations too.

Canada needs to have another *Sir John A. Macdonald moment* – one that demands achievements that seem completely improbable and require much boldness and patience. The first such moment was

Sir John A.'s bold and brave decision to build a railway that would extend this sparsely populated country from coast to coast and thus be able to withstand American expansionism.

Globally, today, we are at another very difficult moment of change in history (as in 1815, 1914, 1945, or 2001). Moments in history come when the momentum and direction of the dominant forces that have overcome everything standing in their way start to weaken, the counterforces become stronger, and the path forward is once again uncertain.

Greatness is important for countries and for leaders. Although great leaders and great countries make many mistakes – some of them big ones – they get the most important things right. Sir Wilfrid Laurier and Canada became great by getting mutual accommodation right. Canada will always be Laurier's country, unless it chooses to abandon its mutual accommodation ways or reaches an impasse where they no longer work.

As for shared stories, they can strengthen *the courage needed to support bold action and confront hard challenges.* These two ideas – courage and shared stories – lie behind the Canadian Narrative Project.

Mr Innes sees Canada's mutual accommodation story as a crucial advantage at home and abroad, an idea central to what we have achieved. I, in turn, foresee several decades of challenge ahead on the scale of what happened internationally after 1910.

We will get the policies we need to survive and thrive only if we find the story that captures where Canadians are now and how they see things – and if we put what we find to good use. This national conversation is key to everything else before us.

Global Implications

Mutual accommodation is the opposite of what is happening in the United States. This great nation is being undermined by extreme emphasis on individual rights at the expense of society, on divisions among different groups, and on the never-ending struggle between good and evil. The global order now faces serious risks of destabilization and disruption. Mutual accommodation looks more and more to be the crucial ingredient needed for the survival of the best of our world as we know it.

There are three kinds of stories: the "how" (the manner of journey), the "where" (the journey's destination), and the "what" (specific events that happen along the way). Mutual accommodation is a how story – a way of doing politics and social living. Science is another great how story – the whats (the discoveries) and the wheres (the specific investigation goals) take place within the science way of doing things. In the years since the Renaissance, science has changed the world by the way it approaches knowledge and technology. Freedom, human rights, the rule of law, and democracy have also changed the world.

Mutual accommodation is not itself a memorable event, although it can make possible uniquely remarkable events. It has changed Canada, but it has not yet changed the world. Europe's postwar successes have come from the continent's growing capacity for mutual accommodation, though its current risks stem from those places where it has fallen short. With the right will, however, mutual accommodation can change the world – just as freedom and science have changed everything.

Canada's mutual accommodation story began when Samuel de Champlain arrived at Quebec in 1608. He came with a vision for a new nation based on co-operation between the Aboriginal inhabitants and the incoming French settlers. Once Canada became a nation through Confederation in 1867, it spent its first 150 years consolidating its northern half of the North American continent into a viable country – again through mutual accommodation between the provinces and the federal government, French and English, Protestant and Catholic, Quebec and the rest of Canada, and settlers and immigrants, though with the glaring omission of the First Nations. Much has been achieved, but more remains to be done.

The next one hundred years will likely be dominated by serious threats to the world's economic and geopolitical order and stability – a world in which Canada's rare combination of physical bounty, socio-political understanding, and living in a good neighbourhood could make a significant contribution. The time has come for Canadians to begin talking about their shared history and how to use it purposefully in the years ahead for the benefit of Canada and the world. As the late Quebec premier Robert Bourassa put it, Canada is for its citizens "one of the world's rare and privileged countries in terms of peace, justice, liberty, and standard of living."

To date, Canada's focus has been on its own internal development – on making things work – and on coping with the United States. Its development has taken place largely separated from events outside North America. The focus in the future, however, will be more external and will extend far beyond this continent. Canada is moving from being a largely disconnected part of the world to being deeply interconnected. This change will make it a very different country, and its mutual accommodation strength will increasingly need to be deployed abroad.

Canada has the water, food, space, minerals, resources, and the political, economic, social, and cultural ways that are in short supply for the rest of the world. These diverse advantages carry both opportunity and risk. If Canada is to seize the opportunities and avoid the risks, it should quickly get on with a national conversation about the shared and separate stories of its different peoples and regions – about how it got where it is, how to envisage its future, and how to seize its place in the world.

The Goal Is to Look Inward

In some senses, Canada is still an unknown country – unknown to itself as well as to others. It needs to hold national conversations about many important issues. Above all, it needs to talk about whether its mutual accommodation narrative captures how most Canadians feel about the country.

If it is to succeed, the Canadian Narrative Project must spur Canadians to think about when mutual accommodation has worked in the past and how in the future it may help us both at home and abroad. For example, what if it were used to manage the fallout from all the current anxiety over extremists claiming links to Islam? If we articulate our narrative well and deepen our understanding of its power – and of the costs where it has yet to work – it will continue to help us and others in the future. Values, stories, ideas, dreams, purposes, and choices together shape individuals, societies, and civilizations. Vision – the sense of what can be and what should be – lures and drives them all.

As the great Canadian critic and thinker Northrop Frye said, identities are always about who you aspire to be, not who you are now. Moving toward some vision of the future for Canada and the world – the two now go hand-in-hand – is really what this Canadian Narrative Project is all about.

Central to all identities – as individuals, organizations, societies, or countries – is how our particular culture shapes us to respond to what is put in front of us. We must understand both ourselves and others and the effect we have on each other. In his book, *The Duel* (1990), historian John Lukacs tells the story of the eighty-day struggle between Churchill and Hitler immediately following the fall of France. Although many others contributed to the ultimate defeat of Hitler, Churchill won this particular round because he understood Hitler better than Hitler understood himself.

So it is with mutual accommodation. It works best when each side understands the other side very well. It's essential to know what the opposing group wants before you can come to a deal that can last, and how best to respond if a deal does not initially prove possible.

The big questions for those who think a national conversation about Canada's mutual accommodation story is worth pursuing include these points:

- Does the mutual accommodation Canada I have described feel like the Canada you live in?
- If it doesn't, what does the Canada you live in feel like to you?
- Do you have an alternative shared story – in addition to or instead of mutual accommodation? What is it? What are your reasons?
- Do you agree with the thought that usable history comes from shared stories and separate stories, and how they may strengthen or weaken one another? If not, why not?

It's time now to get the conversation started.

4. JUSTIN TRUDEAU'S SUNNY WAYS – AND A STORM ON THE HORIZON*

The results of the October 2015 federal election were so startling, and the likely effects so huge, that it will be some time before we can grasp them fully. But let's start with three major outcomes that go beyond the usual fallout from elections.

First, this was much more than a fight between three leaders and parties of varying degrees of acceptability. It was also far more than a poll on the economy or how Stephen Harper went about his business. It was an election about the kind of country Canadians want. A vast swath of voters was determined to hold on to the Canada they have come to love and not to lose it to divisive themes.

Second, Quebec returned to be part of the country's government. Throughout the long campaign, the province was more engaged in a federal election than it had been in almost thirty years. Some 80 percent of its voters supported a federalist party.

Third, the Liberal Party came back from near death five years earlier to win the first federal vote since Canada's existential crisis – its battle with Quebec separatism. The first such provincial election was also won by a Liberal – Premier Philippe Couillard, who dispatched the Parti Québécois in March 2014. In both cases, a political realignment is under way that will leave the crisis behind and look to the future.

The People's Election

Quite simply, the election belonged to the people – it was more about trust than leaders, parties, or policies.

The Liberals recognized that mood best, with their program, their campaign, and their leader, who seemed to grow a little every day in full public view. From the beginning of his Liberal leadership run three years ago, Justin Trudeau trusted Canadians to be fair and give him a chance, despite inevitable miscues as he gained experience – and they did. The Conservatives' "not ready" attack ads recognized that public patience and shifted to "not ready yet."

* Published in the *Globe and Mail*, November 6, 2015.

Over time, the public obviously learned to trust, as well as tolerate, Justin Trudeau. Canada's political system proved that it works (a challenge still to be met by the American system). Their trajectory from a third-place start through a three-way tie to a majority shows that the Liberals had struck a chord with the people. Across the country, the cumulative votes of Liberal, New Democrat, Green, and moderate Conservative voters meant that some 70 percent of the Canadian electorate was on side with seeking mutual accommodation on the niqab and on security issues. At the end, Canadians preferred what they saw as a moderate economic risk over losing who they feel they are as a people.

The election's most striking feature was the level of energy from almost every direction and the number of people actively engaged in the campaign. From time to time, Canadians have strong feelings and worries, but they usually want leaders who are less extreme and worried than they are. The Trudeau victory message – the return of Sir Wilfrid Laurier's "sunny ways" and Canada as the country where better is always possible – added to the historic, stunning scale of the win. It will also move Trudeau into new territory where expectations of what is possible could be too high. He needs to figure out quickly what economic expectations are reasonable and explain them to Canadians. This election was not about the economy. The next one almost certainly will be.

The Harper Legacy

Every Canadian prime minister faces the same three big challenges: the economy, national unity, and the United States. Mr Harper did not do well on the economy: by the end of his term he was burdened by the highest consumer-debt to income ratio in the G7 and the frightening total of $400 billion of accumulated borrowing from abroad to fund consumption. This excess credit masked Canada's economic vulnerability.

Most people do not yet realize the extent of that vulnerability. Mr Harper inherited an economy and fiscal position from the Mulroney-Chrétien era that set him up for a decade. Unfortunately, his natural make-up does not fit with mutual accommodation: he did not trust other people, yet insisted they trust him, and he was determined to manage everything from inside his own mind – an impossible task in a complex and fast-moving world. As a result, he leaves Canada with an economy that is weaker than necessary, and with a decade's worth of policy challenges that will involve some voter pain.

Mr Harper did not get along with the United States, but political leaders there cannot get along with each other. Mr Trudeau may have a better chance, but relations with our southern neighbour will be difficult until the political turmoil there subsides.

Counter-intuitively, Mr Harper did well, over all, on national unity. His greatest skill in terms of mutual accommodation was political calculation. His understanding of Canada's political reality kept him from crossing the line most of the time. In the end, the power of Laurier's Canada prevailed: pursuing public purpose through compromise.

The only time Mr Harper faltered seriously was in his policies toward Muslims and terrorists. Otherwise he leaves an important set of unity achievements.

- When he took office in 2006, the West wanted in and Quebec was still undecided about getting out. Ten years later, the West is in, and so is Quebec – perhaps in part because Mr Harper passed the "Québécois nation" resolution in the House of Commons.
- During the controversy over the proposed Charter of Values in the 2014 Quebec election, he asked premiers and his own Cabinet to keep out of it, knowing that Quebeckers do not want outsiders intruding in their affairs.
- While other countries have serious divisions over immigration, abortion, and same-sex marriage, Canada does not. The opposition on these issues was inside the Conservative Party, and Mr Harper kept it quiet.
- He gave the First Nations the apology they wanted and needed.
- He established the Truth and Reconciliation Commission, whose thoughtful and balanced summary report came out in the spring of 2015.
- He presented a First Nations education bill that awaits implementation by the Trudeau government (and can be quickly achieved by an opt-in approach for those that want to get moving for their children now).

In the final analysis, Mr Harper was an exceptionally skilful political operative, limited by an ideology and a political style that relied on a base that was strong but proved too small and difficult to reach the majority of the population.

Ideology can be like celebrity – a form of shouting. It lacks real substance, the ability to get lasting things done or to provide reliable paths forward. As well, ideology is always trumped by reality – and mutual accommodation can help to keep us within its bounds.

Mr Harper's approach sometimes seemed to be that of a doctor who just shouts: "Bad disease, go away!" And, of course, it never does. For example, Vladimir Putin's Russia is a huge and potentially destructive force that a globally televised snub from a Canadian prime minister does nothing to curb.

Whatever his shortcomings prove to be, Justin Trudeau appears to have the patience, the inner confidence, and the toughness to find very good people to work with as a team. Together they will pursue a strategy that can help, over time, to get the disordered parts of the world to a better place.

Left Behind

The New Democrats and the Parti Québécois have made strong contributions to shaping what Canada is today, but each now seems to have run out of space on the runway.

The federal NDP has never, since its 1933 beginning, offered a single constructive, doable, fresh proposal on any of the fundamental challenges every federal government must face: the economy, national unity, and the United States. Meanwhile, its substantial contribution in social policy and rights has been largely achieved. Unlike Britain, there is no political room here for more mainstream, Tony Blair–style socialism.

The Péquistes, meanwhile, likely have a future in Quebec – but only if they abandon separatism (the BQ has no future federally). If they cannot, some other party will emerge as the primary contender to the Quebec Liberals. The PQ of René Lévesque and Lucien Bouchard gave Quebeckers the choice of in or out. Ironically, that choice and the PQ language bill saved Quebec for Canada, and Canada for Quebec.

Federally, the Conservatives may become the main alternative to the Liberals in Quebec. They can also become federally competitive again if there is more room for Progressive Conservatives. I see no real right-left shift in Canada (the world is too diverse and complex for the left-right split to be useful).

So, federal third parties may now recede. If they return, it will likely be more for regional reasons.

Challenges Going Forward

In the years ahead, October 19, 2015, will take its place among the important elections held since Laurier became prime minister that have involved national unity and solved our problems through mutual accommodation.

The first such election, in 1917, brought to power the Borden conscription coalition, which Laurier would not join and which divided the country fatefully along English-French language lines. It represented the greatest failure of mutual accommodation in Canadian history.

The second was the 1940 victory of onetime Laurier protégé William Lyon Mackenzie King. His policy of "conscription if necessary, but not necessarily conscription" avoided deep divisiveness over a war most francophone Quebeckers did not support.

The third was the election of Pierre Trudeau in 1968. He could be even more averse to mutual accommodation than Mr Harper, but he subsequently faced down Quebec separatism and preserved Canada.

Now we have Justin Trudeau, who matches his father in moral and physical courage, but brings more emotional intelligence and a less intellectual approach to government. Perhaps this approach is more in tune with how young people today go about things and what today's world necessitates.

Spirit of the West

Aside from Quebec, the other great challenge to national unity has come from the West. The Laurier-King political coalition that led to Liberal dominance of federal politics from 1896 to 2006 was based on francophone Quebec finding common cause with western Canada.

That came to an end with John Diefenbaker's sweep in 1957. Thereafter, whether Liberal or not, prime ministers from Quebec seemed largely unable to understand the West, causing alienation that reached its peak with Pierre Trudeau's National Energy Program and his unilateral efforts on the Constitution.

But the fact the Liberals in 2015 won thirty-two seats west of Ontario means that the Harper defeat need not leave the West on the outside. All will depend on the eight members it has in the new Cabinet, how much scope and profile Mr Trudeau allows them, and how they can work effectively with Western Canadian governments.

The major unity problem now is the First Nations. There is every reason to expect Mr Trudeau to do his part of what's needed. If he does, that will put pressure on the First Nations to do their part too. The outcome will depend on patient mutual accommodation.

Trouble Down the Road

Justin Trudeau has the ability to harness mutual accommodation and strengthen unity at home and, when the moment is right, to foster better relations with our southern neighbour.

However, mutual accommodation is a means to an end – not an end unto itself. It must serve a purpose, and a primary purpose at the moment is to get Canada on a sustainable economic path. The country has been living beyond its means (by $60 billion a year), has the G7's highest debt as a percentage of household income, and is not competitive internationally in enough goods and services.

Canada's economic ship is headed for the rocks. Mr Trudeau must chart a new course – and soon.

5

Governance and Political Issues
for the Twenty-First Century

INTRODUCTION

Canada's 150th anniversary in 2017 proved to be a pivotal year in our history. Internationally, we face uncertainty as our traditional allies experience massive changes – Brexit in the United Kingdom, the election of President Donald Trump in the United States, and the breakdown of the global trade and alliance system we have known since 1945. Domestically, our economy is losing competitiveness, and we are accumulating massive household-sector and net country debt. We continue to live beyond our means. We desperately need to boost our productivity, expand our markets, and encourage private-sector investment and entrepreneurial drive.

On the positive side, Canada still has the best overall range of assets in the world – vast space, water, natural resources, and agriculture. Our politics are moderate and broadly stable (though Ontario and Quebec provincial politics, for different reasons, have each become less well attuned to the world each lives in), and our capacity for mutual accommodation satisfies almost all our citizens. But the assets are being diminished and Canada's immediate prospects are getting more challenging in regard to the United States and the economy than they seemed in 2015. Our first-past-the-post electoral system has proved to be the best for Canada. It represents our regional nature, empowers individual voters over politicians, and works against extremist groups. Western alienation (especially in Alberta) has for the moment reasserted itself, but the outcome of the October 2019 federal election will hopefully mark the way forward. Now that

Quebec separatism seems to be satisfied and the key points in the historic NDP agenda have been absorbed into our national policies, Canada needs two hard centre parties. It does not yet quite have one.

Canada still enjoys a good neighbourhood, but it has a less good neighbour, where many disturbing things are going on beyond Trump. What is the United States today? Is it up to the big historic pivot it must now make for the different world ahead? Can it handle its growing political extremism; gun violence; its rising family breakdown and its inequality/left-outness challenges? Great nations, to remain great, have to make big pivots when big changes in their worlds arrive. Was the United States in the 1932–2000 period an aberration? None of these queries are likely to get firm answers any time soon. The uncertainties around the United States make it all the more important for Canada to maintain its vision and practice of inclusiveness and to do better on the Canadian economy. Canada's post-war politics at the federal level have been a blend of Progressive conservatives and conservative Liberals. Both Pierre Trudeau and Stephen Harper departed from that blend during their times as prime minister, and Justin Trudeau now has done so too.

1. CANADA'S 150TH YEAR COULD BE AS PIVOTAL AS 1867 AND 1967*

The year 2017 is not the same as 2015. Sunny ways need real sunshine. It felt sunny in Canada in late 2015: equal numbers of women in the Cabinet, a country with broadly good politics at federal and provincial levels, and a Canadian voting public that rejected Islamophobia. The identity and existential crises, from the Quiet Revolution to the challenge of Islamophobia, were behind us. The problems elsewhere – in the United States, Britain, and Europe – have since then become bigger. In 2015 no one foresaw Brexit or the election of Donald Trump. In 1910 no one foresaw two world wars started in Europe, a global depression, a Holocaust, huge human losses in the Second World War (60 million killed), and a Europe that almost committed suicide. However, although 2017 is not a normal moment, we should not panic.

* Published in the *Globe and Mail*, March 19, 2017.

Canada's Special Opportunity

Canada could be the first country to get on the right political and policy tracks to go forward into the emerging new world. Will Canada seize, or miss again, this second great opportunity of the twenty-first century? Five years ago Canada emerged from the post–Lehman Brothers crises with the best economy among the G7 countries – an opportunity lost for two main reasons. First, the prices for its two big exports – oil and commodities – dropped sharply. Politicians tend most of the time to be lagging indicators, and none of them saw this coming. Economic foresight is a political rarity.

Second, the Harper government made two basic economic policy mistakes. It left all the post-recovery expansion effort to monetary policy and withdrew fiscal stimulus prematurely. It moved into fiscal surplus, not to build the economy but for personal tax cuts for a country already spending more than it was earning and for a household sector that was already piling up debt at a fast clip. This error left too much of the economic expansion burden on the Bank of Canada. One result was a half-trillion additional debt that Canada owed to overseas lenders. The new Justin Trudeau government inherited a poisoned economic chalice and an incipient housing bubble. Both problems have worsened under the Liberal regime.

Dangerous instabilities are already here, and more could come. By 2020 the US economy could be in recession; another divisive US election could be underway; and Russian President Vladimir Putin could be running out of domestic political runway. Chinese President Xi Jinping, who had seemed to be nearing the end of his time in office, instead consolidated his power and was re-elected president indefinitely. Still, domestic political pressures appear to be rising, with a pulling back from freedom and a rapidly growing surveillance state – not a sign of confidence. The Trudeau government must ready itself for more economic self-reliance and the hard political steps such independence may require. If Harper had seized Canada's post–Lehman advantage, Canada would be better placed, and he might still be prime minister. Trudeau now faces a similar need to prepare.

The Federal Budget

Canada has not had a federal government with an intuitive sense of what drives the private sector since the Mulroney/Chrétien era – nor has Ontario had such a government since the end of the Frost/Robarts/Davis era. This omission urgently needs to be repaired in both Ottawa and Ontario.

The jolts to the Canadian economy so far from Mr Trudeau's fiscal stimulus, and as proposed by the government's economic growth council led by Dominic Barton, is mostly fine as far as it goes, but something more transformational will be needed. If not done voluntarily, an abyss moment will force it. Canadian business needs to get behind something transformational now. The Liberal federal government needs to pass this economic test in 2017. Everything else they want to do depends on a transformed economy.

New Politics for a New World

New politics and policies are needed. Philip Stephens, from his British/European perch at the *Financial Times*, has asked how best to confront the destructive side of populism. He sees parties of the left and right consigned to history, and a party of the "hard centre" as the way forward. Thomas Friedman, from his American perch at the *New York Times*, also sees new political parties ahead, but doesn't say what kind will emerge

What we need is a balanced policy of radical entrepreneurialism and a strong safety net. There will still be much to fight over, but ideology of both the left and right will not do the job.

This change will be hard for Americans. It requires a capacity for compromise. The idea that public purpose can be achieved through government is deeply divisive in today's United States. Populism is better at recognizing who and what has been overlooked than at remedying the problems. The blend of politics and policy that both Mr Stephens and Mr Friedman propose is a "what it takes to get there" way of thinking. It is hard to see any other practical political or policy way forward. Canada seems a fit candidate to give it a try. This country could be back as head of the class, where it was after the post–Lehman Brothers crises. Political risk and hard work will be required.

Back Against the Wall

Canada is usually at its best when its back is against the wall. It could be there again before 2020. It has just been through one of its at-its-best periods on the existential and identity fronts. Canada could also take its back off the wall and become complacent. Right now, Canadians feel they have a much better politics and society than Americans do – perhaps neither is as good as each country thinks.

Actually, our backs are always against the wall, no matter how well we have done or how good things appear. Canadians need to understand they are not doing nearly as well as the Americans are on the economy and why, under Mr Harper from 2011 to 2015, Canada lost its comparative economic advantage. The new Trudeau government has had both stumbles and real successes. Mr Trudeau shuffled his Cabinet to prepare for the Trump world and needs to rebuild the public service.

If it is well-paced and scaled, the Trump infrastructure spending and fiscal stimulus could extend the current US expansion – and that could also be good for Canada. But personal and corporate tax cuts could also make the United States more competitive. If too much, too fast is added to an already strong US economy, it could cut short the US expansion. The post-Trump US economic way ahead remains uncertain.

Big Challenges and Strong Assets

Canada confronts five big economic challenges:

- to live within its means;
- to achieve stronger productivity improvement;
- to expand the globally competitive supply side of its economy;
- to make itself more competitive globally in terms of risk/reward opportunity for the best people; and
- to do something bold and strong on the longer-term, private-sector growth side – such as a lifetime capital pool

approach to capital gains taxation (a potentially unique-to-Canada game changer) – to help better match greater private-sector strength with better public-sector infrastructure.

Canada will need to meet all five challenges to survive the emerging destabilized and more dangerous post-Brexit, post-Trump world – a world whose fundamental dynamics have changed and where the outcomes remain unclear.

Canada's new vision and branding aim should be to become the best place in the world to build solid and desirable personal lives in a country that combines dynamism with calm and common sense. This goal needs to become Canada's vision for itself and its brand to the outside world. It will need all Canadians, not just governments, onside. It could be a long time, if ever, before the world is as supportive for Canadian aspirations as it was from 1945 to 2000. Canada will be more on its own and have to count on itself more than ever before.

World's Best Overall Assets

Canada today has the best overall range of assets in the world. It has, arguably, the best perch to observe and figure out the world's two biggest players – the United States and China – accompanied by the least baggage and with the best positive relationship potential. Canada has ample space, water, food, energy, metals, and minerals, and it borders three oceans. It also has, arguably, the West's best politics and a steadily stronger mutual accommodation capacity.

In addition, Canada is still in the best neighbourhood in the world, despite the United States being in political turmoil. And it benefits from a growing diaspora of Canadians around the world, especially in the United States but also at the very top in Britain, with Mark Carney at the Bank of England, Dominic Barton as the global head of McKinsey, and Stephen Toope as the new head of Cambridge University. Finally, it is one of the few countries that might benefit economically from the effects of climate change on its agriculture and living space.

A Hard-Centre Government

What would a hard-centre party in Canada look like, the kind favoured by Philip Stephens? Could it work to keep destructive populism at bay? It would not be old-style right or left, but more like a twenty-first-century version of pragmatic Progressive Conservatives or conservative Liberals. The Liberals are not yet there on the private-sector side. The Conservatives have not decided where they need to be on several key fronts. The NDP is not in the game.

Political success would require use of Canada's full range of assets on the hard side of centre. Canada as a country, and its household sector, are spending much more than they earn for current consumption. Not enough is used for building the country's future economic health. The politics and economics of getting the right blend of federal borrowing and paying-as-we-go will not be easy. Prime Minister Trudeau and Finance Minister Morneau must explain where we are, what the correct balance will require, and what we will all get if we do the right things.

What the Middle Class Needs

A strong, growing middle class is the best antidote to destructive populism. Mr Trudeau faces challenges on the economy and with US relations that could undermine his middle-class ambitions. The middle class is a lot about electoral politics, but even more about managing today's centrifugal forces within the West. Hierarchies and charismatic leaders are no substitutes for stronger and larger middle classes in every country. They are the ultimate source of stability in a world that distrusts institutions and hierarchies and has never been simultaneously more connected and disconnected.

Canada's politics suit that environment. It has the assets it needs, except for enough of the best people and a more diversified and entrepreneurially driven economy. Every political leader, government official, and business leader needs to support that goal. Canada needs a fairness balance that is easier to achieve when both the economy and politics are doing well. The post-Brexit, post-Trump right-track-opportunity world is there, waiting (more clearly than anywhere else, including the United States). Everything depends almost entirely on what Canada's political and business leadership offers, and what the public followership decides.

Standing on Shoulders

Doug Saunders's brilliant New Year's op-ed in the *Globe and Mail* suggests Canada should be celebrating the last fifty years. If so, the first two fifty-year periods after Confederation should also be celebrated. Our 150th year, 2017, could prove to be as pivotal as both Sir John A. Macdonald's 1867 and Saunders's 1967. The last fifty years have consolidated a new kind of great country on the shoulders of the first 100 years. The next fifty can perhaps be Canada's second Macdonald moment as it adapts to the different kind of world now emerging.

The world needs more of Canada's mutual accommodation capacity. Today's powerful centrifugal forces within the West can be contained by spreading that capacity. Canada's politics have been getting lots of outside praise recently but, regrettably, not its economy. Canadian public opinion often needs a negative outside economic story to wake it up and make possible what is necessary.

Canada must always maintain its economic and social-inclusiveness strengths. It can strengthen its compassionate and mutual accommodation sides to help rebalance the driving forces of freedom and science that are making the West harder to govern. It can help Europe and the United States re-anchor the Atlantic West. All four better ways of going about things are inexhaustible – freedom and science explore possibilities; mutual accommodation and compassion offer needed limits. No individual or country can be equally strong on all four – so each must make room for those who are strong where they are not.

Further Reading and Viewing

Mark Mazower, *Dark Continent: Europe's Twentieth Century* (1998).
Mark Shriver, *Pilgrimage: My Search for the Real Pope Francis* (2016).
Charles Dickens, *A Christmas Carol*, with Alastair Sim (1951), DVD.

2. WHY A FAILED BID FOR ELECTORAL REFORM IS A WIN FOR CANADA*

Canada will face some challenges in a Trump America, post-Brexit world. The potential for geopolitical instability and difficulties with a United States in political turmoil is considerable. As Canada feels the rise of divisive politics elsewhere, Canadians need to better understand why its own political system has worked so well.

Shortly before he left office, US president Barack Obama said he wanted to be described as someone who cared for American democracy. His final speech to Americans revolved around how America's democracy is threatened more from within than without – a position opposite to that when the Second World War broke out.

When Justin Trudeau pledged during the 2015 election campaign to get rid of our first-past-the-post electoral system, it seemed to his party a good idea at the time. It did not turn out that way. The case for change was never made. There were two possible outcomes. One (any form of proportional representation) would hurt the governing Liberals immediately, so was a non-starter. The other (a ranked voting system) would ostensibly help them, but could end up hurting them electorally if the change was seen to be to their advantage.

Canada today has the best political system in the world. It is essential for Canadians to understand that fact, given the governance stresses in the United States, the United Kingdom, and Europe. Canada has come through a forty-five-year-long existential crisis in which Quebec not only survived the transformational Quiet Revolution of the 1960s but became a postmodern society with prosperity and social peace. In its 1995 referendum, Quebec had the choice to stay in or leave confederation. For Canada, having the choice was more important than preserving the country at all costs. For the United States, preserving the country with the Civil War took priority over choice – at a huge cost that continues 150 years later. Since Confederation, Canada's politics have arguably produced the best mutual accommodation society in history, making Canada the least troubled by irreconcilable differences.

* Published in the *Globe and Mail*, February 11, 2017.

Practical Politics

The Liberals would have faced a *realpolitik* challenge if they had decided to proceed with electoral reform. When I fought federal policy overreach in tax- and competition-law reform in the 1960s through to the 1980s, I learned an important lesson: although the public finds it difficult to assess complex public policy questions, they believe they can figure out whether the process is fair or is for self-serving politics. The excesses of the Pierre Trudeau government's economic policy bumped up against accepted norms in the 1970s and 1980s. The same would likely apply to electoral reform today.

Mackenzie King would have never got into the electoral reform mess in the first place. Canada's longest-serving prime minister seemed to know both what was right for Canada and how to govern Canada to get there. This talent enabled him to consolidate much that was right on many fronts – national unity, the economy, social advances, and relations with the United States.

Like Canadians, King had his own aspirations and principles. His particular political genius enabled him to achieve both his goals and their desires. The former Progressive Conservative leader Robert Stanfield once privately said that Mackenzie King was Canada's greatest leader because he had the most patience with the Canadian people.

The proponents of electoral reform never stated how any change would bring about improvements on either governance or aspirational fronts. The current government could never make a strong case for any change that would command broad support. The good news is that a project they should never have proposed has now been dropped.

The Nature of Canadian Politics

No one has shown how any alternative voting system would enable Canada to govern itself better. Rather, the first-past-the-post system is well-rooted in Canada's dominant political reality – its regional nature. It preserves the local-constituency roots of the House of Commons and works against extremes – the curse of the American system.

A system that factored in overall national or provincial numbers would sharpen ideological differences and make Canada's regional challenges harder. The first-past-the-post system, on the other hand, requires compromise to come in the first instance from the voter – the safest place. The voters, not a group of competing politicians, have to make compromises between their policy aspirations and what is politically achievable.

Some think reform may get more people engaged and voting. But reform isn't needed to do so. When voters see high stakes, they become politically engaged and their turnout increases. The Quebec referendum and the 2015 federal election are two examples. The other suggested rationale for reform is that people who vote for parties that are underrepresented in seats in relation to the national vote are not fairly represented. That criticism depends on the idea that a proportionate share of the national vote is preferable to regarding the local constituency as the heart of the system – a national-ideology preference over Canada's regional reality. The result would likely be endless minority governments. This would shift the need to compromise away from the voters and make mutual accommodation more difficult.

Former prime minister Joe Clark was derided when he called Canada a "community of communities." The idea seemed weak opposite Pierre Trudeau's strong federal stance. As things turned out, Trudeau's efforts to centralize proved an overreach and weakened the federal government. Former prime minister Brian Mulroney's looser approach and focus on the economy strengthened the country. Centralization was the wrong remedy for both Quebec separatism and Western Canadian alienation. Today's Canada is both a country and a community of communities. The regional nature of Canada's politics is rooted in its communities, alongside a strong nationwide conviction we are blessed to live in Canada.

A ranked-voting system, which drops candidates off and transfers their votes to their next preferred person until there is a majority, would not necessarily offend Canada's regional political reality. But it would so favour the Liberals right now that it would be dangerous politics and might result in underrepresentation of regional views. Proportional representation comes from Europe – a completely different world divided more by ideology and class than Canada. Nor is Europe an example of a politics that is working well. Any version of proportional representation can only increase the role of third parties and make mutual accommodation more difficult. With the partial exception of First Nations, Canada's mutual accommodation challenges are primarily regional. Canada works best when its choices come out of its own distinctive particularities – not an abstract idea.

An Amazing Political System

The Canadian political system meets the most fundamental of all tests – it works in real life and has done so over long stretches of time and through many challenges. It is dynamic, resilient, flexible, and responsive. Things get done. Laurier got it right for Canada in 1887 when he said his guiding political principle would be to pursue public purpose through compromise – to move from aspirational to practical politics. The difference with the US political system and culture could not be more fundamental. In Canada, it is compromise to achieve public purpose. In America, it is no compromise, which makes achieving public purpose harder

Canada's first-past-the-post, community-rooted, regionally driven, compromise-based electoral system has delivered. Regional differences are always a challenge, but not as difficult as differences of class, ideology, language, religion, ethnicity, identity, and culture elsewhere. Almost every decade has seen Canada get closer to Laurier's vision and to broaden beyond it to pluralism and inclusiveness – that is, mutual accommodation.

Fooling around with how we got where we are would be bad policy and politics. Canada works because there is space between communities and regions. It is held together by two official languages and shared territory; values, including the Charter of Rights and Freedoms (with another Canadian mutual accommodation in the "notwithstanding" clause opt-out); and our do-what-it-takes mutual accommodation ways.

How Reform/Alliance and the Parti Québécois Helped

Canada's political challenges from the beginning have come from its difficult and vast geography and its complicated history. Historically, Canada has been divided between the two founding colonial groups, French and English, each with their own language, religion, and law, and with First Nations, now on the path to reconciliation. It has shared the continent with its powerful and wealthy neighbour, the United States.

Europe and its battles, in contrast, originated with nationalist, class, ideological, and economic differences. These also exist in Canada, but not with the same intensity as in Europe. Canada has always needed a practical "what works" approach. Regional third parties have played a big role in helping Canada make that happen. They have lost ground or disappeared when less needed.

In the 1980s and early 90s, the great centrifugal forces of Quebec separatism and Western Canada alienation were underrepresented in Canada's Parliament. Two third parties emerged to fill the gap – the Reform (later Alliance) Party and the Bloc Québécois. Each made it once to official Opposition status. One of Stephen Harper's greatest achievements was to take the regional Alliance Party and make it into a national party. His greatest success lay in satisfying those two groups: in 2006, Western Canada wanted to join in the national discussion, and Quebec was not sure about staying in it; by 2015, Western Canada was in, and Quebec had decided to remain.

Also under Harper, immigration and various forms of social-conservative divisiveness prevalent in other countries were shut down. He understood the political importance to him of immigrants. As most anti-immigrant sentiment resided within his party, he was able to shut them down. Harper is owed more than most Canadians realize for this achievement. Unlike other Western countries, Canada has so far avoided serious anti-immigrant politics. The Canadian system has brought prosperity and social peace to more and more people. Canada's political system constrains excesses from its leaders and voters. The American system makes them worse. Mr Harper and Mr Trump each understand their own countries on this matter.

Canada's System Delivers

The Orlando nightclub massacre in June 2016 is another reason to be grateful for our political system. Sometimes quickly, sometimes more slowly, it mostly delivers what the public wants. A majority of Americans want assault weapons banned; 85 percent want stronger background checks. But their system cannot deliver. In Canada, when a government gets a policy wrong – the National Energy Program, for example, or the long-form census – a change of government allows for swift remedying. Timing and patience are important for big changes.

Mackenzie King called the CCF "Liberals in a hurry." Most of the broadly acceptable changes the CCF/NDP wanted have, over time, been enacted to the extent a majority of Canadians supported them. The CCF/NDP have seen a lot of their agenda enacted, though for good reasons they have never achieved power federally (they are too class- and ideology-oriented to make the needed regional accommodations). Justin Trudeau referred to Conservatives as our neighbours, not our enemies. Hillary Clinton called Trump voters the "deplorables."

Our two most ideologically driven and uncompromising prime ministers of the last century, Pierre Trudeau and Stephen Harper, were constrained by mutual accommodation – Mr Trudeau more overtly than Mr Harper. Mr Trump and the Tea Party were spurred on by division. Mr Trudeau was forced by Canada's system to abandon unilateral constitutional patriation and accept the "notwithstanding clause" override to his Charter of Rights and Freedoms. This accommodation made a Quebec language bill possible and helped keep Quebec in Canada. It also came from the intervention of Western premiers, who would not accept the courts as the final word in every situation. Mr Harper's regionally based Conservative politics failed him in the end but enabled him to unite the right side of the Canadian electorate. He left office with a strong party that can be a serious contender for government once it better understands today's world and Canada's economy – and how best to fit in.

A System That Gets What Is Needed

Most Canadians increasingly like the strengths and pleasures of their inclusiveness. Too few grasp its political foundations. Strong political goals and ideas are essential, but they need consensus. The path is compromise through creativity and patience. Canada has done better than other countries in getting both. Canada's electoral system has made it possible to govern what would otherwise be a hard-to-govern country. Over time it has delivered what most Canadians want and what the country needs – and that's pretty damn good when you look at the United States, the United Kingdom, and Europe in 2017.

3. NEXT STOP FOR THE NDP: THE END OF THE ROAD *

The federal New Democratic Party may soon be out of runway. Not only is it now a non-regional player searching for a place in a political landscape that the regions dominate, but it is ideological in a country where ideology has never really taken hold.

Its predecessor, the Co-operative Commonwealth Federation (CCF), emerged from the Great Depression's fights over class and ideology in Europe. But that world never really existed in Canada, which has almost always had one strong centrist party in power, with another waiting in the wings. Stephen Harper's political gospel was to erase the centrist Liberals and create a great divide between left and right. He failed. Can anyone do it?

The NDP has a fundamental problem: because ideology is divisive and excludes too much reality, the party's core instincts rule out mutual accommodation, which is something vital to Canadians. At the same time, the "movement" wing of the party has never felt entirely comfortable edging toward the centre to achieve power. The NDP's federal success between 2011 and 2015 derived mostly from other parties' weakness.

The abrupt dismissal of Tom Mulcair as leader at the NDP convention, along with pushing through a discussion on the hard-left Leap Manifesto (anti-fossil fuel, anti-pipeline, and anti-trade deal), provided some excitement. But neither move is likely to change fundamentals. The NDP breakthrough in Quebec in 2011, the provincial success in Alberta, and the initial prospect of a federal victory in the fall of 2015 did not reflect the underlying forces at work in Canada's federal politics.

The NDP has never stood on one side of the main issue in a federal election campaign or got beyond a protest role alone or pie-in-the-sky aspirations. Only two other third parties – the Bloc Québécois

---

* Published in the *Globe and Mail*, May 6, 2016.

and Reform, in addition to the NDP, have once become the official opposition. For the NDP, it grew out of the existential crisis fallout in Quebec, the near-death experience of the Liberal Party after 2006, and the collapse of the Bloc Québécois as separatism waned.

Battle for the NDP Soul

Commentator Chantal Hébert sees the decisive repudiation of Mulcair as round one in a proxy war over the manifesto being advanced by Stephen and Avi Lewis – son and grandson of former federal NDP leader David Lewis – and their supporters. She feels Mulcair is "only the first casualty of this potentially self-destructive battle for the soul of the federal NDP."

But is there a serious place in Canada for a moderate left-of-centre party or a harder-line, narrower, "conscience" party? What if party members are facing not a defeat caused by a disappointing campaign and leader but by existential issues to which there may be no lasting answer?

Conscience Is for Movements

Perhaps the conscience movements of the future will come less from parties and more from social media – which is more immediate and can form and re-form quickly. Justin Trudeau may be on to something in trying to make the Liberal Party into a movement – presumably both movement and party.

What that change would really mean, what difference it would make (if any), and whether it would work all lie in the future. Meanwhile, if the Lewis dynasty succeeds in its takeover attempt of NDP policy, the question will be the same as the one asked after all takeovers: what did they get for what they paid? Might the price be too high? If the Leap Manifesto unexpectedly makes the NDP relevant, it would turn Canadian politics upside down.

The NDP is the only serious third party in Canada's history that has not just come and gone. But it may now be facing its exit moment. Justin Trudeau is the most immediate cause of where it finds itself, but the fundamentals go deeper. Canada's federal politics since 1945 have been dominated by two strong mutual accommodation parties – the

Progressive Conservatives and the Liberals. Now that the Liberals have been resurrected and the Conservatives are moderating their tone and policy, there is no obvious room for a moderate third party.

It is also far from clear that there is enough demand for an uncompromising party. Mutual accommodation runs against the strong "we know best" attitude of many federal NDP activists – certainly of the Lewises.

The NDP is almost surely at a crossroads unlike any before. Its leadership is unresolved, its identity is in crisis, and its path forward is difficult – perhaps impossible over time. The party began to see itself in a new way with the surprise federal breakthrough in Quebec in 2011, the unexpected win by Rachel Notley in Alberta in the spring of 2015, and the brief period in the fall 2015 election when it went from a three-way tie with the Conservatives and Liberals into the lead. Unfortunately, all were political flukes. Canadians were not suddenly seeing the world through NDP eyes.

Canada's Third Parties

Over the last century, Canada's politics has often required three or more parties to manage its fundamental regional character. The first three third parties came from Western Canada. Later third parties originated in Quebec. Sometimes there have been up to five federal parties (in 1993, in addition to the Progressive Conservatives and the Liberals, there were Reform, Bloc Québécois, and NDP). The Reform and Alliance parties became so vigorous that the Alliance moved from a third party to a main party by taking over a Progressive Conservative Party that had been sapped in the post-1976 existential struggle.

The NDP is now unlikely to ever again become a contender for official opposition, let alone government. Third parties find it difficult to survive in Canada: they emerge from particular moments (such as economic depression, Quebec separatism, and Western Canadian alienation) that run counter to Canada's non-ideological, mutual accommodation ways.

More relevant is the fact that, over more than eighty years, the CCF/NDP has never stood for a single positive way forward on any of the three great challenges every Canadian prime minister faces: the economy, national unity, and the United States.

Something for the West to Hate

This policy limitation is the real reason the NDP's runway is so short. What does it offer that enough Canadians want and can get only from it? The convention revealed two continuing NDP challenges. First, the party is not good at national unity: it initially put an excessive emphasis on centralized social policy (too much so for Quebec); more recently, there has been its separatism-friendly policy that 50 percent plus one single vote (on a clear referendum question) is enough for Quebec to irreversibly destroy a country that has taken shape over the past 150 years.

Now comes the pipeline and fossil-fuel threat in the Leap Manifesto – a new national energy program for the West to hate. The NDP desperately needs public trust in its economic management. Even discussing the manifesto will make that problem worse.

Tony Blair centrism appears to have failed, and the NDP's "we know best" DNA (usually extreme and uncompromising) is now trying to come back. But the election of a non-extremist, centrist-tending Liberal Party has left no easy space to fill. Most of what the majority of people want from government is being attended to. They see further extension of government's role as unwanted or too much risk.

Is there an acceptable NDP diagnosis and consensus about how to respond? If not, could a lack of consensus lead the party to break up? Or could the wrong diagnosis, in a world where there may be no viable NDP-friendly consensus among voters, lead to its near-disappearance or lack of relevance? With the recent defeat in Manitoba, only one NDP provincial government remains – in Alberta – a strong common-sense opponent of the Leap Manifesto. Its poor recent provincial performances are not a good federal sign. (*Update*: The NDP did better than the Liberals in the 2018 Ontario election – not because the Ontario electorate had become more NDP but because it became more Ontario. The NDP also won a minority government in British Columbia after a long sixteen years out of power.)

The group behind the Leap Manifesto is up to something bigger than dismissing Thomas Mulcair. They were ready to muddy his election chances by bringing their "back-to-the-future" manifesto out in the middle of the 2015 election campaign. Climate change is serious, and the oil and pipeline industry has been stupid. But Premier

Notley was right to describe the manifesto as naive. No matter how well meant, it will be seen as a threat to Western Canada, if not the economy as a whole.

What Lies Ahead

The bleak future of the NDP, with nowhere obvious to go, may be the opportunity the Liberals need. Right now, Canadians are looking for ways that work for them and their country.

If the NDP left becomes more extreme at a time when the right is moderating, the political threat and opportunity for the Liberals will shift to the right. The Trudeau government has launched some big, full-hearted, multi-year journeys on the social-advance side of the ledger. How well they do involves an ongoing set of political challenges. What's needed is a stronger economic advance to go with them: pipelines (for both economic and national-unity reasons) and a new approach to private-sector investment and entrepreneurial drive.

Where Could the NDP Go?

It appears that the government knows the importance of pipelines. (*Update*: When Kinder Morgan dropped out, the government was forced to take the only responsible action it could and take the project over. The St Laurent Liberal government followed a similar route when it forced through the TransCanada Pipeline in 1957.) It is not clear yet where or how it sees the private sector fitting in. Could it see a unique Canadian opportunity for big tech-creative-scientific research clusters all across the country with strong links to its universities?

The belief inside the NDP in a social democratic party is strong, but where does it go now? If, as seems likely, the next election will be about the economy, nothing at the spring 2016 convention suggests that a newly led NDP will be united behind anything politically competitive on the economy.

The party's moment has likely come and gone – a moment never as big as it seemed. That means the Liberals, as they think about the economy, must and can safely look somewhat more to their right flank.

The NDP had one enormous federal impact – the introduction by the first Saskatchewan NDP government of provincial medicare, which later became national. Otherwise, the NDP's federal impact has come mostly from what the party prompted the Liberals to do on social policy, reflecting the Mackenzie King dictum that the CCF were just "Liberals in a hurry."

Canada's Federal Future

The Progressive Conservatives and the Liberals brought Canada through its post-1976 existential crisis. Today, there is no Progressive Conservative party and not much of a Bloc Québécois. The Liberals went into near-death intensive care, but have come back. The Reform/Alliance/Progressive Conservatives merged Conservative Party was in office. This is where things stood when the 2015 federal election was called and the NDP had its high hopes.

Third parties may, for the moment, no longer have a major federal role. If that proves true, there will be big changes in Canadian politics. If the NDP is indeed coming to the end of its federal run, minority governments will likely become largely a thing of the past. Since the first third party arrived after the First World War, almost half of Canada's federal elections – twelve of twenty-eight – have resulted in minority rule.

Two parties – the Liberals and the Conservatives – will now shape post-existential threat federal politics. The regional nature of Canada's federal politics seems unlikely to be expressed through third parties until something changes. And ideology does not seem to be the way forward in today's world.

No party has yet expressed a viable view on Canada's overall debt and economic-growth future. The Conservatives' pre-election economic and fiscal view did not pass muster politically or economically. The Liberals' view will likely not become clear until its 2017 budget next spring. (*Update*: When the budget was tabled, it left Canada with a live-beyond-its-means economic narrative and with the private sector as a secondary element in Canada's economy.) Inevitably, there will be a political battle over growth and debt. Historically, the NDP has never had the right offer when the economy was the fight – and, with discussions within the party focused for the next two years on the Leap Manifesto, this is not likely to change. (*Update*: Both the Leap Manifesto and the federal NDP have gone nowhere since the NDP dismissed Thomas Mulcair.)

If the federal NDP cannot get there with Jack Layton/Tom Mulcair centrist moderation when the Liberals are down, when can they? The big question for Canada is different. The NDP and Stephen Harper were spenders – not builders – one through social spending, the other through tax cuts. What happens if the Liberals are much the same, just sunnier and more expansive? Who and what will the country be able to look to then? (*Update*: So far, the answer is no one. It will likely take the narrowness of the upcoming recession to flush out real policy and the leadership to carry it through.)

6

The Rule of Law Still Matters

INTRODUCTION

The rule of law is one of the West's great achievements – both political and economic. It is central to all its other achievements. Two recent Canadian trials – one about political power (Senator Mike Duffy) and the other about sexual behaviour (CBC host Jian Ghomeshi) – prove that the rule of law still prevails in Canada, even against the power of the ruling government and the weight of public opinion. Individuals are still held innocent until proved guilty; every offence deserves the best defence; and accused persons have the right to remain silent, protecting themselves against self-incrimination. (It was also at the centre of the recent SNC-Lavalin affair and has so far prevailed.)

For this reason, some offences, such as lesser forms of sexual abuse, might best be dealt with outside the criminal justice system – by mutual accommodation, social-control, or self-control measures. The arrival of the MeToo movement will likely prove one of them. If that movement over the next ten years is followed by better gun control laws in the United States in response to the Florida Parkland shootings, guns and sex, two powerful symbols of the still dominant (declining much more slowly in the United States than Canada) patriarchy will decline for the better by force of both laws and social control. A decline in patriarchy would likely help mutual accommodation inside the United States. A failure to do so, if it results in the

Published in the *Globe and Mail*, December 21, 2017.

Supreme Court of the United States reversing *Roe v. Wade* (which permits abortion), could see the United States move beyond its current identity crisis into an existential crisis revolving around patriarchy. It is striking that, in addition to these two rule of law trials in Canada, the biggest non-economic political issues that have been undermining Justin Trudeau in 2019 are each about the rule of law: the detention of Meng Wanzhou of Huawei and the SNC-Lavalin fiasco.

The great Western achievements of the past six centuries rest on two fundamentals: the rule of law and democratic governance – both of which are now under increasing stress. Politics and the rule of law matter to the economy, to a functioning society, and to security. If lost, a great deal will be undermined or destroyed.

Canada's fundamental freedom under the law was strengthened in two recent celebrity trials – one about political power (Mike Duffy), the other about male sexual behaviour (Jian Ghomeshi). The Duffy verdict withstood the power of the prime minister and his office. The Ghomeshi verdict withstood powerful public opinion about how best to address abusive behaviour against women. A trustworthy criminal justice system is central to freedom and to our liberal democracy. It needs to be understood to survive.

The Duffy and Ghomeshi trials and verdicts generated much media and public interest. Federal politics changed after the Duffy trial. And the Ghomeshi trial started a national conversation about the reporting of sexual assault.

Criminal trials may change the world – but it is never their goal. Most are entirely about what happens to a particular individual. The only issue is proving guilt beyond a reasonable doubt. This confinement is fundamental.

No Due Process in the Senate

The Duffy case raised big concerns. The Senate suspended three senators without due process – telling Canadians, in effect, that the only place affecting individual rights that does not require due process is Parliament. This absence of due process was not primarily about depriving the dismissed senators of their rights. It was about avoiding unwanted evidence of what the prime minister and his PMO had been up to and the Senate's own lax policies. Due process could have brought a "political show trial" in reverse – hurting the representatives of the state more than the accused.

The power of the state is awesome, even in a free society operating under the rule of law. My wake-up call came from Peter Mansbridge's interview on March 29, 2016, with Marie Henein, the lawyer representing Mr Ghomeshi. Ms Henein was compelling. She passionately conveyed her belief in how fortunate Canadians are to have the protection of the rule of law and how few countries really possess it. She also conveyed how heavy the weight of the state can be on anyone charged with a crime. She said every person who enters her office charged with a crime is changed forever, no matter the outcome. No one is guaranteed a desired outcome – only a fair trial based on tested evidence.

The Duffy and Ghomeshi trials showed that our justice system still works against the raw force of both political power and public opinion – even that of a public with strong and justifiable feelings about the sexual abuse of women.

People can have different views about the alleged behaviour of Mr Duffy and Mr Ghomeshi, but only one about a criminal justice system that can deprive accused individuals of their liberty. Convictions must come from credible-beyond-a-reasonable-doubt evidence independent of the accused. This standard accommodates two great societal purposes: the protection of society from criminal behaviour, and the protection of individuals from loss of liberty unless proven guilty.

John Henry Wigmore, the great Northwestern University dean of law who wrote *Wigmore on Evidence*, made clear that the rule that convictions must be based on independent credible evidence may protect the guilty more than the innocent. But it protects something greater: the kind of society we live in. Our criminal justice system is not perfect, but no other system is better. Ours is not a "truth" or "absolute justice" system. It is a human construct – a system based on the fair and independent assessment of testimony tested by cross-examination.

How Far Should the Criminal Law Reach?

Every society needs behaviour controls. History has seen a variety of them: the raw force of authoritarian regimes, tribal customs, social norms, and religion. In the West today, we have five broad sources of control: the criminal law, the civil law, societal control, mutual accommodation, and self-control. We must rely on all of them to achieve our goals. If we can lessen our dependence on enforced legal control and rely more on societal control, mutual accommodation, and self-control, the freer and stronger society will be.

Former Supreme Court chief justice Beverley McLachlin, in her Aga Khan Global Centre for Pluralism lecture in Toronto in 2015, said the law should tolerate as much difference as it reasonably can. The stakes in criminal justice are very high, affecting an individual's freedom. What we choose to make criminal is a big issue. It changes over time, as in legalizing marijuana and medical assistance in dying. Our criminal law involves the Charter of Rights and Freedoms and raises issues of effective reach and alternatives. The Charter, Canada's ultimate law, is based on perhaps the biggest mutual accommodation of all: the balance of individual rights and freedoms against the needs of society to govern itself.

Not a System for Accusers

Canada's justice system is based on one fundamental idea: the greatest threat to a free and democratic society almost always comes from a too-powerful and self-protective state – authoritarianism in all its guises. Bad individuals are ranked a lesser threat, unless organized crime or general corruption co-opts the state. Our justice system does not encourage accusers – either individuals or the state – nor does it normally clear the names of the accused.

The Ghomeshi trial did not find out what happened, nor did it clear him. It found only that he was not guilty beyond a reasonable doubt on the evidence before the court, which the judge found lacked credibility.

The Duffy case was a rare exception. The judge cleared Mr Duffy of criminal wrongdoing, but not of every kind of wrongdoing. In effect, he found the previous Prime Minister's Office to be wrongful accusers for improper political purposes.

The Limits to the Criminal Law

The widespread disappointment following the Ghomeshi verdict came primarily from wrong expectations about what the criminal justice system can properly deliver. Ms Henein was castigated as a traitor to women because she took on Mr Ghomeshi's defence. The heart of the justice system stands against any predetermination that a particular kind of alleged offence should not get the best defence. It is fine for those upset about such alleged offences to stand together. It is not fine to do so in ways that could subvert the justice system itself.

The criticism focused on the fact that complainants were cross-examined on their evidence while the accused was not. Such condemnation demonstrates a misunderstanding of the fundamental rule against self-incrimination at trial. Exceptions to this rule would subvert the entire justice system. For this reason, the criminal law will likely disappoint in many situations involving sexual assault or abuse.

One positive outcome of the Ghomeshi trial would be for Canadians to examine the root nature of the relationships and behaviours on the sexual-abuse front and which means of control have the best chance of making things better. The criminal law will always be needed for clear-cut cases, but many troubled sexual situations may require something different. An effective solution may emerge from the groundwork being laid by Ralph Goodale, the minister of public safety, for a national strategy to deal with sexual-assault cases in a way that ensures both the police and the prosecutors are dealing fairly with victims of sexual assault.

Lessons Learned

The Ghomeshi trial revealed that sexual-relationship challenges can go beyond those cases that the criminal law normally handles well. The needed controls for abuse are far more likely to be found in a wide range of self-control and social-control measures.

The Duffy trial showed that, even in Canada, high-ranking individuals can use state power to protect themselves rather than society. It was our criminal law system, not our politics, that protected our society.

If we wonder why we need to pay attention to how well our criminal justice system is working, take a look at Turkey; what is happening to the Pakistani bar; the disappearances in China; the president of the United States undermining its justice system by referring to an American judge of Latin American origin as a "so-called" judge. All these examples undermine the rule of law. In a political world where facts seem to matter less, a world of fake news and demonstrably outrageous lies, Canadians must become more alert to the foundations and importance of their criminal justice system.

The criminal justice system must always be able to withstand political power and the pressure of public opinion. The state or public opinion may sometimes be right, but a strong justice system that protects the freedom of the subject must always prevail.

7

A Fine Balance in Culture and Languages: Overcoming Islamophobia

INTRODUCTION

Canada is home to about one million Muslims, out of a total of 1.6 billion worldwide. Despite claims by al-Qaeda and the Islamic State that the violence they commit is done in the name of Islam, there is no real connection between Islam and terrorism. In a globalized media world, there is always a risk of contagion. Michael Adams, in his new book *Could It Happen Here? Canada in the Age of Trump and Brexit* (2017), answers that yes, contagion could happen. But the last election showed "we don't want to fight to see who is right. We want to talk and talk ..." Talk that still largely prevailed in the 2019 federal election has been the Canadian way. It may move very slowly, but it mostly works over time. Adams sees the demography from our immigration as "the engine that injects values of openness, tolerance and compromise into every sphere of social life." If you have to spend time in a Toronto hospital, these values and practices, and their benefits, are everywhere.

The more serious flareups of Islamophobia in recent years have occurred in Quebec, with isolated cases elsewhere. Quebec has always been a distinct society within Canada, driven by a determination to preserve its own identity, culture, and language. In 2008 the province fought to ban people from wearing conspicuous religious symbols (turbans, hijabs, crucifixes) in public spaces – and that proposed law led to particular rejection of Muslim women wearing face-covering niqabs. In the provincial election later that year, the Parti Québécois lost. A somewhat less restrictive version has now become law with the election of the Coalition Avenir Québec (CAQ) in the recent provincial election.

Leaders within the Muslim community need to find some means of their own to deal with the tiny group of potential terrorists in their community, just as Canadians in general need to educate themselves about Islamic history and culture – and Muslims need to learn about Canada's history and culture. Ultimately, the only long-term solution for peaceful co-existence lies in mutual accommodation – with both Muslims and non-Muslims actively interacting more with each other. A Muslim woman saw me pushing an empty wheelchair at Sunnybrook Hospital in Toronto recently. Unrequested, she wheeled me to the intensive care unit. It is this spontaneous kind of interaction that will win the day – but with help from our leaders.

Quebec after the Quiet Revolution in the 1960s moved beyond the authoritarian bent of the Quebec Catholic hierarchy. The recent new anti-Muslim law against wearing religious clothing or symbols by persons in authority in the name of secularism (though much less extreme than a similar law in France) makes one wonder if the real issue for Quebec is that some francophone Quebeckers need a new secularist authoritarianism to replace the Catholic authoritarianism they chose to abandon sixty years ago. Should it prevail, this attitude will hurt a society whose economy needs more immigrants. We can only hope that this necessity will, over time, gradually cure Quebec's cultural anxieties as the province keeps on its path of thriving, not just surviving.

———

There is no valid reason for Islamophobia, no matter what Islamic State or homegrown extremists claiming to act in the name of Islam do in Canada, the United States, or other countries. We cannot let 0.003 percent of the Muslim world speak for the other 99.997 percent. Canada must avoid this error – and it can. The answer is simple. It requires a willingness by us all to think for ourselves, to be open with others, and, most important, to engage in conversation. Fortunately, that conversation is already under way.

Published in the *Globe and Mail*, August 14, 2015.

Fear can goad people into action, but it is never a good guide for that action. For some reason, Americans seem to be more naturally fearful than Canadians, and the media there stoke that fear more than Canadian media do. The primary danger for us is succumbing to that heightened fear through contagion. The best antidote is calm, common sense, and fair-minded discussion. We all have a stake.

Mackenzie King, arguably Canada's most successful prime minister, once said he wanted to be remembered not for what he achieved but for what he avoided. Most important, he avoided the breakdown of unity during the Second World War. Today, in a world preoccupied by extreme terrorist violence, it is essential that Canada, in relation to its Muslim population, avoid a repetition of its failure so far to deal with its First Nations in a mutually accommodating way.

The numbers tell their own story. There are about a million Muslims in Canada, and 1.6 billion around the world, one-quarter of whom reside in India and Indonesia. Despite the current problems particular to Islam, there is no irresistible link between Islam itself and terrorism. No Muslim country is in the world's top 20 in terms of homicides per capita, nor is Islam associated with any of the 10 largest genocides in history.

The only long-run solution to the relationship between Islam and the rest of the world is rooted in mutual accommodation. Whatever is being done to fight terrorism must always keep that reality in mind. Words matter, and we should avoid to the extent possible including the terms Islamic or Muslim in our descriptions of extremism or terrorism, even if the violence is being done in the name of Islam. Readers already know that's what al Qaeda and Islamic State claim.

Religions Need to Re-evaluate

Islam is no different from any other religion in its need to examine itself critically. The thinking mostly has to come from within, while the challenges will often come from outside events. The recent US Supreme Court decision upholding gay marriage is a good example. Religion not only challenges the world; the world challenges religion. Institutional religions, if they are to survive and thrive, need to communicate with their adherents and with everyone else. For example, the Pope challenges the world to do better at the very moment when the acceptance of gay marriage challenges his church (and not long after it was challenged by the adverse reaction to its reluctance to respond to the sexual abuse of young people in its care).

David Brooks, the insightful conservative columnist for the *New York Times*, described the current post-gay-marriage situation in the United States very well. True believers – mostly of a religious persuasion – have a choice, he says; one way is to keep fighting for what they believe by seeking to change laws so that they can impose their views on society. The other, as Mr Brooks and I both believe, is for these groups to accept that they are special communities of individual believers who can make their best contribution to their members and to society not by trying to impose their views on others, but by the strength of their own communities of faith.

In June 2015 the racist massacre in Charleston, SC, provided yet another example of how our world desperately needs more compassion and a larger purpose than individuals themselves. It is difficult to imagine anything more powerful than the personal, face-to-face forgiveness of the deeply mourning relatives to the murderer of their loved ones. The authenticity of this forgiveness could come only from the force of their deep faith.

Issues with Muslims

We have an urgent need to find the best strategy to address the double challenge presented by terrorist acts in Canada and terrorist recruits from Canada. Aside from that issue, how big a problem are Muslims? Or, from another perspective, is Canada a problem for Muslims? Canada's history is all about a growing capacity for the inclusion of more and more differences in our society. Covering a woman's face with a niqab is certainly incompatible with the openness that has become part of the Canadian way. Yet it represents no threat to anyone except on those occasions when there is a clear need to see someone's face, such as for identification purposes or during testimony in court.

CBC-TV's Rosemary Barton conducted a constructive interview on this subject with two Muslim women in November 2014 shortly after two soldiers were killed, one in Quebec and the other in Ottawa. She spoke first to a middle-aged Quebecker who said that all head coverings, and especially niqabs, are the result of religiously imposed male oppression. She presented herself, I thought, as a supporter of a secularist authoritarianism reminiscent of the religious authoritarianism from Quebec's past.

The other woman was young, lively, and wearing a hijab. She said her personal preference was to wear a niqab as well. It was not a male-imposed choice, so she opposed any unnecessary restrictions against it. Asked by Ms Barton why she didn't have one on for the interview, she replied: "Because other people don't like niqabs." In other words, she respected mutual accommodation. If non-Muslim Canadians felt uncomfortable in her presence when most of her face was covered, she would voluntarily respect their feelings. I hope that impulse will become the way forward. It would see both sides accommodate each other, not by coercion but by choice.

The Situation in Quebec

Over the last few years, there have been some sporadic flare-ups on the Muslim front in Quebec. Quebec is a distinct society, but it is subject to the same demographic pressures as other parts of Canada. How it reacts, however, reflects the special Quebec drivers of culture, language, and identity, which are no longer as different as they have been at times in the past. Separatism may be finished in Quebec, but nationalism and some socio-cultural anxiety still remain.

Philippe Couillard seems to be the province's first post-separatist-threat premier. He knows the power of freedom and science as opposed to a narrow nationalism. He encourages mutual accommodation. Like Robert Bourassa before him, he recognizes that a sound economy and the ability to live within its means are crucial to the survival and prosperity of the province.

Quebec's political preoccupations have always revolved around the survival of Québécois collectivity within an English-dominated North America. The Quebec family quarrel following the Quiet Revolution in the 1960s now seems pretty well resolved, and the majority of the population accepts that it will be more protected than threatened by being a part of Canada. This was the position of all of Quebec's great francophone federal leaders before Pierre Trudeau.

So what have these intermittent disputes over Muslims in the province been about? In the past, issues in Quebec around others who are different have been linked to identity insecurity – essentially to language insecurities. After some wrangles in small communities over the "threat" of Muslims they had scarcely ever seen, Premier Jean Charest felt compelled in 2007 to establish the Bouchard-Taylor Commission into cultural and religious accommodation as a political necessity. The recommendations in its 2008 report over the wearing of conspicuous religious symbols such as turbans, kippot, hijabs, and crucifixes in public institutions were mild and never really implemented. Then in 2013, Mr Charest's successor, Pauline Marois, launched the extremist Quebec Charter of Values, which inflamed the issue once again – and worked against her Parti Québécois in last year's provincial election, when the Liberals returned to office.

The "accommodation" bill that Premier Couillard introduced last fall maintained the religious neutrality of the state even as it protected Quebec "values." Mr Bourassa had recognized Quebec nationalism as something that could not be ignored, and, similarly, Mr Couillard initially seemed to realize that, since the Quiet Revolution, equality for women had become a fixture of the Quebec political scene. Thus it had to take precedence over other considerations, so anyone performing (or receiving) a public service in the province could do so with a covered face.

After the terrorist incidents in November 2014, however, Premier Couillard delayed bringing the bill forward. "I am here to defend the freedom of all Quebeckers of all origins," he said, "and I say no to exclusion and discrimination." This is the kind of firm political leadership that may be needed right across Canada.

A Muslim Response

How might everyday Muslims best respond to these challenges? One initiative I heard about recently is The Next Generation, a modest symposium held in Toronto a few months ago. Some of the most accomplished Muslims in the province were invited to discuss two central issues: how to engage the tiny minority of Muslims who develop strong anti-Canadian views, then act on them violently; and how to reduce Islamophobia.

Similarly, I would add: How might non-Muslim Canadians engage intelligently in the conversation we all need to have?

To begin, I suggest that they follow this program:

- Read two books by the thoughtful English writer Karen Armstrong, entitled *Islam: A Short History* (2002) and *Muhammad: A Prophet for Our Time* (2006). Also read *Globe and Mail* columnist Doug Saunders's *The Myth of the Muslim Tide: Do Immigrants Threaten the West?* (2012) and Michael Adams's *Could It Happen Here? Canada in the Age of Trump and Brexit* (2017).
- Visit the Aga Khan Museum (as well as its gardens) in Toronto and appreciate the rich culture included in the exhibitions. Also, as a caution, visit the Mosque-Cathedral of Córdoba where, after the Muslims were driven out of Spain in the thirteenth century, their monumental mosque was converted into a Catholic cathedral (to my eye, a monstrosity, even though I normally love medieval cathedrals), marring a place of rare peace and beauty.
- Watch *Islamic Art: Mirror of the Invisible World* (2011), a documentary film that has been shown on PBS and is available on DVD.

We are at a hugely important moment in history – possibly comparable to the transition from the Middle Ages to the Renaissance. Canada lives in the world's best neighbourhood, with an unparalleled array of space, resources, and food. It is strong in all the best ways to live: compassion, freedom, science, and mutual accommodation.

If we consider Canadian Muslims in this broad context, two issues have been identified as potential problems: terrorism, which, though involving only very small numbers, must be curbed; and women's head and face coverings – a purely socio-cultural matter. Consequently, only very limited changes in the law and in the use of state force are needed. The recent Senate committee report on terrorism goes much further. It recommended, among other items, training and certifying imams – a suggestion the Muslim community immediately condemned as religious discrimination. The sensible response to the report will be to use it to have more conversation on these issues among all the stakeholders.

All Canadians – Muslims and non-Muslims – need to put their faith in the proposition that every valid value is safe in the Canada we know. It is for those values that Muslims came to our shores in the first place. If Canada holds to its mutual accommodation heritage, the power of freedom and of Canadian inclusiveness will prevail.

Certainly, a well-thought-out strategy that includes force on the terrorism front will be needed. Ultimately, however, to secure a lasting cure for excessive fearfulness and for keeping limits on the necessary use of law and force, we Canadians have to rely on ourselves and on our ability to find a mutually accommodating way forward.

In 2006 the Environics Institute for Survey Research delivered *Muslims and Multiculturalism in Canada*, a useful and interesting study. It provides a vast array of information that could be very helpful in guiding the discussion, especially as it is being updated.

As Walter Isaacson, the acclaimed biographer of Benjamin Franklin, predicted a decade ago, the dominant battle in the twenty-first century will be against intolerance, especially religious intolerance. The only way to handle it will be by mutual accommodation. Canada, if it is true to itself, is as well positioned as any country to succeed.

8

Toronto: From Good to Great

Two powerful transformations – Toronto and Canada – are happening right under our eyes. The limited "Toronto the good" of my childhood is morphing into "Toronto the great" of my old age. Moreover, Toronto is not the only Canadian city undergoing positive change: Montreal and Vancouver are in major transition too. Toronto is simply bigger, with a broader range. It has moved beyond its English and post-war European immigrant roots to be an Asia Pacific city too – arguably more so than any other North American city not on the West coast. Toronto is now English, European, and Asian (with large diaspora communities and external cultural, educational, and business connections).

It's the same with Canada. It was a good country in its first 100 years; and it is now a different kind of great country for a different kind of world. It has been shaped by a difficult coast-to-coast geography; Quebec French alongside English; two major Christian religions (Roman Catholic and Protestant); resistance to a United States intent on its manifest destiny to occupy the North American continent; and its own expanding mutual accommodation ways. Toronto's fundamental values come from these forces along with its own early English conservatism and sense of civic virtue.

In finance, Toronto is second to New York within North America. In terms of jobs in the financial sector, Toronto's share has been growing faster than in all other cities except for Beijing and Shanghai – a 25.2 percent increase from 2012 to 2017, almost five times as much as in New York, Boston, and San Francisco. Toronto is third in the world in English-speaking theatre, after New York and London (with the

Stratford and Shaw festivals nearby). It may now be the lead Western city in AI (artificial intelligence). Its proximity to Waterloo – with Mike Lazaridis and the Perimeter Institute for Theoretical Physics he established (a match for Albert Einstein's Institute of Advanced Study at Princeton) – makes the Greater Toronto area a world leader in quantum-based technologies. Its health research makes academic medicine in Toronto among the top ten in the world. And Toronto is headquarters for one of the great global news organizations, Thomson Reuters.

Toronto's hi-tech employment growth rate is now the highest on the continent. The relocation of the major Collision Tech Conference to Toronto in 2019 speaks volumes. The University of Toronto edged out MIT in 2017 as the North American university with the most startups. Microsoft's Canada headquarters will now be in Toronto. The Ottawa-based Shopify e-commerce retail entrepreneurship platform plans to occupy some 450,000 square feet at the edge of the Toronto city core. And the *Globe and Mail* recently reported that Canada (largely Toronto) now graduates more students with international MBAs than does the United States.

Toronto and Canada can form a powerful combination in the increasingly competitive and entrepreneurial global economy. As Paul Volcker, the esteemed former Federal Reserve chief, recently said: "Toronto has become a true international city in more than size, with the cultural variety, energy, and outlook that implies."

When I arrived in Toronto from Montreal in the late 1940s, it was a one-horse WASP town. My mother grew up there, and both my parents went to the University of Toronto. Slowly but steadily it has transformed itself into a prosperous and inclusive city with social peace. In 1953 the thirteen-lawyer law firm I joined needed a labour lawyer. It bypassed the only candidate because he would have become the second Catholic lawyer – one too many in some eyes. By the mid-1960s that same much-larger sixty-lawyer firm had employees who spoke fifty different languages. Today, 50 percent of downtown Torontonians working in offices are immigrants or first-generation Canadians.

Former US president Calvin Coolidge said, "The business of America is business." But no nation can succeed alone. The countries, cities, and industries that will move ahead in the intensely competitive global world of the coming decades must recognize that they need collaborators – and have the ability to work with them. Right now, the United States is engaged in a long-term technology fight with China. It cannot win, let alone remain great and become even greater, if it loses talent to other countries – as Germany did with its Jews in the 1930s. The identity crisis in today's divided United States will not quickly disappear. It will not help them, in their global competitive challenges.

Toronto/Canada can help the United States reduce the economic cost of its divisiveness and identity crises by benefiting from the US loss of competitiveness for the best people. As America works through these challenges, Toronto/Canada can attract and then help make the best entrepreneurial and technology personnel available to US-based companies. The Nomura Group chief economist, Richard Koo, told me in Tokyo thirteen years ago that Toyota had no interest in making more money out of its large pot of cash, as Japanese and non-Japanese investment banks were pushing it to do. Cash was "not a Toyota core business," they said, and the company did not have enough good managers for its core business. Today, Toronto could play a key role on behalf of the United States and its businesses in the coming US-China technology struggle. This core struggle requires the best people. The new Toronto/Canada generation is increasingly focused on business (primarily in the hi-tech and financial sectors) even as it becomes ever more inclusive.

Toronto's good stories come together around things that work – big, small, international, national, and local. Professor Robert Vipond at the University of Toronto has written a fascinating book, *Making a Global City: How One Toronto School Embraced Diversity* (2017), about Clinton Street Public School. It began with the Jewish Clinton (1920–52), moved on to the European Clinton (1950–75), and became the global Clinton (1975–90) – meaning that diversity was central to the school's life long before the expansion of Canada's multiculturalism after 1945. This story shows how Canada became a mutual accommodation leader at the community level.

In his fine book *Partnership for Excellence: Medicine at the University of Toronto and Academic Hospitals* (2013), Dr Edward Shorter, a professor of medical history at the University of Toronto, gives two key reasons why Toronto's medical research and patient medicine have moved from good to great. First, compared with other major medical cities in North America, where there is usually only one academic hospital per university medical school, the University of Toronto Medical School is fed by nine teaching hospitals. Second, thirty-five of the world's major languages are spoken in this increasingly multicultural city. Toronto today also has the third largest biomedical cluster in North America.

A new Canadian vision seems ready to emerge: Canada as the best country for every kind of successful people from anywhere to live a good life, earn a living, and build their businesses and wealth. (The *Economist* recently ranked Vancouver, Calgary, and Toronto as three of the ten most livable cities in the world.) That vision is Toronto today. Right now, it is on track to be one of the great global cities of the next fifty years. It needs to be a leader in keeping everyday housing affordable in a city where costs are escalating – due to its success. It also needs to encourage ways of outsourcing its hi-tech jobs to regions outside Toronto as a way to help moderate the newly emerging urban/rural political and cultural divide in North America and keep its own housing costs reasonable enough.

Toronto and Vancouver each has one real estate market divided between two systems – one, a safe global real estate for capital preservation by non-Canadians in a dangerous world, and the other, a domestic real estate for locals to live in. In 1973 I advised the Bermuda government on its tax and fee structure and the influx of non-residents capital to buy residential real estate in a small island with limited space. I recommended a special tax on real estate acquisitions by non-residents – an idea Bermuda accepted. The goal was to even out the real estate competition between locals and outsiders and to raise revenues from this scarce resource. Big cities have to be careful to ensure that their residential real estate is not priced out of the reach of locals. Great cities like Toronto will have to make sure that the global population does not disturb the local population too much.

Nouriel Roubini, an economics professor at New York University, forecast the 2008 financial and economic crises before most other people did. Early in 2018 in the *Financial Times*, he foresaw new financial and economic crises ahead in 2020. These crises are not the same as the previous ones, and their timing might vary (right now they seem more likely to come one or two years later than expected). He also said that current global upsets were symptoms of the much deeper rivalry to determine global leadership in the technologies of the future. Toronto can play a leading role in that struggle by providing a place for top people who cannot or do not want to go to the United States. A big economic future will require a strong political governance system that delivers economic and social advances hand in hand – and much depends on Ontario premier Doug Ford's next steps in shaping future governance in Toronto. So far, not so good on the Ford front.

Toronto continues to ride high in 2019. The February 27, 2019, *Financial Times* had a one-page "Big Read: Technology" entitled "The Canadian Brain Gain" (no longer the Canadian Brain Drain – a historical shift of potentially huge long-term significance for Toronto and for Canada). The headline read: "Toronto has created more tech jobs over the past five years than any other North American city, including San Francisco." Then came the possibility of Google affiliate Sidewalk Labs making a successful push for the right to create a 100-acre Toronto waterfront community. As written in the *Globe and Mail*, June 25, 2019: "Cameras and sensors could capture data that Sidewalk and companies could use to get a better understanding of how people move around cities and possibly develop new technology to improve city life." Finally, in late June 2019, the Raptors basketball team became the first non-American team to win the NBA championship. The win was seen on TV globally, showing off Toronto and Canada at their best. It was a "gift" in some ways, maybe best seen as the latest icing on the Toronto cake.

Toronto's recent success streak has been seriously damaged only once by the Ford government's self-inflicted harm in withdrawing Ontario's $200 million investment commitment to research in artificial intelligence – bizarrely done just weeks after Gerald Schwarz and Heather Reisman made a $100 million investment commitment to AI research in Toronto.

The *Financial Times* article mentioned above – "Canada from brain loss to brain gain" – was followed a few months later on July 25, 2019, with a Bloomberg Opinion piece, "US – Hands Canada an opening in tech by making immigrants unwelcome." America does a favour for aspiring hubs in Toronto and Vancouver. "They're beautiful, safe and fun – just the kind of place that your educated workers should enjoy living in" – and more affordable than San Francisco, Los Angeles, or New York.

Canada is a vast country. Toronto has an advantage over Canada's other two largest cities – Montreal and Vancouver. Montreal was Canada's largest until Toronto seized its growing advantages over Montreal after the Second World War. Toronto was favoured by its proximity to the United States industrial heartland – the primary location for the next several decades of Eastern Canadian economic growth. But Montreal has the longest history as a major Canadian city. It is the second largest French-speaking city in the world, after Paris. Historically, Montreal (originally Ville Marie) survived conflict and wars in its colonial period and political instability engendered by more recent referendums on sovereignty and linguistic and identity conflicts. Throughout it all, Montreal has become an increasingly dynamic and diverse economic and cultural centre for Quebec and Canada. In one sentence, it has moved from survival to thrival, some sixty years after the Quiet Revolution that took both Quebec and Canada through existential and identity crises.

Vancouver has the best climate and the worst weather among Canada's big cities. It sits at the edge of some of the greatest and most beautiful mountain ranges in the world. As in Toronto and Montreal, there is explosive hi-tech growth. Vancouver became Canada's Pacific outpost when the transcontinental railway made the town in 1886 into what would become Canada's door to Asia. In the decades since, it has become many diverse things at their best. Vancouver could be East China but for its huge influx of South Asians. The rest of Canada watches and welcomes the future of the world that is Asia primarily through Vancouver.

9

A True Partnership with Our
Indigenous Peoples: Truth and Reconciliation

INTRODUCTION

The final report on murdered and missing Indigenous women and
girls (*Reclaiming Power and Place*) came out after I wrote the updat-
ing introduction below. The report has two dimensions. One is what
needs to be done (231 individual Calls for Justice directed at government, institutions, social service providers, industries, and all Canadians). The other is the claim that what happened and kept happening
was genocide. Many people wished that the term "genocide" had not
been used in this context. They believed that, by making the politics
more difficult, this blame could distract from getting on with the
large challenges identified in this report. Interestingly, an early public opinion poll showed that a comfortable majority of Canadians
accepted the genocide description. This reaction may mean that the
genocide label will not in fact make the politics more difficult. If so,
it may suggest that the understanding by everyday Canadians of their
relations with Indigenous people has been growing.

However, even if the genocide description of what happened does
make the politics more difficult, it had to be heard because it reflects
the deep pain, sorrow, and loss endured by those who went through
what happened to them, their families, and their communities. More
and more Canadians seem to understand this grief. No matter what
you call the tragedy, it is not possible to fathom how it could have
been allowed to happen to anyone. For this reason, the report had
to say what the most deeply affected people felt. The Canadian public opinion response to the genocide part of the report is further

confirmation to me that I was right in my late 2015 essay on the Truth and Reconciliation Report: "This time will be different."

The bottom line about today's Indigenous people can be expressed in a few words: Champlain, the visionary, soldier, statesman, and explorer, saw the way forward for settler/Indigenous relations – that both peoples were equal. Sadly, for them and for Canadians, the French authorities in the early seventeenth century did not follow that vision. Now, after centuries of "cultural genocide," more and more Canadians are open to Champlain's way.

Great individuals and great countries make many mistakes – sometimes very big ones. But they get enough of the greatest things right. Canada got two of these greatest things right – a coast-to-coast country, and one that is increasingly held together by persuasion, not force. Canada's biggest mistake was in failing to see and try to achieve Samuel de Champlain's vision of equality between European settlers and Indigenous people. The cultural genocide of the residential schools compounded this big mistake. The results are traumatized people still living out the abuse they suffered from the original European settlers and, until very recently, their heirs.

Changes on the Indigenous front are underway in increasingly positive ways at the political, business, university, and media levels. Big challenges remain and will take decades to fully overcome. There is even more to accomplish at the ground level of everyday life. Although that is barely happening right now, it has begun. Until five years ago, I had never known an individual Indigenous person well. Now I know three under the age of fifty, and I have the greatest possible regard for each of them and feel privileged to call them friends. This kind of interaction was long overdue for me personally just as it is for both Indigenous and non-Indigenous Canadians too.

There is room in our inclusive ("both/and") Canada for every kind of Indigenous/non-Indigenous relationship. It takes a long time to change individual hearts and minds, but change is essential before we can get to a lasting good place. Now is the moment of catch up. Once that has been achieved, the true partnership of Indigenous and non-Indigenous people will become more about shared new visions, ideas, and projects for the future – about future shared things that can work for both groups, and less about past things that failed.

I repeated in my original *Globe and Mail* essay what Shawn Atleo, the former chief of the Assembly of First Nations, said his grandmother told him: "They are beginning to see us." To be really seen for who you are is a deep human need. I feel that in the three years since I reported that comment, the Indigenous people are indeed being acknowledged and seen by more and more people – but there is still a long way to go by both Indigenous and non-Indigenous people. When we see clearly, both the seer and the seen are strengthened.

Toward the end of 2015, two political events came together that augur well for a real accommodation between Canada and its Indigenous people: the election of Justin Trudeau as prime minister and the release of the full report of the Truth and Reconciliation Commission established by Stephen Harper. The Commission was bold in its conclusions, calling the residential school system "cultural genocide" – a description used earlier by the Rt. Hon. Beverley McLachlin while she was still chief justice of Canada. The Commission report calls for action on a broad range of reforms for Indigenous education, health, justice, job training, and preservation of culture and language. There is no justification for continuing gaps between what Indigenous and non-Indigenous people get in public services. Change is now underway, though it will require persistence and patience on both sides. Unfortunately, in his rush to identify himself with Indigenous issues, Trudeau over-promised on implementation of the Commission's ninety-four Calls to Action.

In recent years the Supreme Court of Canada has usually sided with Indigenous land claims and rights to natural resources. The business community is now catching up. It is gradually learning that, if Indigenous people support projects, it is more difficult for one-sided environmental groups to block them. It is also learning that if there is honest communication with the Indigenous peoples from the start, a majority of them will be open to finding agreed ways forward through discussion. These court decisions can lead to conflict with provincial governments or development groups. Nonetheless, despite serious frustrations and higher costs, fundamental issues are almost always best settled by open discussion among all the concerned parties, even though this process takes time, and time is money.

Champlain, the founder of Quebec, said that full equality between the local inhabitants and the incoming settlers would forge a strong nation – an exceptional vision. His missed dream can now be realized four centuries later through mutual accommodation. Champlain got it right – the Indigenous people were both equal and, in some ways, perhaps even superior. Most were better at talking things through than were the settlers.

I wrote in December 2015 that I thought the time had truly arrived for achieving reconciliation between Indigenous people and other members of the Canadian population. I remain hopeful. Tangible results can already be seen in many areas. To cite some examples: the University of Toronto has a pervasive "truth and reconciliation" program, and almost every night the CBC National News includes an Indigenous story. The National Arts Centre in Ottawa has launched an Indigenous Theatre Department. Many of the major public art galleries have appointed Indigenous curators who, in turn, are organizing exhibitions of Inuit and First Nations art. In 2018 the important CBC Massey Lectures were delivered by Tanya Talaga, an Indigenous journalist at the *Toronto Star*, on the theme "All Our Relations: Finding the Path Forward."

In addition to responding to today's challenges from the past, more recognition is needed of what Indigenous people did for the early settlers and for pre-Confederation Canada, including fighting off the Americans in the War of 1812, as well as of how Indigenous Canadians are contributing to Canada today. Indigenous people in remote settlements must figure out for themselves how best to blend their attachment to their remote communities with their need and desire for participation in what the modern world offers.

Canada is now paying for some of its early "constitutional" failures with Indigenous peoples. Indigenous "nationhood" and representative political organizations (including First Nations, Métis, and Inuit people) are complex, as are the challenges of negotiating with a multitude of them. They could easily be overwhelming for both sides. In recent years, Quebec made its choice between well-articulated Canadian and Quebec alternatives. A similar choice for the Indigenous people is not possible, given the sheer number of separate Indigenous "nations" and how interconnected they and their lands are with Canada. Some kind of mutual accommodation solutions must be found. They cannot be inflexible ("either/or") or only about the past. They must also be about the future.

The overwhelming failure of non-Indigenous people in their relationships with Indigenous people derives in large part from their failures to see and listen. Indigenous people come from an oral tradition. Their history is one of stories that have powerful meaning. Europeans generally come from a written tradition – and this medium has dominated their relationships. Indigenous people need to tell their stories and be heard, and in this way be acknowledged. Once heard, their tradition enables them to reach agreement among a broad range of views – their own form of mutual accommodation. Heather Atleo, Shawn Atleo's wife, helped to reach an agreement on the design and delivery of health programs by and for First Nations in British Columbia. An agreement was predicted to be impossible, given the range of interests and needs among the 203 First Nations, the federal and provincial governments, and five provincial health authorities. After nearly four years of listening to every community through their Chiefs, Elders, and health service providers, they were able to craft a collective agreement that serves both First Nations people and the Health Authorities well.

Reconciliation will require a whole new set of skills for Indigenous people. Indigenous politics has historically been dominated by objecting to the status quo (with good reason). Now, Indigenous leaders are moving forward with their own new thoughts and creative potential solutions. Their views are being accepted on new language, child services, education, and health proposals. Non-Indigenous people need to be patient and actively encourage this process. Canadians and Americans have traditionally been too impatient for the challenges Indigenous people face. More time is needed for many of them.

The Indigenous skill and will to take the time to hear and explore are increasingly becoming the only workable way forward. The idea of mutual accommodation has challenging resonance in this context. Our current situation is the product of history, much of which has been exploitive. We can and should acknowledge the injustices of this history. However, history cannot be reversed, and both sides need to accommodate to this reality. There are always at least two ways of going about things – to seek solutions or to push your own agenda too far. The former has generally worked best for Canada.

The Federal Court of Appeal decision in August 2018 on the two shortcomings of the Trans-Mountain pipeline approval process was initially seen as a shock and, possibly, an insurmountable obstacle to moving forward. Martha Hall Findlay, in an intelligent *Globe and Mail* op-ed analysis, suggested otherwise. Later Trudeau announced that the government would reopen "meaningful consultations" with the Indigenous people in an effort to work together to bridge or minimize the gaps between them.

A friend who works in the Ontario government has been meeting with Indigenous groups in northwestern Ontario for nearly thirty years. She reports that, previously, they used to be angry and spent much of the conversation trying to educate the visitors on broken promises and their bad shared history. Recently, Indigenous leaders have focused more on what is working and what needs to be done to build on successes. Important changes have included government representatives looking more to Indigenous communities and leaders to identify what is needed and how to make it happen. Until recently my friend was always met with complaints when she arrived. Now she is greeted with enthusiasm about what the Indigenous communities are working on themselves. So mutual accommodation ways can work and transform Indigenous/non-Indigenous relationships in the future.

The Western world today faces many severe negative outcomes from its excessive faith in a natural world it can control. The recent floods, droughts, forest fires, tornadoes, hurricanes, landslides, and earthquakes are reminders of just how far beyond human control much of nature remains and how much harm humans can do to nature. It is Westerners, not Indigenous people, who have the most to learn. While many of these terrible natural events may be attributable to human activities, we are not yet ready to do things that would reduce their scale and impact. Indigenous people better understand man's dependence on nature and the need for a mutual relationship.

It will be important to remember in relationships with Indigenous people that reconciliation does not mean assimilation by other means. Rather, it requires "decolonized" ways of thinking as well as mutual accommodation of the many competing ways of looking at things. The pre-Renaissance world and the so-called primitive world were for the most part worlds where spirit and nature were one, not two.

The Indigenous peoples of Canada have always been of that mind. The stresses of the centrifugal forces in today's West may make the Indigenous way of looking at things more relevant than it has ever been since Western settlers arrived in North America.

The bottom line right now is that, while the truth and reconciliation path ahead will be hard and slow, the Indigenous peoples and their issues are no longer missing in action. One test for both will be what more must now start to be done to ensure that Canada returns to living within its means. We lost the opportunity to get the relationship right in the early seventeenth century with Champlain. It is critical not to lose the second chance we have right now.

———————

Three individuals responded in a special way to an early version of this update of my original *Globe and Mail* essay by focusing on how a true partnership between Canada's Indigenous and non-Indigenous peoples could now be achieved. One is a wise young Indigenous woman. Another is an older and very experienced non-Indigenous Ottawa man. And the third is a leading psychotherapist at Toronto's Hospital for Sick Children (SickKids) who has done a great deal of professional work with challenged Indigenous youth. I will first set out the response from the young Indigenous woman in her own words, and then give a summary of what the Ottawa man and the psychotherapist wrote. Finally, I will reproduce my original *Globe and Mail* essay.

To me, these are three responses from a perfect trio – different but compatible. The real reconciliation will come in our country when all Canadians can move on from past failures and work together to solve the big challenges for the future.

A Young Indigenous Woman's Perspective

"Truth and reconciliation" within Canada is a very sensitive and neglected subject. Our educational system has failed us, our government has segregated us, our history has been subjectively portrayed, and I see only long-lost solutions. However, it is never too late to amend multiple centuries' worth of pain. It always comes down to process. Pieces of the truth have already begun to be exposed, though many aspects have been sugar-coated – to no one's surprise – which, honestly speaking, sets back the idea of "reconciliation."

I admittedly have something of an ethnocentric attitude toward the history of the Indigenous peoples within Canada, as I am mixed with Haida. I come from a dying culture, and there are only a few dozen people who still speak our tribe's language. Unfortunately for us, a majority of those speakers are elders who have never passed the language down. Research studies have proved that after European contact, our population fell by about 95 percent. By 1915, it is recorded that there were approximately 588 Haida left. Gratefully, we now number about 4,000 (on and off the island of Haida Gwaii). Through these fluctuations, our elders have worked hard to preserve our traditions and culture.

I have seen different sides of the spectrum of how Indigenous families handle their pain – and it has been painful to see. At one end, you have the very motivated, very diligent Indigenous people who work hard in every aspect of their lives to change the stigma against them. On the other, you see people still suffering from memories of their past or from the effects of trauma caused by our history.

It's an easy concept to understand, once you know what really happened. The first residential school opened in 1851, and the last one closed in 1996. Yet the government didn't issue an apology until 2008 – and that's a long time for former residents to wait. Residential schools were initially established by the churches in Canada, though they later became government funded. In total, some 150,000 children were taken from their families into these establishments. Of those, 90–100 percent experienced severe physical, emotional, and/or sexual abuse.

In 1868 Prime Minister Sir John A. Macdonald deemed it necessary to separate Indigenous children from their parents. In a speech before the House of Commons in 1883 he stated: "When the school is on the reserve, the child lives with his parents who are savages; he is surrounded by savages, and though he may learn to read and write, his habits and training and mode are thought to be savage." In the 1920s Duncan Campbell Scott, the deputy superintendent general of Indian Affairs, noted: "I want to get rid of the Indian Problem ... Our objective is to continue until there is not an Indian that has not been absorbed into the body politic, and there is no Indian question, and no Indian Department."

Soon after the first residential school was opened, the government decided they were too expensive, so introduced amendments that led to starvation, dehydration, and abuse. An early study revealed that the children were working from 6 a.m. to 9 p.m., providing seven and a half hours of physical labour in addition to five and a half hours in the classroom. The long-term effects of these multiple forms of abuse are still affecting our Indigenous communities to this day, and little effort has been made to offset them.

Somewhere along the way, in the mid to late 1900s, Canadians began to question how the government treated its Indigenous people. It began with the realization of how much Indigenous soldiers had contributed in both the First and the Second World wars. As the residential schools were becoming more exposed, the federal government decided on a "positive propaganda" response by releasing favourable videos about the effects of residential schools.

I come from a rural area in Ontario along the coast of Lake Huron. My education in my own culture was extremely limited. When I was in school, I remember learning about "Indians" and the aggressive, savage traits ingrained in our blood. I learned how we were fortunate that European settlers came here and established a government for us, because we were unable to govern ourselves. We learned much about the "great pioneers" who led us to where we are today, as well as how Canada became colonized. One of the many things I never could understand is why I grew up with a family that was embarrassed about our ancestry. As a young girl, I was puzzled why I was so different from everybody else and why my peers couldn't seem to get past my pronounced features. Fortunately, I was able to forgive myself for being different. I was able to see through everybody else's lenses and establish myself as a confident Indigenous woman. I have nothing left to fear, and I will proudly stand for what I believe.

One key component to reconciliation would be our language. I'm not talking about our national languages (neither of which come from any Indigenous tribe), but the way we communicate when it comes to Canada's original inhabitants. Words such as "prehistory," "Indian," "redman," and "savage" can all be offensive when used in reference to an Indigenous person. The way we use our language and the context in which we speak affect the reconciliation process. History has not been our friend, but we're in a world now where there's wide recognition of human rights. There is absolutely no excuse for disrespect and racism. In this era of mass education and multiple movements, having respect for other peoples' cultures shouldn't be a topic of discussion. Unfortunately, people have become so desensitized, especially through anonymous online platforms such as Yahoo, that they don't care who is hurting as long as their own way of life isn't compromised. When the hurt is pointed out, they respond, "What does it matter?"

One of the simplest solutions that is commonly overlooked about truth and reconciliation is acceptance. Acceptance is our key to reconciliation – acceptance on behalf of both Indigenous people and our non-Indigenous brothers and sisters. To our fellow Canadians, it is important to accept history as it is. There is no such thing as sugar-coating history. History is what it is and never will change. If a fact is a fact and it offends you, it is still a fact. It is very understandable, especially from the European perspective, that no one is proud of what has happened to the Indigenous peoples in Canada. It is a horrific idea to imagine that your ancestors, perhaps even your grandparents or parents, could have contributed to the downfall of our Indigenous partners.

However, it is also very important to remember that accepting your history is not accepting defeat or blame. Acceptance is the stepping stone for recovery. We are grieving for cultures lost, people lost, children lost, women lost – as a nation, we are grieving. As for our Indigenous partners, we need to accept that the history will remain as it is, and, unfortunate as it was, there is nothing we can do about it. If we hold on to the pain and suffering that our ancestors endured, we will always be held back by the pain. The desire to inflict blame does not get us anywhere, and it will only slow down the reconciliation process. As a nation, we have multiple choices to make: Will we stand together, accept our histories, and move forward hand in hand? Or will we continue to point blame at the other person? Will we subject ourselves to pain and anger and hold on to centuries' worth of hostilities?

I would love to go on in depth about the Hudson's Bay Company, Nestlé, the initial French/Indigenous interaction (which was very positive), the 1884 anti-potlatch laws, and the fact that the thesauruses still uses the terms "indigenous" and "native" as synonyms for "savage," but that would make this response too long.

For non-Indigenous Canadian perspectives on Indigenous peoples, go to Yahoo News and review the comments on articles about

Indigenous societies. To this day, the average Canadian is uneducated on many Indigenous matters, and that needs to change in order for us all to reconcile.

An Older Non-Indigenous Man's Perspective

When I first met this man nearly four decades ago, he was one of the best of the contemporary Ottawa public servants – which means he was very good. In his reaction to my essay and update he focuses not only on the Indigenous/non-Indigenous relationships within Canada but also on the larger challenges every Canadian faces. My bureaucrat friend described my view on Indigenous issues as possibly simplistic optimism – one that needs some tempering. I am wrong to suggest, he says, that the road ahead will be easy if only we agree to settle our problems by mutual accommodation. But I say, while my views are indeed optimistic, they are also realistic rather than simplistic. I have always held that although the reconciliation path will be hard and long, the first essential step is to get Canada on the path. Now I see more and more evidence that we may at last be on that path.

This wise retired Ottawa mandarin argues that Canada's currently unfinished Indigenous business will have to be addressed alongside three other major imperatives that will take energy and resources away from Indigenous issues. I agree with his caution. The reality of politics means that Indigenous issues will not have the floor to themselves. The issues he raises involve politics, social values, and science, and they will affect the resolution of major Indigenous issues.

- Internationally and nationally, we are witnessing a drift away from liberal democracy. In Canada, the change is most recently visible in Quebec and New Brunswick, where, respectively, anti-Muslim and anti-French prejudices are emerging in the guise of secularism and mutual non-accommodation. Abroad, the move to right-wing politics is developing quickly in Europe, especially in Poland and Hungary, but also in Sweden, Germany, and, with Brexit, in England. Already it is obvious in the Philippines and in various regimes in South America and Africa. Most seriously, it is blatant in the United States, where the traditional political parties have lost their way and where illiberal currents are on the rise after seven decades of rising domestic and global inclusiveness.

- Globally, we see the rise of identity politics. The old prejudices in Canada – for example, between French and English, Catholics and Protestants, whites and non-whites – are increasingly subdued. In their place, the new social media has unleashed a proliferation of ever more minor but increasingly vehement divisions among people. To name but a few: urban populations have less understanding for rural Canadians, men are finally getting their comeuppance from women, progressives (especially in the United States) avoid communicating with conservatives (and vice versa), Crees look down on uppity Mohawks. Everybody is either a victim or a person to be blamed. The tone of much public debate is moving away from tolerance toward envy and even anger. Mutual accommodation is hard in this kind of environment.
- Climate change, no matter its causes, is challenging our way of life and our very existence on earth, as recent UN Climate Change reports are warning. As temperatures rise and the ice caps melt, higher sea levels threaten our coasts and cities. Extreme weather may be becoming the norm, resulting in major droughts, floods, tornados, hurricanes, landslides, and fires. Ironically, this climate-warming may help Canada by making more of its huge land mass agriculturally productive.

These negative forces are real, but they are starting to be countered. Although Brexit lacks the support it needs in both major UK political parties and in the House of Commons, it is still moving to a mutually (UK and EU) destructive hard Brexit. In 2018, the United States also elected a non-Trump House of Representatives.

My friend warns that all these critical issues will need to be addressed as we move toward reconciliation with our Indigenous people. He hopes that the Indigenous nations can begin to define themselves, to make political and territorial arrangements, and to take responsibility for finding positive outcomes, rather than focusing primarily on grievances – no matter how well founded they be. He understands that accomplishing all these goals within the broad framework of the Charter will be challenging but, he says, not impossible. I think that change is starting to happen, though it will sometimes seem to be demanding impossibly much. I hope and believe both Indigenous and non-Indigenous people will choose to keep at it.

I agree that we must strive for a balanced response to all the challenges we face. We live in a very big and demanding world. In essence, Indigenous/non-Indigenous relations today have three dimensions: the wrongs of the past; gaps in how Canada today is meeting its obligation to respond to current Indigenous needs; and future challenges that all of us will need to address together. A little more listening, a little less talk is what the world, including the Canadian Indigenous/non-Indigenous relationship, needs now. We may be in some form of inclusiveness overreach that needs less elite preaching and superiority and more real inclusiveness – one that takes everyone into account, both the preachers and the preached at.

A Professional Psychotherapist's Perspective

I met my child psychotherapist friend some thirty-five years ago when he was at the Hospital for Sick Children. Over his career he has had a lot of experience with First Nations' youth.

The outcome of the last four hundred years' history in Canada is that many of today's most challenging Indigenous issues are family and developmental problems. Listening and hearing are vital functions within any relationship – and many factors affect those capacities. The first has to do with individual maturation and the ability to hear and understand others. In the fields of development and psychology, that capacity is called "reflective function." It is the ability to recognize that other people have minds and feelings, and to consider that fact when dealing with them. Listening and hearing require recognition that the other has something to say, something that needs to be understood. Stress interferes with reflective function. The more stressed people are, the less capacity they have to see or hear the other as a complete person – one with a mind and feelings. Reflective function is developed from infancy. Parenting that does not include successful reflective function limits the child's ability to develop its own reflective function. Reflective function also fluctuates over time within individuals and groups; in times of stress, they have less reflective function.

"Group think" is the opposite of reflective function. Health-promoting groups allow, even facilitate, individual thought. Respect of individual differences is central to seeing the other as human too. The growth in the number of First Nations' artists, professionals, and politicians will, for some Canadians, make them seem more "human" – more like us. That's a good thing because it will encourage more listening. But more human like us will work only if our idea of the human is inclusive enough.

Another issue is stigma. Repeatedly, groups see others as threatening and dehumanize them – there is no reflective function. What "the other" does is seen as posing a danger that must be combatted. Often it is seen as a threat to entrenched advantages that more privileged and more powerful groups hold in society. The powerful groups perceive the other as inferior – their actions misperceived as arising from inferiority or worse. The powerful believe that things will be worse if the other is given more power or rights. The system deprives and stigmatizes the other and, in that way, keeps the other poor, "sick," or "bad." The powerful often do not feel as powerful as they really are, so they are fearful and think they are threatened.

Stigma creates more stressed and less healthy individuals and groups. These individuals and groups in turn may incorporate the perceptions foisted on them by the more powerful and behave as though they are inferior, accepting maltreatment. Other stigmatized individuals may argue or even fight for their rights. Both responses can be seen as "proof" that the other is inferior or dangerous. It takes careful listening and hearing to overcome this reaction. Stigma is both individual and systemic, and it is often hard to recognize. Many laws, policies, and traditions support and reinforce stigma.

This last comment is central to many First Nations communities and individuals. No blame should be attached in it, except perhaps to the colonizers, but the dysfunction is real. It is a serious impediment to autonomous and healthy functioning. The lack of economic, educational, and health resources and of developed governance, extreme levels of poor health, poverty, and isolation are all huge unresolved problems. How can a community build a life for itself and its members when it is being attacked from the inside, as well as from the outside, by factionalism, violence, widespread sexual and substance abuse, and the consequent damage to the brains of parents and unborn children?

Truth and reconciliation is the only real way forward. Truth demands hearing. There is "not hearing" inside the communities as well as from the settler society. Reconciliation also demands capacity within the First Nations communities. Although there are encouraging developments and growth in many communities and for numerous individuals, huge challenges still remain.

I feel confident in making one assertion about the post-2015 developments on the Indigenous Canadians front. Non-Indigenous peoples are beginning to see Indigenous peoples. I first met Shawn Atleo when he was coming to the end of his first term as chief of the Assembly of First Nations, shortly before he was elected to a second term. He liked my idea that the relationship between our two peoples was Canada's biggest piece of unfinished business. As his grandmother had told him, the non-Indigenous population is "beginning to see us." Seeing each other and seeing ourselves will be the foundation of almost every good thing – for both the seer and the seen. It is best when the seeing is mutual. It will be a long time before this seeing gets good enough, but at last we are on a better mutual seeing path.

The American poet Henry Wadsworth Longfellow expressed what needs to be said: "Let the dead past bury its dead." Or, as stated earlier in the young Indigenous woman's perspective, "history is what it is and will never change. If a fact is a fact and it offends you, it is still a fact." Non-Indigenous Canadians must remember and mourn what their forebears did to Indigenous people. Indigenous Canadians must also remember and mourn what was done to them in the past. Then each must move forward on what the present and the future require of them.

I said in my original essay that this time would be different on the Indigenous and non-Indigenous front. The point is made by this update – many times longer than the update of any other essay (other than China). There is a lot that is positive that is now going on.

TRUTH AND RECONCILIATION: WILL THIS TIME BE ANY DIFFERENT? *

The year 2016 offered Canada its best chance in four centuries to reach an accommodation with its Indigenous population. At the end of 2015 the Truth and Reconciliation Commission (TRC) published its full report – six volumes totaling nearly 4,000 pages – on how best

* Published in the *Globe and Mail*, December 18, 2015.

to cope with the fallout from the residential-school era. It comes six years after the commission began its work and six months after the release of the report's highly acclaimed executive summary. Change is in the air, and Prime Minister Justin Trudeau was present when the final documents were released. During the campaign that brought him to power, he promised that, if elected, he would enact all ninety-four of the commission's recommendations.

A skeptic may recall that almost exactly twenty years ago another large report appeared – the report of the Royal Commission on Aboriginal Peoples. It had no fewer than 440 recommendations for sweeping changes that would recognize Aboriginal self-government and address social, educational, health, and housing needs – at a cost of $35 billion over two decades.

The federal government responded, more than a year later, with an action plan that was much more modest. But it led eventually to a pact between Aboriginal leaders and then prime minister Paul Martin that was very encouraging. Unfortunately, the plan was aborted after his Liberals were voted out of office in 2006.

So, what will happen now? Will history repeat itself as Canada falters once again in trying to deal with its biggest item of unfinished business: mutual accommodation with Indigenous people? Just saying that this time will be different (as Neville Chamberlain famously told reporters after his "peace in our time" meeting with Adolf Hitler) is not enough. There are signs, however, that Canada's quest for a more just and equitable relationship with its Indigenous people may be coming together.

Champlain's Dream

It's still too soon to see what can and should be done, and the path is not an easy one. But we would do well to remember the example set 400 years ago by Samuel de Champlain. The founder of Quebec did not set out to conquer the Indigenous people, whom he regarded, according to biographer David Hackett Fischer in *Champlain's Dream* (2008), as "fully equal to Europeans in powers of mind, and … superior in some ways."

Had such an attitude persisted, the residential schools would have been inconceivable. Exposed as a young man to the brutal treatment of Indigenous people in New Spain, Champlain envisioned a society in which settlers and local inhabitants would intermarry and, together, forge a strong nation. He was ahead of his time, but that dream may yet come true because we now have what seems to be our best chance at mutual accommodation since he was alive – the cost of failure have become too high.

The TRC was established specifically to redress the residential-schools tragedy, but the six years of research and public hearings led to a report on a wide swath of issues – from the sociological, economic, and political impact when children are separated from their homes (let alone disappear altogether) to what happens when people lose their language, culture, and sense of identity. The ninety-four recommendations for reconciliation range from how to heal families and communities and revitalize Aboriginal cultures, languages, spirituality, laws, and government systems to building respect for and a relationship with First Nations at all levels of government.

No Mean Feat

Despite Justin Trudeau's promise, implementing all the recommendations will be easier said than done. If another Trudeau promise – more open discussion – is kept, the best early use of the report will be to provide the basis for proposals by many actors. Input must be real and come from all who are affected. The members of the commission clearly believe that First Nations have been missing from almost every part of our national life. Many changes will be needed to break this pattern. Every significant institution and segment of Canadian society needs to take an honest look at itself from this perspective.

These action calls cover child welfare, education, language and culture, health, justice, Aboriginal equity in the legal system, public servants' training and development, youth programs, museums and archives, missing children and burial information, commemoration, establishment of a National Council for Reconciliation, church apologies and reconciliation, media and reconciliation, sports and reconciliation, business and reconciliation, Aboriginal information for newcomers to this country, Canada and the United Nations Declaration on the Rights of Indigenous People, and a new Royal Proclamation and Covenant of Reconciliation. Given all these demands, the devil will be in the details and in the need for goodwill.

The TRC report described Canada's residential-school tragedy as "cultural genocide," which some people consider inflammatory. But what happened is what's truly inflammatory.

The residential schools are part of a much larger problem in the Western world. Over the last few centuries, thinking that it knows more than it does, the West has sometimes felt it has the right (or the obligation) to impose its views on others. Even those considered socially progressive were still captive to their times. For instance, J.S. Woodsworth, the first leader of the Co-operative Commonwealth Federation (predecessor of the New Democratic Party), once praised a Toronto church for sending a minister to a residential school in western Canada "to do God's work." Even if people mean well, superiority and arrogance can be very destructive; add abuse to the mix, and the results can be fatal.

The TRC report addresses all these problems and, in its recommendations, seeks to find redress for them. A key factor is recognition – it matters to everyone. The apology former prime minister Stephen Harper gave to Aboriginal people was important, but his failure to call a public inquiry into the murdered and missing women remains a need for recognition that the Trudeau government is promising to address.

Historically, there have been many similar breaches of trust and respect. The UN Declaration on the Rights of Indigenous Peoples and a jointly developed Royal Proclamation and Covenant of Recognition recommended by the TRC are more important than many Canadians realize. Restoring broken trust requires both mutual recognition and much encouragement.

We must recognize that the sizable gap in the funding for education between reserves and everywhere else is unfair – and stupid. Despite the imbalance, a number of Aboriginal-education initiatives are in progress across Canada, many of them innovative and privately funded. Canada's public-school system could learn a lot from them.

First Nations are united in their belief that education is the way to strengthen and sustain their cultural, linguistic, social, and economic development. They want it to prepare their children to walk in two worlds: to know their language and culture and be proud of their identity, and also to have the skills they need to succeed in the dominant society and the modern economy.

This objective applies to Aboriginal students both in reserve and public schools – just as it applies to all Canadian students. Everyone lives simultaneously in two worlds – inner and outer. Literacy facilitates access to culture; fluency in two or more languages brings cognitive, social, and economic benefits; and a strong sense of identity improves academic achievement and social behaviour.

The Missing

When I saw the recent revival *Flare Path*, the 1942 Terence Rattigan play about British airmen and their wives, I was reminded how, during my youth, the nightly radio news almost always ended: "One of our aircraft is missing." The wives would know if an aircraft had not returned – it could be one of their husbands.

Indigenous people still experience too many such moments. We are constantly reminded of the women who are missing – and perhaps murdered – but many in the community are missing as well from Canada's mutual accommodation ways. Our school system fails to provide everyone with a good education, and our child-welfare and justice systems do not shield everyone who needs protection.

The TRC report is essentially about a large number of Canadians who have gone missing, or are at risk of going missing. How will Canada reduce that number? Shawn Atleo, former national chief of the Assembly of First Nations, described Aboriginal Canadians as a "traumatized people." The high incidence of Aboriginal Canadians gone missing only serves to prolong the trauma. The institutional critical mass that is needed to respond effectively encompasses key government leaders and their governments, the courts, educators, the media, public opinion, and business at large along with affected industries.

Aboriginal leaders and their communities will have to do part of the heavy lifting. The TRC Report is focused on what Aboriginal groups want and need, so they will have to get the different balls moving by thinking through what they specifically want and how best to achieve it.

In my experience, no matter how good your case, governments and businesses tend to act only when your proposal helps them deal with specific immediate challenges – not their longer-term interests. And the time is finally here for movement on relations with Aboriginal peoples.

Political Stars Aligned

Mr Harper did more on the First Nations front than he is generally credited with, but he was limited by a reluctant voter base. His successor doesn't have that problem: Mr Trudeau's heart and mind are open – the Aboriginal issue is one of the more important challenges he wants to address. The premiers of the four largest provinces are in the same place. There is a strong political basis for moving forward.

The Supreme Court of Canada has consistently found that the law on Aboriginal title favours First Nations – decisions that, along with their protest-based clout, gives them greater leverage on big resource projects. Although some businesspeople and their advisers find the Supreme Court uncertainties hard to manage for practical business decision-making, I doubt they present an insuperable problem. Legal reality may help businesses see that they need more social licence for what they do. We will see.

This combination of evolving politics and Supreme Court decisions should encourage Canada's First Nations to believe that the political and legal system can work for them. In the last federal election, First Nations' engagement was higher than ever and a record number of ten Aboriginal members were elected as MPs. Having the First Nations on side would be a huge asset for credibility on the environment, although the federal and Alberta governments and the oil and pipeline industries have been very slow to grasp that idea.

The media seem to get it. So, for the most part, does the public, as long as whatever steps taken are discussed openly and thoughtfully first. There will, however, still be strong differences on the particulars.

Optimism among Aboriginal people about the combined potential of the TRC report and the new Trudeau government is palpable. Mutual accommodation and improved relations by both sides will be needed to flesh out these expectations and to seize what is now possible. Continuing political leadership from the prime minister and the premiers will also be indispensable.

Looking Ahead

The whole tone of the report presented by the commission (whose chair, Murray Sinclair, was Manitoba's first Aboriginal judge) was forward-looking, using truth, not blame or anger, to move toward reconciliation.

In the early seventies, I used to go fishing on Georgian Bay with Barney Danson, Pierre Trudeau's minister of defence. On one occasion, when he talked about doing business with West Germany, I asked how, being Jewish, he could do that, given the Holocaust and the fact that he lost an eye as well as many comrades during the Second World War. "You have to move on," he replied, expressing an idea that is the most powerful message for our times.

This same idea underscores what an Indigenous professional I know and respect told me when I asked what she considers the best way to address the TRC report. In her words: "Governments should move on matters under their control, especially funding for education and child health. All sides should focus on how to bridge the gaps between them. First Nations should take more responsibility for their own future."

The world is driven by feelings and limited by facts. Right now, there are high hopes for reconciliation and mutual accommodation, and we must seize the moment. We can achieve these goals by open discussion, very hard work, and much patience over a long period. What matters now is to get on the right path – quickly.

Further Reading

David Hackett Fischer, *Champlain's Dream* (2008).
The CBC has an interactive page called Beyond 94 where individuals can investigate progress on each Call to Action: https://newsinteractives.cbc.ca/longform-single/beyond-94?&cta=1
The federal government publishes progress reports on official responses to the 94 Calls to Action: https://www.aadnc-aandc.gc.ca/eng/1524494530110/1524494579700
The National Centre for Truth and Reconciliation at the University of Manitoba – the principal repository for the TRC archives and the monitor of the Calls to Action.
#Next 150 Challenge: 94 Calls to Action (featuring Murray Sinclair), website for the film *Indian Horse*: https://next150.indianhorse.ca/challenges/94-calls-to-action
A multitude of TRC reports can be found at http://nctr.ca/reports2.php

For non-Indigenous Canadian perspectives on Indigenous peoples, go to Yahoo news and review the comments on articles about Indigenous societies. To this day, the average Canadian is not well informed about many Indigenous matters, and that needs to change in order for us all to reconcile.

10

How to Foster Enterprise and Innovation

INTRODUCTION

Three years ago I said that Justin Trudeau's government could not afford to ignore Canada's two major economic challenges – living beyond its means as a country and doing something to strengthen its private-sector goods and services competitive supply capacity. Unfortunately, my advice has been ignored. Consumer spending and foreign borrowing were the major culprits then – and this situation has not changed. Canada's fiscal and monetary disciplines are still too weak. Trudeau is making the same mistake his father, Pierre Trudeau, made in largely ignoring the private-sector economy. His early "sunny ways" were not followed by the foresight to see that the Canadian economy would be heading toward the rocks – despite an increasingly strong US expansion reinforced by a synchronized global expansion. Fortunately for Justin Trudeau, the crisis will not take place until after the fall 2019 election, and the next government will still have time to get onto a better economic growth path – no/low carbon oil sands, a Quebec Hydro Energy corridor, and a capital pool approach to taxing entrepreneurs to support investing in Canadian hi-tech global competitiveness advantages.

The bottom line is simple. The Harper government mismanaged the strong position Canada emerged with after the post–Lehman collapse crises. Justin Trudeau's government has failed to take advantage of Canada's post–Lehman strengths and the subsequent emergence of a broad, synchronized, global expansion now ending. Its problem is not primarily its government's deficits. Rather, it is what the deficits are being spent on – consumption. The government deficits are proportionately much smaller in Canada than in the United States, but the household-sector debt has become so high that Canada's strong private-sector consumption is bound to weaken. Finance Minister Bill Morneau's first budget failed to get Canada started on the right path. His next two budgets also failed. An election year budget early in 2019 had no chance of making a stand on getting the needed strengthened economic and financial disciplines. That discipline will be the hard challenge for whoever forms the government after the October 2019 federal election.

The Bank of Canada under Governor Stephen Poloz remains confused, with no effective policy for a country living beyond its means at a time when it should have been moving strongly toward living within its means. The Conservatives and the media focus today on federal government deficits. Their real focus should be on Canada's high current account deficits and rising household-sector debt. Understandably, the Conservatives avoid both issues because real economic adjustments and the inevitable political pain would be involved.

Three years ago, Canada needed more balance between natural and human resources (that is partly happening now, but mostly not thanks to federal economic policy) and between indebted sectors (three of Canada's four biggest provinces, the exception being Quebec, are getting more indebted, alongside households and the country as a whole). Only Quebec, in 2019, has retained Canada's good post-war balance between social and economic advance. To make it in the big leagues, even a politician needs more than one pitch. Justin Trudeau has not yet shown he has that ability, nor have the federal Conservatives.

The Trudeau government got an economic wake-up call three years ago. It may now be too late to show it has heard it. Both the federal government and the Bank of Canada have provided too much stimulus for too long for the wrong purpose – consumption. Instead of spending to help build a stronger and more competitive private sector, they have been spending on consumption. That is unsustainable. A recession is likely (but not certain – we are in a different world from that in 1945) within eighteen to thirty-six months. The Bank of Canada will be of little help this time round, and public spending cutbacks will be unavoidable. This dire forecast did not have to be.

Canada would benefit from a new hard look at its economic future:

- The premiers of the four largest provinces (Ontario, Quebec, Alberta, and British Columbia) should already have called for a Canadian Economy of Tomorrow Conference in the way Ontario premier John Robarts and Quebec premier Daniel Johnson did in 1967 when they invited other premiers to Canada's Confederation of Tomorrow Conference.
- Ottawa should propose a lifetime capital pool approach to capital gains taxation – an incentive to make, save, and reinvest capital gains (a reward for those who pitch in).
- We should have a federal public review of the tax system, with a strong emphasis on competitive private-sector growth. It should be a much narrower review than the Royal Commission on Taxation (Carter Commission) launched by the Diefenbaker government in 1962, one more focused on economic growth and less on abstract "tax purity" concepts (the basis of the Carter report).
- Top Ottawa policy makers should take a hard look at (and do some serious fresh thinking about) how best to address the structural imbalances at the heart of today's economic policy management challenges (see Chapter 22).

None of this kind of adult and professional discussion is taking place anywhere in Canada. It is now overdue. It will be required for the kind of new visions, new ideas, and new projects that Canada needs for the new world. Lester Pearson launched a Royal Commission on Bilingualism and Biculturalism; Pierre Trudeau launched a Royal Commission on the Economic Union and Development Prospects for Canada. The results of both inquiries helped to shape Canada in positive ways for challenging times.

Canada should have moved overall on all these fronts after it and the global economy started to recover from the post-2008 crises. Instead, it moved in the opposite direction under both Harper and Justin Trudeau. Trudeau should have seized the strengthening US and global economies to meet some unavoidable and difficult challenges. Now the global economic expansion is coming to an end and is being severely threatened by Donald Trump, Brexit, and China. Neither federal leader did what he should have done. These proposals are still the right things to do, but they will not be done until after the 2019 federal election. Whoever forms that government will then have to play painful catch-up.

As I pointed out three years ago, it is possible for leaders to have foresight. Neither Harper nor Justin Trudeau so far has shown the kind of foresight that Franklin Delano Roosevelt did, for example, two years before Pearl Harbor. Harper had the advantage of Canada coming out of 2008–09 stronger than any other country, but he did not use it to strengthen Canada's economic and financial disciplines – just the opposite. The country got a second chance under Justin Trudeau, with growing US and global expansion strength, but he chose to spend, not to build. The country will now face a hard number of catch-ups when a recession likely hits in 2020–22.

Three years ago, I reported that Prime Minister Trudeau said at Davos that Canada would not just manage change but take advantage of it. It has since been an increasingly hard three years for Canada. We have to conclude that, so far, Canada has neither managed the big changes well nor taken advantage of them. Canada is not helpless, but right now it continues on its path of weakening economic and financial disciplines. It has no new approach for the worlds of Brexit, President Trump, and President Xi Jinping. Nor does any other country. Whoever forms the federal government after October 2019 will have no choice but to find and implement a new approach to the new world we are all living in.

1. JUSTIN TRUDEAU CAN'T AFFORD TO IGNORE CANADA'S ECONOMIC CHALLENGES*

Late in 1939, Franklin Delano Roosevelt called Harry Hopkins, his closest aide, into his office. "Harry, up until now, I have been the New Deal president," he announced. "From now on, I will be the 'war president.'" Pearl Harbor was still two years away, but FDR could see what was coming.

Now that a new year is dawning, Justin Trudeau is in need of similar foresight. He should have the wisdom to call Gerald Butts, his

---

* Published in the *Globe and Mail*, January 1, 2016.

closest political partner, into his office and say that, so far, he has been all about who we are and "sunny ways." From now on, however, he will also be paying close attention to something far less esoteric: the economy.

Trudeau can still be the prime minister he campaigned to be – the champion of mutual accommodation and the notion that "better is always possible" – but only if he also goes in the right fiscal direction.

Canada's economy is heading toward the rocks. Consumer spending and foreign borrowing to cover it are the major culprits. Trudeau must convince the country to accept a fair balance between what we want and what we can afford – between an activist government and one that rebuilds the economy. He will not want to make the same mistake his father made. Asked, after leaving office, if he had any regrets, Pierre Trudeau said yes – he wished he had paid more attention to the economy.

If his son doesn't learn from that, we will all pay a higher price. Not only are the Canadian and global economic fundamentals weaker now than they were then but the economic legacy left by Stephen Harper is challenging.

Doing the Math

The challenge is not the deficit: Canada has the best ratio of government debt to gross domestic product in the G7. But one good number is not enough when two other key indicators are so bad that they have the economy well off course.

The first tough number is the current account deficit – that is, the gap between the value of the goods and services we import and those we export. That deficit will likely hit $67 billion this year, the result of consumer spending, not productive investment.

Another pair of dangerous numbers involves the level of household-sector debt (higher than both the comparable US figures during the 2008 crisis and that of any other G7 country today) and high prices for houses, particularly in Vancouver and Toronto.

Private-sector debt on this scale can cause people (and companies) to suddenly stop spending (and investing) so that, instead, they can pay off what they owe, which can in turn spark what's called a balance-sheet recession. Richard Koo, chief economist of Japan's

Nomura Research Institute and a global guru on such recessions, recently said that Canada is risking one.

If it happens, the Bank of Canada will be powerless to use monetary policy to offset economic weakness, as it did in 2008–09, by lowering the interest rate. Those already focused on reducing their debt won't go out and add to it just because the carrying cost is down a bit.

The political news is perhaps as good as it could have been. The new federal government has a majority and is broadly in tune with large numbers of Canadians. And the economic news is not in panic mode – the federal deficit forecast in the latest fiscal update from Finance Minister Bill Morneau, although higher, is not significant yet.

But it is likely to get larger because the economy, already weak, keeps declining as the price of oil drops, alongside accumulating debt challenges and not enough internationally competitive supply capacity.

Spend Only Where It Counts

This government has big plans that involve spending, but that spending must be limited to top priorities. Deficits are not Canada's primary challenge, but if the economy is not earning its way, government spending that fails to restore its ability to do so could pose a problem.

Harper's priorities were smaller government and reduced personal taxation – valid goals if based on living within one's means. Instead, taxes were cut and the budget balanced even as Canadians were living beyond their means on a scale never seen before.

The new government's spending promises and growth aspirations will make its deficit goal (a surplus by the last year of its mandate) harder to achieve. Paul Martin's first budget as Jean Chrétien's finance minister failed to get the country back on track – he needed a second one. Morneau's first budget may meet the same fate.

Moreover, by Canada's next federal election, the current US economic strength will be fading and oil prices could well be worse than expected, meaning slow growth, if not a recession, and reduced revenues in Canada. The huge household-sector debt needs to be carefully displaced by federal deficits that support investment to build the economy. There is no need for Keynesian consumer-demand stimulus – $60 billion a year in foreign borrowing is already too much.

What is needed is investment in public infrastructure and private-sector job creation to broaden the competitive supply capacity of the economy. Growth fuelled by the private sector is the only practical way forward on jobs, rising middle-class incomes, and reduced deficits.

The federal policy inherited from the Harper government, which combines rising foreign and household-sector debt used for consumption, is not sustainable.

Something Is Wrong

The Bank of Canada, among others, expected that consumer spending would be followed by investment and exports. Neither has happened or seems likely. Why has the United States experienced this rotation but not Canada? Why is US consumer strength greater than that of Canada?

The fundamental answer is that US competitive-supply capacity has been broadening, while the Canadian capacity has been narrowing. This difference calls for new creative thinking. To do well, a country needs at least one of three basic economic strengths:

- A big domestic market. Canada can never have a huge population, given its geography and climate. Trade agreements to expand markets are not the same.
- Space, food, water, minerals, and energy. Canada has them all in abundance. When it comes to natural resources, only Brazil and Russia are in the same league as Canada.
- Competitive rewards and opportunities for the best people – entrepreneurs, professionals, managers, creators, and innovators. In this vital area, Canada desperately needs new creative policies and initiatives.

Canada's natural resources are certainly a great long-term strength, even if resource markets are cyclical. Canada's only choice is to match strength in natural resources with strength in human resources – and we already excel in such fields as financial services, medicine, hi-tech innovation, and architecture.

Our two current economic challenges are, first, to reduce overall debt and rebalance it away from households toward the federal government; and, second, to strengthen the role of human resources in the economy. Canadians' standard of living is declining because of its negative terms of trade (the oil-price collapse and low commodity prices), the lower dollar (which makes imports more expensive), less income growth (the weakening economy), and less consumer room to borrow. A successful new policy is essential.

The Debt Anesthetic

Canada had a huge advantage over other countries at the end of the Brian Mulroney–Jean Chrétien era, as the world fell into the post–Lehman abyss in 2008. This advantage should have been used to build our means – instead, it was used to live beyond them. Understandably, no political party has wanted to talk about it.

The problem is hardly a new one. I recall, twenty-six years before the Lehman Brothers collapse, speaking to a senior Canadian businessman who wanted me to agree that Ronald Reagan, although he had been president for just a year at that point, was a great man. I argued that Reagan was getting into too much debt, but the businessman wanted something positive out of me, so he said: "You have to admit Reagan has made Americans feel good about themselves." I agreed, but I pointed out that if I spent more than I earned on my wife, as the president was spending on the American people, she would feel good about herself, too.

In recent years, that is exactly what Canada has done. The challenge is to take away the debt anesthetic and help people feel better about themselves by doing real things that build a more productive Canada for the future. It is what the greatest leaders are for.

Building for a better future always requires deferring consumption. That is the biggest political persuasion and policy task the new Liberal government faces. It requires a balance between personal reward and societal reward – a balance that recognizes society's role in private opportunity and the role of privately driven economic achievements in societal opportunity. To have success that truly lasts, each side must accommodate the role played by the other.

What Should Be Done?

How might these challenges best be addressed?

- *High house prices–household-sector debt.* The Bank of Canada must follow the lead of the US Federal Reserve and raise interest rates as federal fiscal deficits grow. We must get on the long, slow path to less household-sector debt and less foreign borrowing for the sake of consumers. We must use prospective larger federal deficits for the kind of growth that brings lasting job creation, rising incomes, and better-balanced sectors.
- *Transit infrastructure.* We need a much bigger program than the one currently planned.
- *Wealth and job creation.* We need the social licence to offer incentives that reward successes that are reinvested in the economy. This approach worked for Canada in the twenty-five years after the Second World War, when the opportunities were in natural resources. A comparable approach is needed for the first half of the twenty-first century, when opportunities lie in human resources.

In the past decade, Canada's economic policy environment became too narrowly political. It lacked a longer-term strategy and discernible national vision for a constantly changing world. That must stop. A policy of tax cuts and no deficits is too limited. Policy and politics must return to the full playing field.

Policy Confusion

The Bank of Canada under Governor Stephen Poloz does not seem to have an effective strategy for the current Canadian economy and debt challenge. Not only do the bank's two rate cuts this year go in the wrong direction, but Mr Poloz has added to the confusion by suggesting a policy of negative interest rates in the event of a crisis, even though he says there is no reason to expect one will happen.

In that case, two questions:

- Why talk now about something that is not needed? Is he trying to say the bank could do a lot about where we might find ourselves?
- How would negative real interest rates help us live within our means and broaden our competitive supply capacity?

Either way, the finance minister must keep on top of his department and the Bank of Canada and demand clear monthly analytical updates on both house prices and household debt. Morneau needs to know:

- What can we do, and are we doing it?
- Is that likely to work in time?
- What do we do if the job is not done in time and the bad possibility becomes real?

Mutual Accommodation Can Help

From 1945 to 1993, Canadian politics was dominated by the Progressive Conservatives and the conservative Liberals (the latter went off economic and fiscal balance under Pierre Trudeau). There were two great postwar dynasties – one federal (rooted in the conservative Liberals under Sir Wilfrid Laurier and William Lyon Mackenzie King); the other provincial (the Progressive Conservatives in Ontario under Leslie Frost, John Robarts, and William Davis).

Each shared the idea that social and economic progress go together. This policy resulted in a sixty-year mutual accommodation of these two powerful sets of aspirations. They came to be seen as mutually strengthening, not adversarial. They made today's Canada.

Canada now needs more balance: between natural and human resources, between indebted sectors, and between social and economic advance. Those who want a strong economy must understand the need for societal strength – and vice versa. Pierre Trudeau overreached on the economy; Stephen Harper underreached. Justin Trudeau cannot get it right if he is governed by a fiscal straitjacket. No one, including the prime minister and his economic advisers, is ready yet for what is needed. A big, bold, prudent, and patient approach is the way forward.

In a recent column, the *Globe and Mail*'s Jeffrey Simpson said that the Liberals don't really have their heart in fighting the deficit.

Nor should they. But if the government doesn't meet the economic challenge it faces, the social policy that is close to its heart will be undermined.

Invoking an Icon

We must echo the boldness of John A. Macdonald in building the transcontinental railway after Confederation. It will take everything Justin Trudeau has to pull it off: a capacity for mutual accommodation, the intestinal fortitude to set the right priorities, and a penchant for what works.

Pierre Trudeau kept the country together; Justin Trudeau saved the Liberal Party. Can he now do the long, hard, and bold things needed to build the country for the twenty-first century? He has shown he can be bold by doing hard politics, such as staying positive in a negative campaign and his out-of-step campaign decision to advocate running deficits. He won big by reassuring Canadians that openness, engagement, and inclusiveness are still the best way forward. Now he must turn to the economy (as well as security, both at home and abroad). If he does not become the "economy prime minister" and get the needed reforms right, he will find it almost impossible to keep his ways – and ours – very sunny.

By knowing when to change focus, Franklin Roosevelt was able to face a conflict and prevail. A quarter-century later, however, Lyndon Johnson could not keep the Vietnam War from destroying his dream of being remembered as the "Great Society president" who eliminated poverty and racial injustice.

To make it in the big leagues, even a politician needs more than one pitch.

2. TO TRANSFORM CANADA'S ECONOMY, TRUDEAU NEEDS TO BE A "BOLD BUILDER" *

Canada's wake-up call has arrived with all the bad economic news – the falling loonie (which raises the cost of living), collapsing oil and

---

* Published in the *Globe and Mail*, February 12, 2016.

commodity prices, a serious bear stock market, reduced government revenues, and weakening employment performance.

But bad news can include good news – and the upside is that the new government and the watching public cannot fail but see what they face. The harsh forces now at work can no longer go unnoticed. The government, four months into its mandate, is getting a clear idea of the challenges ahead – and that will help it explain to Canadians what has to be done.

The last five years were largely lost ones for the Canadian economy, which has suffered from three major vulnerabilities:

- Our growing household-sector debt and (because we have failed to live within our means) foreign borrowing.
- China's impact on oil and commodity prices, which stems from the fact that a once-explosive economy is growing more slowly and reducing its investment in physical capital.
- Finally, the looming – and unavoidable – end to the current US expansion.

Some of these troubles were self-inflicted; others came from outside, but were at least partly foreseeable. Either way, the end result is very, very real. What matters now is to assess where we are and find the right policy and political ways forward. Canada was unprepared to deal with the first two problems. It is urgent that we get ready for the third by using US growth while it lasts.

A Hard Global Environment

The global economy is still being held back by two huge deflationary, or recessionary, drags.

CONTINUAL AFTERSHOCKS FROM 2008

We forget that the world never really came out of the Great Depression of the 1930s – rather, the economy was revived by a global war. Nor has Japan really recovered from its twenty-five years of economic malaise. In both cases, the premature withdrawal of measures to stimulate a recovery brought recession back.

This context helps to explain why the US Federal Reserve Bank has been so cautious since the 2008 meltdown – and, now that it has begun to raise interest rates, why *Financial Times* columnist Martin Wolf writes that the increase perhaps was a blunder. He may be right, but for once I think not – just as I don't feel the Fed's action is the prime suspect in triggering the current global stock setbacks.

THE CHINA FACTOR

The overwhelming shock of China's economic rise has now turned into the shock of its lowering growth adjustments. Wendy Dobson, a China expert at the University of Toronto's Rotman School of Business and the author of *Canada, China, and Rising Asia: A Strategic Proposal* (2012), points out that, while Western economies make mistakes, they have way-forward charts. For China there are no charts for moving 1.4 billion people forward, with an authoritarian government and an economy hindered by the fact it's partly state-owned. We don't like today's destabilized Middle East. A politically destabilized China could be much worse.

But Canada has to look out for itself in a world of insufficient demand. Just as it needs what Prime Minister Trudeau calls "sunny ways," it needs to be deeply rooted in reality and what works.

The Way Forward

Right now Canada needs major initiatives in three key areas: public infrastructure, natural-resource infrastructure, and incentives designed to foster the creation of wealth.

Following the 2015 election, Canada emerged with a government that supports the first of these initiatives (developing public infrastructure) and promises a more positive approach to First Nations and climate change, which could help with the second initiative (developing natural resources). Unfortunately, none of the three main parties advocated anything to help Canadians to start living within their means.

In the immediate aftermath of the financial crisis, Canada famously did almost all the right things, using the strengths from its Brian Mulroney–Jean Chrétien heritage to overcome the worst of the fallout. The Bank of Canada under Mark Carney edged interest rates up 75 basis points – an amazing accomplishment compared with the rest of the G7 developed nations. The bank no doubt wanted to do more but was held back by elections and volatile external challenges.

After the return of majority government in 2011, there was a shift, but for political, not economic, purposes. And those changes rested on an unsustainable foundation: too much foreign borrowing and too much household-sector debt.

Now, the rough new economic world Canada faces will be much more powerful in shaping future policy. No matter what the Liberal government does, any tendency to live beyond its means will be shaped more by market forces than by policies.

The Liberals put forward two positive ideas: enhanced infrastructure financed by a larger deficit and better relations with First Nations – initiatives that, together, could help to get big pipeline and resource projects moving. However, the centrepiece of its platform – a better life for Canada's middle class – requires some heavy lifting on the economy.

The Need for Change

Canada's overall policy is badly unbalanced: there is too much stimulus from private credit and too little from federal deficits. Interest rates are so low, housing prices in some areas so high, and many households owe so much money that the Bank of Canada is now essentially powerless to provide relief when the next recession comes, as inevitably it will. A recent poll shows that Canadians' prime financial goal is to cut their debt, which would help even if it slows consumer demand in the process.

Now is the time for the Bank of Canada to spur debt reduction. It could do so by matching the Federal Reserve rate increases and even by retracting the two unnecessary decreases it made last year. As for the lower dollar, by raising prices it tightens domestic spending while at the same time spurring foreign demand for Canadian goods – not that earning less for what you sell is the fast track to prosperity.

It was heartening that the Bank of Canada resisted the urge to cut interest rates yet again this month. After seeing the federal budget, which is expected to land next month, it should consider an early 25-basis-point rate rise. Such an increase would signal a better sense of policy reality than its actions and talk indicated before a speech by Governor Stephen Poloz early in the new year. In it, he essentially acknowledged for the first time that we are in a world beyond monetary-policy help, one that will require hard and painful adjustments.

Canada must use the stimulus provided by the fiscal deficit the Liberals have promised to raise interest rates slowly to help achieve four goals: a stronger dollar, less inflation, somewhat lower household-sector debt, and more moderate housing prices.

Currency-exchange and interest rates are good or bad depending on whether they reflect a sound policy framework, and Canada's overall framework has been askew for three to four years.

Too little stimulus has been focused on the economy's true challenge: building longer-term productivity and expanding the supply capacity. Too much has gone to creating jobs in other countries because Canada has spent billions more on imports than it earned from exports.

The possibility of more personal financial prudence is a positive sign, but right now the dollar and interest rates are both too low. The federal government and central bank need to work carefully together to achieve great balance, with less risk than we are now running and a bigger cushion for the future.

What the Policies Should Be

And how do we build that cushion? Imagine the nation's economic policy as a stool that is supported by three legs, and the first is public infrastructure, especially transit and communications. The government is making a start, but the investment will need to be bigger than it has promised and focused almost totally on what will make the economy more competitive in the longer term.

Leg two is pipeline infrastructure. Here the Liberals can benefit from their approach to policy on Indigenous affairs and global warming – issues the previous federal and Alberta governments, along with the oil and pipeline industries, were sharply criticized over during the past decade.

The third leg should be a powerful incentive for the best people to come to live and invest in Canada and for businesses that are bold enough to expand in the face of uncertain times.

The old way to promote initiatives of this kind was through tax breaks or direct government spending – and there is still a role for both approaches. But something big and new is needed on the globally competitive goods-and-services front to match the infrastructure incentives.

We need a creative way to reward those who create wealth and jobs – and who then put their gains back into the Canadian economy.

Serious Bargaining Ahead

Canada's economics and politics tend to be more regional than national, whereas elections that bring about change are usually national, like the one last October. The provinces and the First Nations have needs – and leverage – so overcoming their differences will require political leadership, based on mutual accommodation.

Today's regional economic tensions are not as severe as the political tensions Pierre Trudeau faced when he was prime minister, but they are still difficult for any federal government to manage alone. The eruption of protest against the Energy East proposal for a 4,600-kilometre pipeline to carry a million barrels of oil a day from Alberta and Saskatchewan to refineries in the East illustrates what may lie ahead.

Back in 1967, there was a void in national leadership before Pierre Trudeau took office. Premiers John Robarts of Ontario and Daniel Johnson of Quebec stepped in, calling their provincial colleagues to the Confederation for Tomorrow Conference. As I've said before, it's time the premiers of the four largest provinces (Ontario, Quebec, Alberta, and British Columbia) did something similar and called a Canadian Economy of Tomorrow Conference.

The Future

Every Canadian prime minister faces three primary challenges: the economy, national unity, and the United States. The wider world has now added two new challenges: security and desperate people fleeing failed states and economies and the effects of global warming.

Pierre Trudeau saved Canada from separatism. Justin Trudeau promises to preserve its identity as a nation that relies on – and thrives because of – mutual accommodation. But the second Trudeau also needs to become the second Sir John A. Macdonald – the bold builder of a stronger coast-to-coast Canadian economy that flourishes both internationally and at home. It is a huge moment both for him and for Canada. The urgent question now is whether he and we can seize it.

The scale of the oil-price and global stock market collapse must be seen as wild cards that would not normally threaten the US and global economies – but could do so. If they do, it does not mean the Federal Reserve was wrong to test the waters with a 25 basis-point rise in interest rates. What it says is how very hard it is to get past the two big global drags – the post–Lehman aftershocks and the challenge of adjusting to China's new path.

Heavy lifting and much need for mutual accommodation lie ahead. The key is to get on the right path with a lot of honest and open discussion. In all likelihood, it will take the rest of 2016 to get started.

For the government to get all parties and provinces on side for what is needed, it needs to explain the problems and the proposed solutions well. At this critical moment, the "right" policies ideally should bring little political danger from the left, and potential support from moderate Conservatives on the right. These policies should not be based on ideology or wedge politics but simply on what works.

3. TO REVIVE CANADA'S ECONOMY, REWARD THOSE WHO PITCH IN*

Vaudeville ain't what it used to be, nor is the Canadian economy. But the economy can bounce back, and this week Finance Minister Bill Morneau announced something to help it do just that.

Largely lost in the fallout when Morneau revealed that this year's fiscal deficit will be much larger than expected was the creation of a special agency – the Advisory Council on Economic Growth.

After years of policies that created debt at home and employment elsewhere, this country must earn its way again. Once it has delivered its first budget on March 22, the government of Justin Trudeau plans to do something much needed: It will devote the rest of the year to

* Published in the *Globe and Mail*, February 26, 2016.

looking to the future. The new advisory council is being asked to recommend ways that Canada can, as the Ministry of Finance puts it, "create the long-term conditions for economic growth."

That is clearly a step in the right direction, as long as the government recognizes what is really needed: a broad set of discussions about how best to increase productivity – especially how to revitalize the nation's competitive capacity to supply global goods and services.

Direct government spending to spark a sluggish economy is effective in the short term, and Morneau insists the rapidly expanding deficit makes the infusion of public money more vital than ever.

But the only lasting strategy for generating jobs that are more plentiful, more satisfying, and better paid is to enlist the private sector. And I have an idea that Ottawa's new advisory council should consider. It is rooted both in the notion that the private sector should drive the economy and the fact that private enterprises deserve a strong foundation built on social licence. In other words, ventures that make a contribution to society should be granted special privileges.

My proposal may not be the only (or even best) way forward, but it takes a practical, "what works" approach that is easy to grasp and would enable Canada not only to live within its means but to prosper.

Invest Now, Tax Later

Building larger, more dynamic pools of capital in Canada would be enhanced if investors could treat their investment capital as a single asset for the purposes of capital-gains taxation. The way to do that is to allow capital property gains to be reinvested without immediate tax.

A simple taxpayer election, like the existing rollover (deferral) provisions for a small category of capital gains, would do it. It would be available to all Canadian resident taxpayers and involve no registration requirement, only a tax-return designation. In effect, until assets in the pool are withdrawn (or so deemed on death or residence change), they would remain at work, creating businesses, jobs, incomes, and tax revenues. There would be no change in the present capital-gains system or level; no fund, plan, or administrator; and nothing directive as to qualified reinvestment. If taxpayers wished to avoid having premature taxation reduce their capital pool, they need only elect to have the cost of the disposed security become the cost of the new security in order to defer recognition of the gain.

If a taxpayer did not reinvest, a taxable gain would be reported. Elections would not be available in the year of a taxpayer's death or when the taxpayer ceased to be a resident. If the full proceeds were not reinvested within some reasonable time (say sixty days), a *pro rata* portion of the gain would be subject to current tax. Income on investments would be subject to taxation, and interest on money borrowed to acquire securities would remain deductible. The plan would be easy for those paying tax and for those who collect it.

Why the Timing Is Right

Several developments suggest that now is the right time:

- The recovery of our oil and commodities strength is likely some years off. Until then, supply will probably exceed demand. We need more strings to our bow.
- Canada has lost ground in some manufacturing sectors. The lower Canadian dollar will help sales, but some lost capacity will not return.
- Recent economic and financial setbacks mean smaller initial revenue losses from deferred capital gains because those gains will likely be smaller for a while. Like infrastructure spending, short-term revenue losses are best seen as a longer-term "investment."
- The plan will counter weak Canadian business investment prospects by favouring reinvestment from successful ventures over immediate profit-taking. These reinvestments have to succeed to benefit.
- It will make Canada's capital markets more efficient. People will decide to sell for investment reasons, unaffected by tax considerations. We don't want our physicians thinking about tax while they operate; similarly with investors.
- The global venture-capital world, one of launching new businesses and moving on from one success to the next, would find Canada a much more attractive place to do that.

The proposal reflects today's realities, not ideology or theory. Canada has huge advantages – resources, space, water, and food; it's still the best neighbourhood in the world, with a proven history of mutual accommodation. The best way forward is to make an already-good Canada more competitive for the best people – entrepreneurs, innovators, creators, professionals, scientists, and managers (the weaker dollar is starting to really hurt here). The ability to build personal wealth by keeping one's gains at work would be an additional powerful magnet, one that is fair and reinforces Canada's advantages.

The proposal would temporarily "socialize" private-sector gains by keeping them at work creating jobs and wealth and enhancing government revenues. When the reinvestment ends, the deferred tax is paid.

We are likely in the early stages of the second quantum revolution. The first one brought us the modern, digital world. Mike Lazaridis, the technology genius behind the BlackBerry and the Perimeter Institute, the cutting-edge physics research group in Waterloo, Ontario, believes the next one will produce an even greater transformation. He says Canada needs to match a university infrastructure that is strong in basic science research with equal entrepreneurial and investment strength. A one-two punch.

US president Franklin Roosevelt realized that science and the government, together, had contributed enormously to victory in the Second World War. He wanted that same collaboration to bring the US economic success in peacetime by combining effective public support for science with effective incentives to the private sector. Canada, being even more willing than the United States to use collective action to advance shared causes, surely can do this.

After the financial crisis in 2008, Canada had an economic advantage over the United States and other advanced economies that could have lasted a decade. Instead, the advantage has disappeared already because we chose to spend now and earn later, at a record level. Nonetheless, we can have another "Canada moment" when our country is viewed positively from abroad, our economic policy approach is regarded as among the most effective, and Canadians feel deservedly good about themselves.

Policy That Makes Sense

For two decades after 1945, Canada had a tax policy that was well suited to its strengths. Special provisions encouraged oil, gas, and mining development. The absence of any capital-gains tax proved a driver to all investors and businesses.

These policies rewarded success, not effort; investment, not spending. We again need a custom-made policy for Canada's particular situation. The controversial report of the Carter Commission in 1966 recommended big changes. One was taxing capital gains as ordinary income – an approach out of tune with how investors and business people behave. This recommendation was rejected in favour of the current 50 percent of gains.

In its December 1970 paper on taxing small business, Ontario accepted that compromise but put the reinvestment-rollover case very simply: "The need for both private savings in Canadian hands and capital-market efficiency strongly favours a reinvestment-related tax-free rollover approach for all shares and business assets ... especially if one regards the taxation of capital as more appropriately having a lifetime perspective ... The Ontario proposals are based on the central importance of savings and investment for economic growth as the only reliable generator of increased revenues to governments ... Ontario does not believe in designing a long-term structure on the basis of short-run revenue considerations."

Get Moving Now

During his recent "rebranding Canada" trip to the World Economic Forum in Davos, Prime Minister Trudeau offered encouraging words. But now is the time for action, and this proposal responds to Canada's needs. It is balanced – everyone gains. It will show Canada in a new light, to itself and to others – a unique made-in-Canada way forward.

The Canadian business community has been absent for twenty years from serious discussion of economic policy. It shows. Neither zero federal deficits nor "shovel-ready" should be the primary focus. The business sector should take a hard look at this proposal and consider whether it would work and whether they could help make it happen. The unions should ask if any other proposal would work better for their members. Is there a safer bet for creating good jobs? At Davos, Trudeau said that Canada would not just manage change but take advantage of it. How? Unless matched by some big deeds, the words will not become reality. Small will not work for tomorrow's world, which is not about to get much better. It will become even more competitive. Mr Trudeau's assertion will happen only if Canada gets better – starting in Ottawa.

The Right Message

The best global economic outcome is a slow struggle forward to 2020. A worse outcome is where the inclusive global order continues to weaken and Canada becomes more isolated in a difficult economic environment, next door to a United States with a weakening economy and a seriously dysfunctional political system. Canadians must drop their moral smugness and economic complacency and engage in serious discussions about the future. Canada was unprepared for the oil-price collapse. There is no excuse for not being prepared for a wide range of potential economic outcomes in a world that is so uncertain.

There may be a better plan than what I suggest, but doing nothing powerful to stimulate private-sector investment is not an option. The low dollar alone is not sufficient. You do not get ahead by making yourself poorer through foreign borrowing and a currency that buys less. In an outside world that's far from favourable, how does Canada do something striking and different – really rebrand itself? We need the start of an answer within the year. If we do not, the populism spreading in other Western countries will reach Canada. Too many think the system no longer works for them. The challenge is to find what can work and get it working before the populist train leaves the station.

Postscript

The creation of the federal advisory council guarantees that the government will have the economic discussion it needs (and one ably led by Dominic Barton, a Canadian based in London as global managing director of consulting firm McKinsey & Company). No doubt the council will explore many options before delivering its report, which fortunately is due by the end of the calendar year.

I have believed in the capital-pool approach since 1970, when I was advising the Ontario government in its fight against Ottawa's tax proposals. I have yet to find a better way forward. We approve of large rewards for sports and entertainment stars because we feel what we give them is matched by what they give us.

The capital-pool idea tries to fit the feeling that "a fair exchange is no robbery" into the broader world of jobs and wealth creation. The idea is win-win – the non-zero-sum world of mutual accommodation, a social contract that works.

Canada Needs a New Economic Narrative

INTRODUCTION

Canada has remained on the wrong economic path for the last fourteen years. When I wrote my two essays in this chapter, we could still retain the hope that change would come. But it has not done so yet, and it is not likely that there will be a reset by the time the current economic expansion ends sometime after the next federal election in October 2019. Nonetheless, there was good economic news earlier this year: a five-times better 2019 spring jobs report in Canada compared to that in the United States; better prospects for NAFTA; the removal of steel and aluminum tariffs; the approval of the Trans-Mountain pipeline; and the emergence over the last three years of Toronto as a competitive global hi-tech employment leader.

On the whole, however, Canada today is being carried along primarily by the United States and the rest of the world, and the danger signs are many and troubling. Canada has real problems with goods and services competitiveness. It is not competitive with the United States in the encouragement of the private sector. Our interest rates remain low for a global economy in expansion mode alongside the persistent size of Canada's current account deficits and household-sector debt. US business investment will be spurred by the new US corporate tax cuts and incentives, but not as much as many hoped. Canada has lost competitive ground as a result. The 2018 Economic Statement did not help materially. The politics of two of Canada's three biggest provinces (British Columbia and Ontario) have or will have more bad news than good news for provincial debt and private-sector encouragement.

NAFTA uncertainties and US steel and aluminum tariffs (now lifted) and US corporate tax reform have been making Canada even less competitive for business investment than it already was. There has been until very recently no export recovery in real terms since 2008–09, despite a more competitive Canadian dollar, an accelerating US economy, and a synchronized global expansion. Canada's share of US imports and of US foreign investment – both direct and portfolio – is also down. So Canada remains on a clear path to continue to spend more than it earns and to borrow more from abroad than it can sustain. There are no good policy reasons for this decline – only political ones.

Currencies have a way of measuring foreign opinion on a country's prospects. The Canadian dollar flashes an alarm from time to time. Many have thought that "made in Canada" recessions were a thing of the past, but maybe not. Canada's $60 billion a year current account deficits continue with no sure end in sight. This is not the best place from which to face rising trade disruptions and the end of the US and global cyclical expansions. If trade threats get out of hand, Canada's recession risk, looking six to nine months ahead, could be high.

The Trudeau Liberals have lost political ground over the last year, largely through a series of unforced political errors of their own making. So far, they have done about as well as anyone could on the US trade front and in standing against single regional issue threats to national unity (the Kinder Morgan pipeline). But they still have no longer-term viable economic narrative – a vacuum that must be filled because Trump's global trade threats are affecting Canadian consumer confidence. The Liberals need a reality-based narrative fast. Otherwise, growing economic anxieties and the threat of a US recession could lose the Liberals not just their majority but the government itself.

The global financial crises of 2008 brought the world a huge balance-sheet recession and, subsequently, to the brink of a global depression. Martin Wolf, the respected economic journalist at the *Financial Times*, sees this breakdown as marking the end of the post-war Western-led era of liberalism and globalization. While I don't yet say it marks the end, it means at least some serious weakening and needed reshaping. There is really no other successful way to go about running an international global economy than through rules and markets.

More important than the causes of this breakdown is the question: what kind of order or disorder will replace it? The new ideas that underpinned the unprecedented peace and broadly based growing prosperity of the post-war era were freer and more globalized markets, active monetary and fiscal policy on the demand front, and international trade and monetary institutions. These policies are under increasing threat from centrifugal forces within the West (such as Brexit and President Trump) and from "strong-man" global players whose values are different. New visions, ideas, and projects are needed to address the world that is emerging. Without them, there can be no basis for a necessary consensus on the way forward.

The central role of monetary policy is ending. It became dysfunctional as it increasingly interfered with the pain needed for timely adjustments in market economies and democracies. Too much money and too much fiscal austerity has proved a toxic mix. The United States got monetary policy and bank regulation badly wrong in the run-up to the Lehman Brothers' collapse. Then, after the collapse, only the United States got the right mix of monetary and fiscal policy. It showed up in the much stronger US economy under President Barack Obama. Large fiscal deficits were part of what worked. Now the United States is pushing its fiscal deficits much higher despite its already very strong economy.

The overriding question is what can replace US leadership of the global economy if it does not reassert its leadership? How do China's and Germany's current account surpluses get reversed? What does the savings glut and the now low-to-negative real interest rate economy mean? Recent policy responses of extremely low interest rates and increasing debt loads in many countries are not the answer. They are making things worse without making longer-term growth sustainability better. Recovery from the next recession will likely be harder – a potentially more worrying economic challenge than in mid-2015, when I wrote these two essays for the *Globe and Mail*. Canada has now lost its post-2015 economic advantage opportunity.

Amid this increasingly troubled global economic and political situation, Canada must get onto a sustainable economic path. No one else can do that for us. Our future economic strength now lies less in natural resources, oil, and manufacturing and more in human resources – in retaining the best people at home and attracting the best from abroad to create businesses, jobs, and capital investment. To make this switch successfully, we need to develop a strong university research infrastructure that will boost science and technology; accept immigrants with excellent qualifications; encourage the private sector to expand our competitive goods-and-services supply capacity; and create a tax regime that takes a lifetime "pool" approach to capital gains. Canada needs a better balance of paying as we go for current expenditures and for building economic competitiveness for the future. It needs to become the best country in which to live a good life, earn a decent living, create new businesses, and build savings and investment. It is encouraging that Toronto currently has the fastest growing hi-tech sector of any North American city. That is where much of the world's economic future lies.

Canada must also curb its headlong drive into ever more foreign debt borrowed for consumption. It is crazy that in 2018 Canada borrowed an estimated $71 billion from abroad for consumption rather than for private- and public-sector investments that build for the future. It should borrow only to build more future earning capacity and to advance stronger First Nations' development, but not to give the middle class or the poor more than Canadians are willing to pay for out of current earnings. The best way to bring down high household debt levels is to return to the economic disciplines of the Mulroney/Chrétien era (1984–2003). Canada has lost ground since then and must turn that around. It also needs new economic ideas for a harder-to-manage global macro-economic world.

Canada's greatest strengths are its stable, inclusive politics. It is still in a relatively secure neighbourhood, with ample space and resources. Alarmingly, though, it has no economic policy to sustain its economy in a "higher risk for Canada" global environment. To forge ahead economically, it will need the federal and provincial governments and the First Nations to cooperate for the good of the country as a whole. That goal will be hard to reach. Over the next few years, Canada will have to adjust to a very different kind of world – one much less friendly to Canada than that of the first sixty post-war years. The continuation of its social policies and inclusive mutual accommodation ways depend on a prosperous Canadian economy. Stephen Harper missed this point – he thought he was on the right economic track, and Justin Trudeau is continuing to fall seriously short.

The US-led post-war era was driven by a vision of peace, prosperity, and social security – a long process of broadening the inclusive order at home and abroad and containing what could not be included at any particular time. We now need new visions, ideas, and projects for the different future the world faces, particularly for the economy. The post-1945 focus on free domestic and global markets and on fiscal and monetary policy for cyclical macro-economic management will remain important, but much more will be needed. Europe and China would not be where they are today without the benefits to them of this post-war world regime. Trump is right that, over the last few decades, the United States has done more than its fair share. But destabilizing this successful, unique, and broad-based order is not the solution. It needs to move forward, not backward.

Economics and politics need to be reunited and brought together again as political economy – the two together. The emergence of the centrifugal and populist Brexit and Trump forces came from the failure to accommodate both politics and economics. Post-1945 Canada has done pretty well overall on both politics and economics, with economics and social advance going forward most of the time hand in hand.

After every great moment of transition conditions change and the expectations rooted in the earlier era can no longer be fulfilled. Today's gaps among recent expectations of continuing expansion, new productivity possibilities, and rising incomes are creating several political and economic difficulties for the Western nations. These difficulties in turn will make it harder to reshape the global order in a constructive manner.

The post-war era has been one of accelerating innovation – more and more ways of doing more and more things. It can create illusions of a world with fewer limits than the real world allows. Awareness of these limits requires some form of pain in order to be noticed. As in the human body, pain killers in the economic, political, and social system – too much borrowing and central bank or financial innovation money – have weakened the message that the limits have been reached. They have separated the financial and real economies from each other in counter-productive and unsustainable ways.

Simply put, a financial sector that grows faster than the real economy, with rewards to the financial players in excess of their net contribution to the economy, needs to be examined. Our monetary policy mainly informs us about inflation, but inflation has not been a problem in thirty years. There is no sign yet that it will become a key problem any time soon.

The United States has elected a man who believes US greatness is about the past, not the future, and he is deferring to "strong man" authoritarian politics in other countries. It is plausible that the United States needs to be more focused on itself, and less on the rest of the world. But it is not yet plausible that this nation of freedom, science, and technology is abandoning its "frontier nature"– as the land of freedom and the future – to become Trump's world of inward withdrawal and the past. Will that fate become the future of the United States? Will it be paralyzed by political and social division between the two options? Or will it revert to being the global land of the future, though in a different way for a different world?

China is a long way from being able to replace the United States if the latter chooses to withdraw from its global leadership role. Trump's preference for two-step (one forward, one backward) dances does not fit the intertwined global world today. Canada can play a role, and the global need for its mutual accommodation skill is growing in urgency. That external role should be part of its going-forward economic narrative, just as it was after 1945. But it faces a new world – one much less friendly to Canada than it has been – and so far it has given no serious thought to how to fit in and look out for itself.

Further Reading

Mohamed A. El-Erian, *The Only Game in Town: Central Banks, Instability and Avoiding the Next Collapse* (2016).

Richard C. Koo, *The Other Half of Macroeconomics and the Fate of Globalization* (2018).

John Lanchester, "After the Fall," *London Review of Books* 40, no. 13, July 5, 2018.

1. WHY THE LIBERALS' BUDGETARY BEST IS LIKELY STILL TO COME*

Aspirations and campaign promises were job one for the Trudeau government's first budget. Getting Canada on a sustainable economic path will be job two for 2017. Finance Minister Bill Morneau mostly did what could and needed to be done. With their wish list on display, the Liberals have kept most of their key spending and tax promises. Still to come is the heavy lifting to get the economy on the right path and to ensure that the overall debt is better balanced and growing less rapidly.

This budget was mostly about putting the past behind. It provides no more than a broad fiscal framework, leaving the Conservatives and New Democrats much to criticize. But in today's world, it was never in the cards that a government just five months into its mandate could figure out where it needs and wants to go.

Unfinished Business

The budget story is bigger and more complex than the front-page headline it was given in the *Globe and Mail* – "Spending in search of growth" – would suggest. (A better one appeared above the editorial that day: "A good start, but watch the future.")

If the Liberals think spending on First Nations and big-city transit infrastructure will help growth, they are right. If they think diverting billions toward the middle-class and the less fortunate is the way to boost the economy, they are wrong.

First, increasing consumer demand to stimulate the economy is not needed; it is already overly (and wrongly) stimulated in that regard. Second, essentially nothing in the budget addresses how to deal with the two great supply-side shrinkages from oil prices and the loss of manufacturing capacity – further threatened if a softwood-lumber deal is not made by next October in today's toxic US trade atmosphere. The policy of Stephen Harper's government that increased household-sector debt and borrowing abroad for personal consumption was unsustainable. The middle class will now have to absorb

* Published in the *Globe and Mail*, April 8, 2016.

some pain on the road back to balance, and next year the government must decide how to make this happen.

This budget involves a shift to more, but not yet big, government. Will that shift be balanced next year with stronger policies for the private sector? Two years from now will Canadians like the shift as much as they do now, especially if the economic and job growth is not there, and they have to start paying for it? Are Canadians as confident about more government as the Liberals seem to be?

Rising deficits come from weak economies as well as from increased spending. We have both. Mr Harper got the country into a big debt hole, a trend it will have to reverse. Canada took more than five years to get there. It will take at least as long to get out.

Rarely About What Is Needed

The last election campaign was still about having us live beyond our means. The Harper Conservatives and the Liberals offered competing personal tax cuts the country had not earned. The NDP did the same on social spending.

All three political parties ignored the reasons why Canada, after emerging from the 2008 financial crisis in better shape than any other G20 country, has only lost ground:

- Rising household debt, which recently claimed its biggest share ever of the gross domestic product, and persistent current account deficits produced a drag that will take years to overcome.
- Consumers living beyond their means, with foreign borrowing that created jobs in other countries, saw Canada lose ground in manufacturing capacity and on unit-labour costs compared with the United States.
- The premature withdrawal of the federal fiscal stimulus left more of this burden on the provinces and more of the overall stimulus burden on household debt – neither of which happened in the United States.
- The collapse of oil prices could take years to get back to a viable oil-sands price, if ever, although a relatively decent improvement in government revenues could come sooner.

None of these issues was discussed seriously in the election. And we still don't know the new government's diagnosis of where we are. A cure requires that it be the right diagnosis.

Although many key determinants of Canada's economic future are known, the budget did not address issues affecting long-term growth. Over the next few months we will need to know the views of both Bill Morneau and Stephen Poloz, the governor of the Bank of Canada. We must act but are not yet at panic stations. It will likely take five to ten years to rebalance our debt and find a strong economic path forward.

Hope for the Private Sector

The economy is the biggest downside risk to the Trudeau legacy. Fresh policy aimed at an expanded competitive goods-and-services supply capacity driven by the private sector will be needed in the next budget. The Morneau-appointed economic advisory council was one good sign – the quality of both its leadership (Dominic Barton of McKinsey & Company) and its membership is encouraging. Another was that neither the promised reduction in the small-business tax rate nor the proposed tax on stock options was in the budget. The government appears to realize that it needs a comprehensive and coherent approach.

Canada must use the strengths it has that are not facing the challenges posed by oil, other commodities, and its shrunken manufacturing capacity. They include basic university research, plentiful food, and strong financial institutions, whose large pools of capital can help stronger Canadian investment and entrepreneurial performance. Pension funds already have a capital pool-taxation approach to their capital gains. If the private and the institutional sides were on an equal capital-gains tax footing, it could give each a powerful added push. The shift from a one-transaction-at-a-time system to a pool-withdrawal taxable event needs no other change. It would help to narrow Canada's reward-opportunity gap for the best of every kind of people. It would help investment and entrepreneurship in every part of the country.

Canada will need a stronger infrastructure program in both transit and basic university scientific research, matched by a broad-based, private-sector tax incentive for risk and investment. Longer term, as well as reducing its household-sector debt and foreign borrowing,

Canada must accept significant federal deficits for some time – as the United States still does. It cannot change the global economy, but it can cope with it better. The last good economic-policy era spanned the Mulroney-Chrétien years, from 1984 to 2003. We need another one now.

The First Four Years

The journey to address First Nations, climate change, and refugee settlement will be a long one – lasting well beyond 2019. Canada has the required capacity for inclusiveness – the ability to operate effectively in an interdependent world. Security and pipelines issues will not be easy but should be manageable. There is no fundamental barrier to success on either right now.

The danger will come from the economy. Canada has about a year to find a better long-term path. Now that the country's existential and identity challenges are largely behind it, everything the new government hopes to accomplish depends on making this transition. A bad or an unfair economy could undermine it. In fact, how the economy goes will determine the success – and length – of the Justin Trudeau era. It has been almost twenty-five years since Bill Clinton campaign strategist James Carville declared, "It's the economy, stupid," but the mantra holds true for Trudeau.

Spending and Tax Reform

Why the need for deficits? They are necessary because preparing the economy for the future will require new program spending that must be paid for. The Harper government used politically targeted personal tax reliefs that cost billions every year. Decades have passed since the last thorough review of the tax system, and Morneau has promised changes in tax expenditures – the tax breaks given to specific segments of the population, such as tradespeople and public transit riders – that will save about $3 billion annually.

Tax reform is needed but takes a long time. The immediate questions about growth and the federal deficit must be addressed first. Tax expenditures and spending cuts are needed for pay-as-you-go program spending. Deficits should be restricted to supply-side growth.

The Fiscal Framework

Two initial points about the projected federal deficits: first, on a proportional basis, they will likely be less than that of the United States, which is still in the $500 billion range; second, the US economy has done much better than Canada's over the last five years, partly because its federal deficit has come down more slowly. The federal government has a year to get a longer-term fiscal framework that makes sense. It has cushions (prudent for uncertain times): a $6 billion contingency to protect against the possibility of oil falling to $25 a barrel, which is below the price forecast by private-sector economists ($35 is more likely, and would increase revenue exponentially); and an estimated economic growth for this year and next that, hopefully, is too low, given that a lower dollar and continuing growth in the United States increases demand for our exports.

The Art of What Is Possible

The politics of more public spending right now are easy. The politics of matching private-sector incentive with spending requires explanation and discussion. Great political leaders can see around corners; they can get their supporters to do things they may not want to do; and they can remind us why politics is known as the art of the possible.

The party politics right now look favourable. The Liberals are said to dominate the "progressive majority," though in the long term, Canadian politics seem to be more regional than ideological. It is more a "what works" Progressive Conservative/conservative Liberal blend of inclusiveness and mutually supportive economic and social advance. On that basis, their domination of "progressive" issues gives the Liberals political room to move on private-sector growth.

The Bottom Line

Canada, for the moment, has politics that are broadly good but also at risk because of its economy, whereas the United States has broadly good economics at risk because of its politics. US politics need to recognize that a good economy works for everybody. Canada's politics need to recognize that a good economy gets everyone working for it.

The inclusiveness the new government espouses must apply not only to the disadvantaged and the middle-class but to those who build and invest. Postwar Canada has thrived because of the broadly acceptable idea that social and economic advance go hand in hand.

The new government is doing well on Canada's brand management, both at home and abroad. That matters, but it has limits. Advertising can get people to try your product, but if they don't like it, the game is over. How the Liberals use their success in managing the brand to address what the economy needs, and how the public feels about it, will determine their success and their legacy.

We won't know if the first budget was good until we see the second. Don't forget that even Chrétien's budgetary maestro Paul Martin didn't get it right on his first attempt. Still, a recent editorial in the *Financial Times* sounded positive: "Japan and Canada show some fiscal good sense – tax and spending stimulus is needed to help the global economy."

2. AN URGENT CALL FOR NATIONAL (ECONOMIC) UNITY IN CANADA[*]

All hands on deck – that's what Canada needs right now. Working together is never easy, but provincial premiers and First Nations leaders must join Ottawa in facing a global economic and political situation that is likely to remain unsettled for decades. It is urgent that Canada figure out where it stands on both counts and which strengths it can bring to bear.

The global balance-sheet recession of 2008–09 came as a huge shock. Suddenly, concern about debt caused a spending dip that threatened to drag the economy to a halt. The world has been fundamentally altered as a result.

Until around 1980, the US economic locomotive pulled the global economy out of cyclical recessions as America's current account surpluses (savings) were borrowed by weaker countries to build their productive capacity. But when those surpluses changed to deficits, because easy credit allowed US consumers to live beyond their means,

---

[*] Published in the *Globe and Mail*, June 10, 2016.

the locomotive ground to a halt, threatening in turn to spark a massive depression.

End of the Postwar World

The United States will never again play the role of economic engine to such a degree. Monetary policy can no longer mask what is going on. A depression was averted, but huge unfinished business remains:

- The aftershocks of 2008 continue, but the underlying causes of the crises remain unaddressed.
- The US economy is good but not trouble-free and remains vulnerable to the nation's disaffection-driven politics and a global economy that is generally weak.
- The central role of monetary policy is ending but its exit poses risks, both from continuing low interest rates and from unconventional tools being used in an attempt to keep it alive.

Avoiding the worst from 2008 was only half of the job. The rest will be more challenging and calls for painful structural adjustments that, so far, only the United States has done much to address. Moreover, the world of the US economic locomotive has to be replaced by something else – an enormous task under the best of circumstances. Current circumstances, however, don't seem conducive to a reasonable outcome.

Wrong Medicine

Monetary policy was part of the reason the world avoided a global depression, but it is no longer the right medicine. That particular cure has been maintained for too long at too high a dose and to less and less effect. It must give way to something better, despite the unavoidable risk of withdrawal shock. Our current monetary doctors do not want to admit defeat, so are administering the medicine in bizarre, untested new formulations (negative interest rates are the latest), making exits ever more difficult and the longer-term negative effects ever more costly.

Two numbers from Richard Koo, chief economist at Japan's Nomura Research Institute and an expert in balance-sheet recessions, make the case:

- the US monetary base has been expanded by the Federal Reserve by 357 percent since the end of 2008; and
- credit to the private sector has increased only 19 percent over seven and a half years.

That's an elephant effort for a mouse outcome.

The message for Canada is twofold. We may not have much time to get on the right path. And what we do must rely on our own strength rather than on the rest of the world, although that process could take decades.

On the plus side, Canada is possibly the only happy political place among Western countries right now. That is true both federally and provincially, and for politicians and parties in office and not. There are fights over policies (as there should be), but Canada's politics are, for the most part, not very divisive by today's standards, especially in terms of populism and extremism.

Use It or Lose It

The nation must use its current good politics, or it will lose them. The federal government, the provinces, and the First Nations must collaborate to find as many win-win, non-zero-sum ways of moving forward as possible – a reasonable expectation.

No provincial premier today needs, or stands to benefit from, national politics that are divisive. This was not the case forty years ago in the era of Pierre Trudeau, René Lévesque, William Davis, and Peter Lougheed, when each benefited from having one (or more) of the others as political foes. Today no leader needs an enemy. In fact, the provinces and First Nations have things they need from each other – and can gain leverage from what they offer in return. This balance of need and leverage should be the foundation for lasting deals that benefit everyone.

Canada's politics and economics are each strongly regional. What is national are its federal-provincial system (which, arguably, has worked better than any other political system) and its strong mutual accommodation ways. When the various economies are not well balanced (something that is often difficult to achieve), regional tensions tend to rise. Right now, oil and many other commodities have moved from hugely benefiting their regions to putting them at a severe disadvantage.

Look to What's Ahead

Effective political leadership must have the ability to look around corners and prepare for what is coming – not just the art of the possible but of making possible the necessary.

Fifty years ago, our existence was threatened when the Quiet Revolution in Quebec deeply unsettled our society and politics, yet Canada got the far-sighted leadership it needed. Prime Minister Lester Pearson responded early to the tensions that the rising forces of modernism and Quebec nationalism would bring. He recruited three forward-looking leaders from Quebec (Pierre Trudeau, Jean Marchand, and Gérard Pelletier), initiated a distinctive Canadian flag, and appointed the Royal Commission on Bilingualism and Biculturalism to address the future. Yet, after 1965, his Liberal government was a minority, and it was two premiers – Quebec's Daniel Johnson of the Union Nationale and Ontario's John Robarts of the Progressive Conservative Party – who called the other premiers to a Confederation of Tomorrow Conference in November 1967. *Globe and Mail* writer Ross H. Munro said that Robarts, "probably more than any other English Canadian, helped prevent Quebec from not reaching into a dangerous isolationism."

Security Threat

Today the threat, here as everywhere else, is the economy. If Canada is to survive and prosper, it has an array of needs: risk-reward opportunities, institutions, and clusters able to compete with those in the United States despite the huge US advantages of domestic market size, large global corporations, and freedom-driven entrepreneurship.

Canada's advantage lies in human resources. Its long-term political security now rests more on its ability to attract and retain the best people, and less on resources that depend on global markets.

Canada's Economy of Tomorrow

The global economy is undergoing irreversible, destabilizing changes. President Barack Obama has done a major service in his measured withdrawal from ground the United States can no longer hold to ground it can better hold. But even if the country escapes the high risk of Donald Trump as president later this year, the forces that produced both him and Democrat populist Bernie Sanders will be back with a vengeance in 2018 and 2020. The crisis will be particularly acute if China and Germany fail to get their current account surpluses substantially down and take pressure off both the United States and Canada.

In the Pearson era, the premiers of the two largest provinces came together to offset potential federal weakness and meet the burgeoning unity challenge. Now, the premiers of the four largest provinces should call the rest of their colleagues to a "Canadian Economy of Tomorrow Conference." This get-together would produce a conversation very different from one led by an unavoidably remote Ottawa.

Provinces Need Federal Growth Strategy

Above all, every province needs growth for revenues and jobs – requiring a stronger federal policy focus on human resources (as well as the First Nations). Each can attract good people, and has done so. But they should push the federal government, as should the Conservatives and the NDP in Ottawa. Resources are a huge continuing Canadian asset, but people are Canada's future.

The federal "people push" needs four major elements:

- a strong university research infrastructure as part of larger technology and commercialization clusters;
- open immigration, supported by a speedy and efficient system;
- encouragement for competitive and collaborative personal initiative – the best people almost always create jobs, not take them, so Canada must offer opportunities that attract the best people and keep them here for the long term; and
- a tax regime that takes a capital-pool approach to capital gains and reflects the reality that building businesses and capital are lifetime, not single-transaction, affairs.

This approach works everywhere, in every activity, and provides a doorway to businesses of the future. It also allows the economy to perform much better when it comes to creating capital – essential in a country that borrows more than $60 billion a year. It would rebrand Canada as the best of both worlds – societally inclusive and economically hard-headed.

The federal government may achieve these goals all by itself, but the provinces have the clout to make sure it does. The federal opposition parties could seal the deal. For the Conservatives, support would show them backing "build-the-economy" taxation rather than "populism wins election" personal tax cuts (which did not work). For the New Democrats, support would demonstrate they understand how growth in the private sector can advance social well-being too.

For more than a decade, neither Ottawa nor Ontario has had a government with a real instinct for what drives a successful private sector. Canada needs leadership that does. It requires stronger collaborative self-reliance, boldness, and the confidence to raise the excellence bar even higher – all in ways that strengthen what both Canadians and non-Canadians like about our country. All groups are needed. But the provinces have the most at stake – and the most political clout. If they do not use it, the price may come high on the revenue and job fronts.

Canada's Three Big Eras

Canada has been through three big challenging eras:

- 1867–96: Confederation and the building of the Canadian Pacific Railway, thereby creating a coast-to-coast Canada;
- 1896–1960: an outlook shift – away from Britain and colonial status toward North America and independence; and
- 1960–2015: dealing with the centrifugal forces of both Quebec separatism and Western alienation.

Canada now appears to be entering its fourth big challenging era – figuring out what it needs to navigate in a deeply unsettled world. As was the case during the last five decades, it will need early, far-sighted leadership for its next long journey of large change.

Justin Trudeau – or some other bold, far-sighted leader – must respond to the challenge and make Canada a very different kind of great country for a very different kind of world.

12

Trade and Free Markets in a Global Economy

INTRODUCTION

The Harper government inherited from the Mulroney-Chrétien era the strongest economic and financial position of any G7 country. Harper did not use that strength to build the robust Canadian economy needed for the future. Justin Trudeau took over just before the global economy began to experience its sturdiest synchronized expansion in decades. Like the Harper government before it, which did not take advantage of its inherited domestic strengths, the Trudeau government, rather than living within its means and building its economy, has used the global economic expansion to borrow for consumption. Both governments used the advantages delivered by others to spend for narrow and immediate political purposes – Harper primarily through personal tax cuts, and Trudeau primarily through spending.

The Trudeau government inherited from the Harper government a Canadian economy borrowing in the order of $60 billion a year from abroad for current spending at home. Almost four years later, that is where Canada still stands. It will likely take a new (though not yet in sight) government and a Canadian recession to force the living-within-its-means standard and foster the more competitive private sector that Canada has needed since 2009. At present the country also lacks imaginative leadership from the business side of public policy. New thinking is needed, but none so far is evident.

The Canada that took root in Quebec City in 1608 has come a long way. It has changed its vision more than once, advanced different ideas, and found big projects – economic, political, and societal – that are now making it a different kind of great country for a different kind of world. A new Canadian vision is emerging – perhaps furthest along in Toronto – as the best country for good people from anywhere in the world to live a high-quality life, earn a decent living, and build their businesses and wealth. To date, though, no party in Ottawa or any of the provinces has found what that track needs to be or how to get on it.

It made sense for me to say five years ago in my July 26, 2015, *Globe and Mail* essay that in today's world, Canada should be moving from backwater to a global role. Today, the competing "separatism" developments in the United States and China will not allow that idea to materialize. They make it premature. In the meantime, Canada needs to do two sets of things. First, we must be more economically realistic on a broad scale. The reduced commitment to an inclusive global order in the United States, China, and the European Union means that our primary focus must be on what works narrowly for ourselves, particularly in the hi-tech areas (Toronto-Waterloo, Montreal, and Vancouver) where Canada is becoming an increasingly strong global leader.

Second, Canada can have a role in helping the West to establish a new approach to collective defence against a China that seems to be adopting a one-at-a-time approach to its targets – as Hitler did in the lead-up to the Second World War. Canada was able to help on both sides of the post-war approach of broadening the inclusive order in the world and containing what could not yet be included. Dealing with today's China will be more complex and sophisticated – knowing how, simultaneously, to include and contain, and to contain not China's future but only its "counter-productive" behaviour. To be useful, however, Canada will need to sharpen its foreign policies: its China edge no longer matters, and its US edge is weakened by a divided United States.

Today, Canada has less potential leverage than it had only four years ago, and few business leaders have emerged to forge their way actively in the new world. Still, it is developing a new potential leverage source as an attractive country in which the very best people can build their businesses and live their lives. Both the United Kingdom and the United States are less attractive to the brightest and most enterprising people from the rest of the world. A *Financial Times* Big Read feature in February 2019 identified Canada as having become a brain-gain rather than a brain-drain country.

Canada has done much too little over the last four years to address its economic policy challenges through structural change. The US economic policy (monetary and fiscal) was well on track from 2008 to 2016. Following the election of Donald Trump, however, this successful strategy changed, and US fiscal and current account deficits have started to rise again.

I foresaw some five years ago that the US federal election in November 2016 might become one of the most dangerous moments of the post-war era. It is now clear that this projection was right. Unfortunately, Canada is almost totally unprepared for this new reality, and its business community still does not see an urgent need for it to play a key role. Canada has not yet started to think seriously about how to operate more on its own. The people-to-people friendship between our two countries remains strong, but, just as Americans are finding it more difficult to get along among themselves, so Canada and the United States are finding it harder to get along with each other.

My assessment that Canada's best prospects would come from a "No Trump America" has proved all too true. Canada has not done very much to address the challenges I laid out in my September 29, 2015, *Globe and Mail* essay. No one in Canada yet talks seriously about how Canada can best approach the new era of huge negative structural change ahead for it. We need to capitalize on the two things that are better for Canada today than they were four years ago: we are on a better path with Indigenous relations; and, especially in Toronto-Waterloo, Montreal, and Vancouver, we are increasingly globally competitive. Right now, only Beijing and Shanghai attract more hi-tech workers than Toronto gains each year.

I. CANADA'S MAJOR CHALLENGES AS IT FINDS ITS WAY INTO THE FUTURE*

Canada has big things to think about, discuss, and do on two major fronts. First, as a country, we must get back to living within our means. Since 2008 we have accumulated massive current account deficits financed by borrowing abroad in order to consume more than we earn, not to build the country. Second, going forward, Canada has a huge set of advantages and vulnerabilities stemming from its unique varied assets, which are in short supply globally.

Two important factors have contributed to Canada's shortfall over the last decade: a failure to understand our mutual accommodation strength and how we can use it; and the overall absence of needed business and political leadership on key economic policy challenges. The coming decades will bring new choices that will determine Canada's role in a changing world of great peril and opportunity. In this world, working within limits may become as critical as pushing possibilities. Limits drive creativity. Canada's mutual accommodation story is overwhelmingly one of creatively overcoming limits – in how we go about governing ourselves and living together.

The national focus since Confederation has been on consolidating the transcontinental nation formed by Sir John A. Macdonald, achieving independence from Great Britain, and avoiding domination by the United States. The focus for the rest of this century will be more on what we want and need to do on our own behalf in a rapidly changing world. Will we have the resilient flexibility needed for this more externally focused task?

What if the twenty-first century is primarily about resources, creativity, innovation, governing diversity, and achieving minimum levels of collective action? What if the population explosion, resource limits, and climate change make management of the planet increasingly difficult? What if the demands of an inclusive global order prove too much for many important countries to handle? How might Canada then fit in? The current inclusive global order, ranged around the West, is becoming less global and less inclusive. The world faces a

* Published in the *Globe and Mail*, July 26, 2015.

new, post-9/11, and post-Soviet collapse mutual accommodation challenge that will increasingly test the stability of the several orders in the world. It must decide what kind of global, separate, and differently connected orders are needed going forward.

Canada should now be moving from a backwater to a global role. England in the early sixteenth century had a freedom, rule-of-law, and constitutional-democracy gospel to spread. Canada today has a mutual accommodation gospel to share. A stronger capacity for mutual accommodation is the only lasting way to achieve sustainable purpose in a crowded and stressed world. This gospel does not require occupation or military victory; it works only if voluntary. Force may be needed to keep the door open, but a lasting mutual accommodation has to be, in some realistic sense, better than the alternative.

Leadership in the Long Term

Canada needs a new generation of political and business leaders who can look beyond short-term votes and profits. Business was at the centre of shaping Canada's economic policy from 1984 to 2000 – a fifteen-year span of fiscal progress. Its absence since then has already begun to damage Canada's short-term future. In time, it will risk its long-term future too. Business leadership in the narrow pursuit of its self-interest does not work (witness the last decade on the pipeline front), but business is needed to make things happen. Someone has to convey to politicians and public officials what drives the private sector. And the private sector has to be reminded of its social responsibility.

Great leaders have the vision and the drive to look beyond their own personal interests and offer the community what is needed for economic progress, political stability, and national security. Right now, there is little public policy leadership from the business community, yet Canada's only real security is its economy. Canada needs a more broadly based and vibrant private sector. Our largely absent business leaders must rise to fill the current economic policy leadership vacuum and become more involved. Otherwise, other forces and interests will step in to take over.

Since 1980, markets and an ideology based on shareholder value have held a kind of moral authority among leadership elites across much of the business and economic community. However, as governments have failed to ensure the basic economic element of any free society – good-quality jobs and decent wages – their credibility and moral authority have begun to erode.

Moral authority comes to those who recognize the real issues in the world. A dysfunctional economy based on favouring Wall Street over Main Street is no substitute. The year 2013 marked the passing of one institutional leader of great moral authority, Nelson Mandela, and the arrival of another, the Pope – men who stand for an inclusive compassion. It also witnessed the courage of a young Pakistani girl, Malala Yousafzai, who stands without fear for the right of girls to be educated.

Challenges on the Horizon

Canadians must start to think about and discuss their future. Staying the course of the last decade will not do it. Politics and political leaders are usually lagging indicators. Fresh policy leadership on competitive growth will almost certainly have to come from the private sector – journalists, academics, and business people. It will also need public officials at their best.

The United States presents another challenge – domestically and globally as well as in its relationship with Canada. It has been clear since at least 2001 that the United States was having its own "George Kennan moment." As predicted by Kennan when he was in the US Embassy in Moscow in the late 1940s, the Soviet Union by 1989 had developed overreach challenges too great to overcome. Putin is now going down the same path, but with much less strength. Kennan saw that the Soviet takeover of Eastern European countries after the Second World War would have two results. First, at least some of those countries would try to break away – as happened almost immediately with the departure of the former Yugoslavia, and in 1956 with the unsuccessful Hungarian Revolution. Second, the Soviet Union would have insufficient public energy to address ongoing internal challenges on a timely basis.

Around the turn of this century, the United States, the so-called winner of the Cold War, realized it would also have to withdraw from its geopolitical, economic, and financial overreaches to ground it could hold. But unlike the former Soviet Union, it is doing so before it is too late. And it is already getting stronger. The post-9/11 geopolitical overreach and the post–Lehman Brothers near-collapses have seen these withdrawals get underway seriously. The fallout is an important part of what is disturbing the United States, inside and out. Retreats are rarely positive affairs. Friendly countries find they now resent the US absence, where before they resented its presence.

This US withdrawal shapes everything in the world today, including the game-changing positive factors about to reshape Canada. Big changes lie ahead in Canada-US relations. A new era of political turmoil in the United States has emerged: the no-compromise Tea Party dominates the Congressional Republicans on fiscal issues and on social economic issues such as immigration. The United States no longer needs Canada in the same way it did during the Cold War, and it does not rely nearly as much on Canada for energy.

Canada still has many sources of potential leverage. It possesses many of the things that are increasingly in short supply in the world – space, a good neighbourhood, and political, socio-cultural, and institutional strengths – along with essential natural resources such as food, energy, water, and minerals. It will soon be a country bordered by three navigable oceans.

This changing future will demand all of Canada's capacity for boldness, firmness of purpose, and internal and external mutual accommodation. Until now, Canada has stood on the shoulders of other countries for much of what it has become and achieved. Now it must operate more independently in thinking and action at home and abroad. Every country in the world must change how it sees itself and goes about its affairs. Canada is no exception. What puts Canada in a different place from most is how much it has of what other countries want and need – its good neighbourhood and its mutual accommodation advantage.

Seizing the Moment

In a world of rising populations, climate change, and resource pressures, does Canada have better long-term prospects than most people realize? If so, what should Canadians be doing right now?

Canada must think more for itself, if it is to protect and preserve what it has achieved. Canada developed into an independent country under the military protection of Britain and then the United States, but that is no longer what Canada will need most. As the

United States is discovering in Afghanistan and the Middle East, overwhelming military strength at 30,000 feet does not translate into on-the-ground security.

In the future, Canada's best protection may well revolve around trade and immigration and a Canada-based economic policy that can drive a stronger competitive supply capability – two areas in which Canada already has solid experience. In addition, Canada's long history of mutual accommodation, ability to collaborate with others, practical "what works" approaches, and small-country flexibility in the face of complex situations will all be to its advantage.

Canada could undergo two huge changes from climate change: an expanded area in its northern regions suitable for agriculture and comfortable human settlement; and the emergence of a third ocean – the Arctic – with new resources and sovereignty issues. So far, Canada's North has been more mythic than "real" – the "true North strong and free." In the near future, that North will need to be occupied, managed, and protected well.

For the past century, Canada has lived in a good neighbourhood. It will now need to think seriously about how political turmoil in the United States and bordering on a third ocean could undermine that position. Canada cannot afford to allow any more of its resources to become hostage to a US political system that is blocking measures simply for partisan advantage, independent of national interest.

The twenty-first century may well belong to Canada, in terms of everyday life for ordinary people, in much the way Wilfrid Laurier said the previous century would. Greater volatility and risk are in every country's collective future, but Canada can improve its chances by exploring developments that are most pertinent to us. Knowing more than other countries about what we see to be central for us and having better relevant relationships could make Canada, with its mutual accommodation culture and solid institutions, a haven of opportunity for good jobs and for wealth creation and protection. It could also provide increasing professional, creative, and entrepreneurial opportunities for the best people in every field. They will be essential for a more productive and competitive non-resource and non-manufacturing-based Canadian economy.

How will Canada get from today's here to tomorrow's there? The United States is back as a reliable, forward-moving economy. Canada has lost momentum from its position of comparative advantage in 2012 and has yet to find a new path. The oil-price collapse has caused major problems for the economy. The recent suggestion of drought in Western Canada could add to the challenge. Canada lacks policies to reward competitiveness in creating new job opportunities at a time when it is declining in its ability to attract the best people to establish themselves here.

The message for today's leaders in every field is simple: if you do not see Canada in a strong and long-term positive way and act on that basis, you cannot expect other Canadians, let alone the rest of the world, to see Canada that way. Right now, Canada needs a far-ranging conversation that combines the best possible growth thinking with a bolder and higher aspirational performance bar – a new balance between big infrastructure and dynamic, knowledge-based entrepreneurship.

2. NO TRUMP:
THE BEST BID FOR CANADIAN–US PROSPERITY*

As Canadians prepare to go to the polls on October 19, 2015, the economy is the campaign's main focus, as it almost certainly will be when the Americans do the same this time next year. What should voters be asking? The basic questions are the same for both countries: Where are we now? How did we get here? What do we need to do as we go into the future? But the answers in the United States are somewhat different, as is public opinion. Canadians perhaps feel better – and Americans worse – than they should. Why? And could that change?

Canada weathered the 2008 crises better than any other G7 nation. It has since lost ground relative to the United States. Why is that? Canada must ask how to best manage public opinion, political leadership, and the gap between the policy that is needed and the political will to make it happen.

The meltdown that almost brought the world's economy and financial system to their knees in 2008 began in the United States. How

---

* Published in the *Globe and Mail*, September 29, 2015.

then did the Americans, the primary source of the collapse, get more corrective actions right than any other country?

And why, despite this success, do the Republicans have a front-runner like Donald Trump? He is an oversize bully, a big-time insulter, and a shameless self-approver. Yet he currently has almost one-third of the support approaching the primaries, based on his skilful response to public fearfulness and frustration. Given that the post–Lehman United States is so much better off, something deeper is at work.

Diagnosis Matters Most

My approach to economic questions comes from a 2007 book by a Harvard medical researcher. It's called *How Doctors Think*, but it is really about how humans think. Author Jerome Groopman makes two fundamental points: If the diagnosis is wrong, the treatment will not work; and, if the diagnosis fails to explain every potentially relevant factor, think again until you find the right diagnosis. If our politicians took this approach, they could help both Canada and the United States get back on the right economic-policy track.

To diagnose where we are and where we have been, we need to go back to the Great Depression. It was never really overcome, but was supplanted by the Second World War. The lack of economic demand in the 1930s made developing sufficient demand the focus of postwar politics and policy. So, for thirty-five years, it was widely accepted (even in the individualist United States) that, after a global depression and war, the focus had to be on jobs and economic security.

That changed after 1980, once Ronald Reagan was elected president and the era of debt and globalization began. The feeling grew that there was too much government, that government was too much in debt and taxes were too high – that the time had come to shift from demand-side to supply-side policies. Macro-policy challenges tend to shift between demand and supply – from being about too little (Keynes) or too much (inflation) demand, and then to too little (inflation) or too much (recession) supply. However, what works when demand is the problem does not work when the problem is supply. By the 1990s, there was insufficient global demand, too high global savings, inadequate productive investment opportunities, too many workers, and global imbalances.

Many countries were beginning to struggle early in the last decade. The United States remained prosperous until 2008, when the sudden flood of Chinese exports overwhelmed its deeply indebted economy. For the United States, the big challenge was fundamentally different from Canada's. It went into a "balance-sheet" recession, which happens when high levels of private-sector debt cause both individuals and companies to focus on saving (paying down debt) rather than spending or investing. Canada did not follow suit because its monetary policy was able to stimulate consumer borrowing. Unlike their American neighbours, Canadian households could still do so.

Now, the situation has reversed: The debt of Canadian households as a percentage of gross domestic product is above the 2008 American level. If a real recession does hit Canada, monetary policy will not be able to generate economic activity as it did in 2008. When Canadian interest rates finally start to rise, they will put pressure on the level of household debt. So would unemployment or lower house prices.

Richard Koo, chief economist of Japan's Nomura Research Institute, is the world's pre-eminent student of balance-sheet recessions. He recently told *Maclean's* magazine that there is a real risk of one happening in Canada, if home prices fall while household-sector debt remains high. Tomorrow's home prices could look like today's oil prices. This is not a prediction but a forewarning.

The Bank of Canada, with its low interest rates, has got us into this threatening situation over the last few years. The reason Canadians feel better today than Americans is that they have adjusted less, and the country lives far beyond its means. This complacency can feel good while it lasts, and was the Reagan-era experience for America. Canada's huge level of low-interest household debt has not yet been felt. Wages here have risen much faster than in the United States. These gains were made possible by Canada's looser stance on macro-economic policy and contributed to a loss of manufacturing jobs and capacity because the country was less competitive. Now this loss has been aggravated by the oil-price collapse and generally low global commodity prices. None of these things will change quickly.

Why do Americans, who have their affairs in better balance, feel worse about their situation than Canadians? A mix of unrealistic expectations, impatience, and the fact they have been through extended rough times. Wage gains have been well below those in Canada. Now, however, the United States is both more competitive in manufacturing and less dependent on foreign energy. That means US growth will help Canada less than before.

Current Challenges

Canada's recent economic history can be summarized in three phases. From 1984 to 2003 (the Mulroney-Chrétien era), it ran an increasingly tight macro-economic policy that put the country in good shape for the post-2008 crises. From 2009 to 2011, a balanced use of fiscal and monetary policy got the country through the height of the crises. Since then, Canadian policy has become increasingly unbalanced, with the emphasis primarily on monetary rather than fiscal measures. Monetary policy is largely about expanding credit (to help growth) or contracting credit (to contain inflation) for business and households. Fiscal policy is about government borrowing to stimulate demand in the economy, and taxing to contain the economy when demand exceeds supply. There is, as a result, excessive total debt; too much household-sector debt relative to federal debt; and too much of the debt funded by a big buildup of foreign borrowing, not domestic savings. Working this debt down to a better balance will not be painless.

Canada's major political and policy challenges lie on the economic front. Four issues are immediate:

- We must stop living beyond our means – which have already declined because of the fall in oil and commodities prices and the loss of manufacturing capacity. We must replace those lost means, not increase our current spending or cut taxes. The brake will come initially through higher prices brought on by the lower Canadian dollar and lower wages.
- We must broaden our capacity to supply goods and services that are internationally competitive.
- We must address our challenging transit-infrastructure needs, initially through federal deficits. High-speed rail, in and between

large urban centres, is a productive time-saver and globally helpful in attracting the best available people, many of whom are used
to very good transit.

- We must figure out a new tax policy that is fair and can power
the creation of new wealth – and, through it, new jobs.

A Rebalancing Act

Over the next few years, the incoming Canadian government will
have to begin to rebalance the economy in several ways:

- Stop relying on debt-fuelled domestic demand and focus on building a competitive supply economy to produce exports.
- Aim for a better balance between Canada's monetary and fiscal
policy.
- Reduce household debt. That would require higher interest rates
from the Bank of Canada and, if needed, more federal debt to
offset the demand loss from less household-sector debt.
- Convince Canadians not to be spooked by the idea of running a
deficit to build the country. Right now there are no grounds for
fiscal deficits to provide cyclical stimulus. Much of the stimulus
we have is going into foreign jobs (that's what a current account
deficit does), so the demand helps them, not us. Building the
country requires more spending inside Canada, so the jobs are in
Canada. The level of household-sector debt is more than enough
demand stimulus.
- Address Canada's current economic weakness through structural
change. We are entering an era of huge global structural change –
much of which will be negative for Canada.

The American challenge is different from Canada's. The economy
is in pretty good shape, but it faces a political threat. Republicans do
not grasp the fact that the issue today is weak global demand, not US
government debt, and weak US supply. Worse, US political turmoil
has raised the barriers to mutual accommodation, both at home and
abroad.

Right now, US macro-policy is about right, but a sweep by the
Republicans next year could put that policy at risk. As Dr Groopman

might say, they could misdiagnose the problem and prescribe a supply-side, anti-debt ideology at odds with the lack-of-demand reality. If the new president adopts any of the Trump approach to the world, the struggling global economy would confront a stark reality: the only country that is on a strong economic path could be undermined, economically and geopolitically.

Voters Decide, Politicians Lead

The task of political leaders is to integrate what voters want with policies they know are needed. Most of the time this task is the art of the possible. At key moments, it becomes the art of making possible the necessary. Democracies and free markets depend on myriad individual decisions. If they are to work successfully, the signals must tell the truth. When those natural signals are interfered with by massive borrowing (which blocks the natural pain warning that all is not well), both voters and the markets will make the wrong decisions.

Politicians are lagging indicators and pain avoiders. If there is pain on the horizon, they tend to try to mask what is really going on. They prefer to keep voters ignorant of reality's pain. Credit excess has become a favoured way to mask unpleasant economic truths. Ideology, based on observation of what works, can be useful in providing direction. If it is applied inflexibly, however, it can do great damage. Some politicians find simple ideological promises a seductive political shorthand to avoid facing the hard measures needed to manage in today's global economy.

For all these reasons, Canada and the United States may not get the political or policy leadership they need in the coming elections. Politics matter, but economics inevitably will dictate a change of course before long. Canada may be able to survive (at a cost) without the political leadership that gets the diagnosis of its economic and financial challenges right. Markets and economic forces will limit how far Canada can go off the rails sooner than in the United States. But over time the United States and the world generally will not be able to escape the consequences of US political and policy leadership that gets its diagnosis wrong. With Henry Paulson as secretary of the treasury, Ben Bernanke running the Federal Reserve, and Barack Obama in the White House, the Americans got the post-2008 financial system and economy diagnosis largely right, but the fiscal side was later threatened by the Republican Congress for several years. Right now there is no sign that anyone who leads the Republicans will get either the economic or the financial path forward right.

Canada's unaddressed economic-policy challenges may prove less severe in the short run than those in the United States. Canadian politics and policy making are not likely to be better, but Canada has less scope for financial misbehaviour than the United States does. Markets will catch Canada sooner than the United States, but at the end of the day, markets and increased geopolitical instability will also affect the United States. If US leadership is not there when that happens, the consequences for the global order will not bear thinking about. The United States may well get through the present dangerous political situation, but Canada should be prepared if it does not. An adequate response will require diagnosis and discussion, not political sound bites.

13

A Different Foreign Policy
for a Different World

INTRODUCTION

The centrifugal forces in the West reflected in Brexit and Donald Trump, and the post–Deng Xiaoping Communist Party domestic leadership anxieties (now aggravated by serious and dangerous Hong Kong protests), have together altered the global economic and geopolitical landscape since my last *Globe and Mail* explorations of foreign policy. As a result, the conditions for Canadian foreign policy have been fundamentally changed. The hoped-for participation of China and Russia in the post-war inclusive order failed to take place on a viable basis from a Western perspective; the post-war global order must now be reshaped. There needs to be two kinds of global structural reordering – a fairer global burden-sharing with the United States, and more reciprocity and structural balance on the part of China. At the same time, Western economic and social policy management also needs to change to respond to the shortcomings of the Margaret Thatcher/Ronald Reagan economic era.

Since 1945 Canada has benefited from the global order, but now many countries and its former allies are suddenly turning against it. Over the last two years, Canada has been unfairly bullied by both China and the United States as well as by Saudi Arabia. Hopes for China that looked good in 2010 appeared dim by 2019. Canada has to rethink what the new world will be like for it and how to focus more of its efforts on strengthening its own economy. It cannot hope to help China and the United States. Canada will now, more than ever before in its history, be on its own internationally. Unfortunately for Canada, it will be more tied to a United States that feels less tied to it.

The world needs a new shared vision with new ideas and projects. Only one country can lead that – the United States – and it has gone missing. The United States at the beginning of this century needed to start withdrawing from economic and geopolitical ground it could not hold to ground it could hold. Instead, the George W. Bush administration made the huge mistake of overreaching further into the mire of the Middle East. President Barack Obama saw the need for both a withdrawal geopolitically and a shift of focus to Asia. Instead, he had to cope with the US/Middle East geopolitical overreach and the Wall Street 2008 overreach that he inherited from the Bush administration. His withdrawal may not always have been ideal, but he was largely measured and on the right track.

Trump saw the overreach, but not the right kind of withdrawal. He has breached three Obama-made deals: the Paris global warming accord; the Iran nuclear deal; and the Trans-Pacific Partnership. Trump is still far more a deal breaker than a deal maker. The last two withdrawals have weakened his hand opposite China and in the Middle East.

The United States was already, before Trump, in its greatest political turmoil since the Civil War. The next election in 2020 will result in a decision fundamental to the prospects for a bearable future for the world. No matter which way the US election goes, Canada has to focus more and more on building its multiple strengths. It will not be able to count on a stable world or as reliable a United States as it has since 1945.

I was wrong five years ago in thinking Canada could play a significant role in strengthening US-China relations. Today's United States and China are different countries from what they were when I wrote the *Globe and Mail* essay (March 24, 2016) seeking to make that case. Canada's edge with China no longer applies and has become largely irrelevant history. Canada's former ambassador to China, David Mulroney, saw that more clearly than most of us. He listed several specific China challenges, and he captured better than almost anyone that the overarching question is "President Xi's vision problem" – his belief that what is good for the Communist Party is good for China. It is similar to the Trump vision problem that what appeals to the Trump base is good for the United States (which in Trump's case really means him).

Canada needs a big rethink of its foreign policy and its current weak-for-the-future economic policy. The Chinese pro-Canada items I listed no longer seem to matter – and they probably never will. Canada's people-to-people US strengths remain, but less so with a United States that is deeply divided within itself. Every aspect of the world needs a Canada rethink that it is not yet on anyone's horizon, let alone getting done.

1. IN DEALING WITH UNCLE SAM, CANADA MUST BE PATIENT AND FIRM *

In 1993 I was in Tokyo to address a group of businessmen on "Coping with a Changing United States in a Changing World." It was a year after George W.H. Bush, then US president, had become violently ill at a state dinner with the prime minister. The uproar had produced a low point in Japanese-US relations, and the shock had yet to subside. So I repeated for my audience what I'd said at the time to a Japanese journalist, who was unsure of what to make of Americans. Just as American jazz is called the "sound of surprise," I said, the United States is the nation of surprise. Then I made three points:

- First, whatever happens in any given week in no way represents the United States as a whole. Even Americans can't see their own country whole at one time. There is simply too much energized purpose in their vast, open society – too much action being initiated. No matter the problem, or the opportunity, someone is taking it on.
- Second, just as it's impossible to overestimate the lack of Americans' collective foresight, it's impossible to overestimate the power they bring to bear when they decide they must do something.
- Finally, after living beside Americans for 150 years, Canadians have learned one key lesson: be firm and patient with them, and

---

* Published in the *Globe and Mail*, May 20, 1016.

you can find a position somewhere between Pearl Harbor and simply handing them the keys.

This fine balance is crucial because no country matters more to Canada – to the world, for that matter – than the United States, and, right now, it's in its greatest political turmoil since the Civil War. The war was an existential crisis, and afterward the United States faced an identity crisis: What kind of country did it want to be? Today it again faces an identity crisis that is an existential crisis for the Republican Party.

Even so, the United States has two very big positives: it is the only major country on the right economic path; and under President Barack Obama it has largely withdrawn from geopolitical, financial, and economic ground it could no longer hold. It's now stronger, but at risk because of America's divisive politics.

The Drive to Divide

The United States has a drive for division, but at critical junctures, under the right leaders, it can also do big mutual accommodations. Canada has a drive for mutual accommodation – one that involves overcoming, not aggravating, divisions. The United States was founded by force and preserved by force. Canada was founded by the mutual accommodation of the Quebec Act of 1774, which was passed just fifteen years after the British defeated the French in the Battle of the Plains of Abraham and allowed the vanquished to retain their language, their religion, and the French form of civil law.

The pattern has been repeated, first at Confederation and, more recently, with the notwithstanding clause in the Charter of Rights and Freedoms. Canada has been preserved by words and persuasion, not arms and force – a contrast that marks the abiding difference between the two countries.

The current wave of US populism, nativism, racism, and fearfulness can be attributed to many factors, all of them valid but only partial. What is happening to the United States comes from the beginning – from the driving force of its freedom and individualism. But these strengths can overwhelm mutual accommodation and collective action.

Canada's mutual accommodation culture is rooted in a different history and geography. Ironically, Canada has become less European than the United States – less divided by nationalism, ideology, religion, class, and cultural differences.

The world is in its first global moment in history – when the momentum and direction since 1945 have weakened and the counterforces have strengthened. This shift will require all the important countries to better understand themselves as well as others. In his insightful book *The Duel: The Eighty-Day Struggle Between Churchill and Hitler* (1990), historian John Lukacs argues that, from May 10, 1940, the day Churchill became prime minister, through the Battle of Britain, the war was essentially a two-man struggle – which Lukacs says Churchill won by understanding Hitler better than Hitler understood himself.

What was apt for leaders then is apt for countries today. Those that do best understand themselves and others, and they use that understanding effectively by following the four great better ways mankind has found for going about things: caring and compassion, freedom under the law, science and education, and mutual accommodation.

The world is becoming less vertical (tribal and hierarchical) and more horizontal (democratic). Freedom has made that happen, and the Internet, along with social and physical mobility, has reinforced it. Nowhere has that happened more than in the United States.

Moral Crisis and Fearfulness

The United States faces moral crises in many of its major institutions. Examples include a Washington barely able to govern and the hierarchical side of both the Catholic Church (in the Oscar-winning film *Spotlight*, sexual predators are attracted to the church because it offers them, as well as victims, lasting safety) and Wall Street (in *The Big Short*, another Oscar-winner, tycoons make profits any way they can, disconnected from the real economy and from those who work and invest in it). Similarly, the current exclusion-style capitalism is also in a moral crisis, reflected initially in Occupy Wall Street and now in the fact that some 40 percent of US voters are prepared to support delusional (Donald Trump) or pie-in-the-sky (Bernie Sanders) politics.

Historically, waves of fearfulness have come and gone in the United States: the McCarthy-era paranoia about "Reds under the beds," for instance, or the attitude to terrorists after 9/11. President Franklin Roosevelt seemed to have sensed this tendency. When speaking of the Depression in his 1933 inaugural address, he famously said, "There is nothing to fear but fear itself." In most countries, leaders do not invoke the idea that the problem is the fearfulness of their own people.

The US election in November may become one of the more dangerous moments of the postwar period. It is hard to imagine what the world could become if the United States were to go into some form of craziness – a world of exclusion and no compromises – opposed to what it has always been about.

The raging US democracy and its exceptional ability to manage extremes are under severe stress. Though unlikely, that craziness scenario cannot be ruled out. Even the best possible result will not assure minimum effective politics. The combination of high levels of partisanship, divisiveness, and disaffection will likely make a sunnier Reagan-like political outcome close to impossible.

The leadership and consensus for a better way forward after November looks unlikely, but a start may be possible. The United States faces an identity crisis about the kind of country it is and what it will stand for in the future. The Republican Party has its own existential crisis. The Republican crisis means that the current danger facing Canada and the world from US politics will not disappear if Trump becomes president. Hillary Clinton has so much political baggage it will be hard for her to bring the country back together again by moderating its extreme partisanship.

The situation is different in Canada. The federal election last fall saw a young, untested leader and a party that had been in intensive care completely change the feel of Canadian politics. Yet the Conservatives still have the critical mass needed to challenge the Liberals and come back, if voters want them.

Big-Time Accommodation

Americans have usually preferred division, yet they have had two historic mutual accommodation outcomes and four great mutual accommodation leaders at critical moments. The United States was launched by war. It was achieved by the mutual accommodation of national and state interests: a president elected by a popular vote (expressed through state electoral-college delegates) every four years; elected individual House of Representative constituencies every two years; two senators elected for every state, no matter its population; and a Bill of Rights that can be changed only with great political difficulty. This complex political system, though frustrating at times, has worked most of the time.

Fast-forward 170 years, and the United States led the greatest statecraft achievement in history. It created a post-1945 global order based on broadening the inclusiveness in the world and containing what could not be included. It did so collectively, not unilaterally.

The first US president, George Washington, won not only a war but the peace. He created a new country through mutual accommodation with a fractious group of founders. Abraham Lincoln, by collaborating with his notorious "team of rivals," could not avoid the Civil War, but achieved some accommodation with the slave-holding South and pre-served America's representative democracy – government of the people, by the people, and for the people. Franklin Roosevelt saved political and economic democracy by overcoming the deep divisions from the Depression and leading the allied victories in the Second World War.

I believe Barack Obama will come to be seen as a great American president and one of its foremost mutual accommodation leaders. The post-2008 economic improvement is finally reaching more middle-class Americans, and his approval ratings are approaching 50 percent. Great leaders make many mistakes, including big ones, but they get the most important things right. President Obama got three: election and re-election as the first black president; keeping the world from a global depression; and bringing the United States back from economic, financial, and geopolitical overreach. Ironically, the absence of the victories Donald Trump craves has made the United States stronger on every substantive front. Obama withdrew from overreach, but the Republican response was to overreach themselves.

How Canada Copes

Canada has always understood that hockey showed the way for deal-ing with the United States. When Americans wake up each day, they find it difficult to see beyond themselves. But they are so interconnected with the rest of the world that, by the end of the day, they realize they have to break out of their US-centric perspective and deal with issues beyond their borders.

Canadians understand that, in their relations with the United States, they are always short-handed. To continue the hockey analogy: they have to rag the puck until an opportunity to score emerges. It usually does – but sometimes, as in the case of the St Lawrence Seaway years ago, only after long delay. Short-handed hockey is punishing, and Americans use punishment as they see fit.

What if the present political turmoil in the United States ends badly? How can Canada best look out for itself? Has it a role to help the world cope?

As I told the businessmen in Tokyo, the United States is always capable of surprise – its politics could bounce back. Even so, now is the time for Canadians and their government to start thinking about and discussing these questions.

- Job one is to use the present US economic positives to strengthen the longer-term supply side of Canada's economy.
- Job two is to build a strong political, economic, and socio-cultural intelligence capacity regarding the United States and other relevant countries.
- Job three is to build Canada's diplomatic relationships and explore its best roles.
- Job four is to reposition Canada's relationship with the United States to reflect present reality: a world where the dominant power is in turmoil, with an emerging relationship with Canada that is moving away from decades of convergence to one of divergence.
- The best way to face any hard challenge is to build on one's strengths, which Canada's ambitious new government must do as it focuses on something better suited to tomorrow's world. It needs more sources initiating action – especially of the economic variety.

2. CANADA COULD PLAY A MAJOR ROLE IN STRENGTHENING US-CHINA RELATIONS*

How much interdependence is possible in today's world? What form will it take? How stable will the way forward be? Zbigniew Brzezinski, the political strategist who advised US presidents Lyndon Johnson and Jimmy Carter, said that the world is still making the transition from the Cold War to an international order that continues to rest on the decisive axis of two great powers but is more complex.

The great powers today, of course, are the United States and China, but two significant realities distinguish their competition from that of the West and the Soviet Union: neither party is excessively ideological, and both recognize that they have to get along – they really need to master mutual accommodation.

In the coming years, the big economic challenge facing China and the big political one facing the Americans will test this view – but Canada has some special qualifications that could make it an important player. Canadians can bring to the discussion both their own capacity for mutual accommodation and the unique relationships they enjoy with the global powers. The connection with the United States is a special people-to-people bond much celebrated during Prime Minister Trudeau's recent visit to Washington and his welcome by President Obama. It is beyond the reach of government.

Canada also has an edge with China, for several reasons:

- Canadian Norman Bethune brought modern medicine to rural China and made such an impression that Chairman Mao wrote a eulogy for him that Chinese students for decades were required to know by heart.
- Northrop Frye, the great Canadian cultural critic, got more serious attention in China than perhaps any other (non-communist) Western thinker.
- In 1958 the Royal Bank of Canada was the first Western financial institution to open in the People's Republic.

* Published in the *Globe and Mail*, March 24, 2016.

- A year later, the *Globe and Mail* became one of the first Western news outlets with a base there.
- In the early 1960s, Canada sold China wheat it needed badly and could find nowhere else.
- In October 1970 Pierre Trudeau made Canada one of the first Western countries to officially recognize Beijing.

China does not soon forget a favour. When President Xi Jinping met Justin Trudeau after last fall's election, he produced a photograph of the new prime minister's parents. It was taken forty-three years ago when the elder Trudeau was making his third visit to China, though the first by a sitting Canadian prime minister.

As well, both China and the United States appreciate Canada's natural resources, so this country has a lot going for it right now. The mainland's most popular foreign TV personality is even a Canadian – Mark Rowswell, the comedian and on-air host better known as Dashan.

We must be sure to make use of this clout, to stand back and feel confident in who we are. Like the West as a whole, we have no choice but to take risks with China, but we must do so with open eyes. Remember what happened when the world failed to find a way to accommodate an ascendant Germany? By the same token, China would be wise to remember that the United States can be slow to act, but it brings a lot to bear when it does.

A Troubled People's Republic

China has issues. David Mulroney, who was Canada's ambassador to Beijing from 2009 to 2012, sees many pressing problems: the unpredictable behaviour of neighbouring North Korea; pollution; uneven development across society; corrosive public criticism of education and health care; concerns about corruption; and uncertainty generated by the Taiwanese and US elections. The overarching question, Mulroney says, is President Xi's "vision problem"– his belief that "what's good for the Communist Party is good for China." At the same time, China has many big positives. The late Deng Xiaoping set his country on the road to economic advancement in 1978, when he made his historic "speech for change." The subsequent speed, scope, and scale of the transformation, and the number of people who have benefited, are without precedent.

Unlike the former Soviet Union, which reformed its politics without reforming its economy, China made the practical political choice to improve economic conditions in ways that would be felt quickly by individuals. It avoided the swamps of Western-style democratic politics, in which neither China's leaders nor the public had any experience. As in the United States right now, the economic results are better than the political.

Success Through Co-operation

Although China and the United States have many shortcomings, they should be seen in the larger context of astonishing achievement and resilience. The task for both countries – one they are up to but may not want to tackle – is to use their strength to co-operate in making an interdependent world work for each of them.

What is the challenge for Canada? Find how best to be useful. Since the Second World War, the external leadership provided by the United States has been unprecedented. There is still no credible or acceptable alternative global order on offer.

The Chinese achievement at home is no less impressive. In 2010, while in China for a week, I asked myself what I would do if trying to bring 1.4 billon people, peaceably and at high speed, through two centuries of the Industrial Revolution and three or more decades of globalization.

What China has done since 1979 reveals amazing strength. Its accomplishment may seem imperfect to Westerners, who took centuries to get where they are today, so some mind-boggling numbers may help our perspective. In 1989, a decade after Deng Xiaoping had launched his economic reforms, China's per capita gross domestic product was still a mere $403, but by 2014 it had topped $7,000. In 1940, average life expectancy was thirty-six years, and the literacy rate was 20 percent. By 2012, people were living to seventy-five, and literacy was over 90 percent.

This rise is unique in human history – but as huge as China's accomplishment has been, so too is what remains to be done, at home and abroad. Beijing painted itself into a corner by relying excessively on the global system to propel the scale and pace of its development. It must now move beyond these dependencies into more interdependent ways.

Similarly, the United States hobbled itself by the scale of its debt, the weakness of its financial system and the unpreparedness of its voters and its political system to address the inevitable fallout as it withdrew from its international overreach. So, just as China is finding its new economic path harder, the United States is experiencing political turmoil. China needs to understand that American workers carried part of its great leap forward on their backs, and this burden is part of what is now playing out in US politics.

Deciding Factors

Certain impressions still resonate from my trip to China: memory, hope, and energy, alongside overwhelming size and speed. All five will determine the success or failure of China's unprecedented experiment of modernization and participation in the global order. It is impossible to see China as a whole, especially in a week or two – and the same applies to the United States. But seven days was time enough to raise one simple question: Can China become an ongoing positive participant in an evolving inclusive global economic order?

Since then, a second question has arisen: Can the United States hang in, or will its internal turmoil lead it to withdraw, leaving the rest of the world more than it can handle? In the last few years, the overall US economy has done well, but the domestic political fallout of the last twenty-five years has become very challenging.

Meanwhile, many outsiders have believed there is no end to the demands that can be placed on the United States. But that era is over – as are the days of the Chinese economy as the great resource and consumer market of the future, as well as the provider of cost-effective outsourcing for the world's suppliers.

The fact that China has vivid memories of the Mao era's extremes (and a deep-seated desire not to return to them) may give its leaders the latitude they need to maintain cohesion. (The United States has no recent memory of such extremes to constrain it.) Hope is less a fundamental for China's current generation than for its children. Like memory, hope stands to last another one or two decades as a source of stability through huge change. These powerful feelings should result in needed patience and realistic expectations. They do not, however, guarantee Chinese political will for needed change.

And then there is energy. The sheer power of the China numbers could yet overwhelm its own positive socio-cultural driving forces and the ability of the global economy to handle them. The math of huge numbers and compressed time frames will continue to test both Chinese capabilities and those of the global economic order.

No Impending Implosion

Not long ago I listened to David Mulroney deliver the annual Bishop White Lecture (which honours the first curator of the Royal Ontario Museum's Chinese collections). He acknowledges China's strengths and achievements and the positive changes within the Communist Party that emerged following the Tiananmen Square crackdown and the collapse of the Soviet Union. He sees a party that has been immensely adaptive but not yet ready to relinquish office. He expects no early Chinese implosion – if ever. If there were such an implosion, it would make the current Middle East mess look minor.

We have to hope that the continued Chinese acceptance of Communist Party rule in exchange for economic prosperity will not become prematurely inadequate politically through some combination of mediocre economic performance and a desire among the younger Chinese for something more than full stomachs. The West should stay out of this difficult challenge on the domestic front, while not letting China forgo its fair role in preserving the global order.

Canada Needs Them to Succeed

Canada played a special role in the global order that emerged in the late 1940s. It should do so again by helping to shape a more sustainable global economic order. Ottawa has in the Bank of Canada and the Departments of Finance and Foreign Affairs a group of officials not surpassed for independence, innovative analysis, broad experience, and an ability to work with others to help achieve this new world.

For a decade, Canada lacked responsive political leadership because Prime Minister Stephen Harper found it difficult to get along with the two countries most important to Canada and to the world. The new government in Ottawa has a role. Canada needs a sustainable global order. It also needs both the United States and China to succeed. The United States is our most important customer by far. China may no longer drive the demand in the important resources sector, but it is still a significant factor. China's population numbers and multiple strengths mean it will matter, regardless of what happens.

Can China and the United States find the capacity for needed mutual accommodation? If you doubt interdependence is the challenge of our time, think again. Take a hard look at the surge in blue-collar support for Donald Trump. Overwhelmingly, it is about trade, which, in turn, means China. I was part of a small group of senior Canadian businessmen who took that message to Shanghai in 2010. We were five years early. (For more on Canada, the United States, and China, see Part Three, Chapter 17.)

Navigating the World's First Global Moment

14

The World We Live in Now

INTRODUCTION

Canadians wanted sunny ways when they voted for Justin Trudeau in October 2015, shortly after my first essays were written for the *Globe and Mail*. He won the most remarkable election victory in Canadian history – starting as a far-behind third party and ending with a solid majority. The rising global warning signs at the end of possibly the most positive era (1945–2018) of human history foreshadowed what has since been happening: the collapse of the Soviet Union; the rise of Islamic terrorism; Brexit; Trump's United States; and a more assertive China. The post-war forces of integration at home and abroad had lost momentum and the centrifugal counterforces were asserting themselves within and between countries.

In recent Western history, bad eras have followed good ones – and vice versa. The bad Napoleonic era was followed by the good 1815–1914 era, then the bad 1914–45 era, and finally the good 1945–2000 era. We do not know yet if we can break this alternating bad/good pattern in our current emerging era. Whether we can is the great issue of our time. It also has meaning for two of my early essays on Canada's role in the world and on Trudeau's optimism in relation to the emerging world of every nation for itself.

The world that is emerging is not one where Canada can effectively play the possible role I foresaw in August 2015. Moreover, Trudeau's sunny ways are out of step with what is happening in the rest of the world and are not strong enough to overcome them. Canada's world at home is under regional stresses, but not at the level of the existential and identity threats it was under between 1960 – the beginning of the Quiet Revolution in Quebec – and the defeat of the minority Parti Québécois government in 2014. Canada has faced one growing urgency since 2006 and the election of a minority Harper government – to address its "living-beyond-its-means" problem and the loss of its global goods and services supply competitiveness. Looking ahead, Canada faces a different, more challenging global economic and geopolitical world as well as rising political stresses among the regions at home. Right now, no political party has a reality-based approach for any of these issues.

1. A NEW ROLE FOR CANADA AND THE UNITED STATES IN A WORLD OF PERSISTENT MENACE*

Mutual accommodation – the willingness to compromise, if required, to settle a dispute or move forward – may not always work, but it should always be an option. Even when circumstances don't seem promising, we should keep in mind the impact that flexibility could have.

Canada's story shows that mutual accommodation is one of the better ways to conduct human governance. Non-violent resistance is another. It sparked the great achievements of Mahatma Gandhi in India, Nelson Mandela in South Africa, Martin Luther King in the United States – which ultimately also became achievements for those who opposed them, those who initially resisted before giving up ground rather than resorting to drastic measures.

Non-violence is a particular way of achieving mutual accommodation, but since 1945 the Western world has developed other effective techniques for avoiding war and achieving peace and prosperity:

- collective rather than unilateral action;
- broadening the inclusive order both at home and abroad; and
- containing (rather than defeating) what cannot be included at any particular time.

* Published in the *Globe and Mail*, August 4, 2015.

Hazards to World Peace

At the same time, three new threats to the inclusiveness and scope of the global order have emerged:

- Vladimir Putin's Russia;
- the multidimensional mess in the Middle East; and
- an expansion-minded Iran.

Each has emerged, in part, because the United States has forgotten what has worked so well for it and the rest of the world since 1945.

Mike Mullen, the admiral (now retired) who served as chairman of the US Joint Chiefs of Staff from 2007 to 2011, recently criticized his country's triumphalism and lack of assistance to Russia after the Soviet collapse. The United States would have been better to approach the diminished Russia the way it did Germany and Japan after the Second World War, even if the two situations aren't comparable. In fact, Russia, like Iran and the Islamic State, has two traits that make it hard to handle – a thirst for revenge and a desire to reconstruct a lost "empire."

These narratives look backward, not forward. They get in the way of seeing a better, more collaborative, and safer way ahead. The approach taken by these states makes it extremely difficult for other countries to work constructively with any of them. The United States, more than most countries, is seeking paths forward that strengthen the global order (though both President Trump and the Brexit referendum have suddenly changed this position). By contrast, these three danger zones have expansionist ambitions that threaten their neighbours and undermine that order.

A forward-looking expansionism that takes the needs and interests of others into account – that operates through mutual accommodation – can exist within a peaceful and prosperous world order. But a fixation on vengeance and lost empires is more likely to respond to a strategy of containment, of "disintertwinement," than to the increasing inclusiveness of the world order.

This fixation demands uncompromising stands and decisive actions rather than the small steps that mutual accommodation allows – steps that feel less risky for all participants because whatever is done requires consent. During the Cold War, this kind of limited accommodation happened more than once in key areas such as arms control.

Russia, the Islamic State, and Iran are each of special importance right now. They pose huge, immediate, and imponderable risks to the global economy and to long-term global security. Their strong geopolitical drivers are not a good fit for what they and the world need right now.

Let's begin with Russia. Vladimir Putin had a real opportunity to become a major player in making the global order better in ways that also worked for Russia. So far he has not followed that route, but he or a successor can still do so at some future date. Looking backward no longer works in a world that, since 1945, has been on a fast and powerful track forward. Both the Soviet Union and China lost ground for decades because they did not acknowledge that fact. Now Russia, from a weaker position, seems back into the same kind of overreach that plagued the Soviet Union before it collapsed. It may have some early success, but over time it will further weaken Russia. The sooner Moscow acknowledges that it must collaborate with Europe, the better it will be. Europe and Russia need each other.

Neither Iran nor anyone else in the Middle East has given any indication of being ready to become a positive participant in the inclusive global order. By its very nature, the Islamic State could never be a partner, but Iran could be – if it set its sights on that goal. Unfortunately, though, in the Middle East and, to a lesser extent, Iran, the revenge and reconstruction stories are reinforced by cultures that have found modernization difficult. Countries in the Middle East cannot overcome these backward-looking drivers any time soon. There are simply too many obstacles preventing them from moving forward. In Iran, however, a large part of the population is looking to the future or is already there.

The West and these troubled places have only one constructive way forward – mutual accommodation. Given their complex history, that is not a natural way for any of these three places to think or operate. One good thing about mutual accommodation is that it is hard to do. It requires minimal illusion among all parties. That same quality makes it safer to try, and safer once it is accomplished.

President Barack Obama and Iran's leaders were right to try to find a mutual accommodation on the contentious nuclear file. That is so, even if the deal fails to achieve its goals. The nuclear talks are limited in scope and aspiration, which is good. Although the purpose is big – to forbid any additional nuclear weapons in the Middle East – it, too, is limited in scope. After fifty years of distrust between the countries, an agreement will not in itself bring trust or peace, but it could be the first step along the way.

Iran may or may not be open to a different way of going about achieving its aspirations. It has a significant population that is attracted to the West, but some of its key players are stuck in the past. Now that a nuclear agreement is near, the West needs to think about the longer-term benefits for both sides in the dispute if Iran can be persuaded that a more collaborative approach will be both safe and productive. In the meantime, policies and active efforts to thwart destabilizing Iranian behaviour will be needed.

At the same time, the United States itself remains a potential global risk due to its hyper-partisan, no-holds-barred politics, which reflect a lot of divisiveness within US society. If that divisiveness were to derail the agreement with Iran, the ramifications would go far beyond nuclear weapons and the rising risk of military action in the Middle East. It would be the United States turning its back on the other four permanent members of the UN Security Council as well as Germany. It is hard today to get other countries on the same page. To get the United States, France, the United Kingdom, and Germany on the same page with China and Russia does not happen often or easily. Having the United States refuse to go along because of what the world sees as its dysfunctional politics could not fail to weaken Washington's ability to attract international support for other geographical and economical challenges.

The Fading US Presence

All three of these troubled places would be better off, as they look forward, if they could view the United States as a less dominating threat than it has been in recent years. In fact, the United States is withdrawing, not because of weakness but because of overreach. This withdrawal is making the country stronger and, simultaneously, less dominating.

There will always be geopolitical dangers in a fast-moving world. The most striking feature of the Cold War and the twenty-five years since the collapse of the Soviet Union has been how containable big crises, including high-risk moments such as Cuba in 1962, have been. In the past, similar events have led to catastrophe. If we consider some significant "moments" in the past two centuries – the bad Napoleonic wars (up to 1815), the good Western Europe era (1815 to 1914), the bad Western Europe era (1914 to 1945), the (on average) good global period (1945 to 1990), and now the post-Cold War era – we have to conclude that we are currently back in a "bad" era. It is not clear where the world is headed. Almost certainly, though, it is in a more manageable state than it was in the first fifty years of the last century. So far, extreme outcomes are being avoided.

Major countries like Russia and China do not consider the current world order suited to their needs. They see it as something imposed by the United States. For that reason, the inclusive global order will be less inclusive and less global. At the same time, no major country wants either the economic or the security foundations of the global order to collapse. Both China and Russia seem to worry about the social and economic risks they would face from a weakening global economic order, even as they build their security strength opposite that of the United States.

In principle, today is not very different from the postwar era that ended in 1990. Both Russia and China are strong military countries with clear borders, and their governments are in control of their territory. The big difference is that they are more intertwined with the global economy, so the idea of containment is not as simple today as it was in 1950. And disintertwinement is a central and difficult-to-implement part of any containment strategy.

Russia could become a second fifty-year containment challenge. There is little immediate prospect of becoming a positive player. That is just not how President Putin sees Russia's future. Western policy has to figure out how to deal with that reality in a way that avoids extreme outcomes.

The several failed states in the Middle East present a completely different set of problems: Islamic State's absolute brutality, the absence of functioning states, the huge number of refugees, the thousands of immigrants fleeing from Africa, all alongside the poor, stressed middle classes and the unemployed youth everywhere. This set of challenges has no real historical precedent. It will be a fundamental challenge to all Western countries and require action from both governments and private institutions.

The United States faces a new and difficult world, one that has never been more connected yet so disconnected at the same time. It is in the late stages of withdrawing from ground it can no longer hold to more limited ground it can hold. Until the collapse of the Soviet Union, it lived in the two-superpower world that marked the years after the Second World War. Then, for a few years, the United States was the only superpower.

But a superpower is not what it used to be. America is bumping up against challenging limits it has yet to think through. Other countries also need to rethink the current global realities as the United States withdraws. It is still a superpower, but it has definite limits on its effective reach. It is still indispensable, but not as pervasive as it used to be.

In *Superpower* (2015), political scientist Ian Bremmer, a consultant and active observer of political risk, has outlined three broad choices for America's role in the world. All non-Americans, including Canadians, should think about his arguments carefully. No country will be more important to the world over the next few decades than the United States. It needs to get the part it should play as right as possible, but its divisive politics will make that very difficult. Just as war is too important to be left to the generals, America's role is too important to be left to the Americans.

A Canadian Contribution

Great powers usually don't feel any particular need for mutual accommodation as they go about their business. But without it, lesser powers like Canada cannot make much progress on anything. To thrive, Canada needs to rethink its role, that of the United States, and how, together, the two countries can use their individual strengths in a world that desperately needs fresh thinking, more vision, and greater collaboration. This reconsideration should be at the top of the new government's to-do list after the federal election in October 2015.

Canadians in the past have chosen a peacekeeping role, but there's now little call for that. Canada will be most useful if it commits its resources and experience to disintertwinement and long-term, humanitarian-based broadening of the inclusive global order.

North America has seen the creation of two improbable countries: the United States in the eighteenth century, driven by freedom and individualism, and Canada in the nineteenth century, driven out of necessity by mutual accommodation and collective action. Now may be the moment when these two neighbours, who are very different but share many values, can work together in a new way. It is possible that Canada's talent for accommodation could join the economic and military strength that are the fruit of US freedom and science – and thus become a dominant and indispensable force in the twenty-first century.

2. CAN TRUDEAU'S OPTIMISM SURVIVE IN A WORLD OF EVERY NATION FOR ITSELF?*

Canada is feeling very good about itself and its new government, especially now in the immediate afterglow of this week's warm Washington welcome for the prime minister and his family. The state dinner at the White House was the first for a visiting Canadian leader in almost two decades, and the media embrace was over the top. "Justin Trudeau," asked the *Christian Science Monitor* in a lengthy cover story, "is he Canada's J.F.K.?"

But the honeymoon may end in a hurry if the economic challenges Canada faces both at home and abroad are not dealt with, realistically and promptly. The optimism that Mr Trudeau and his team generate is hard to find anywhere else. Witness what happened when G20 finance ministers met in China recently for the very first time, supposedly in a collective bid to rescue the world from the economic doldrums. And how did they fare? Not very well, according to David Loevinger, a former China specialist at the US Treasury Department. "Investor hopes of coordinated policy actions," he said afterward, "proved to be pure fantasy."

Canada has taken 150 years to consolidate itself as a coast-to-coast country, a journey made far from the world's troubled places under the protection first of Great Britain and then the United States. Its growing capacity for mutual accommodation brought Canada

* Published in the *Globe and Mail*, March 11, 2016.

through its growing pains and made it one of the world's most successful countries – a fully fledged young-adult nation.

This independent Canada now enters a world whose disturbances are no longer thousands of miles away but impinge on the everyday life of its citizens. So, less than eighteen months after it finally emerged from almost forty years of existential crisis focused on Quebec, Canada must now face a world it could not have been expecting. It is a world that is fast-moving and prone to extremes and anomalies – the oil price collapse, the Chinese stock-market selloff, and the Republican Party in utter disarray even as it enjoys the biggest majority in both houses of the US Congress it has had in eighty-five years.

What is really going on? We need a better fix on the problem, which begins very close to home.

Across the Great Divide

Despite the world's political troubles and weak economic climate, Americans have by far the world's best economy. Yet their domestic politics are dysfunctional. Just as tribalism and populism are making the world more difficult to lead (as well as more dangerous), they (along with nativism) make it increasingly difficult to bring the United States together. More and more observers are seeing a rise in authoritarianism in the American population. Even after the dust from the presidential election in November 2016 settles, a political honeymoon is unlikely.

As well as battling each other, both major parties are increasingly divided within themselves. In fact, the challenge for the Republicans is existential. The primary reason isn't even the parties or the political leaders; it's Americans themselves. John Kasich, the Republican governor of Ohio who placed an unexpected second in the New Hampshire primary, has some idea of what has gone missing. "Slow down," he tells his audiences, and "take time to listen" to what others have to say. But his is a lonely adult voice at odds both with his party's angry, hyperpolarized base and with a country that is evermore divided.

Not that divisions are unique to the United States. The ruling British Conservative Party is seriously split over staying in the European Union. Anti-immigration feelings and parties have gained strength in Europe and could create an identity crisis for the European Union, alongside a British exit, if not a threat to its very existence. The big question is: Will the centre hold?

A Brave New World

The hardest post-9/11 lesson for the West is that the world does not revolve around it, despite what Francis Fukuyama, usually a smart political scientist, naively concluded in *The End of History*, his 1990s paean to the American way. There have been so many opportunities for young Western people that a sense of entitlement has understandably emerged; they expect to be able to do what they want. The reality is that those who get what they want must usually play a big role themselves. Now more opportunities are opening for people from other nations, and the major danger in the United States and Europe comes from people – and politicians – who refuse to accept that.

Meanwhile, the West faces some new key political challenges: security and identity issues. But even the economics landscape has changed, with two big serious changes at work.

First, oil – one of the world's most important prices – is currently affecting financial markets and the real economy. Not only have oil prices collapsed (for some time) but so has the supply-demand structure. Saudi Arabia no longer acts as a swing producer, and the OPEC cartel no longer has pricing power. Demand growth is slow, and excess supply will be difficult to run down. Any price improvement will immediately bring more US shale oil back into the market.

Second, central banks are now out of fashion: The change started for me after 1985, when monetary policy in Japan proved no substitute for needed structured change. Now financial markets are losing confidence in central banks. In fact, in his excellent book *The Only Game in Town: Central Banks, Instability, and Avoiding the Next Collapse* (2016), Mohamed A. El-Erian, chair of the US President's Global Development Council, says that overreach on the part of central bankers is the primary source of the current instability. As the former chief executive officer of the US investment manager PIMCO (and now an adviser to the parent company Allianz), he sees another major collapse within the next three years if reliance on central banks is not reduced. Canada seems about to move that way – but it will be hard to do.

The Banks Became a Problem

That overreach came from global imbalances that emerged in the 1990s and culminated in the post–Lehman crises. By the 1990s, the world was back in the 1930s, with inadequate consumer demand and more savings than available investment opportunities. This slump lasted as long as Americans used foreign savings to consume more than they earned, much as Canada has done since 2010–11. (This situation happens when a country like China wants to earn more than it wishes to spend, which required the United States to spend more than it could earn. That imbalance was possible because, due to its export surpluses, China was willing and able to lend it the money.) Fortunately, the world is now back to the 1990s, but with a more prudent US consumer.

Two central questions: How do we get more global consumer demand and more global investment opportunities? If things go badly, two big issues will emerge: how to reduce inequality without undermining savings and incentives, so consumers have more money to spend; and how to use long-term public investments in big transit and communication and in large-scale university-centred scientific research infrastructure. These issues will provoke political challenges – something the United States in its present mindset would find hard to handle.

Simultaneous Journeys

One way to look at what is going on as well as our best way forward is the reality and metaphor of journeys. Humans have always been driven to move on – initially for food, but then for dreams of glory and power, and for better ways to live. One could say Adam and Eve were the world's first refugees – pushed out of their Garden of Eden home by God himself. We are all immigrants who move from one place to another; from accustomed lands and families to places where other languages are spoken and different cultural ways are the norm. By choice or necessity, virtually everyone chooses or feels forced to move on from where they are in every kind of way. It can be very unsettling and provocative.

The challenge of this pervasive mobility in almost every aspect of life is that we all find ourselves in spaces where we are not yet comfortable – a version of the Tower of Babel. Who can know the way ahead in this uncharted world of changing geographies, sophisticated technologies, and political upheavals to engender the genuine trust necessary to lead? Science and mutual accommodation are likely to be at the heart of what we will need.

Every individual, society, and country is always on a journey. We are all explorers of possibilities, confronted by limits that require creative solutions. Even the greatest of these explorations – geographical, scientific, intellectual, cultural, or spiritual – must proceed one step at a time. Journeys go best when purpose, strength, boldness (when needed), and determination are present. Canada's mutual accommodation ways, along with freedom, science, and compassion for others, are the four best ways that humans have found over history to go about things. The more an individual, group, society, or country can move on all four fronts together, the stronger each will be – the only bearable path forward.

What It All Means

Canada has a massive array of strengths to work with. It has reached an independent adulthood that can help at home and abroad – and be useful to the rest of the world.

We need to understand and see these strengths well and also to comprehend what the outside world requires. The twenty-first century will be dominated by two massive sets of forces:

- the huge numbers of desperate people with not enough safe places to go; and
- the proliferation of every kind of way forward, with vastly different ideas about where and how to go, and at too fast a pace for necessary balance and stability.

So far, Canada has found ways to provide safe places, accommodate different ideas, take multiple ways forward, and achieve longer-term balance and stability. The Trudeau government is listening and seeking guidance. But it also faces a severe challenge with the domestic economy which would be easier to get wrong than get right, even without all the campaign promises it made.

Family therapists note that the shocks and setbacks we undergo are often external but also can come from within. As well, some, such as adolescence, are paradigm shifts, and others, while painful, are less pivotal. If, however, you are being shocked simultaneously inside and outside, as well as experiencing paradigm shifts, as Canada now is, you have to ask what you must do as well as what you want to do.

By year's end, the Trudeau government will almost certainly recognize that this is where it's at – and its immediate priorities have to be the economy, security, refugees, and the Indigenous people. Together, these challenges are more difficult than those most governments have to face. They demand two major sets of decisions:

- Apart from what the government campaigned on and wants to do, what else must it take on in the current economic and political circumstances?
- Given what those "no choice" items will demand in terms of money, political capital, and stamina, how many promises can the government delay or cut back, without paying an unacceptable political price?

The year 2017 will be primarily about how the federal government answers these questions, and what comes at it from an increasingly unsettled world.

No White Knights

The prospect of help coming any time soon from anywhere other than the United States is unlikely. So, rather than wait, Canada must do what it can for itself, and the best outcome right now is to keep things from getting worse. That means improving its overall policy and business performance, but it is unlikely that much of what needs to be done can be done in this month's budget or even in the rest of the year. The required shift away from monetary policy and growth-driving structural change are both too big and too bold to really get going until next year.

Meanwhile, the government has a lot to absorb about the world in which it must govern and how its aspirations can be made to fit the economic limits it faces. The previous government did not comprehend what was happening in the rest of the world, and so it missed the economic-policy boat.

Above all, the Trudeau government should not allow its domestic inspirations to get in the way of what Canada must urgently do, both at home and abroad, to cope with an economic world that is still becoming harder, even as it struggles to leave the post–Lehman crises behind it. Or as David Loevinger put it after the G20's meeting in Shanghai: "It's every country for themselves" – an approach that has real limits for today's world.

3. IDENTITY AND CULTURE: THE NEW DRIVING FORCES

The wonderful Harry and Meghan (Duke and Duchess of Sussex) wedding showed the world that making room for the cultures and identities of others – in their case, the British and African-American – diminishes neither one and enhances both. The inclusiveness of the wedding was reinforced by a bride and groom who had gone through very personal hard things and come through whole; who had real achievements in challenging professions (the military and acting); and who genuinely embrace humanitarian causes.

Identity and culture are the new driving forces of the twenty-first century. They change slowly, and they always matter. They have an impact on the dominant military, political, and economic forces. They shape aspirations and anxieties; they divide countries and societies. They also bring them together. Canadians and Americans share the New World of North America, but are very different. The United States has been shaped by force: slavery – later race, minimum compromise, and seizing what it sees as opportunities without limits. Canada, in contrast, has been shaped by persuasion, accommodation, and overcoming limits.

Culture is how we go about things – how we face challenges and conflict, seize opportunities, and live and dream. Identity gives us our sense of difference and who we are – of borders and feelings that separate us from others – tempered by how we live and work with others. The new global world is so intertwined that separatist nationalisms and nativism are delusions. The more we are able to accommodate other's differences, the stronger our own identities. The choice between inclusive and exclusive identities is central to the future. Alongside the economy and internal and external security, that choice will shape the next decades.

Culture and the Human Imagination

Culture is paradoxical: it is about inner and outer factors that must always be reconciled. The outer is the uncaring horizontal world of nature, technology, markets, rights, and democratic majorities (exemplified by the United States). The inner is the vertical world that, at its best, recognizes and cares for what is special in individuals (as in Japan). In the West, the impersonal horizontal has been steadily gaining on the personal vertical. It has given the West tremendous dynamics and power. But the lack of balance may explain why so many feel left behind. It has also contributed to the horrors of the twentieth century and today's populist and authoritarian dangers.

The West was born in the Biblical story of the Garden of Eden before the Fall, when the inner and outer worlds were one. Nature cared for man within the Garden, but not outside. God made refugees of us all when he drove Adam and Eve out of the Garden. Canada's Indigenous people have a different image – where spirit and nature are always one. In the Western way, the two are separate; in the Indigenous way, always somehow together. The world needs both ways.

Culture as Redemption

Adults assert themselves in ways that enhance the ability of others to do the same. Asserting oneself is perhaps more masculine; seeking to enhance others more feminine. A culture that survives and thrives must accommodate both masculine and feminine traits.

The universal appeal of Lucy Maud Montgomery's novel *Anne of Green Gables* comes from a human Garden of Eden (Prince Edward

Island) that appears to care for its residents. Although individuals assert themselves in ways that adversely affect their own happiness and so divide their society, the world ultimately redeems itself. Everyone is reconciled and reunited. This dream is set deep in human hearts. Canada has always leaned toward mutual accommodation as the way – all parties get some of what they want. Compromise and inclusion make Canada different from the United States and China, the world's most powerful countries.

The Challenge Today

The half-century following the Second World War focused on jobs, social security, and peace. Since 9/11, the challenge has been different: to help those who cannot keep up; to reshape an inclusive global order; and to find safe places for desperate people everywhere. This enormous and vital task requires new visions, ideas, projects, and help from every country and individual. The divisions from the old producer-dominant world do not fit the new consumer-dominant world.

The United States is much more patriarchal than Canada. Michael Adams, head of Environics Research Group, found that, today, 50 percent of Americans believe men should dominate at home; only 23 percent of Canadians share that idea. Now, the "MeToo" movement (against male sexual overreach) and the youth protest following the mass shooting at the Parkland, Florida, high school (the maleness of guns), since followed by more and more mass shootings in the United States, could over time bring a less patriarchal US culture and more mutual accommodation. If so, these developments could lead to changes, first in US politics, and then in policies. If the United States cannot become less patriarchal, its current identity crisis could at some point lead to an existential one.

The Flight from Freedom

The disruptions of our era risk repeating Germany in the 1930s – the "escape from freedom" described in Erich Fromm's book of that title published in 1941. Our culture and identity must prove able to fight for, rather than flee from, freedom. If they are not based on fact, we are doomed.

Pope Francis brings compassion to a Catholic Church in desperate need of redemption. This kind of compassion and Canada's mutual accommodation ways are two culture and identity beachheads for the future. We must also learn and teach each other how being inclusive of others' differences can strengthen, not weaken, our identities – the overwhelming message of the Harry and Meghan wedding. The old maxim "United we stand, divided we fall" is still true within countries; it is now also true for the whole world.

The culture wars are back in the United States. The Trump midterm politics in 2018 dictated a fire-up-the-base strategy over one of the best post-war US economies. He continues on this track as he heads toward the 2020 presidential election. A new book – *Prius or Pickup? How the Answers to Four Simple Questions Explain America's Great Divide* (2018) by Marc Hetherington and Jonathan Weiler – lays out how deeply entrenched the drive toward division is in the United States. It goes back to its original sins: force in its creation and preservation, excessive individualism, post-slavery racism, and too much fear of collective action – a phrase used by Henry Kaufman, the insightful Salomon Brothers chief economist, who predicted the US bear stock market in the 1980s

The United States has already had one existential civil war over slavery. The elevation of Justice Brett Kavanaugh to the US Supreme Court could create a new existential crisis over culture and the patriarchy. This court is very unrepresentative of the American population, as is the Senate that appointed it. There may or may not be a majority in today's court to overturn the *Roe v. Wade* 1973 Supreme Court decision that protects the right of a woman to have an abortion. Chief Justice John Roberts may yet have to put the public opinion legitimacy of the court ahead of his own social conservative views by supporting the precedent on the abortion front. It is difficult, for example, to see New York and California accepting any decision against this long-established right. Canada has, for the moment, put its great existential and identity crises over separatism in Quebec behind it – but it took Canada almost forty years to get there. Based on US past performance, it would take the United States a lot longer – if the deeply divided Americans can do it at all.

The geopolitical struggle of the next decade will be between the United States and China. Who does best will depend on technology and on the success of an inclusive society. The United States started this century with a huge edge on both, but its identity fearfulness is rapidly undermining that edge. A major pivot from divisiveness to mutual accommodation is the American challenge of the next several decades. It has made big socio-cultural-political pivots in the past, so it can do it again if it once makes the collective decision to follow that route. It can also stay stuck for very long periods – racism and force over compromise and persuasion, division over inclusion.

Religion has been a source of division and inclusiveness and of comfort and anger or hatred. The Judeo-Christian religion – especially the Old Testament part – has a strong (but not exclusive) focus on the power and glory of God. I have started to wonder if that is the best focus. Using my language of separateness and connectedness as a central way to look at things, power and glory emphasize human separateness from God. But what if He is not primarily about power or someone to be glorified? What if God is both limited and without limits at the same time? What if, regardless of one's own particular religious tradition, we should now explore a more God/man inclusiveness (both/and) alongside the traditional separateness (either/orness) of things?

The most important new idea from Christianity may be that of a suffering God – that the most amazing thing about God is not how powerful or glorious He is but that He is a fellow sufferer and embracer of joy, vulnerable, and, like all who love, He too needs to be loved – perhaps more to be loved than adored.

What if my idea of separateness and connectedness and of both/and and either/or in everything should also apply to the God of all religions? This idea suggests to me that, while physical and institutional power still matter at the heart of things, real progress to a better world may require a God who is both separate from us and connected to us. Exploring the idea of a suffering God, who not only loves us but wants us to love Him, could be what brings the biggest positive potentials to a world where authoritarian societies are once again reasserting themselves. It will be hard to fight the dangers of political authoritarianism if our religions are also authoritarian.

The power of military force, strong economies, or hierarchical status will not disappear from the world. They are likely to prove durable, with both positives and negatives. If identity and culture are indeed already the new driving force of this century, do they also have to become the latest war zone of new culture wars, or can they become a shared source of inclusiveness?

I have said elsewhere that God's ejection of Adam and Eve from the Garden of Eden made refugees of us all – it separated us from the Garden of Eden but did not disconnect us from God. Separateness (free will) means that God's power and omniscience has limits, though they remain far more vast than the power and knowledge of humans.

What if God is like us and keeps learning? What if, like us, not knowing everything and not having all power makes things better for Him and more amazing for us? Further, what if the only way that He is without limits is in his love for us and his world? What if the world's religions could further explore themselves along this line? Might that bring more of what we need more of – mutual accommodation and compassion? If all religions could explore these possibilities alongside the essential elements of their own religion by making room for other identities, they might find greater strength in inclusion and less identity fearfulness. (I am indebted to Dr Charlotte Stuart for the core idea explored in these final paragraphs. See Appendix B.)

Further Reading and Viewing

Michael Adams, *Could It Happen Here? Canada in the Age of Trump and Brexit* (2017).
Erik Erikson, *Childhood and Society* (1950); *Identity, Youth and Crisis* (1968); *Identity and the Life Cycle* (1980).
W.A. Macdonald, *Culture: The Driving Force of the 21st Century* (1997)
A Place to Call Home (Australia TV drama series – 58 episodes).
Far from Home (PBS, Dick Nielsen: Canada in the First World War – 3 episodes).

4. FRAMING THE NEW WORLD WE LIVE IN

As we look ahead in the new world we live in now, I see three sets of ideas to consider:

- monopoly is a good way forward – if acquired and gone about in the right way;
- framing better ways to look at what is going on is essential if we are to cope with the complexity and rapidly changing dynamics of this new world; and
- Canada's second "Sir John A. Macdonald moment" needs to match the first moment's huge Confederation and nation-wide railway achievements with comparable building achievements to shape a different great Canada for a different world.

Monopoly

After the speeches at our oldest son's fiftieth birthday celebration, a lawyer nearing his mid-sixties told a few of us assertively how very competitive he was. He then paused and, looking at me, continued: "I guess you're competitive too." I paused before answering, "Not so much. I'm more into monopoly myself." I have always been looking to know more beyond the law than my competitors did, and to bring to the table something not brought by others. This strategy has served me well over my forty-three years as a lawyer, and even better in my last twenty-eight years as a consultant.

The reason I am more into monopoly than competitiveness is obvious. I was an only child, so throughout my childhood I had an unearned monopoly at home. I naturally did things my own way because my way was the only one on offer, without the influence of a sibling. In my high school graduation year-book, my favourite expression was said to be, "I have a better proof, sir." It seems I always wanted to take my own approach to whatever was going on. Once I became a lawyer, I sought to be competitive on the narrow legal task at hand, and, at the same time, to bring something more of value to my basic legal services.

I started going to Ottawa to seek federal policy changes for companies over sixty years ago. I began with approaches that would work for all affected: the country itself, the particular government of the day, the industry competitors, and, finally, the particular client I was acting for. I later worked for the Ontario provincial government on a wide range of large public policy challenges. Over the same period, I started two different CEO groups, one over forty years ago on Canadian public policy, and another over thirty-five years ago on the global economic environment.

Monopolies can be good for both the monopolist and the customer/client so long as you earn them and keep renewing them. They come from knowing more about what is important to your own vital interests than anyone else – including governments and competitors. The keys are knowledge and relationships, on knowing more than any other relevant person as the one way to stay ahead of others – to keep your monopoly.

Framing Better Ways for Our New World

In the fifty years following the end of the Second World War, the United States led the Western World in developing an inclusive global order within and between countries and containing those countries that could not be included. This project gave the world the most peaceful and prosperous era in history. The positive momentum of this era ended with the arrival of global terrorism on 9/11 and the great balance sheet recession of 2007–08. How should we prepare for the new world ahead?

Eras start with a new momentum and direction that overwhelms the counterforces until the prevailing momentum weakens, the counterforces strengthen, and the old momentum and direction are replaced by a new momentum and direction. Since the Napoleonic era, bad eras have alternated with good eras. A bearable future for the world depends on breaking this good era/bad era pattern and finding a way to follow the good 1945–2008 era with several minimally good eras.

The rising populist and centrifugal force of the last fifteen years threaten a new bad Western era – this time coinciding with the first global moment in history. This first global moment marks the end of the Western era that started when the Middle Ages and Renaissance were followed by six centuries dominated by the inflexible (either/or) forces in the world – freedom and science. Now the either/or forces need to be better balanced by the inclusive (both/and) forces of mutual accommodation and compassion. The East and Indigenous people everywhere have for the most part thought more in both/and ways; the West since the Renaissance has operated in more either/or ways.

Great powers tend toward overreach. The great American Eastern Europe diplomat and scholar George Kennan saw this danger when he served in the US Embassy in Moscow immediately after the war as the Soviet Union was taking on more than it could manage in Eastern Europe. He foresaw that this extension would leave the Soviet Union with insufficient political energy for the necessary internal domestic changes. He did not foresee, however, that it would lead decades later to the collapse of the Soviet Union itself. Now Vladimir Putin's Russia is heading toward its own new overreach, failing to use the US withdrawal from overreach as an opportunity to become a co-shaper with the United States – and later potentially China – of a better balanced new global order – the best way forward for Russia to regain its sense of lost respect.

I foresaw the need early in 2001, before 9/11, for the United States to withdraw from geopolitical, economic, and political ground it could not hold to ground it could hold. Unfortunately for the United States and the world, instead of that starting to happen, George W. Bush took the United States further into multiple overreach (Afghanistan, Iraq, and the post–Lehman Brothers financial crisis). Donald Trump, like Barack Obama, understands that the United States needs to withdraw from every kind of overreach. Unfortunately he does not see his own overreach and seems to know that the best way to accomplish this goal is by preserving US alliances and agreements as it pulls back. He prefers disruptive and disorderly withdrawal to orderly withdrawal (the Obama way).

Each of the United States, China, Russia, the European Union, and the United Kingdom faces pivotal moments ahead, but none of them have demonstrated any ability recently to manage the upcoming big challenges they face. This ignorance will make for a global environment of increasing danger, as many major countries need to change how they go about their basic political business in a world that is demanding big pivots from them all.

The post-1980 era of US overreach led to the Obama era of increasing US political turmoil, which was accompanied by the growing division and rising breakdown in political leadership in the United Kingdom. That has led in turn to the associated existential and identity crises in both the European Union and the United States – the result of the deep structural imbalances that have grown in the West since the end of the Renaissance. US political turmoil did not originate with Trump. It preceded him – goes back to the very beginning of America – one might call it America's original sin. It has been made worse by Trump and will be highly dangerous for the peace and prosperity of the world until he departs. The United States is currently undergoing an identity crisis. At some point it could end up in an existential crisis.

The best thing for Canada is that it has already undergone its identity and existential crises – from 1960 to the defeat of the last PQ government in Quebec in 2014. Quebec still has a left-over identity crisis. But it shows no signs of returning to separatism as the way ahead. Francophone Quebeckers are thriving, not just surviving, so in all likelihood, cultural fearfulness will continue, slowly, to lose political salience in Quebec.

Domestic politics in Western countries were, until some twenty-five years ago, dominated by divisions in class and between left/right and socialist/capitalist. Those splits have now largely changed in advanced Western economies, primarily brought about by the shift from a producer-dominant world governed by scarcity to a consumer-dominant world in which scarcity is no longer the primary driving force of economies (see Chapter 22).

The post-1945 world has moved from a fifty-year Cold War to a multipolar world in which many see China as a rising power vis-à-vis the United States – a rivalry that could lead to a Sparta/Germany-like war outcome (see Graham Allison's important book *Destined for War: Can America and China Escape Thucydides's Trap?*, 2017). This comparison is a parallel but not an exact one. Several major differences make a China/US "rising power war" less likely than those historical conflicts between Athens and Sparta or, in the twentieth century, the Allies and Germany. Half the world is now middle class, so huge numbers of people have a large stake in a peaceful and prosperous global order; the degree of intertwinedness of economies was not a factor in the earlier case, but it is big today; and finally, Sparta and Germany did not depend on the economies and technologies of other countries such as the United States and the rest of the West in the way China did during its rapid rise to power. Quite simply, China could not be what it has become without the United States and the West.

China claims that the rise of populism and centrifugal forces in the West has proved that China is the model of the future. That seems most unlikely. In particular, the Chinese in Hong Kong and Taiwan do not see things that way in 2019. Nonetheless, Western countries will keep losing political ground for the way they go about things until their troubled internal situations turn around. Such a sudden change happened in Greece when it abandoned a decade of unsuccessful populism in its 2019 election.

The United States is currently going through an identity crisis – cultural white racism has been rising ever since Obama was first elected in November 2007. If there were to be an existential crisis too, it could come from a US Supreme Court endorsement of patriarchy by reversing the abortion-permitting *Roe v. Wade* decision. Politics will probably find a way back from that brink, but it could become a high-stress political moment. The United States manages political extremes better than any other country, but it failed to manage slavery in a way that avoided war. The US political turmoil will remain, whether or not Trump wins the next election. Its main elements have been present ever since the United States was formed: force over persuasion; slavery and racism; and excessive individualism at the expense of the community.

The big global question is whether the world (especially the United States and China) can find a path that combines mutual accommodation and mutual containment. The Hong Kong protests make it clear that the one country, two systems policy is easier said than done. It is potentially good for the future of both China and the world that it is protesting Chinese in Hong Kong, not Western powers, who are putting this idea to a real test.

What could it mean that Canada is a different kind of great country for a different kind of world? It would be best if it could mean that the rest of the world gets itself on the same kind of path that Canada has been on – namely, learning to use limits as creative opportunities; to strengthen the use of persuasion, not force.

Our different world needs a different kind of greatness. My view of greatness in individuals, societies, institutions, organizations, and countries is that they make many mistakes, including big ones, but they get the most important things right. My favourite individual examples are Churchill, who got almost nothing right except the most vital of all – Hitler; and Canada's Pierre Trudeau, who got

almost everything wrong – the economy, the United States, and relations between East and West in Canada – but got the biggest issue
right – Quebec separatism.

A Second John A. Macdonald Moment

Matching the scope and scale of our first prime minister's national
achievements for a second time will require real determination
between now and 2040. I see three issues in particular.

First, Canada already has much of what is needed to be competitive and to attract the best people in the world to come here to live
and do business. It needs two more things. One, the ability to get
technology-driven no/low carbon oil from the oil sands. The other,
tax change to push it over the top and put it in a class of its own –
namely, a capital pool approach to capital gains taxation.

Second, Canada needs to improve its global coverage of factual,
in-depth news, both international and of Canada's place in the world.
It should join the United States and the United Kingdom to bring
Canadian news and public affairs television to the world as those two
countries do, respectively, with CNN and the BBC. It could do so in partnership with one or more others or on its own with an international
CBC service. The goal should be to present the most insightful and
balanced daily assessment of where every relevant part of the world
sits in relation to Canada and how the situation seems to be changing.

Third, Canada has the potential for monopoly power of the kind
discussed above – a country whose access to enough facts, thinking, and important relationships is unmatched by any other country
in terms of government, business, and university-level research. We
need the very best of thinkers about the world we live in, in every
area where what happens could be important to Canadians. The
next prime minister should launch an independent group or think
tank, insulated from political marketing and with broad-based
strengths, which would focus on knowing more relevant international news and more key people than any other similar group,
especially about anything that could matter to Canada. This group
would be made up of top federal and provincial public servants
along with their counterparts from the private business sectors and
from universities.

5. TODAY'S FOUR BIG POWERS

The era of unquestioned Western dominance is now clearly over. There are four major players today. Two are Western: the United States and Europe; and two are non-Western: China and Russia. India may soon join them. And other big countries will increasingly matter and have to be accommodating. Europe and the United States have huge strengths in freedom and science, but they are now being challenged from within by the populism and nationalism fallout from those strengths and by the destabilized global disarray that the resulting imbalances have brought in their wake. Great powers are not quite what they used to be – but they still matter a lot. Today, great powers can do more harm than good if they primarily rely on and actually use military power. The United States and Europe together still have a much greater array of strengths than China or Russia do. The primary problem in the West is a sense of diminished strength and lost confidence amid a rising sense of increasing numbers of its citizens being left out on the economic and identity sides.

Between 1945 and the early years of this century, the West became ever stronger. Then, quite suddenly, internal and external imbalances emerged and disruptive changes from fast-moving technology and globalization undermined the cohesiveness within the West and within individual Western countries. During the last seventy-five years, the West's record has been mixed. It helped China make an unprecedented economic leap forward at the same time that it failed on the Russia front. The United States did the opposite to Russia after the collapse of the Soviet Union to what it did for Japan and Germany after the Second World War. It gloated on this triumph rather than bringing Russia into the Western alliance and providing economic help. Mikhail Gorbachev and Boris Yeltsin also fell short. Gorbachev put more democratic politics ahead of market-driven economies, but the policy did not work. The result is a Russia that, unlike Japan, Germany, and now China and India, is looking backward and inward rather than forward and outward. Vladimir Putin sees trouble-making, not helpfulness, as the way forward that is best for Russia – to regain the respect it lost when the Soviet Union collapsed.

China is the only one of the four big powers right now that, at least on the surface, is confident and steadily looking forward and outward. It has a long way to go. It is finding that a stable path into the future for 1.4 billion people will not be easy. Right now, China feels confident in itself and in its capacity to move both forward (strongly) and outward (more cautiously and uncertainly). It has great post-war achievements under its belt. So have the United States and Europe. However, those Western achievements have produced centrifugal counterforces that threaten to undermine them.

In 2019, then, the world has four great powers alongside big troublesome powers like North Korea, Iran, and Middle East Islamic countries that have yet to find a stable and positive way forward. How these four big powers relate to each and how far they are able to work together to shape a different kind of inclusive global order is their primary challenge today. China has a great civilization to build on, but, so far, it lacks sufficient useable history to prepare it fully for the new world. The United States has the most useable history for the world that Europe launched at the time of the Renaissance. However, to fully succeed in the new world, it needs one more huge pivot toward more mutual accommodation. Pivots are responses to crises. All four big powers will almost certainly face crises that will require great pivots, but how they will handle them remains to be tested. Great countries get great things right, but they also get great things wrong.

Russia right now is in some ways nowhere at all. It is a threat to global order – not a help. It is subversive and invasive, with no outward-looking strengths. Its history has not yet found a lasting forward path. It also has no useable history for the new world. What it needs is an outward path forward that includes both Eastern Europe and China as well as an economic dynamic to match that in either Europe or the United States. Unlike China, Russia has not found a way to combine more outwardness with more reliance on market forces. Russia, under Putin, has become sullen and troublemaking toward the rest of the world, and it resents the lack of respect it feels it gets from the West. It had a huge opportunity to gain global leverage and respect as a helpful filler of the vacuum when US overreach led President Barack Obama to start the long process of withdrawal to ground it could comfortably hold. Instead, Putin's Russia chose to be a sore loser (after the United States chose to become a gloating winner), to become blatantly anti-American, and to employ every kind of disruption. To cite some examples: Russia became physically invasive, as in the occupations of Crimea and Eastern Ukraine; it intervened to help President Bashar al-Assad in Syria; and it engaged in cyber intrusions in US elections and the UK referendum.

The question becomes, how to respond? The West needs boots on the ground to protect Eastern Europe and ever-stronger sanctions to bring Russia to the table. It also needs to begin a peaceful and globally helpful path forward that is matched by offering Russia appropriate better access to the global economy. If the United States and China can move beyond trade wars, get a denuclearized Korean peninsula deal with North Korea, and agree on a reshaped, less Western-dominated, more asymmetric but still rules-based, global order, that achievement would isolate Russia and create the potential for sufficient pressures to bring Russia over time into this new world order. The major remaining trouble spot then would be a more isolated Middle East of divided Islamic countries. They would become easier to contain and to help when they were ready to be helped.

Too many Islamic Middle East countries do not seem to have a viable and stable path forward. They have got the most global attention since 9/11, but so far they offer the least prospect for positive progress. Many cannot yet be helped very much. Mostly they have to be contained and provided with humanitarian aid to the extent that such aid can work. Progress will happen when they are in a better position to do more to help themselves. Post-2019, the path forward will not come from Russia or the Middle East, but from the United States and China. This realization underlay the Obama idea to move the American foreign policy focus from the Middle East to China – a decision that was made easier with the exploitation of shale oil in the United States.

The United States has almost always looked forward; Trump and his rear-view-mirror-looking domestic followers are aberrations. China is not historically a strong look-ahead country, but that is where it is now. Trump won the presidency by looking back. The 2020 US election will be decisive on whether to look ahead or to choose the Trump way as the path forward. When and how the United States rediscovers that it has been paying too much attention to its weaknesses and not enough to its strengths is by far the most important question of all. How China goes forward is the second most important question for the world. There is some counterproductive ideology and nationalism today in both China and the United States. Both countries have tended over history toward pragmatic realism – but not always. The sooner they find and use their realism roots, the more likely they can find a mutually agreed way forward that reshapes the global economic and trading order and makes Asia safer by denuclearizing the Korean peninsula. The world needs a successful United States and China working well together.

The two biggest immediate sources of great power strength are the military and economics. The United States and Europe still have overwhelming economic strength – and each one of them can more easily do without China and Russia than those two countries can do without the United States and Europe. Sanctions against Russia, Iran, and North Korea have shown that steadily stronger and well-conceived sanctions can be increasingly effective over time. But they have limits and are not lasting solutions. The US economy among the four is the one best able to do without the rest of the global economy. The Middle East is where Western strengths are least effective, with the possible exception of Iran on the economy. The United States and Europe should concentrate their economic strengths on China and Russia – China first, and Russia later, most likely after Putin has gone. His ways of going about things will not change, and they do not fit with what either Russia or the world needs.

Political, organizational, and societal structures are always deeply rooted in their history. They do not change easily or quickly. Changes either take a very long time or are forced by extreme levels of stress. The best structures for the long haul are usually successful blends of the vertical and the horizontal. Russia is the most vertical and centrally directed of the four big powers. Some thirty years ago I was told at a private meeting in Moscow with the head of Novosti, Russia's international news agency, that Russians always looked to Moscow for direction. Democracy – a more horizontal way of going about things – is socio-structurally alien to Russia. It will require a difficult and historically alien pivot to get there. For this reason, Russia, among the big four powers, is the furthest removed from what the post-2019 new world requires for lasting success. It lacks a relevant past history to draw upon.

China today is a blend of the vertical and the horizontal that, for the moment, is working pretty well in the perspective of Chinese history.

Its first task is to hold its 1.4 billion people together within a country that works at home and also plays a major role to help achieve a stable world order that works for it in the long term. However, if China is to move forward, its economic behaviour has to improve. It needs to follow the rule of law and act with more economic integrity and reciprocity. China must also lean less on the global (primarily the US) economy, which on the trade side it is doing gradually.

Europe and the United States are different blends of the horizontal and the vertical. The United States needs to become more compromise-oriented within its own territory. Its first task abroad is to work with Europe and Japan to find, along with China, a reshaped global path forward. Europe has to take Russia more seriously and be ready to reduce its economic dependence on Russia. China and the West can best bring Russia into a more stable global order if they work together to reshape this order as they deem necessary and apply further sanctions against Russia when they are warranted. This isolating economic pressure is probably the best way to force Russia to change its aggressive approach to the Western world. Russia deserves respect from the West, but it also needs to behave in ways that give it its own self-respect.

Right now, the greatest long-term advantage the United States and Europe possess over China is that they have more useable history for the kind of world that lies ahead. The United States and China seem set to be rivals in the twenty-first century, but the key question becomes how they conduct themselves. Will they fall into "Thucydides's trap" – the conflict that ensues when a rising power (Athens) challenges a ruling one (Sparta), as Harvard scholar Graham Allison describes in *Destined for War: Can America and China Escape Thucydides's Trap?* (2017). The alternative is to be rivals within the limits of a reshaped global order – a win-win versus a win-lose approach. In the best-case scenario, they will build together on the post-war inclusive global order that has served both of them amazingly well by the standards of history. As Las Vegas magician Jeff McBride puts it, "accepting the limits that lead to creativity" is the best way forward for all countries.

15

US Protectionism and President Trump

INTRODUCTION

The biggest single danger to the world in mid-2019 is the possible re-election of President Donald Trump. A majority of American voters did not want Trump as president in 2016, but they wanted Hillary Clinton even less. That could happen again if, by the time of the 2020 election, the Democrats fail to find the right candidate and acceptable policies, and if they are too divided. If Trump was to win a second term, he would become largely uncontainable. He would have shown three times in a row that he was the smartest political guy in the room – unexpectedly winning each of the Republican nomination, the 2016 presidential election, and the 2020 presidential election.

Canada once again faces having to play another long game opposite the United States. It has previously endured challenging times with its southern neighbour. At the very least, Canada will increasingly diverge from the United States in important ways. Americans find it difficult to get along with each other – and that divisiveness will extend to the relationship between Americans and Canadians. In the meantime, Canada's economic policies need a major reboot. Fourteen years of borrowing abroad to consume at home leaves Canada owing some three-quarters of a trillion dollars borrowed so Canadians could spend more than they earn. That is not a good position to be in as the current US and global expansions approach their end. It is even riskier in a Trump world.

The basic thinking of my essays on US protectionism and President Trump remain what they were when I wrote them. The world has so far avoided the worst immediate outcomes. The longer-term impact, however, is that the United States is making itself less and less trustworthy. The recent abandonment of the Kurds to Turkey is only the latest example – one bad enough to alienate Trump's strongest allies in Washington. Trustworthiness is not something Trump sees as an asset, but it is, in fact, huge. Nor does he see how falsely treating imported steel and aluminum from Canada as security risks undermines American claims that Huawei is a security risk. The good North American trade news is that there will almost certainly be an acceptable trade agreement – whether it is the old NAFTA, the old Free Trade Agreement, or the new NAFTA.

The answer to my question "Has Brexit and now Trump brought about a new world?" is yes. What we do not know is what kind of world that will be. It will primarily depend on the next US election outcomes because, for the foreseeable future, the United States is the only country with the range of strengths able to lead on a global basis. But it will need more help than Trump recognizes. There are too many threats to US interests for it to handle them all alone.

The Russia cloud over Trump has dominated Washington since before the Mueller Report. Something about Trump and Russia does not add up, but in mid-2019 it looks as though he will not lose the presidency because of Russia. Meanwhile, the "Washington swamp" has not been cleared up (which may not matter in 2020). Trade and immigration are not so much real policy challenges in Trump's mind. They are more political opportunities to pursue with his base as long as the fallout does not hurt his voters too much economically. They will not be made any better off, but Trump needs these issues as "fighting words" for his base.

Canada remains behind the same three eight-balls I mentioned in my June 2015 essay, though, as I explain, there are some promising improvements:

- none of the current political leaders is yet fit for what Canada's economic future needs (this problem remains, but the growing global hi-tech competitiveness of Toronto, and to a lesser degree of Montreal and Vancouver, is an increasingly positive development);
- real trade wars exist (fortunately, they have recently moderated somewhat); and

• possible Canada unity problems over pipelines are a danger (again, they are far less ominous than they were before, and a way out may be emerging with the real technological possibility of no/low carbon oil sands oil).

I said four years ago, before Trump and Brexit, that Canada needed to rethink its global role. It has not done so. The Trudeau government by and large has done as well as possible with US and European Union trade. It has, however, been largely naive and, at times, even juvenile, in Asia.

Trudeau's "sunny ways" optimism of 2015 has not served Canada well in the world of "every nation for itself" that has emerged since his election in 2015. The biggest Trudeau government failure to date is that Canada has kept living beyond its means, has underperformed in preparing Canada's economy for the world of the future, and has no fresh thoughts about how to cope with the way the future seems to be shaping up. Bottom line: in 2019 Canada faces a lot of debt.

I. NAVIGATING THE WORLD DURING THE TRUMP ERA*

"You can always count on the Americans to do the right thing – after they've tried everything else," said Winston Churchill. This observation is key to navigating a Donald Trump–led United States in political turmoil. Voters do their best with what is on offer. Last November, American voters chose Trump and the Republican Party.

Reserve Judgment, But ...

Seasoned commentators said, first, that Trump could not get the Republican nomination, and then that he would not become president. He did both. Many now say he cannot succeed as president, but perhaps he will. There is much to worry about. The United States has for some years now experienced its greatest political turmoil since

---

* Published in the *Globe and Mail*, May 20, 2017.

the Civil War. We must be watchful and careful. We should also keep open the possibility of Trump's success.

Success was never more than a possibility. Unless the web of Russia questions can be quickly resolved, the challenge will not be whether he can succeed but whether he can last. The US turmoil he exploited could now bring him down.

The Big 2017 Question

The United States built and led the post-1945 global order by broadening the inclusive order at home and abroad and containing what could not be included. The big 2017 question is whether a new world order can be reshaped under some form of US/China co-leadership. Or will the centrifugal forces within the West and between it and the rest of the world undermine that possibility? If or how Trump survives will be crucial. It is an ominous moment.

The Trump-led United States and Brexit are the greatest challenges to the West since the 1938 Munich Crisis. They are key to how things now turn out with Western Europe, Russia, and China. Russia has an increasingly hostile policy of combined aggression (in the Crimea, Eastern Ukraine, and Syria) and subversion of political institutions in Europe and the United States. A West subverted from the outside and undermined from within will become a weaker defender against overt external aggression (Russia).

China understands that a destabilized West would hurt a Chinese economy still dependent on Western economies. A denuclearized North Korea could help make possible a United States and China-led reshaped global order. This reorganization could in turn help fend off Russian aggression and subversion – step one of a long journey to bring Russia back into a new global order. Fortunately, the important members of the initial Trump foreign-policy and security team are of high quality.

Is the United States Still a World Player?

The Munich failure to face up to an expansionist, authoritarian Germany came when the United States was not yet a world player. Winning the Second World War and creating the postwar inclusive global order were possible because the United States became part of the solution.

Today's Munich comes from centrifugal forces within the West. The United States is part of that problem. If this challenge cannot be countered, the world will enter a darker, more authoritarian age. The post-1980 Ronald Reagan/Margaret Thatcher world of free markets and democracy has proved to be the trigger for the first global transition moment in history. Can the rest of the world help the United States as it pulls back from the Reagan/George W. Bush era of economic, financial, and geopolitical overreach? Barack Obama started the country on its withdrawal path. Can a now weakened Trump (if he survives) deal with the still unfinished US overreach without falling into underreach or dangerous new overreach?

The Arrival of Trump

Donald Trump rode to the US presidency partly on voter disaffection with a Washington that no longer worked (primarily because of no-compromise Republicans). The other, bigger but related forces stemmed from the founding nature of the United States and the rising challenges of the American-led inclusive global order. There are big questions – Trump himself; what he most deeply wants from being president; his personal strengths and limits; and the kind of country the United States has become. Can its strengths be mobilized and its shortcomings overcome so it can move beyond its current identity and existential crises? Can it be relied on to help contain the centrifugal forces in itself and the world?

Trump is faced with enormous, fast-moving, unavoidable, and interacting systemic challenges from America's technological change, global trade, and inclusiveness strengths, now in manageability overreach. What they have brought is increasingly hard on more and more Americans. Can Trump and the Congress get on track to do better? The Republicans lack a sure governing majority, and the uncompromising Democratic side (Bernie Sanders and Elizabeth Warren) stridently oppose Trump. Now the Trump presidency has been weakened by its inability to put Russia behind it, making its prospects worse.

There are now two Americas – the people who can cope with the forces of change and those who feel they can't. Mutual accommodation is the answer, but it goes against America's natural drive for division. Russia has become more than a distraction. At best, it is creating a wounded presidency, with reduced leverage at home and abroad.

Is America Still about the Future?

The United States has always been about the future – a "new world." Now, more people are looking to the past, not because they are unwilling to move forward (only a minority are "deplorables") but because they are afraid they cannot. They need recognition and concrete sources of encouragement. Where that encouragement can come from is one of the big questions for the West's future. Ideology, individualism, and a culture of winners and losers are all barriers to figuring out how to move forward as one country. Both the Republicans and the Democrats have deep-rooted ideologies that exclude, divide, and interfere with thinking and seeing – making mutual accommodation almost impossible.

Trump realizes the need to compromise to make deals. Sometimes he shares more policy instincts with Democrats than with the no-compromise Republican Party he has taken over. But he needs more inclusiveness before he can become a full leader. That may require a national crisis. What will the future US glue be? Trump does not believe in American exceptionalism. If Americans lose faith in the American dream, what will happen? Could the only American glue become shared fearfulness and enemies?

Is America No Longer Forward-Looking?

Can Trump communicate confidence in a United States able to mutually accommodate its strengths and the everyday economic and identity challenges its strengths bring? How will the political fight go between fearful (hesitant to move forward) and confident (raring to go)? Can the two come together? It could take years unless forced by some crisis.

Many saw the Obama coalitions of 2008 and 2012 as threats to the country itself. Some version of them may return. If the 2012 Obama coalition had held in only three key states in the 2016 election, Trump would not be president. The Republicans chose as their presidential nominee a man whose policies, had he been a Democrat, they would condemn out of hand. The hard-line Republican no-compromisers must now compromise to "clean up the Washington swamp." The history of the Obamacare bill so far shows how difficult that will be.

The Trump of "the deal" had only himself to satisfy. He could always leave the room. Now he has political supporters, a country, and a world all with a stake – a room he can't leave. No US president can. Trump understands that successful business deals require "enough" for all parties.

Politics is harder; governing even harder. Trump is not stupid – he knows he cannot always get what he wants. But he has never had so much reality to respond to, with so many people affected, or so many people out to get him. Does he get what is great about the United States, and what keeping it great will take? Does he realize that the ability to attract more and more followers is how one becomes great?

Which Mr Trump Has Come to Washington?

Voters will pressure Trump on his vow to make Washington work – a promise even bigger than ending Obamacare. His leverage with the Republican Congress will increase or decrease, depending on how the public likes what he does. Two Donald Trumps will likely emerge in this Dr Jekyll/Mr Hyde world. The US political system works only if the president has political leverage, but the growing Russia issue risks losing that power. It makes Trump much harder for the Republican Congress to live and work with.

Trump faces a series of mutual accommodation challenges, beginning with himself. Then there's the challenge of mainstream Republicans on both the domestic and foreign-policy fronts, where he's considered, respectively, too liberal and too isolationist. Other challenges come from his own base.

Negotiators should warily take the slow and bumpy path toward one-at-a-time normalizations (real relationships likely beyond reach) and reasonable accommodations. The world is in a dangerous situation right now as it waits for what happens in Washington. The United States began to lose its domestic post-1932 capacity for mutual accommodation after the civil-rights legislation split away the Southern part of the Democratic coalition. After the 2008 election, mutual accommodation became almost non-existent. If the United States is to move forward, some mutual accommodation is essential.

Have Brexit and Trump Brought a New World?

The post-1945 forces of integration and disruption on the world stage are becoming unmanageable; the centrifugal pressures from within, hard to contain. Trump cheered them on, particularly during the US election. Meanwhile, Britain decided to pull out of the European Union (Brexit). As the United States experiences its most divisive moment of political turmoil since the Civil War, the remaining months of 2017 will tell much of the story. Will the big systems push back and find a focused path forward that works? Or will things move farther further down a path of divergence and dangerous division? A defiant Trump doubled back to his earlier calls for closer Russian ties after firing FBI director James Comey. Will he bring himself down?

Since its foundation, the United States has followed an individualist and isolationist path, except in the period from 1945 to 2000 (when it responded to the global failures of 1914–45). The current US political turmoil, and the challenges coming from the European Union and Britain, have created a dangerous global moment. The United States has huge economic, military, technological, and innovation strengths. These strengths are vulnerable in a racially divided country split between rich and poor, the confident and the left-out fearful; a country awash with guns, drugs, and more demoralized people.

The world has to figure out how to deal with this deeply challenged nation led by a man who uses people of opposite views to create a chaos of differences which he then navigates for his own purposes. As president, he inherited an ongoing chaos of views among his own base voters and the Republican Congress. He has never had to deal before with systemically interconnected markets, the responses of other countries, and uncompromising Republican and Democratic parties at home. More divisive decades likely lie ahead, as American limitations from its past and a weakened president interact with today's global centrifugal forces.

Is a New-Compromise Washington Possible?

The biggest realistic hope of the 2016 election – a new-compromise Washington – was dealt a big blow with the failure of the first Obamacare bill. However, no one becomes president of the United States without having many strengths. Trump's greatest survival strength may be his remarkable "dot-connecting" ability (though, so far, he has not done a very good job on connecting the domestic politics of the Russian dots). His greatest weaknesses may be his short attention span and self-centredness. What Trump proposed to Ohio governor John Kasich as his possible running mate now looks prescient. Kasich as vice-president would look after domestic and foreign policy, leaving it to Trump to make America great again.

Trump's first job is to move immediately on Russia and reconstruct his White House team with one or more people able to play the role Trump envisaged for Kasich. The second is to face how difficult it is to develop policies that work in today's complicated world. The third is to overcome the deep divisions within the Republican Congress and to combine Republican and Democratic votes when essential. Trump could still surprise one more time. If not, who then knows? There is always the possibility of another deal – but not of another United States. Can Trump extend himself once more and expand the art of the deal to include a capacity for leadership based on more inclusiveness and accommodation? This very notion goes against both Americans' and Trump's natures.

Trump may prove to be an agent for two of the changes the United States and the world need: a return of compromise to Washington, and a reshaped, somewhat less inclusive and less global order, co-led by the United States and China. The post-war inclusive global order is now under threat. It will survive only if it can become somewhat less inclusive and somewhat less global. The element needed to get there would be the containment of a nuclear-threatening North Korea. That would give China the stable trading order it needs and avoid a potentially disruptive United States on the trade front.

The possibility of a new world order is a huge opportunity for China and the United States – a safer world, a reinvigorated global vision, and a new project. But how to get from here to there? The increasing US-governance and rule-of-law stresses do not help. No matter what, there will not be much rest on the Trump journey ahead. Until it is behind Trump, the Russia problem will at best get in the way of success on all fronts; at worst, it will bring the end of his presidency. The United States has two sources of political turmoil – its own historic nature and Trump. The first will last long after Trump.

Breaking Good News

The Department of Justice announcement of the appointment of former FBI director Robert S. Mueller as special counsel to an investigation into Trump's Russia ties will stanch the bleeding for the moment. Nothing less could do that. Adults are at last in charge.

2. CANADA'S PATH FORWARD DURING TURBULENT TIMES*

First, Quebec separatism. Now, US separatism. Fortunately, separatism is something Canada knows how to handle.

Canada is behind three big eight-balls: an economy not yet fit for the future; real US trade risks; and a possible Canadian unity problem from pipelines. Prime Minister Justin Trudeau could now simultaneously face all three of these challenges. Canada must get its economy back on a strong track, particularly with a United States in political turmoil led by a wounded president, and Alberta/BC could be the new unity challenge.

The United States Is the Long-Term Problem

President Donald Trump is a high-risk US president. He will not change. Reliable relationships are not possible, and if you get too close to him, you could get badly burned. What Trump says matters less than what he does; the internal and external pushbacks matter even more. The underlying sources of the deep and persistent division in his country will take years to sort out.

---

* Published in the *Globe and Mail*, June 10, 2017.

Canada has a unique combination of US strengths – an unmatched understanding of dealing with a difficult, powerful neighbour as well as broad and positive continuing relationships with key institutions and individuals there. Americans in general know that Canadians lend a hand when they need it. How Canadians use these connections matters. Ottawa, so far, has reached out well. Other Canadian communities, starting with business, need to address the big picture better and leverage Canada's particular positions in the United States where it counts.

Canada in an America-First World

Global fundamentals within and between countries will be a primary world challenge over the next 25 years. Canada probably has the best chance of succeeding in a Trump America-first world. Current flows in trade and services between the two countries are in broad balance (right now, Canada is in deficit). When you take into account net investment-income flows, Canada has always been in overall current account deficit with the United States. Canadian imports matter in politically key US states. A retaliatory Canadian border tax on non-business tourism, for example, in big Trump states such as Florida and Arizona would quickly hurt politically.

Trade is not the only area affecting Canada's relationship with the United States. Canada also has important relationships through the North Atlantic Treaty Organization, the North American Aerospace Defense Command, and the Group of Seven, as well as close security working arrangements with the United States. Trump may be learning that this is not a world where going it alone works.

Canada, from its beginnings, has experienced the best and worst of the United States. For its part, the United States has often recognized that the asymmetrical relationship means that Canada sometimes needs exemptions from US global policies. In the current fear- and enemy-driven US politics, Canada is not seen as an enemy or a people to be feared.

Canada Has a Lot to Work With

Canada can help Trump get political wins that also work for Canada. Ottawa got off to as good a start as possible – not just with Trudeau's Washington visit but in mobilizing long-standing relationships with both US government and non-government players.

The challenge is to use the above talking points with all kinds of US contacts. The Canadian business community, in particular, must use and create opportunities to tell these stories. If all parties work hard on the Canada side, the outcome can become a win-win story for both countries – economically and politically. It can be done but won't be easy.

Canada always has to play the long game with the United States. Between 1945 and September 11, 2001, both countries were closely aligned on most things. But on many fundamentals, Canada and the United States are very different: mutual accommodation versus division; persuasion versus force; use of collective effort versus extreme individualism; and openness to the use of government versus an overwhelming distrust of government.

US Strengths in the Postwar Era

The United States after 1945 had two great abilities: to attract almost everyone from everywhere (though not Russia or China, initially) to its larger purposes; and to get others to follow. No other country in history can match that record. Canada can help Trump and the United States get back to these strengths. It also needs to bring these strengths to a new vision and a new global order. Only the United States can take this leadership role.

Every era ends in either overreach or underreach. The years from 1945 to 2000 were largely productive. The way forward is not to undermine but to build on their achievements. Churchill said he looked backward to get a better view of the future. If the United States in the 1980s and 1990s had looked backward, it would have had a better sense of what had worked so well and avoided much of the Reagan/George W. Bush overreach that must now be undone, and the dangerous kind of Trump underreach on climate change and the Trans-Pacific Partnership.

The NAFTA Challenge

One major strength for Canada is that it is part of North America, but the basic imbalance within the North American free-trade agreement is a problem. NAFTA trade disproportionately benefits Mexico, which has big surpluses with its partners. US politics and the United States' and Canada's global current account deficits will make it impossible to continue the disproportionate trade surpluses that Mexico has with each country.

Any NAFTA renegotiation has to start from the fundamental balance of Canada-US economic relations and the fundamental imbalance of Mexico's economic relations with its two NAFTA partners. The three countries have become economically intertwined, and it will not be easy for the United States to avoid doing itself more harm than good on its Mexican flank.

There is merit in the Mexican president's idea of a stronger North America opposite a rising Asia, but it is one that would have to be based on a vision shared by all three countries. Mexico will have to do some heavy trade lifting to make that happen.

North America's large current account deficits are supporting the rest of the world by importing their goods and exporting jobs to them – an untenable situation given the current US political landscape. Canada is right to want to keep NAFTA, but it cannot do for Mexico what Mexico must do for itself to get a better three-way balance.

How Best to Cope with the United States

Canada has had an unstable United States to deal with several times in the past, such as the threats that came from the American War of Independence, the War of 1812, and the Civil War. But if war comes today, it will be over trade. The trade wars of the 1930s brought global depression and the Second World War.

At that time, the big countries could not find the shared vision or the project to move from the old world before 1914 to a new global one. Today, with the world once again in the midst of huge and troubling transitions, the challenge for Canada, North America, and Western Europe is how best to move forward with a divided and unpredictable United States embroiled in a bumpy process of with-drawal from overreach.

What ideas and steps should guide Canada's diplomacy with a strongman US president who has been steadily weakened since his inauguration and is now wounded – possibly fatally? Most politicians are more driven by pain avoidance (losing) than pleasure-seeking (winning). Trump's driving force is the pleasure of winning – as both he and others see it.

Canada's way forward is to explore all the possible positives and negatives for Trump. The pain that matters is any that affects Trump directly or indirectly. Diplomacy that works requires the opposing side to understand the political pain that an agreement can help to avoid. Canada's strongest approach to the contentious trade issues surrounding NAFTA – softwood lumber, a border tax, and a "Buy America" policy – is, first, to know more about everything that matters to us than the other parties do; and, second, to have and optimize the best set of relevant relationships.

Negotiating Amid the Chaos

Chaos was something Trump could always manage as a business-man. Chaos does not work so well for the White House. The firing of former FBI director James Comey is a good example, with its con-fused and conflicting stories. This erratic messaging is impossible for both the White House staff and everyone else to handle.

The combination of multiple Russia problems and an out-of-control White House will make it difficult to move anything forward in Washington, including NAFTA renegotiation. This stalemate makes the task of Canadian and Mexican negotiators decidedly high-risk and, at some point, perhaps impossible. Amid all this chaos, slow will likely be better than fast.

What Canada Must Do

Canada needs to work harder on doing everything it can to build its economy. Its biggest shortcomings of the past twelve years have been living beyond its means; the failure to build an economy that is better suited to the future; and the failure, in the post-Brexit and Trump world, to adopt policies that will attract the "best people" to drive a successful private sector. A stronger private-sector-driven economy will make it easier for Canada to live through a period with a self-centred United States – and to prepare for a possible fight ahead.

Trump is cornered by a combination of economics and politics. There is no money for his election promises. Right now, with the Russian investigation and a chaotic White House, he has lost the presidential leverage that hard congressional politics require. With the president and Congress all under the Republican banner, if the United States cannot pull itself together now, when will it? Fortunately for Canada, this turmoil may be its greatest protection against a bad NAFTA outcome – a border tax and Buy America.

Mexico has got itself through its share of foreign economic crises. The NAFTA review comes at a time of domestic political stresses that will be very difficult for Mexico. Canada and the United States could help more if their current accounts with other countries could get better. Canada so far has not been destabilized by the US political turmoil. Its stronger politics and economics make it less vulnerable to destabilization than Mexico. All three partners will have to help improve the Mexican NAFTA imbalance in a way that strengthens stability in each.

Canada needs both a pain-exaction and a pleasure-giving strategy. Its task now is to know how to execute it. It must also put its mind to a post-NAFTA renegotiation vision and project for North America that is more suited to the world ahead.

3. CANADA MUST ACT FAST ON TRADE AND COMPETITIVENESS TO COUNTER TRUMP*

Nine hundred days make a difference! It's 2018, not 2015 – neither the best nor worst of times. Sunny ways and the middle class still matter. But federal Liberal politics and economic and trade policies need a huge reboot.

Everything for everyone now depends on the United States, but it's a tale of two Americas: the isolationist America of a century and a

* Published in the *Globe and Mail*, August 6, 2018.

half after the War of Independence, and the global-leader America that emerged between 1932 (Franklin Roosevelt) and 2016 (Obama). Was the latter an aberration or one more step forward for an increasingly great America able to make its next big forward pivot? Is Donald Trump's America a temporary setback or a revived American isolationism? Canada must now assume the mostly safe – for Canada – United States of the past eighty-five years may be gone for many years.

Canada must move quickly – before the US midterm elections in the fall – on trade, debt, and competitiveness. For eighteen months, Canada has tried to negotiate with an intractable Trump, for whom facts do not matter. NAFTA is still alive and may, or may not, largely survive. Tariffs on steel and aluminum are not a response to any unfair Canadian imbalance.

Trump may yet put recession-causing tariffs on automobiles, which Canada would have to counter. One possibility might be a per diem tax on Canadians for every day beyond two or three spent in the United States. Such a penalty would hurt in at least two Trump states – Florida and Arizona.

Trade wars are not the way. In an intertwined world, no country can win. Canada – despite the solid balance in the overall economic relationship – is still the most vulnerable to a trade war with the United States. (China, with its big US current account surplus, is a close second.) It must start to explore, first with Europe but also China, what kind of "second-best" trading order may be possible. It would not have to exclude the United States. It's the best alternative to a trade war and a go-it-alone United States (the kind of world Trump has long believed in).

While the United States is free to go it alone, there is no place for a United States of bilateral deals free to undo multilateral ones. The numbers are irrefutable that Canada is a net US economic plus. Canada must make that case as it works for a different collective global response. The United States can hurt Canada greatly, but has never successfully bullied Canada. Before November, Canadians must talk directly to ordinary Americans – quietly, positively, as friends – about how fair and balanced our economic relations are with them. This people-to-people relationship is still beyond the reach of governments, but that could change. If the United States cannot get along with Canada, with whom can it?

On the trade front, the United States is about to make the geo-political mistake the Soviet Union made when it took over Eastern Europe. American ambassador to Moscow George Kennan foresaw that overreach would weaken the Soviet Union at home. In the end, it resulted in its actual collapse. Now, the postwar order could also collapse if Trump underestimates the damage to the United States of losing long-time friends and family.

Canada must move quickly to get a "second-best" trading order on the table. This might help drive the Republicans to finally end their Munich-like appeasement of Trump – either containing trade wars or providing a second-best alternative.

At home, Canada must reverse the weakening of economic disciplines prevalent since 2006. Prime Minister Justin Trudeau's current weak fiscal discipline and Bank of Canada Governor Stephen Poloz's weak monetary discipline see the country headed for an estimated $71 billion current account deficit in 2018 – crazy at a time of the strongest and most synchronized US and global economic expansion in decades (repeating the Stephen Harper mistake of 2009 of borrowing from abroad, not to build Canada's economic strength, but to spend on current consumption).

Canada needs a new macro policy to strengthen private-sector global competitiveness and address Canada's now $2.1 trillion of consumer-sector debt, some $560 billion from borrowing abroad. Despite a weakening dollar, Canada is becoming less competitive. One real and symbolic policy for investment and entrepreneurship would be a capital-pool lifetime approach to taxing capital gains. This would make Canada entrepreneurially more competitive, and the reinvestment of capital gains would help reverse its savings shortage ($71 billion this year).

Trump is a zero-sum guy. Trade is not zero sum. The global trading order is a system. Trump does not understand the fundamental system's nature of things. China and Germany have unjustifiably big current account surpluses. The United States has moderate current account and steel surpluses with Canada. Canada helps global growth with huge (unsustainable) current account deficits. There is a basis for fair-trade US compromises from China, but not from Canada. Over all, Canada-US trade is already fair. Any changes need to be two way. The best global trade compromise would be substantially reduced Chinese and German current account surpluses.

Private-sector market behaviour may be the only way forward in today's dysfunctional US political scene. For example, the biggest long-term challenge the United States faces is the technology battle with China, but its politics are hurting its chances of attracting the best people from everywhere. A far-sighted Amazon private-sector decision to have its second headquarters in Toronto would mean Amazon, the United States, and Canada together could all have unbeatable best-people access.

The shared Trump-Putin goal is to destroy the Western order. But Trump may be dangerously cornering himself. He finds it easier to break than make deals. Canada was at the centre of the US-led postwar effort to build a safer and more prosperous postwar world. If there is to be a new "second-best" trading order, Canada again needs to be at the centre. Trump's America of trade wars with friends and broken alliances has become too dangerous not to respond to.

Putin understands one thing Trump does not. Weakening America's alliances helps him and hurts America. This is a bigger moment than ending the postwar global order. A new Dark Ages could be the result.

16

Brexit: The UK Withdrawal from Europe

INTRODUCTION

It is now virtually certain that Britain will leave the European Union. History will in all likelihood see this uncoupling as one of the great mistakes of the early twenty-first century. It stems from several different causes.

- Weak British and EU political leadership and bad choices (especially the Brexit referendum called by Prime Minister David Cameron which unexpectedly, to him, careened out of control).
- Brexit voters seemed only half aware of what the real choice was – they saw only half of what was involved. The "leave" voters reflected the world of middle-aged English-born voters who said at the time, "We are an island people." They did not get the other half that the great English poet John Donne recognized, "No man is an island, entire of itself."
- The EU (with Britain in it) and the United States provided the fundamental post-1945 geopolitical stability on which the fifty-plus years of growing global peace and prosperity rested. Hillary Clinton understood the significance of this alliance, so she would have had the United States weigh in on the side of that geopolitical stability (of keeping Britain in the EU) with the help of Germany's Angela Merkel. Her presidential defeat and the simultaneous weakening of Merkel at home undermined the needed US/EU foundation for fending off the rise of populist forces in Europe.

- No leader in the United Kingdom or the EU saw (has yet seen) the need for a less rigid, symmetrically structured EU. Only President Emmanuel Macron of France seems to realize the necessity to counter the populist forces. But the United Kingdom and the EU are largely weak in terms of political leadership and followership right now, and the EU needs a United States that is once again able to lead the global alliance.

IMPORTANT BREXIT LESSONS FOR AN ANXIOUS, FRAYING WORLD *

For many people in Britain, Europe, and the United States, things are changing too fast – life is unfamiliar, and far from what it used to be. They no longer feel at home. While some may be doing well, others are not keeping up. These feelings of discontent and inequality underlie much of the political turmoil in these countries today and lead to three key questions: Is there a way for Britain and Europe to turn the shocking Brexit referendum result around? How long do they have? And will the United States avoid its own Brexit moment?

A Dangerous Time

Dangerous moments require higher-than-usual levels of leadership and followership. In his recent story in *The Atlantic*, "How American Politics Went Insane," Jonathan Rauch argues that the current world (never more connected, yet dangerously disconnected) has left US leaders without the tools to bond with their followers. Britain, Europe, and the United States all have great strengths. They would do well to re-establish the model of the US-led postwar approach: broaden the inclusive order in the world at home and abroad; contain what is not includable at any one moment; and act collectively, not unilaterally. This model produced more peace and prosperity for more people than ever before in history. Trump and Brexit seek to undo it.

The outer challenges in this global world are big, but the biggest come from within. The forces that created today's overreach have

---

* Published in the *Globe and Mail*, July 15, 2016.

been at work for some thirty-five years. The counterforces they provoked have produced a populist politics with nothing better to offer – and likely very much worse.

Striking at the Postwar Foundations

Brexit may not happen, should not happen, but could happen – maybe in some form it is even likely to happen. If it did, it would strike at the twin foundations of the post-1945 era – globalization and its inclusive world order, as well as a stable and prosperous Europe. It's imperative now to confront the rising centrifugal forces within the Western world.

Brexit must not become our generation's Munich. At Munich, France and Britain failed to confront the rising authoritarianism, racism, and expansionism of Germany. Now, the West must not fail to confront a different centrifugal political turmoil in Europe, the United Kingdom, and the United States. Brexit is the biggest wake-up call since Munich, but, unlike Munich, the danger comes from ourselves, not from outsiders. Europe was saved from suicide by the United States, and Europe's inclusive postwar journey is the foundation for seventy years of relative European peace and prosperity. The world cannot afford to have the United States, Britain, or Europe falter now.

Two Bullets to Dodge

The world needs to dodge two bullets in 2016 – Brexit and Donald Trump. Both can be dodged if Trump does not win the US presidency, or perhaps even if he does. If the leaders of Europe and Britain can delay Brexit, time could favour the Remain side, even though 58.1 percent of the ruling Conservatives voted to leave. Immigration is the touchy issue. A majority of the older and more numerous Britishers are bothered by increasing numbers of newcomers. The young generally hold the opposite view, but they failed to vote in sufficient numbers (36 percent of those aged eighteen to twenty-four voted, versus 80 percent of those over sixty-five).

Like separatism in Quebec, Brexit is largely a family quarrel in the United Kingdom. Quebec separatism was primarily about different visions of Quebec – one inside Canada, one outside – not about

Quebec and the rest of Canada. Brexit is primarily about different visions of Britain – not Britain and Europe.

"He Knew Me"

On the night US president Franklin Roosevelt died, a man on a subway platform began to cry. "Did you know him?" a bystander asked. "No," the man replied, "but he knew me."

The elites know a lot about how to deal with world complexities, but they failed in Britain, Europe, and the United States to understand how today's world affects people less able to cope with it. Losing our sense of identity, our jobs, and our money are powerful forces. Austerity in both Europe and the United Kingdom has reinforced the sense of loss. In the United States, the biggest challenge has been the increasing winners/losers, zero-sum, no-compromise approach of its politics.

The best mutual accommodation techniques are objectivity and empathy – or, to use former Canadian prime minister John Turner's phrase, "free enterprise with a heart." That empathy was missing in the post-Ronald Reagan/Margaret Thatcher dominance of markets and globalization.

Where Does Brexit Stop?

The biggest question now is whether Brexit stops with Brexit or goes on to reinforce the centrifugal forces in the world. The first task is to contain the forces of Brexit and Trump. The second is to move beyond the creation of credit by central banks to real economic advance. The third is to abandon fiscal austerity in a world that is short on demand compared with supply. Three people are needed to meet the challenge: Theresa May, the new grownup UK prime minister; Hillary Clinton, internationally experienced and a good listener, and soon to be on the ballot for US president; and Germany's broad-based Angela Merkel at her political best.

Short-term stakes matter. But the big stakes are containing the centrifugal forces. China needs – and knows it needs – a stable US and Europe. Russia may not want to know it, but it needs that same stability, too. The whole world must see the high-stakes risk that Brexit is as the first big postwar centrifugal force to emerge in the West.

A Divided Country and Weak Politics

The United Kingdom is a divided country: London, Scotland, and Northern Ireland against the rest; and the old versus the young. Both major political parties are weak, but that could change under Ms May. Labour is divided between Tony Blair's New Labour and its current hard-left leader, Jeremy Corbyn. The Conservatives are divided between the Leave and the Remain factions.

Once Theresa May settles into her job, there will be new opinion polls and new financial markets and economic developments. Then there will be a new US president. Calm common sense and patience will be the best approach until more Brexit political and economic fallout emerges.

Former Quebec premier Robert Bourassa privately told me and two senior Toronto business leaders, following the failure of the Meech Lake Accord, that even if Quebec voted to separate, it would not be able to do so. Quebec and Canada were too intertwined. The same may apply to Brexit. A more precise referendum defining the realistic choices may at some point become essential.

One thing is for sure: Brussels has been too intrusive. Two decades ago, for instance, an apple grown for centuries in the United Kingdom was banned; and teenagers who had paper routes were prevented from working weekends at supermarkets. At times, too, there may be small surges of too many migrants from Europe.

Brexit, if it happens, will further unbalance an already beset European Union. Right now, the EU needs less austerity and more flexibility; less bureaucracy and more control over internal migration. It also has to find a way to manage the unending flood of refugees.

These problems have to be worked out — collaboratively. The idea of a new European identity and the institutions of a new European superstate would benefit from rethinking – not just to avoid Brexit but to better accommodate many of its other European members. Brexit is a British, an EU, and a global challenge.

For Canada: Risk and Opportunity

Are we looking at the breakdown of the postwar era of peace and prosperity? There are threats from outside – austerity, terrorism, and millions of refugees – but the threat comes primarily from the elites and winners within Britain, Europe, and the United States who are not addressing what globalization has cost too many people inside their own countries. The threats call for a Franklin Roosevelt rather than a Winston Churchill.

Brexit sends many messages to the world – mostly of risk and danger, but also of opportunity for the EU to get onto a more sustainable structural and economic path. It also sends a message of risk and opportunity for Canada – to become the place where those with big aspirations can set up lives and businesses. Brexit could foreclose much of the anticipated future for Britain's younger people. If Canada adopted a lifetime capital-pool approach for ventures and investments that succeed, it would brand this country as the world capital of hardheaded economics and mutual accommodation.

Canada knows something about the power of centrifugal forces and the interaction of identity with the economy. In just fifty-five years, francophone Quebec emerged from pre-modern to postmodern status. Canada knows that a firm competitive stance tempered by flexibility is the ideal. It knows that strong identities can be made stronger if they create room for other identities. It knows that mutual accommodation can take a long time to achieve. The world would be wise to look closely at how Canada got to where it is today.

No More Status Quo

Brexit is an extreme response to legitimate concerns. The Leave campaign was based on the false promise that Britain can have its cake and eat it too. The EU needs to use the Brexit vote to respond to the reality that large numbers of ordinary Europeans do not share the enthusiasm of the successful elites for "a utopia of Europe without nation states" – as a former Polish prime minister recently expressed it. The EU will remain in existential crisis until that problem is faced and until the austerity-based, slow-growth structural economics of the Eurozone is replaced by a more strongly and evenly balanced growing Europe.

The status quo is not an option – that is the message of today's disconnecting populism in the United States, Britain, and Europe. Some big rethinking is crucial before any potentially fateful action is initiated. Following three decades of disintegration, integration may have overreached in the European Union. But acceding to the forces that would pull nations apart is the wrong way forward.

17

China's Ambitions at Home and Abroad

I. A CHINA RETHINK IN 2019

China's Communist Party was able to retain power and legitimacy at the same time as its high growth rate kept increasing the size of the middle class and its standard of living. That is no longer so. The Hong Kong protests; President Xi Jinping's tightening grip in mainland China; and the US/China trade war now mark the end of an era for China. Like the United States and other countries, it has to change and find new ways for its politics in the global economics that are now emerging.

This essay was not included in the *Globe and Mail* series, nor does it refer to what I said about China then. It has been written especially for this book, and it is primarily a look-ahead think piece. It attempts, first, to match the underlying forces at work in the world with those in China, and, second, to suggest what will need to happen for things to progress and be bearable for both the world and for China. The situation has changed so quickly that my original China-related essays that follow in this chapter are almost entirely about a China and a China-Canada relationship that no longer exist.

China in the World

The United States and China are together fuelling the world's rising geopolitical risks. At some point, each will have little choice but to find a mutual way forward. The failure to do so would disrupt the whole world. China's long, largely successful era launched by Deng

Xiaoping has ended, just as the post-1945 era has ended for the West. To succeed in this new world, China and the United States need a stable global geopolitical and economic order. There is always more to both countries than we can see at any one time. Things will not end well if the West at all levels of society does not better understand China – and vice versa. Right now, China may realize this need better than the United States. In terms of trade, a much larger share of China's GDP comes from trade.

Larry Summers, a former president of Harvard and former secretary of the US Treasury, said recently that the transformation in China over the past forty years will probably go down in history as a process larger than the Industrial Revolution. He pointed out that since China joined the World Trade Organization, its GDP has increased ten times over – a result possible only because China embraced the liberal international order. Beijing realizes this connection. The critical issue is how China would do under two systems in one world if the current one system in one world proves too much for it to handle. Somehow, the United States and China have to find a way to mutually accommodate a competitive Chinese domestic order within the liberal global order.

Kishore Mahbubani, a Singaporean and former president of the United Nations Security Council from January 2001 to May 2002, stated in the Munk Debates on China in May 2019 that China is threatening the global balance of power, but not the global order it needs in which to succeed. He said China went through a hundred years of hell from 1842 to 1949 and then, when the liberal international order began, China discovered two big principles that worked well for it: sovereignty and rules. With sovereignty, every country can decide its own future; with rules, every country knows what it can and cannot do in the international space. What Mahbubani did not discuss was how to accommodate both sovereignty and rules or that China still had a long way to go on that front.

Essentially, Mahbubani says you need to judge China's international behaviour by asking yourself how the rest of the world is reacting to China's rise. He claims they're welcoming it and co-operating with it, but in my view it may be too early to draw this conclusion. Chinese in Taiwan and Hong Kong have reservations. So now does Canada. The issue is how hermetically sealed off can the domestic and international orders be from each other? The China

Belt and Road initiative has resulted in a lot of pushback from countries involved in it. The good news, however, is that China seems to have been able to find enough mutual accommodation with these pushback countries. That means China can practise mutual accommodation when it chooses to do so. Both the United States and China have to find a way to mutually accommodate a competitive Chinese domestic order within the liberal global order.

Mahbubani puts today's China in a personal perspective. He acknowledges that China lacks a liberal democratic society and that it has a lot of problems and challenges. But he adds: "When I first went to China in 1980, people there couldn't choose what to wear, where to live, where to work, what to study; and zero Chinese could travel overseas as tourists. Today, when you go to China you see that the Chinese people can choose what to wear, where to live, where to work, what to study; and each year, in this amazing land of 'non-freedom,' 134 million Chinese travel." That is indeed a huge achievement – something important for the West to understand. Right now, however, the freedom is being pulled back a bit under President Xi.

Mahbubani points to the paradox in our global situation: the biggest threat to the liberal international order is not a non-liberal society such as China but a liberal society such as the United States. The American scholar John Mearsheimer from the University of Chicago agrees, as do I. In the words of John Ikenberry from Princeton University, the liberal international order faces a danger not from murder but from the suicide of its creators.

China, Mahbubani concludes, is the only major power on Planet Earth that hasn't gone to war in forty years and hasn't fired a bullet across its border in thirty years. By contrast, under the peaceful term of President Barack Obama in the last year of his presidency, the United States dropped 26,000 bombs on seven countries – and Russia occupied Crimea and part of the Ukraine.

China needs to do three things quickly and firmly, or it will face rising collective containment and growing limits in its access to the global economic order – particularly as the West recovers from its current disruptive surge of centrifugal forces:

- reaffirm, in both word and deed, that it accepts the principle of one country/two systems (mainland China and Hong Kong);

- affirm, in word and deed, that it accepts the idea of one world/two systems; and
- affirm that it is moving away from hostage diplomacy.

These urgent moves will be a hard pivot for China to make. Although some policy people in the Chinese Communist Party would likely agree, we may well be seeing the beginning of a factional struggle within the party which could incline President Xi to double down on Hong Kong. So far, that has not happened, and we can only hope that China's leaders have learned the lesson from Tiananmen Square that Canada learned from its 1917 conscription mistake. (In the almost sixty-four years after 1920, the Conservative Party in Canada had thirteen years in office, and the Liberal Party had fifty-one years. Mistakes, and learning from them both matter.)

A better outcome would be the successful emergence of a less assertive, more cautious and conservative faction that seeks a return to consensus-based rule within the Communist Party. This group could become a hedge against international brinksmanship and aggression. The chances of success right now look to be less than 50 percent. If the one country/two systems approach were to fail in Hong Kong, the chances for China to live in a one world/two systems global economic world would be reduced. Is this comparison something today's Beijing can both see and act upon?

The moment of history-making decisions is upon every country. Recently, some potentially good news has come out of China, though it is not guaranteed. Where the usually astute Deng Xiaoping made a huge mistake at Tiananmen Square, in July 2019 China made an equally huge right decision – to drop the extradition treaty with Hong Kong. If that holds, it could contain the recent anti-democratic, anti-rule-of-law developments in China. There is, however, a new danger from within Hong Kong itself: that Hong Kong Chinese will turn against the current one country/two systems arrangement. Right now, the big test of China's ability to access the global economic order on the terms it needs is whether it can preserve a viable one country/two systems arrangement with Hong Kong. If China cannot find agreement with Hong Kong, it will become less and less possible for it to settle with the rest of the world. The shift from anti-extradition protests to pro-democracy protests may become too extreme for China.

Beijing may feel it cannot allow Hong Kong pro-democracy forces to appear too strong to its own population inside China. That result would be tragic for both China and the world.

The Big Global Question

Most people (I was one of them) in the West got China wrong at the end of the twentieth century and in the first ten years of this century. The reasons were two: first, the changing feel of China after it opened itself to the global economy and to a larger role for markets, both domestic and global, with a lot of freedom for Chinese citizens; and second, the naive view, best expressed by Francis Fukuyama, that the world under Western (US) leadership had come to the end of history itself – "that is, the end point of mankind's ideological evolution and the universalism of Western liberal democracy as the final form of human government." Today's populism and powerful centrifugal forces make it clear that something big was missing from that proposition.

The big global question right now is the Hong Kong question writ large. At home, can the Hong Kong/China one country/two systems arrangement work under the current mainland Chinese government? And beyond, can the China/rest of the world one world/two systems arrangement work under that same government? In June–July 2019, China's attempts to change the accommodation it had accepted with Hong Kong in 1997, when UK administration of the colony ended and control of the territory passed to China, met with massive street protests.

It is also becoming clear that the West does not like the accommodation China has required with it and is increasingly ready to resist. China, in its massive surge forward, has leaned too heavily on Western economies. It has been overreaching at the same time that Trump's America is both underreaching and overreaching. It will help if China can keep two things in mind as it reflects on the reality that, in just four decades (since 1978), it has lifted 800 million people out of poverty and created one of the largest (perhaps the largest) middle classes in the world. First, this historic achievement would not have been possible without China's access to Western technology and markets. Second, China may not want to follow the Western path to democracy, but if it cannot become a real rule-of-law country, it will find that its market system will suffer. Successful market economies need a rule of law that can be trusted.

It will also help if the United States and the West accept that the right approach to an overreaching China is to work toward a workable reciprocity on economic matters – one that does not have to be identical for everyone. The United States and the West should not try to contain Chinese growth and competitiveness. The global order needs China, and China needs the global order – and both sides should work with this basic leverage. It will be best for all sides if they compete. When the United States tried protection for its motor vehicles over competition with Japan, the Big Three auto makers lost competitive ground. They regained it only when protectionism was dropped. Similarly, the new era should be inclusive of China to the extent possible, but alongside a contemporary form of NATO to contain China's unacceptable behaviour (such as taking two Canadians hostage) and its gross human rights violations (the detention of hundreds of thousands of Uighurs). To this end, we need to explore a different kind of non-military global NATO for a different kind of world.

In the twenty-first century, China has been confronted by a new global economy and a new geopolitical order at the same time that the global system itself has been subject to huge disruptive and destabilizing forces (to which it also contributes). China, for its part, has been rapidly catching up with this new global order even as it experiences a different kind of West that is less ready or able to tolerate what it had previously accepted in the relationship between them.

China is one of the world's great countries and one of its oldest civilizations. In the last one hundred years, it has experienced huge change: the civil war between the Nationalists and the Communists, the occupation of much of the country by the Japanese, the return to full Chinese control under Mao Zedong, and the remarkable economic achievements under Deng Xiaoping, 1978–92. Deng chose a freer market economy over freer democratic politics – the opposite of the Russian choice and one that has been much more successful. As a result, China has quickly developed as an economic and geopolitical leader. It was able to advance for two reasons: its own strengths and ambitious qualities, and its ability to rely on a growing and stable global order that gave it a lot of room.

China Today

Over the last three centuries, development in the West has been marked by a series of alternating eras: the bad Napoleonic era followed by the good post-Napoleonic era (1815–1914), then the bad (1914–45) era of global depression and wars succeeded by a good (1945–2008) era. The prosperous and stable era the West enjoyed after 1945 was led by the United States – a global approach that was based on broadening the inclusive order at home and abroad and containing what could not be included at any one time. We don't yet know what the direction of the post-2008 era will be. Right now, containment is likely to be what is required for Russia, which shows no sign of being interested in any feasible form of inclusion. China needs global inclusion, but also to be contained – not its economic advance, but in its unacceptable behaviour, if it wants to fully participate in the rules-based inclusive global order. It remains to be seen whether China can reconcile minimum standards of mutual inclusiveness (fair reciprocity) at the same time that it preserves its domestic political system under the rule of the Communist Party – and whether it can ever achieve a trustworthy rule-of-law system. The accommodation of its present domestic political needs with global inclusion will likely be the dominant factor for China over at least the next two decades.

How much inclusion of China will prove possible and how much containment of Russia will be needed, alongside how the current US political turmoil finally turns out, will determine what all our futures will be. All discussion of China needs to be looked at within that primary framework. It will also require that more people in the West better understand the last 150 years of Chinese history.

Today's China under President Xi Jinping cannot be trusted. The United States has also become much less trustworthy since the arrival of President Donald Trump – but it is still more trustworthy than China. The growing US loss of trust needs to be reversed. Right now, China is singling out and picking off individual countries one at a time – Canada being a perfect current example. The United States is less extreme, though on a similar path. The world desperately needs a new US-led strategic and collective deterrence-based approach against the wide array of harshness that China can cause other countries to bear. China appears to be culturally more strategic and patient than the United States; Xi Jinping more so than Trump. However, the current Chinese approach is not a sustainable way to live with others and can end only in heartbreak. Meanwhile, in most other countries, "China-beware" will increasingly be the order of the day.

The Chinese economy is more dependent on geopolitics than is the US economy. It needs the rest of the world economy more than the United States, Russia, or Europe do. It is short of resources, and its productivity growth has become more challenging. At some point, internal political pressures will force the Chinese government to try to achieve the level of accommodation needed to give China adequate access to the inclusive global economic order that it has depended on. Meanwhile, the United States may or may not be starting to fall behind China in the long-term hi-tech struggle that lies ahead. If it does start to lag, the way it responds will be critical. In the best-case scenario, it will repeat what it did in the late 1950s when Russia launched its first spacecraft *Sputnik 1*, giving Russia a short period of space supremacy. That achievement jolted the United States to catch up and move ahead. It quickly won the space race with Russia to the moon.

What kind of a country, really, is China – and, for that matter, what kind of country is the United States? Can the real United States and the real China find ways to compete, to collaborate, and to co-exist peacefully? In the new world order, China and the United States need each other for a stable and sustainable world. The alternative is some version of the 1914–45 era and/or a new Dark Age for the whole world.

The time of European naiveté around China is over – as French president Emmanuel Macron put it in April 2019. The arrival of Trump ended America's Chinese naiveté, and Canada has been hard hit by its own naivetés about China. Looking ahead, there is no way the guaranteed centrality of the Communist Party to Chinese governance will change any time soon. There is also no way the Western belief in democracy and the rule of law will change, unless there is a complete collapse of Western civilization. The pressures of the current huge scale of change in the West and in China mean that the Chinese Communist Party and the West will each have their work cut out for them. Moreover, neither side's way of approaching things right now appeals to the other as a better way for going about things. The base of Western naiveté about China was that the Western way would almost inevitably come to appeal to China politically and economically. There is no sign that could happen for decades, if ever. The base of Chinese naiveté about the West is the idea that China has found the way of the future. It does not look that way to me in 2019 about China any more than that today's US has found the way.

The recent book by Harvard Kennedy School professor Graham Allison, *Destined for War: Can America and China Escape Thucydides's Trap?* (2017), investigates the failure of the established power, Athens, to cope with the rising power, Sparta. It is a timely and important thesis, one we should apply to the current relationship between the West and China. However, there are three huge differences between today's world and the worlds in which Athens (in the fifth century BC) and Germany (1914–45) were new rising powers. First, the United States, despite Trump-inflicted self-harm, is on the whole still relatively stronger than China, though that advantage cannot be guaranteed forever. Second, the world is simply too intertwined for either the United States or China to separate from it. Third, China's big middle class will resist being held back.

Canadians know from its Quebec existential crisis in the late twentieth century that it would be very disruptive, if not impossible, for Quebec to separate from the rest of Canada. Today, one-country separatism from the rest of the world is even less viable than Quebec separatism was then. Accepting the reality of "intertwined" is the only feasible path forward for both China and the United States. Whichever country can accept that reality in practice and find a shared way forward will do best over both the short and the long haul. Each has big middle classes that will do better if both countries can find a mutual accommodation way forward. In his June 8–9, 2019, op-ed in the *Financial Times*, George Magnus, the author of *Red Flags: Why Xi's China Is in Jeopardy* (2018), made the key point that China and the United States are too intertwined (his words) to go their separate ways. The same idea holds internally too: countries that are disunited politically and socio-culturally will almost certainly fail. Right now, China looks, though it may not really be, less divided than the United States, but the ongoing Hong Kong protests are testing that idea.

Our ever more deeply intertwined world needs to understand that mutual accommodation is the best pragmatic way forward for everyone, including the United States and China. Zbigniew Brzezinski, the national security adviser for President Jimmy Carter, asserted shortly before he died in May 2017 that the world's greatest need was for "mutual accommodation" (his words) between the United States and China. He added the thought that each had the capacity to achieve what was needed because neither country was fundamentally ideological. Since he made that remark, China has moved away from increasing freedom under the law. It has become more politically ideological. The United States has become more isolated and fearful. The post-1945 American idea was that you could build both a stronger America and a stronger world – that they went hand in hand, making both America and the world stronger, inclusive (both/and), and rigid (either/or). This idea is now under threat. The United States needs to regain confidence in its ongoing idea, and China needs to rediscover its historic confidence for the first time in its modern history.

The world got post-Mao China wrong, just as China got the world wrong. In 2019, China under President Xi seems to be deciding that making China great again (as it was before there was a strong global West) is better for China than building hand-in-hand both a stronger world and a stronger China. President Trump, too, is determined to fulfill his mantra of "making America great again." Both countries are committing the same big mistakes at the same time. These must be contained if the future world is to be worth living in. There will be no stable global era until they can form a practicable consensus on a stable and balanced way forward for the world economy that works not just for them but for everyone. At one time it seemed that China and the United States could work things out – albeit not easily. This hope is not so clear today as it seemed then. New shared ideas and projects will be needed for a new sustainable global order. For the West, it will require a return to collective action and away from bilateral battles. The United States would be much stronger in its trade battle with China if it had stayed in the Trans-Pacific Partnership and better fostered its European alliances.

My belief is that the West – for all its own errors – is still much stronger than China (in the sense that it is better suited for the world that is upon us), even though Trump is undermining, rather than using, US and Western strengths. If Britain had abandoned Brexit, and Europe had chosen to be more flexible in how the EU works, Europe and the West would be stronger economically and also geopolitically opposite Russia, just as they would be better able to help opposite China. Right now, however, a potentially more isolated China is rediscovering Russia as a partner. China may be buying support in Africa and South America, but that support cannot match the Western alliance, even with Trump (so long as it does not further weaken too much). Asian support for the West is much stronger. Japan, India, South Korea, and other Asian countries are greater sources of long-term sustainable strength for the United States and the West than Russia and North Korea are for China.

The United States and China

The early Chinese mistake was to choose a domestic economic structure that leaned too much for too long on its ability to sell more to the United States and the West than it bought. The American error was to reinforce that Chinese mistake by living beyond its means, thereby leading to the excessive Chinese current account surpluses and rising US external debt. The resulting structural imbalances are the main (but not the only) source of the current US-China trade war threat. They are also a medium to long-term threat to viable global economic growth.

The United States has a stronger hand than President Xi for the current trade dispute. China's economy is the weakest it has been in three decades. China needs the global economy more than the United States does, and it likely will for some time to come – perhaps forever. On the US side, Trump needs a deal for political reasons – but not just any deal. Unlike most Western elites recently, China understands it has a social contract with its citizens. The recent slowing of Chinese growth, perhaps among other things, appears to be seen by President Xi as a threat to the Communist Party itself. If so, the recent tightening in Chinese social and political life may be quite revealing about the domestic political challenges felt in Beijing today. China will have to learn the hard way that bullying does not work, though the lesson could take decades to sink in.

The United States has a much more self-sufficient economy than that of China, which is vulnerable in both agriculture and oil. The United States has export strength in agriculture and, after decades of oil dependency on others, it will soon be a net oil exporter. It will then have three key, though fixable, vulnerabilities: political divisions at home, though they should sort themselves out as the country adapts its economy to better serve all Americans; the Chinese threat to US superiority in high technology, though with renewed investment and focus, that could still be remedied; and the loss of trust among its allies and other countries. The sooner the United States resumes its position as a trustworthy leader of the free world, however, the better it will be for all and the better for an America that continues to be great.

Two challenges must be faced immediately before President Xi and President Trump can turn their attention to more basic issues: the United States can no longer handle a world where it is expected to buy more than it sells; and the inclusive global order (both economic and geopolitical) is increasingly unstable. First, the US-China trade imbalance became more balanced in 2018, but is now getting worse again, as the Chinese economy is slowing, and the US economy still has strong monetary and fiscal stimulus – likely too strong. Together, these trends have been increasing China's current account surpluses despite Trump's trade protectionism, and that risk has given rise to the current China-US trade war. When our group of Canadian corporate leaders visited Shanghai and Beijing in 2010, one of the top Beijing economic advisers said that China would get on a path toward better current account balance (more consumption and less investment). Unfortunately, as happened earlier with Japan in the 1980s, that has proved difficult to do. Second, the post-1975 domestic China economic structures (the massive investment share of GDP and the excessive reliance on exports) no longer fit with the Chinese economy – either for China or for the rest of the world. Global economic stability and China's domestic political stability are each dependent on getting this structural balance right before time runs out.

China has one huge long-term post-2010 weakness: ever since President Xi Jinping came to power, it has been reducing freedom (instead of the West's hoped-for expansion of freedom). Hostage-taking outside the rule of law does not bode well for a China as part of the global economic order. Freedom and science have dominated Western strength since the Renaissance. If China curtails rather than extends freedom, that approach will become a long-term weakness for it.

China's economic strengths are large and real, but it also has three serious structural economic limitations at this stage in its economic development. First, the need to avoid the middle-income trap, where the success that comes with higher incomes also brings higher wage costs, leading industries to send production to lower-cost countries. Second, China, because of its demographic imbalance, faces a drop in its share of global exports by 2040 – an imbalance that could mean China becomes old before it can become well off. Third, China's growth has been heavily unbalanced: domestic imbalances, used to spur its rapid physical production surge, are no longer helpful and have become counterproductive. China now needs more consumption (requiring stronger safety nets that reduce the incentive to save) – a significant economic shift. Its domestic imbalances have been creating global imbalances that the global economic order can no longer manage politically or economically. They have led to the US/China trade wars and accelerated the breakdown of the Thatcher/Reagan economic order – although the vast changes of that breakdown were inevitable (see Chapter 22).

China overdid it in 2005, with its huge global export surge. It was foreseeable that this surge, unless moderated, would affect US politics negatively for longer-term Chinese interests. During my visit to China in 2010, I predicted this outcome in both Shanghai and Beijing. I also said, one year earlier at a Japan Society symposium in Toronto on the crises following the Lehman Brothers collapse, that there was a real risk that the post-war inclusive economic and financial global order would not be sustainable. That was in part because China's unsustainable export surge, made possible by the United States living far beyond its means, was bad for both the United States and China.

That is one of three big things any US-China trade deal has to help overcome. The other two are reciprocal access to each other's economies and an end to technology theft. These changes will take time and require patience as well as mutual trust. Neither country is there right now. Today's China is in too much unsuccessful and unproductive overreach. The United States was in geopolitical underreach from 1914 to 1942, and in increasing geopolitical, economic, and financial overreach after 1980. The recent return to rising economic imbalances – excessive demand in the United States and insufficient demand in China – are not a good development. They led to the post–Lehman crises and persist as the current economic expansion moves toward its end.

In the years before President Xi Jinping and President Trump came to power, China was primarily seen by most countries in the West as a market opportunity and a low-cost supplier. Now, China is increasingly seen to be using its growing economic clout coercively and going too far in stealing Western technology. A US-China mutual accommodation – what the world most needs – looked doable before Trump and Xi. It should still be achievable. The United States benefits from a stable global order, but in the short run less so than China does. Its social contract does not rely on it to the same degree that China's does.

China has not so far had to face hard choices between running its own country as it chooses and its increasing participation in the global economy. It will now face increasing demands for reciprocity that will be very difficult for it to meet. That will mean hard choices that affect both its domestic politics and economy and its acceptability in other countries.

China misunderstands if it thinks the United States is bent on containing China's advance. No doubt many Chinese do hold this belief, and some of China's current behaviour is reinforcing that notion with some Americans. However, China should remember that it was active US openness under President Bill Clinton to China's participation in the global economy that made its recent fast economic rise possible. The United States, and many other countries that supported this acceptance, have lost faith in how China has responded and gone about its economic business. If China wants to be part of a rules-based global economic order for the long term, it will have to do better on what that requires. If it does not, its access to the global economy will decline over time. A non-rules-based and unreciprocal global economic system cannot work. China will never be able to give the West enough to make it give up the basics of the current, albeit imperfect, rules and market-based global system. The domestic political costs of inclusion and the economic costs of exclusion are what the next decade of Chinese challenges will likely be largely about.

Although some in the United States see China as a long-term military threat, the primary negative strategic views of China focus on its lack of economic fairness and reciprocity and its role in the current global economic imbalances. There are plenty of able Chinese in Beijing who are capable of understanding this concern.

The pro-China West in the years since Deng Xiaoping was naive about how easy it would be for an undemocratic China, facing the scale and speed of its development aspirations, to meet minimum free-market openness, integrity, and reciprocity norms. At present, Xi Jinping is moving in the opposite direction to what China needs if it is to co-lead a strengthened and balanced global economic order (and so, too, is President Trump). The United States has more strengths than either its own president or China recognizes. The two biggest issues today are when and how the United States will begin to make better use of its strengths, and whether China can make its perceived domestic political needs compatible with the way it needs to participate in the global economic order. If it cannot do both, its economic advance will be slowed – and over time that could have serious consequences for Chinese domestic stability. Putin lost Russia's co-leadership chance. Will China make the same mistake?

The world does not stand still. China may soon find India an increasing rival in Asia. A recent *Financial Times* story showed India's growth moving ahead of China's. India has two advantages over China: democracy and freedom under the rule of law. China has two advantages over India: no caste system and an economic head start. However, China has a third disadvantage: it still does not understand how to do what it needs to do on the global economic participation front. It strikes back against Western restraints on Huawei, but still resists reciprocity. As an example, the January 14, 2019, *Financial Times* reported that China thwarts market entry for groups wanting to pay by credit card – thereby interfering with its global economic aspirations. Beijing, before Xi Jinping, understood better how to participate successfully in the current global economy. China now faces a less lax and tolerant West, one that no longer has the economic or political margin to carry an unfair China on its back.

The Trump administration claims there are security concerns around Huawei. That may well be true. The trouble for American credibility is that the United States also claimed security concerns to justify tariffs on Canadian steel and aluminum. The US needs to remember that it lost ground to Japanese car imports until it stopped protecting the Big Three auto makers. It regained strength when it started to compete again. It needs to be careful not to overdo security and lose global competitiveness ground to Huawei.

Once the West pulls itself back together (as it almost certainly will, though not quickly), China will face an increasingly uphill job to get the kind of participation in the global economy that it wants and needs. The West, in its fight for the rule of law and the need for reciprocity, will try to avoid a fundamental break with Chinese participation in the global economic order. But it will be China, by and large, that will have to make the biggest and hardest changes.

The world that emerged from the multiple horrors of the 1914–45 era brought the new ideas, visions, and projects that led, after 1945, to a long and much more prosperous and peaceful era for more and more people. These initiatives made China's amazing economic achievement possible. The direction and momentum of that era are no longer as strong as they once were, and the centrifugal counterforces have increased in intensity. The world once again needs new ideas, visions, and projects if it is to go forward to a better place. Great power dominance that works solely for the great powers should no longer be conceivable to even the most super of superpowers. In 1945, the global leadership task fell to the United States. In 2019, it falls to both China and the United States. Both are strong powers, and both face the need for big and hard-to-do changes. How each does will primarily depend on which country can attract the most other people and countries to follow it. Right now, even under Trump, the United States is better able to do that.

There is always a lot of fear in the world. Fear is a good goad to action, but a bad guide. The Gardiner Museum in Toronto recently held an exhibition of Ai Weiwei's ceramics. Looking at the beautiful objects he produced raises questions as to why the Chinese Communist Party fears him so much that he would be imprisoned if he returned to China. His treatment signals a lack in political self-confidence and strength. Similarly, in Trump's current bullying tactics, the United States is exhibiting its own signs of fearfulness and a lack of inner confidence. Both countries need to make big pivots if they are to move ahead. Each of them has enough underlying strengths to undertake these turns, but whether they can get the leaders and followers to make them happen will be what the next decades are primarily about.

China and Canada

In this kind of world, Canada cannot have a China policy of its own any more than it could have had a German, Italian, or Japanese policy of its own in the 1930s and 1940s – or, after 1945, a Soviet Union policy of its own. As then, the US/China struggle today is forcing Canada and other countries to choose sides. The United States for the moment, despite Trump, is still the better choice for most. This trend will continue unless and until there is a US/China reconciliation and a broadly agreed path forward. As never before in its history, Canada will have to fit its own challenges into the much greater ones facing the world. No country (including the United States and China) will prove big or strong enough to avoid doing the same to varying degrees. The China of 2010 looked like a China that was perfect for Canada, and Canada looked somewhat perfect for China. Less than a decade later, that is no longer so.

China is supposedly more long-term in its approach to the future than are Western countries, but in recent years that has not been so for Canada. Bullying is a short-term approach, not one for the long term – as the Americans have learned from their dealings with Canada. The first things Canada can and should tell China is that short-term bullying will not work – neither for China or any other country:

- if China wants to think long-term about Canada, it should reflect on two important reasons why a more trustworthy relationship with Canada can help China in their future:
  - China could face a bigger food challenge that it now does, according to the recent UN report on the risk due to climate change on world food supply, and Canada is a rich agricultural producer;
  - Canada can become helpful to China in its relations with the United States in challenging times, given the long relationship Canada has had with both the United States and China.

Canada should recognize that its oil sands and its agriculture are two areas that need investment in order, first, to make Canada's oil sands more no/low carbon competitive and, second, to reduce our reliance on China as a customer for beef, pork, and grain. Canada has a new emerging unity crisis around these products. We must remember how Prime Minister Lester Pearson always kept ahead of the rising Quebec separatism crisis in the 1960s. Whoever becomes the next prime minister must get a firm grip on the oil sands and agricultural challenges and opportunities Canada is facing. China, in one way or another, will be key on the agricultural front – either by restoring China as a trustworthy long-term market for Canadian agricultural goods (which will not be easy for China to do) or by finding new markets to replace it.

Unfortunately, China and Canada have got each other increasingly wrong ever since China became a greater part of the global economic order. Our relationship in the future will largely depend on how three things unfold on the China side.

- China needs a better understanding of what works with a country like Canada. Its current bullying will not work, simply because Canada is so much smaller, and submission would mean no end to Chinese bullying. Successful bullying always leads to more, so standing up is Canada's only choice. Canada, over more than two hundred years, has from time to time been faced with unacceptable pressures (including actual war) from the United States. It stood up then to its southern neighbour, and, once again, it is having to do the same against Trump's America. Canada must now face China with the same determination.
- China needs to reconcile how it wants to do business in the West with what Western countries regard as fair rules. That will increasingly be the only way they will let China's businesses participate fully enough in Western economies.
- China can no longer take unfair advantage of the West through technology theft and by persistently selling more to the West than it is willing to buy. Over time, China will face much stronger demands for reciprocity. The task will be to find Chinese equivalence, where it cannot provide symmetrical reciprocity. Asymmetrical balance is how Canadians have been able to make Canada itself work.

It may be some time before the West and China can figure out what the outcomes of the present standoff are likely to be. Canada has big China troubles, mainly because it is dealing with a different China in a different world, a China that has yet to learn about the limits of its strengths. None of the major players – the United States, China, Europe, Russia, India, or Japan – yet have what it takes to lead the world with a new vision, new ideas, and new projects. Leadership on each of these issues is needed, but everyone right now is too self-preoccupied to see, let alone do, what is needed.

China is far from ready for across-the-board global leadership. Its response to the arrest of Meng Wanzhou under the Canada-US extradition treaty showed a lack of understanding of Canada's system of the rule of law (it is possible that the United States will fail to prevail once the extradition has been heard by a Canadian judge). The Chinese ambassador to Canada has handled the case extremely poorly in his public statements, which no doubt are being directed by a myopic Beijing. Meng Wanzhou is not in jail and can talk to whomever she chooses. The two Canadian detainees are not free; their access to anyone is almost zero; and the charges against them remain unclear. The ambassador's claim that Canada's actions show "Western egotism and white supremacy" is farcical. His false claim will not sell with Canadians, and it clouds Chinese thinking about Canadian reality. Canada has relatively more immigrants from everywhere (largely from Asia) than other countries. The number of immigrants from China grew 63.9 percent from 332,825 in 2001 to 545,535 in 2011, making Chinese the second largest foreign-born group in Canada at that point. China's misunderstanding of Canada's political and legal system and its ambassador's slander of Canada will hurt China over the long term – not just in Canada but with many countries that matter. It is more a sign of Chinese weakness than strength.

The way back for Canada with China will first be through the United States, and then through stronger Chinese tourism and more Canadian business deals in China. The immediate problem is that even if China wants to encourage tourism and business relationships with other countries, for people ready to risk trips to China, the fear of being taken hostage on issues that have nothing to do with their own behaviour will be a long-lasting barrier. Both China and Canada will pay a price for what is happening between them right now. Until the recent hostage takings and the abrupt cancellation of trade deals, many Canadians were seeing China as a potential counter-balance to the United States. That opportunity has now been lost. Similarly, there is little effective room right now for a Canadian diplomatic role between the United States and China. That will not change until China is able to be helpful in getting a stronger global order in a manner consistent with what it sees as necessary for its political challenges at home. This restraint will limit China's ability to replace the United States in the leadership role it has been abandoning.

The disasters of European history are the consequences of too many "destiny" nations that got in each other's ways and could not mutually accommodate. The dangers today from China and the United States are that they could repeat some equivalent of the horrifying wars of European history. Canada's advantage is that it combines its multiple strengths of space, resources, water, food, and a relatively good neighbourhood with a less grandiose and practical mutual accommodation approach to survival and thrival. Canadians do not see themselves as a "destiny country." They do see themselves as having ways of doing things that could work elsewhere. And most love being Canadian.

Three years ago (before Trump and Xi), Canada appeared to be in a position to play a useful role in strengthening US-China relations. Since then, China has changed, the United States has changed, and the relationship of each to the other has changed. Canada right now has more to handle in its own relations with China and the United States than it can manage successfully. It is not, at the moment, in a position to help much on the China-US front. Rather, it needs help from both the United States and Europe. China has always had residual trust challenges with segments of the Canadian public. Its recent behaviour has only exacerbated that mistrust. The next step will have to come from China – and lost trust is hard to regain.

Canada's former reasonable hopes for bigger and stronger ties with China will not likely be realized anytime soon. This new reality requires a fundamental rethink by Canada about its approach to China. Canada has two roles to play. One is a leader's role in helping to get the kind of collective action that will be needed to deter a range of unacceptable actions, such as the recent hostage-taking, and to explore how to mutually accommodate Western and Chinese joint participation in a global economic order that is minimally reciprocal. The other is for Canada to reduce both its export and import reliance on China until there is no longer the threat of China's bullying Canada on this front.

I concluded my *Globe and Mail* essay on Canada-China relations on October 20, 2017, with these words:

"Canada understands that mutual accommodation is now the only good way forward for great powers. China and Canada can and should harness their complementary strengths as they seek to reset their relationship and support an inclusive global trading order.

"President Xi told the 19th Communist Party Congress in 2017 that China had entered a new era. It's a good time for the Canada-China reset."

Although it is now a less good time, the reset is even more urgent. The bottom line is simple: China needs the United States, and the United States needs China to share the visions, ideas, and projects the world needs for a bearable future. But Canada can fully reset its relationship with China only when the United States and China agree on how to move forward.

Further Reading and Viewing

Wendy Dobson, *Living with China: A Middle Power Finds Its Way* (2019).

Thomas L. Friedman, "China Deserves Donald Trump," *New York Times*, May 21, 2019.

Richard McGregor, *Asia's Reckoning: China, Japan and the Fate of US Power in the Pacific Century* (2017).

George Magnus, *Red Flags: Why Xi's China Is in Jeopardy* (2018).

Kishore Mahbubani, "What China Threat? How the United States and China Can Avoid War," *Harpers Magazine*, February 2019.

David Mulroney, *Middle Power, Middle Kingdom: What Canadians Need to Know About China in the 21st Century* (2015).

Munk Debates, *Is China a Threat to the Liberal International Order?*, May 29, 2019.

Evan Osnos, *Age of Ambition: Chasing Fortune, Truth, and Faith in the New China* (2014).

Martin Wolf, "How the Beijing Elite Sees the World," *Financial Times*, May 1, 2018.

Xu Jilin, *Rethinking China's Rise: A Liberal Critique* (2018).

The Bitter Tea of General Yen, directed by Frank Capra – a film about the Communist/Nationalist Civil War in China (1933).
The Story of China, written and presented by Michael Wood (DVD series, 2016).

2. THE UNITED STATES AND CHINA: THE WORLD NEEDS A GRAND BARGAIN*

The world has two great powers – the United States and China. And though being a great power isn't what it used to be, great powers still matter. Their reach has been much reduced since 1945, not so much by competitors as by their inherent natures. In future, the most successful will be those that can use their multiple strengths (both hard and soft) to get others to follow them. The will and the skills for mutual accommodation will be indispensable.

The world needs a grand bargain between the United States and China that combines a rebalancing and reshaping of the global order along with a solution to the North Korea crisis. Henry Kissinger, the US secretary of state who took Richard Nixon to China, recently said we are at a rare moment when the interests of both America and China coincide. Zbigniew Brzezinski, Jimmy Carter's national security adviser, said something similar in 2014: "The post-Cold War era was not really an 'era' but a gradual transition from a bilateral Cold War to a more complex international order that still involves … two world powers. The decisive axis of the new order increasingly involves the United States and the People's Republic of China. The Sino-American competition involves two significant realities that distinguish it from the Cold War: neither party is excessively ideological in orientation; and both parties recognize that they really need mutual accommodation." The arrival of Donald Trump may have changed this prediction.

The Rise of China

China's sudden global economic surge in 2005, and the United States' excessive borrowing spree after 1981 and its geopolitical overreaches

* Published in the *Globe and Mail*, October 13, 2017.

into Afghanistan and Iraq, led to the 2009 financial crisis, chaos in the Middle East, the Russian annexation of Crimea and military interventions in Ukraine, Brexit, and the election of Trump. These developments resulted from the unsustainable global imbalances that now dictate America's withdrawal from ground it can no longer hold.

This withdrawal began in a measured way under former president Barack Obama, but now, under Trump, the United States has moved on to a disruptive undermining of the global order achieved since 1945. There is no practical alternative to mutual accommodation and a largely rules-based global order. Today, China's president Xi Jiping seems to understand that better than Trump.

The United States and China, 2017

The centrifugal forces within the West and between the West and the rest of the world must be contained. When the European countries failed in 1914 to find an inclusive path for a rising Germany, their behaviour led to the Western-driven global horror story that culminated in the Second World War. A comparable horror story now awaits the world if it does not find a path to a reshaped world order. As Harvard professor Graham Allison writes in his indispensable book *Destined for War: Can America and China Escape Thucydides's Trap*, "It was the rise of Athens and the fear that this instilled in Sparta that made the war inevitable." With China and the United States, we face this ancient conundrum all over again.

Unlike in the 1914–45 period, the United States and China are among the world's destabilizing forces. Although they both have strengths to work with, they face huge domestic challenges. After 1945 the West sought two goals, both through US leadership: to bring greater peace and prosperity to the world; and to contain the Soviet Union and China until they were ready to join the inclusive order as leaders. Today, the potential danger in Brexit/Trump populism and a subversive/aggressive Russia should bring China and the United States together to lead a new effort for inclusive global order – order that would be more responsive to differing needs, and yet still be based on equivalence.

China's Xi may, right now, be the only leader with the strength and the willingness to try to preserve a largely rules-based inclusive global order – and he should act sooner rather than later. He has the motivation: China, more than the United States, depends on the global economy, especially for resources.

The Post-2010 World

In 2010 a group of Canadian business people sponsored a symposium in Shanghai. The objective was to alert China to the danger in its excessive reliance on high net exports to the United States. Though the Canadians did not predict Brexit or Trump, they made these points – which I've commented on in light of the situation today:

- Today is a high-stakes moment in human history. The postwar achievement of an inclusive global economic order is at risk and may prove to be beyond the collective ability of the world to sustain. (*This prediction is now happening.*)
- China played no role in creating the conditions that led to the debt crises – trends that had been forming over twenty-five years. But China's strong arrival on the global scene early in the 2000s overwhelmed a global system that had become vulnerable to adverse shocks. China will be central to when and how we get out of the current mess. (*Although China's too great a reliance on exports over imports has lessened, it still has a long way to go.*)
- American politics poses the greatest single potential danger to global prosperity and to preserving the inclusive global economic order. (*In 2017, this prediction is beyond doubt.*)
- The US Administration does not yet have it right on the economic challenge. (*It has been able to get the monetary/fiscal balance largely right, but has been unable to carry out much needed tax reform and infrastructure investment because Congress has refused to compromise.*)
- Economic activity and markets are important, but balance sheets and the gap between policy and political will are even more important. (*That is generally still the case.*)
- During the past twenty years, three of the world's largest economies – first Japan, then Germany, and now the United States – have had balance-sheet recessions. (*The United States has come through, but can no longer play the role of global economic*

*engine; Europe, Japan, and China have been struggling, but
are now doing much better. China has not yet found the right
economic path forward but is trying.*)
- The best scenario going forward requires the United States to
get some reasonable level of natural, self-sustaining recovery
and some help with growth from countries with a surplus. Even
then it will still be a long, slow struggle to achieve assured, stable
global growth. (*We are not there yet. The United States did not
really get any help from surplus countries after 2008. A boost
did come from shale gas, but not the needed balanced growth
in global demand. Now, after a long absence, global growth is
synchronized.*)
- Canada, although a small country, can play a helpful role. (*That
is even more true now, with the arrival of Trump and the
inward-looking electorate mood of 2017 America.*)

China's Astonishing Path

China started down its new path in 1979. The Industrial Revolution
began in Britain 250 years before and sustained globalization sixty-five
years ago. By 2005 China had compressed these two massive transformations into twenty-five years. China's sudden export surge and
current account surplus – the result of jobs outsourced from the United
States and money borrowed to enable this increasingly debtor nation
to live beyond its means – created huge systemic vulnerability in the
overall global economy. No country in history has ever improved its
economy as quickly as China has in recent years. However:

- The United States and its blue-collar workers bore too much of
the burden, as the 2016 election proved.
- History will likely say that 2005 marked a fundamental transition
moment, when emerging-market economies, led by China, began
to help shape the global economic order. China's fast ride initially affected financial markets primarily. The 2005 China surge,
however, was a key cause of the post–Lehman Brothers mess that
emerged two years later in the United States and of the Brexit/
Trump mess in 2016. The Trump United States sees the negatives of
the trade deficit role, but not its own debt complicity. The United

States and China must now begin to listen to each other and to others. US diplomats do it, but Americans in general less so. What Canada can bring to each country is the listening skills it has developed to survive, along with more fair-mindedness. These qualities can help the two big guys, so long as they are ready to use them.

Strengths and Stories

When my wife practised family therapy, she always said that in looking ahead we should start with reflecting on strengths and good stories. One of America's weaknesses is that the majority of its population has little understanding of its strengths and stories. China is very conscious of its thousands of years of history and its amazing post-1980 achievements.

The United States, in contrast, has no understanding of why or how it successfully led the creation of the postwar inclusive global order, and, partly for that reason, it began to overreach after 1980. The neo-conservatives intruded into the domestic orders of other countries and espoused regime change, putting the world order at risk. The world today needs to find political consensus to use its many strengths to avoid another 1914–45 horror story.

Getting to a Grand Bargain

China and the United States have to find a path toward a "grand bargain" in reshaping the global order. No one really believes that war will break out in North Korea (though it could happen), and that reduces the US leverage against China and North Korea, as well as China's against North Korea. However, the United States can get its leverage from its own interest, and China's, in preserving and reshaping the global order and keeping the Korean peninsula and Japan nuclear-free. Achieving this goal will likely need some private-sector leadership, especially from China, along with finding a way to bring Canada's successful mutual accommodation ways into play on both sides. What North Korea needs is its independence guaranteed, along with its freedom from externally imposed regime change.

In shaping this new global order, China has four long-term challenges: economic reform; respect for the rule of law; devising a political system for the future; and expanding its role in the world. The United States in turn has one big challenge: to contain its persistently divided nature reflecting its win/lose, black/white, no-compromise political and societal culture. In addition, Americans must come to better understand the huge array of strengths they possess – and use them to maintain peace, prosperity, and security.

China and Russia

Great countries make mistakes, some of them big, but they get the most important things right. Since the end of the Cold War, China, unlike Russia, has got the greatest things right in three very big ways:

- China chose economic reform first; Russia embarked on political reform first;
- China chose to be mostly constructive in its growing international role; Russia has been aggressive and subversive; and
- China has looked backward to its history and used that inheritance to move forward; Russia has looked to its past in order to go backward.

Canada Has a Real Role

Canada is well placed to play a real role in shaping the new global order so long as the United States and China are open to working together for their own advantage and for the world. Canada has to move quickly and carefully on two fronts:

- First, to establish steadily improving trade arrangements with China.
- Second, to bring its strengths in mutual accommodation to each of these countries to help them achieve this single most important goal in the world. Both the United States and China have the strength and the ability, but they need to have a better understanding of themselves and of the other. They need to find a way to respect not only each other but other countries, too. That is difficult for nations that regard themselves as exceptional.

Further Reading

Graham Allison, *Destined for War: Can America and China Escape Thucydides's Trap?* (2017).

Wendy Dobson, *Living with China: Finding a Middle Power's Middle Way* (2019).

3. WHY CANADA MUST WORK WITH CHINA IN SHAPING GLOBAL TRADE*

Canada has two big China opportunities. First, an expanded relationship with China is important and timely. Second, China's Xi Jinping is the only major world leader who may have the strength and will to preserve a largely open-trading and rules-based global system on which postwar peace and prosperity rests. Canada can play an important role in this effort, which is crucial to its future.

An increasingly protectionist United States poses a threat to the current order. The last time the United States turned protectionist, in the 1930s, there was a global depression that lasted for a decade. There is no case to take such a stance on trade when growth is strong, as it is in the United States today.

The most sensible alternative is to do as much business with China as possible, providing it is conducted within Canada's fundamental value system. Despite considerable societal and political gaps in values and interests, we can work together – though those big gaps call for wariness and patience on Canada's part. There will be high hurdles in the so-called Trudeau reset, but with sufficient will, we can find the way.

Canada is well placed to help if the United States and China are open to working together for a win-win result for themselves and a win for the world. Canada has to move on two fronts: first, to get on a path to a steadily improving set of trade arrangements with China; and second, to bring its capacity for facilitating mutual accommodation to help the single most important relationship in the world to work – the relationship between China and the United States.

* Published in the *Globe and Mail*, October 20, 2017.

Canada's Good Intentions Are Not Enough

The Trudeau team is "sunny" and eager about many things, including a reset of its relations with China. The differences between Chinese and Canadian political and legal systems mean that reset would be challenging under the best of circumstances. President Donald Trump's upending of the global order, his negative views of China, and his pro-Russian tendencies all complicate the matter. They also open up an opportunity for Canada to help itself by helping China to get through its current domestic and global challenges.

The less Canadian the public face on any China reset is, the safer and better – not because of China, but because of Mr Trump. A United States that breaks agreements – whether with Iran or NAFTA – is not the best of partners, and Canada must ensure that it does not aggravate an easily aggravated Mr Trump.

Canada needs to be wary on two fronts: there must be no extradition treaty with China as the price of a new trade agreement; nor must there be any Chinese high-tech acquisitions of Canadian firms that have military implications, such as the O-Net Communications purchase of ITF Technologies. The fact that somebody wants something they should not have as the price for a deal is seldom reason enough to give it to them. Appeasement does not work.

China is a long way from having the values that Canada shares with the United States, let alone the capacity to replace or offset the United States as Canada's key economic partner. But right now, the United States is a better neighbour than partner. David Mulroney, our former ambassador to China, warned in a *Globe and Mail* op-ed in 2017 against Canadian naivety in relation to China. Former prime minister Stephen Harper was slow to grasp the need to deal with the reality of 1.4 billion Chinese because it ran counter to his and the Conservative's ideological stance against China. The Trudeau risk, in contrast, is proceeding too fast. Canada needs to take as long term a view as China always holds.

China's Place in the World

China has earned its way to the centre of the world stage, but it is still not seen as a leader that weaker countries can trust and the world as a whole can count on. It does have money, however, and the currently unreliable United States gives China an opening to change its place in the world – though it will take time.

The Trudeau government is right to seek a stronger relationship with China, but if that means violating the rule of law, it will undermine the reset. We have no choice but to live in the same world as other countries that we believe abuse human rights, and to make deals with them. But that does not require us to turn over people protected by our criminal justice system to a country without those protections, as any compromise with our extradition system would do.

On expanded trade and investment, the bigger practical problem with China will likely be to know at any particular time whom we are dealing with. China is not transparent. Canadians will have to get better at background checking individuals and at knowing what to do when things go wrong. The Chinese, in turn, will have to provide better and more timely information so Canada can keep the unwanted out.

Canada-China Reset Matters for Everyone

Canada has enormous strengths in relationships among people in both China and the United States. A successful mutual accommodation approach can help the United States move forward with China in a reshaped but strong inclusive global order.

On the China trade reset, Canada must not be too eager or opportunistic. We must stand back (as China does), take time, and be wary. Big changes are under way in China, the United States, and Russia. Canada can help – but it needs to be strategic in the larger context of world politics: the possible US retreat into a philosophy of "every nation for itself"; Russia's trouble-making; recent weak leadership in the United Kingdom and continental Europe; and much of the Middle East destabilized or in flames. China is the only major country today that says it supports an overall global economic order that remains inclusive but needs reshaping – a statement that should now be tested.

What Trump Needs

Trump is in a hurry. He has to keep winning, and no win ever seems big enough or lasts long enough. But it is not only the United States that wants disruptive change. Others, including Canada, need a shaking up, too. China, in contrast, is being changed inexorably by its own huge moves forward; it has very big challenges, but it is in less of a hurry. It has already experienced a lot of wins in its great leap forward. However, the combination of corruption and excessive restrictiveness at home and a protectionist global trading order could result in a great leap backward for China if it becomes unable to sustain the large rapid growth on which its social contract depends. This instability would be bad for everyone.

China can best enhance its strengths collaboratively; it can be strong in today's world only if it can get others to follow its lead. Much of the US postwar strength came from that ability, which is now at risk. Trump has exploited the adverse outcomes of US financial, economic, and geopolitical overreach in order to get a mandate to undermine many postwar US achievements. In Trump's view, throwing others off balance is the way to get what he wants and needs.

Canada's unique, broadly balanced strengths in its relationship with the United States can be important to China. Canada is not the "danger" or "enemy" Mr Trump likes and seems to need; China may be. In a Trump world of increasing US isolation, Canada will always end up still standing. The US/Canada trade and current flows are big and in broad balance. Canada's current account deficits (which must come down) help other countries in the global economy.

Trump is at heart a deal maker. But if he wants to be a man of global hard populist vision, Canada's task will be to work with others to contain the damage. If he exhibits an insatiable need to bend policy toward his own personal view of reality, all bets are off, and extreme care and attention to building one's own strengths will be very important. Alternately, he could demonstrate a mix of all three. The biggest sources of instability among the United States, China, Russia, and Europe all go through Trump. This global context must be remembered by Canada as it works with China, and by China as it works with Canada.

Big Strengths to Work With

The United States is coming out of a period of foreign and domestic overreach and domestic underreach. China is coming out of a period of too much reliance on the global (largely US) economy for coping with the domestic challenges brought about by its huge economic leap forward. Unlike the United States, China needs resources, many of which Canada has. Canada has a large Chinese diaspora and has enjoyed a good relationship with China over the past seventy years. China needs to work collaboratively with the United States, and in this Canada can help. Canada understands that mutual accommodation is now the only good way forward for great powers. China and Canada can and should harness their complementary strengths as they seek to reset their relationship and support an inclusive global trading order.

President Xi told the 19th Communist Party Congress in 2017 that China had entered a new era. It's a good time for the Canada-China reset.

18

A New Surge in Moral Authority

INTRODUCTION

Canada is still hanging onto a positive attitude toward immigration in a world of post-Brexit and Trump populism driven by rising centrifugal forces. Canada got its internal domestic balance between symmetrical integration and asymmetrical decentralization about right throughout the whole post-war period. This equilibrium enabled it to overcome both its existential and its identity crises. Europe over-integrated in too symmetrical a way. The United States overreached its global role at the expense of its economy and domestic political stability. It continues to find domestic compromises out of reach and still prefers divisiveness.

Moral authority matters. In Western eyes, China, Russia, and Iran have varying degrees of moral authority within their own countries, but not yet very much outside. China's moral authority is not as strong as it would like among Chinese in Hong Kong, Taiwan, and Tibet. Western moral authority is weakening outside, but the perceived continuing reliability of its freedom strengths and its post-war capacity for alliances are still stronger than those of other countries.

Since the Second World War, the West has been the world's safest place for refugees and those seeking freedom and economic opportunity. The result has been massive mobility within and between countries. The numbers seeking to move are now probably too many to be acceptably managed by populations that are themselves under the multiple pressures of today's disruptive forces. It is likely that ways will have to be found to improve the safety and opportunities where people now live, so they will rely less on ever more mobility.

Canada is unique among Western nations in the absence of seriously poisoned immigration politics. It owes this generally positive attitude to Stephen Harper, who mostly shut down excessive anti-immigration sentiment because it was primarily in his own party, and also to the Canadian voter, whom Harper was smart enough to gauge and mostly follow in this regard.

Moral authority ultimately comes from what people see as working for most of them, in both their personal and their work lives, and for communities and countries.

Freedom, a rising standard of living, large geographic space, a big population, military strength, alliances, and trustworthiness have together produced for the United States the kind of moral authority that fuels the highest and strongest leadership. The United States had this status for five decades after 1945. It started to weaken after 9/11 – a time when the United States never felt stronger and at the same time more vulnerable.

Agriculture, natural resources, and manufacturing are the traditional sources of a higher standard of living. Hi-tech is the new source. This switch has produced a fundamental shift in Canada's economic prospects, which are already moving up not just in Toronto but also in Montreal and Vancouver. The challenge will be to move enough of the new opportunities to places where Canadians want to live, rather than the reverse.

Canada's moral authority has always come from within. Given the "unfriendly-to-Canada" world we now live in, that will not soon change. Meeting hi-tech needs for a huge global market is Canada's transformational way forward. It will work best if the job opportunities are not over-concentrated in only a few cities. That model will, moreover, suit a small-market country better for a world with less reliable trading arrangements.

THERE'S A BIG RISK IN DOING
TOO LITTLE FOR SYRIA'S REFUGEES*

Munich – we did not face up. The Holocaust – we looked the other way. History may not repeat itself. Europe today is not the Europe of 1938, and the West is more aware of the interconnectedness of peoples and countries than it was back then, but sometimes, as the old saying goes, it rhymes – that is, it takes a different route and still winds up in much the same place.

Canada is struggling to cope with an influx of 25,000 Syrians. In Europe, so many refugees from Africa and the Middle East have reached its shores and its borders that its welcome mat is wearing thin. The situation calls for more than compassion, but for vigilance too. The full context is much bigger than that, and more complicated and urgent after the Paris attacks.

The danger lies in doing too little. We don't want to wake up and find, once more, that we failed to meet the challenge, and stood by as Europe broke down and mass tragedy struck again.

Humanitarian and Geopolitical Issues

The lack of response at Munich to Hitler's aggression against Czechoslovakia came at a high cost and almost ended with the suicide of Europe. Today, Western nations cannot back down; they must confront the geopolitical and humanitarian implications of the refugee challenge as well as the implications for domestic security (the Paris attackers were homegrown, after all).

That challenge presents two serious problems: potential actions by terrorists who get through the screening process; and the many hazards posed by a destabilized Europe. There is no Hitler, no Stalin, backed by a national army. So, while Europe is multi-challenged, overt threats to its inclusive order cannot as readily lead to world war.

But no one knows how far Russia under Vladimir Putin may try to go – and stability is already an issue. The refugee crisis has the twenty-eight members of the European Union divided and threatens

---

* Published in the *Globe and Mail*, December 4, 2015.

Chancellor Angela Merkel's governing coalition in Germany – a very dangerous development, given the existential crisis that has begun in the eurozone (the nineteen countries that use the euro). Having a common currency is stressing the social contracts of EU members with weaker economies, and we cannot foretell how the crisis will unfold.

Meanwhile, the situation is being aggravated by a host of other factors, from high youth unemployment, antagonism over migration between EU countries and the risk Britain may withdraw from the union, to the crisis in Ukraine and the carnage in the City of Light.

Canadian Voters Helped

None of this may seem to apply to Canada, which has just gone through an election in which its tradition of mutual accommodation prevailed yet again. In a way, what Canadians voted for was almost more important than who won. Some 65 percent of voters opposed attempts to stir up Islamophobia (such as discriminating against women who wear the niqab) and supported the three parties that favour a stronger refugee performance.

More Muslims than ever cast ballots (their participation rate may have been higher than that of the population as a whole), and a record eleven Muslims were sent to Parliament. Also, the campaign was affected by the refugee crisis, beginning with the heartrending photographs of a little Syrian boy washed up on a Mediterranean beach. The ensuing compassion was fuelled day by day with images of migrants as they boarded flimsy boats and trudged through Europe.

Parts of the election were far from uplifting. We had a prime minister falsely charging that his two main opponents planned to bring in hundreds of thousands of refugees with no security checks, proposing a law against "barbaric" cultural practices, encouraging citizens to spy and report on each other, and using cultural and religious differences as a vote-getting wedge issue.

But two-thirds of voters rejected these divisive themes. Polling strategist Michael Marzolini told me many years ago that a majority of Canadians favoured capital punishment but did not vote for a candidate who did. They wanted leaders less extreme than themselves. This election showed that they haven't changed.

Where There's a Will ...

In any event, the great danger to Canada is not its own refugee security, which can be managed. Rather, it is the geopolitical situation – the stability of Europe, and containment of the instability in the Middle East. Munich was a failure of will and collective action, at unimaginably great cost. And it could happen again, in a different way.

In a recent *Financial Times* column, Martin Wolf discussed why Europe could not have escaped the current crisis. "The last thing the EU wanted to deal with was a tide of refugees ...," he explained. "The desperate human beings landing on European shores pose daunting moral, political and practical difficulties. But a way has to be found to manage them without sacrificing the values on which modern Europe was built." The same is true for the entire West – and most especially for Canada, which has long known that it and the rest of the world are inescapably interdependent.

Serious thought must now be given to the disruptive, large-scale human mobility that may lie ahead. Canada needs to figure out in the short term how much it can realistically do and the logistics of how to do it. Terrorist acts in Paris have made the goal of accepting 25,000 Syrians even more challenging. Longer term, the government must engage in a broad, substantive conversation about how to make the influx a success, both for the refugees and for Canada. As well as assistance, newcomers deserve recognition for the strength they showed in leaving home and respect for what they can bring to Canada.

At the same time, varying attitudes toward and fear of anyone different are inevitable and must be taken into consideration. If done well, reaching out is good for us all.

We Are All Migrants in a Way

The story of humanity is about journeys. Some of us choose to leave home and everything we are accustomed to, while others are forced to do so. A successful transition always requires two things: we must come to stand on our own two feet; and we need some help to attain that independence.

Refugees rarely choose to cross borders. They are driven by fear into a decision that is less under their control than the product of chaos. If the danger subsides, they may return home again. At present, however, what they need is Canada's capacity to do what works and, through mutual accommodation, to transform chaos into a stable way forward. Then they can meet the challenge all immigrants must face: learning to stand on their own in unfamiliar surroundings.

How well they fare is mostly up to them. Almost forty years ago, our family participated in an effort to assist draft dodgers, who had left the United States illegally to avoid serving in Vietnam. When they arrived, many had a plan and showed strength, independence, and self-esteem. But that did not last for some, who slipped into a pitiful form of dependence, pleading "Please let me stay."

How independent and self-sufficient the Syrian refugees prove to be will determine whether their adventure ends well. And taking in 25,000 is only a small part of what is needed from this country. Canada is in a special place to start collective thinking, which can lead to collective action on all three aspects of the problem: humanitarian, domestic security, and geopolitical stability. The new government has members with a multitude of diverse experiences suited to the task.

We are all migrants in a way – life itself is a form of migration in space and time, but most of us are not fear-driven refugees. Yet many people who are physically safe in Canada still feel unsafe because of the multiple changes going on around them. They feel that Canada is somehow leaving them behind. Perhaps no one ever feels quite at home in a world where death comes to everyone. Death is the ultimate existential threat and mystery – and that is why the meaning of life has been fundamental to most people through the ages.

It should not surprise us that sociocultural and religious differences can disturb us unless our understanding of the world has grown large enough to become more inclusive. These deep-seated feelings can be intense around war-zone refugees from societies where very small minorities become terrorists. We all share death, but we differ about what it means. British author Karen Armstrong focuses on faith and modern society in her writings, and, she says, religious extremism derives from fundamental fear. That same fear constitutes part of the fuel for the brutal conflict in Syria and the attacks in Paris.

Islamophobia

Of course, the newcomers may pose a security threat – a Syrian passport, either counterfeit or stolen and used to obtain refugee status, was found near one of the Paris bombers. But a bigger danger is the impact the refugees may have on society at large: an outbreak of Islamophobia.

Over the past few months, we have seen three remarkable clips of Muslim women on television. On election day, the woman who won the right to wear a niqab in her Canadian citizenship ceremony was shown, as she emerged from a voting booth, her eyes sparkling. A second clip featured a woman telling a CBC reporter that she too prefers the veil but, instead, covers just her hair because that makes Canadians less uncomfortable. Finally, another woman in a hijab was shown handing her baby to Justin Trudeau and promising to vote for him so her daughter will live in a country where she can make her own choices. Each of these women is enthusiastic for Canada and its values – and yet the lawyer who won the niqab case is receiving hate mail.

Islamophobia is part of the refugee challenge everywhere and it could get worse, especially if oil vulnerabilities become a reality in the Arab Gulf states and their social contracts become unsustainable. The resulting chaos could be serious and mean even more migrants. Now is the time to prepare and forestall. Every government, institution, and individual must get involved. Realpolitik math – Muslims account for almost one-quarter of the global population – makes it vital that we head off Islamophobia before it happens.

A New Pearson Moment?

The immediate challenge is doing what it takes amid the chaos of hundreds of thousands of Syrian migrants fleeing a war zone. Looking ahead, failed states and climate change will likely prompt global migration on a very large scale for decades.

These crises will require a collective strategic approach. Lester Pearson was right, as Canada's minister of external affairs when the North Atlantic Treaty Organization was formed, to want NATO to focus on social and economic challenges as well as military ones. The Vietnam War and various US-led military adventures in the Middle

East have validated the view that collective military action and social and economic action fare best when they go hand in hand. Too often, they do not, and in the fight against Islamic State, they must.

At present, the humanitarian aspect of the refugee crisis calls for compassion. But the geopolitical part will be a long and arduous journey needing consensus and patience. Large-scale migrations will slow only when we have a better world.

Having a role that goes beyond military intervention may also give NATO a more certain future. Canadian global leadership and skillful diplomatic effort can help to make that happen. In the meantime, we must start talking about what we can do and what is needed next.

Recent terrorist acts – the Russian plane downed over Egypt, then the bombings in Beirut (leaving forty-five dead) and in Paris a day later – may bring an abyss moment leading to stronger collective action to counter the Islamic State (which has bitten off more than it can chew). The new government faces tough decisions on the role Canada should play – and ordinary Canadians must consider what they can do too.

While making his curtain call after performing in *Hamlet* at the National Theatre in London, actor Benedict Cumberbatch recited a few lines from "*Home*" by Warsan Shire, a rising young poet whose family came to Britain as refugees: "*No one leaves home unless home chased you ... no one puts their children in a boat unless the water is safer than the land.*" Then he asked the audience (including a British Cabinet minister) to donate to Syrian-refugee relief on the way out.

It's an idea well worth applying here. Why not have groups such as Lifeline Syria provide collection boxes, so that anyone attending a public event can contribute? Allowing them to express their generosity helps Canadians get involved. Not that a good many aren't involved already. In a world that often seems anti-immigrant, Canada provides some good news. Its resettlement-aid organizations are being overwhelmed with offers of people's time and money – and both are badly needed.

19

Why Mutual Accommodation
Is Essential Today

INTRODUCTION

The Justin Trudeau team wanted to be inclusive, but they have too often been primarily inclusive of their own particular group – the middle class, women, Indigenous people, and those under the age of fifty – and too quick to exclude the rest. Selective inclusiveness in the end becomes counter-productive. The best forms of inclusiveness come from shared purposes and projects that benefit everyone. Brian Mulroney and Jean Chrétien got that right. Post-war Canada got it mostly right too – at that time, social advance and economic advance moved forward hand in hand.

Over the last fourteen years, Stephen Harper, and now Trudeau, have both failed on this score. Harper was primarily interested in Conservative political advancement and Liberal political retreat, at the expense of economic and social advance. Trudeau has focused on his chosen groups and social advance – leaving too many people out and ignoring vital needs: to live within Canada's means and to foster a globally competitive private sector. In this scenario, the danger is that economic advance becomes too weak to sustain social advance.

Going back to the future does not work. The United States, Russia, and the European Union are all on this path right now – looking back. Among the great powers, only China is on a going-forward path – but one that needs to move beyond the narrow route that got it where it is. It has done enormously well over the past forty years on growing its domestic economy, but much less well on becoming a trusted rule-of-law country that works at home and abroad.

The stakes are high in the world today – and becoming higher. For the first time in history, it will take two super-powers – the United States and China – to each pivot enough to the realism of mutual accommodation to reshape together a more stable global order. Mutual accommodation is needed more than ever as countries withdraw from international organizations and treaties and as trade disputes fester, China surges ahead with its ambitious but not trouble-free Belt and Road Initiative, and the United States resigns its position as leader of the post-1945 global system. There is still no other palatable path forward. Even more than when I began the series for the *Globe and Mail*, this statement has become both more true and more urgent.

The stakes are high because, for the first time in history, the United States and China are two great superpowers that can still choose to use consensus to enable a good era (1945–2008) to be followed by yet another good era.

1. THE TROUBLE WITH GOING BACK TO THE FUTURE*

Canada has just had perhaps its greatest election when it comes to advancing the cause of mutual accommodation. The country faces some very difficult economic challenges, for which it and its new government is not prepared. But even before Canadians cast their ballots this week, the polls showed that roughly 65 percent of them – Quebeckers included – would vote against policies steeped in divisiveness and exclusion.

Contrast this with political forces at play elsewhere. For example, Russian president Vladimir Putin and US presidential candidate Donald Trump may appear to have little in common, but they are, in fact, on the same wavelength. Mr Trump, whose slogan is "make America great again," may employ the key elements of mutual accommodation – negotiation and compromise – in business, but not in politics. When he complains that "we have no victories," he's clearly thinking in terms of winners and losers.

As for Mr Putin and his supporters, their strategy is "like some kind of conservative cultural revolution," one of his former advisers

---

* Published in the *Globe and Mail*, October 23, 2015.

(who has since left the country) told Mark MacKinnon of the *Globe and Mail* not long ago. "They are going back to the past, saying everything modern is bad, and everything old is good." If, instead, Mr Putin could move forward along a path of greater mutual accommodation, Russia would gain far more lasting influence and would be, along with Europe and the rest of the world, far better off.

"Men of destiny" such as Vladimir Putin and Donald Trump live in a world quite different from that of most people – who are trying to get ahead or just keep up. Jean Piaget, the pioneering Swiss child-development psychologist, saw the path to adulthood as that of a child taking from its environment and accommodating. This strategy worked for static, self-contained societies whose greatest challenge came from nature. Now, we live in a big, ever-faster environment that we have made for ourselves. Taking from and adapting to it is not enough. Only ever-expanding mutual accommodation can work to sustain it and manage the huge transformations now underway everywhere.

Strength Leads to Success

Two powerful sets of ideas concern the individual (separate) in relation to the mutual (connected): the more separate you want to be – as a person, society, group, or country – the more connected you need to be. And vice versa.

Accommodation is most successful and long-lasting when both parties are strong and believe in it. Throughout history such powerful partners have been few and far between – Canada has had more than its share, which is why the federation thrives as well as survives. The lack of good partners makes mutual accommodation more difficult, but not less relevant or important. It is a big, two-way idea that involves sharing with, and making room for, others. The "mutual" part is as essential as the "accommodation." In fact, force may be required (preferably not) to make it possible. For example, the force of law is needed to deal with the immediate threat of domestic terrorism. But in the longer term, we need faith that the power of Canada's freedom and inclusiveness will prevail. The right anti-terrorism strategy is to broaden Canada's inclusive order and, at the same time, to contain whatever rejects inclusion.

However, not every mutual accommodation is necessarily a good thing. If its purpose is evil, negative, destabilizing, or dysfunctional, the fact that mutual accommodation is the best way forward will not redeem it.

Views from Outside Canada

Despite the appeal of President Putin and Mr Trump, mutual accommodation is gaining the attention of serious people outside Canada, primarily because world events are driving them in this direction.

Martin Wolf, chief economics commentator at the *Financial Times* of London, has written two well-reasoned essays on the subject. On June 11, 2014, he wrote: "We are doomed to co-operate. Yet we remain tribal. This tension between co-operation and conflict is permanent. In the past century, humanity has experienced extremes of both. The history of the next century will be shaped by how we approach very similar choices." Then, on January 13, 2015, he asked how we can share the world with the "true believers behind global turmoil" – the Islamic State and its fellow jihadists, in particular – but what he says also applies to less extreme true believers, such as the "no compromisers" within the US political system.

Mr Wolf rightly finds a direct relationship between extremism and frustration. Anyone – rich, poor, or otherwise – can qualify, and the most deeply frustrated are those who see a threat to the essential meaning of their lives. He also compares the challenge presented by terrorist-driven true believers with that facing post-1945 Europe – collapsed, morally degraded, and even suicidal after four terrible decades of war, depression, and political extremism. The essence of his advice for today is to adopt the same approach that the US-led West took at that time: a long strategic commitment to broadening the global inclusive order, containing what cannot yet be included, and acting collectively. The global moment for mutual accommodation will arrive when the cumulative pain of non-accommodation finally becomes too great.

Recently, two Americans – Paul Volcker, possibly the greatest of central bankers, and Zbigniew Brzezinski, a former US national security adviser now teaching foreign policy at Johns Hopkins University – also have had encouraging words about mutual accommodation.

In June 2015, the University of Toronto presented Mr Volcker with an honorary doctorate. In his acceptance speech, he said: "A good Canadian friend of mine … makes a point of extolling what he sees as the essential point of Canadian history and its governance – he calls it a capacity for 'mutual accommodation' … What has happened here is truly remarkable and has lessons for others," he continued. "The Canadian nation, built out of different national instincts and cultural traditions, whether Indigenous or from abroad, has in the end held together. The narrow bank of population stretched over 3,000 miles of difficult landscape no longer seems so subject to centrifugal force. Today, we need some of the Canadian genius of mutual accommodation, of a shared order."

Mr Brzezinski, in turn, stated in a recent interview that "the decisive axis of the new order increasingly involves the United States and the People's Republic of China. The Sino-American competition involves two significant realities that distinguish it from the Cold War: neither party is excessively ideological in its orientation; and both parties recognize that they really need mutual accommodation." Also, if we are prudent and lucky, he predicts, a more politically assertive liberal middle class will reappear in Russia and "quite naturally wish to live in a society like that of Western Europe. A Russia that gradually begins to gravitate toward the West will also be a Russia that ceases to disrupt the international system."

As well, in the fall of 2015, "mutual accommodation" essentially received a Nobel Peace Prize when the Tunisian National Dialogue Quartet – a coalition of national agencies – was recognized for its efforts in helping Tunisia become the only country to experience the Arab Spring and see its democracy survive. The way the Quartet fostered a dialogue between Islamist and secular parties to arrest a growing crisis was similar to the way in which francophone Louis-Hippolyte Lafontaine and anglophone Robert Baldwin worked together to make Canada the sole country to preserve (and without violence) the reforms that swept Europe in 1848.

Events are slowly starting to teach the world two things: one must go forward; and the only safe way – for individuals and for countries – is through mutual accommodation.

The Old Canada's Return

Canada's role, as the global movement for mutual accommodation starts to arrive, could be central. Its new prime-minister-designate has already announced that the old Canada is back.

The right kind of laws are often key to internal accommodation. As Chief Justice Beverley McLachlin of the Supreme Court of Canada said while delivering this year's Annual Pluralism Lecture at the Aga Khan Museum in Toronto, the law should lean toward tolerance, not restriction. It should stay out of sociocultural differences as much as possible.

Or, as the late Northrop Frye, one of our great visionaries, put it:

The reasonable person proceeds by compromise, half-way measures, illogical agreements, and similar signs of mature human intelligence ... But even a system of law based on precedent has problems with the pressures exerted by the majority on individuals and minorities. In Canada, before the Charter, our own 'inspired' document, we had a series of ad hoc agreements and compromises like the Quebec Act [of 1774], which made some effort, in fact, a rather remarkable one for the 18th century, to keep the civic rights of both English- and French-speaking Canadians in mind.

But the indigenous peoples, the Japanese-Canadians during the Second World War, and other such groups would tell a different story.

United by "What Works"

Over the last three decades, my wife, Molly Anne, and I have put together a collection of seventeenth-century Kakiemon export porcelain from Japan, as well as the European porcelain influenced by it. We were attracted by three qualities in Kakiemon wares: their asymmetry (unlike Chinese ceramics and most classic styles), imperfection (like Zen), and negative (empty or unfilled) space.

There are similarities between Kakiemon porcelain and Canada. The success of each comes from this special combination: neither is bound by imposed restrictions; instead, both take a practical, "what works" approach. These qualities lead to a different kind of freedom, with less political, social, or cultural restriction. In each case, there is both the outer (physical) space and the inner (imaginative) space to make room for finding what works. In everyday life, this means looking at things practically, not ideologically, and more individually than meeting expectations from others.

Many of the world's mutual accommodation challenges come from unfinished business – from the past and looking backward, not ahead. In 1992, political scientist Francis Fukuyama argued in his influential *The End of History* that what America had achieved was the model for all – a way of looking at the world that always brings trouble with it. Now, more than two decades later, Russia as well as the Islamic State and Iran are mainly about the past, and the huge unfinished business of race in the United States and the Indigenous people in Canada remains.

The time to start mutual accommodation is before there is a resort to violence. Those who enjoy detective series on television know that many of the plots are about personal unfinished business where the victim and the perpetrator did not find mutual accommodation. Two insights from my wife's years as a family therapist are relevant. First, people often fail because they are afraid they cannot do something they should do, not because they are stubbornly against it. Consequently, they get stuck or they feel cornered – as Japan did in 1941 and Russia does today. To move forward, they have to find the inner confidence that they can do it. Second, some form of conflict may at times be necessary (hopefully, not war), because fighting is the most powerful form of communication. But there's always a risk when you fight: you have to know when to stop and how to negotiate. Most fail both tests.

Mutual accommodation also requires discipline: What do I need, and am I up to it? What do the others need, and are they up to it? Is the particular mutual accommodation what each of us needs, and will it last?

Every country faces domestic mutual accommodation challenges. The most immediate one is the probable emergence of an existential eurozone crisis that, we can only hope, will not lead to crisis in the European Union itself. The United States and China each have internal challenges too, but the one between them is certainly the most important in the world. Canada has a role to play with each of these great powers – and Canadians need to think about how best to act.

Canada's first order of business is our relationship with our next-door neighbour. The biggest challenge is to balance our strengths – to put Canada's mutual accommodation skills at work in the world alongside US economic and military strength, and vice versa.

The Drive Forward

The question the world always faces is whether it will move forward, and doing that in a way that can work for most people requires all four of the better ways of going about things: compassion, freedom, science, and mutual accommodation. It is the angry, the left-out, the unsure, the fearful, and the cornered who lean backward and gravitate to simplistic, either/or, win/lose leaders. It is those with reasons to be confident and hopeful who have the forward drive.

Canadians have those reasons to be confident; the United States needs to regain them. Right now, Donald Trump is responding to those Americans who are focusing on their sense of the loss of what they used to be. Many of them do not see how much stronger the United States has become since the post–Lehman Brothers crises and its withdrawal from geopolitical, economic, and financial over-reach. They find it hard to understand how much the United States has gained relative to others in economic strength and to accept the implications of the current withdrawal (amazingly successful so far) to ground they can hold.

The refugees from war-torn countries in Africa and the Middle East are the latest source of destabilization in the world. But the single most worrying development today is a buildup of fear and frustration in the United States that could lead to a Trump presidency. He is the opposite of mutual accommodation. He is domestically divisive and would quickly become globally divisive, unless he were to go through one more transformation. He reflects US thinking that is very different from the thinking that prevailed among Canadian voters in the fall 2015 election.

Canada stands to have a government more inclined to solve its problems through mutual accommodation. But expanding this approach in the United States will be very difficult, no matter who the next president may be. This divergence may well give Canada a large edge going forward. In today's world, mutual accommodation alongside strength is what works best and maximizes influence.

2. HIGH STAKES AHEAD*

After six centuries of expanding freedom and technological development since the Renaissance, the West has weakened and provoked counterforces both within and beyond its borders. As it relinquishes its role as leader of an inclusive world order, drastic changes will test every country in the years ahead.

The world we have known since 1945 focused on fairness, peace, and prosperity, supported by good jobs and economic security. By 2000, these ideals had given way to lesser visions, such as shareholder value and regime change. This consumer-driven society brings different policies and political battles to the fore as the effectiveness of the old policies declines. Postwar growth seems to have peaked, as have the central banks, free markets, and government-sponsored social security programs it fostered. Only technology remains a big growth story; the rest will continue, but without the same potential for expansion.

The year 2018 resembles 1945 in many important respects. In 1945, after thirty hellish years of two world wars, a global depression, a Holocaust, and a Europe that almost committed suicide, the US-led West advanced new visions, ideas, and projects powerful enough to get a broad global consensus on the direction to follow, though without support from China, Russia, and Iran. This momentum lasted for the rest of the twentieth century and transformed the world – mostly for the better. We need a comparable consensus now, though it must come from determination and skill, not war and economic decline.

Today's rising power is China. Over its long history it created an impressive civilization, and it is emerging as a great country again. It has an important contribution to make as a world leader, though it still lags behind Western countries because of its limits on freedom and mutual accommodation. Its social contract with its citizens is

* Published in the *Globe and Mail*, April 3, 2018.

vulnerable because of its economy, which in turn is dependent on the global economy. Still, over the past few decades, China has built on the strengths of its historic achievements, bolstered by access to the US-led economic order.

Over these same few years, American achievements have been undermined by overreach and underreach. The United States started withdrawing from overreach under Barack Obama, but it has since moved into disruptive disarray under President Donald Trump. He has an uncertain political future, and his goals are measured in hours, not decades. By contrast, China's president Xi Jinping has a long view and a seemingly assured political future.

We need a multi-country approach led by the United States and China if we are to attain a world worth living in. The basics of the postwar Western approach still apply: broaden the inclusive order within and between countries, and contain what cannot be included. Our first task is to find the political will and consensus for an orderly path forward in our closely connected world. It's not possible for any country today to go it alone – mutual accommodation is essential.

The West needs to focus on strengths, not weaknesses, and finding a renewed global order for all. Its strengths in politics, economics, resources, and values are unmatched, as are its military power, alliances, sense of inclusivenesss, and capacity for change. Today, no other countries, ideas, or civilizations can threaten the West. We are threatened only by our own inherent contradictions.

China and a deeply divided United States will make the decisive choices of our era. Can they find a grand plan that will create a peaceful, prosperous, and inclusive global order that works? Ideally, they will discover a way to reduce terrorism, contain broken states and civil wars, abolish walls between countries, and establish safe places for refugees.

Mr Xi seems to understand elements of the situation and believes he can look out for China, the Chinese Communist Party, and himself in a reshaped global order. The West is still stronger than China, but its advantages are being undermined by centrifugal forces and populism. It must recognize that its strengths rest on five institutions: the rule of law, democratic ways, free markets, a robust media, and fear-free universities. The United States is floundering in Mr Trump's "no man's land" as he bullies his enemies, threatens to withdraw from trade agreements and international deals, builds walls, blusters and contradicts himself, all in the name of making America great again.

Faced with this crisis, the West would be wise to draw on Canada's mutual-accommodating ways. We do what it takes to make things work, and every outcome is custom-made.

PART FOUR

New Thinking for New Ways in a New World

20

The Need for New Fundamental
Ways of Thinking

I have believed from early in my professional life that getting the full context right was indispensable to getting decisions right. That meant I was always looking for new and better frameworks for investigating and thinking. Then came 9/11, and I realized that everyone needed to better understand themselves and each other, especially in the West and among Muslims. We all required ways of looking at things that, to the extent possible, were not culturally or power position biased. We also needed approaches that minimized the negatives of limits in our experience and the tendency of language to reflect existing power relationships. The new terrorism world we live in has been developing for over twenty-five years now. It requires both a fuller context and better ways of going about things. One of these ways is how we think. Everyone has to improve how they see what is actually going on and find ways to mutually accommodate all of it, not just part of it.

In November 2002, fourteen months after 9/11, I wrote a fifty-page essay for private distribution titled "The Return of History, the Reassertion of Politics, the Driving Force of Culture, and the Need for New Fundamental Concepts." My goals were twofold: to show the need for a new post-Thatcher/Reagan political and policy focus that went beyond free markets/globalization/shareholder value; and to discover unbiased root ideas that encompass everything about which there is nothing more fundamental to say.

The basic idea was that the economically advanced part of the world (the West) would shift its focus from the economic performance of the previous twenty years (1980–2000) to

- the return of history;
- the reassertion of politics (both global and domestic); and
- the driving force of culture (see Chapter 14, essay 3: Identity and Culture: The New Driving Forces).

The forces of history, politics, and culture would have a rising impact on domestic economies and the global economy. Also, economic performance would continue to be a major factor in how well societies, organizations, and individuals would cope with the stresses created by the need to adjust to those disruptive forces (for better and for worse):

The primary thesis of that essay was twofold:

- the foremost order of future Western politics and policy would be to continue successful Western economic performance, alongside improving economic performance beyond Western economies; and
- the other primary order of Western politics and policy would be to address the real-world consequences of the rising salience of history, politics, and culture on everything in all countries.

By and large, the events of the last seventeen years have confirmed that thesis. The shift in forces I foresaw has since given rise to Brexit as Britain readies to leave the European Union, the election of President Trump in the United States, and the spread throughout the West of populism and centrifugal forces within and between countries.

I also saw then and still see a need for new fundamental concepts as free as possible of cultural-experience and power-relationship bias. The events of 9/11 promoted the idea that people in the West and Muslims need to find more truly objective ways of talking to each other, while they still retain what was distinctive about their own cultures and identities. The fundamental concepts I advanced were not intended as a theory or philosophy about anything, let alone everything. The test is whether they ring true to what most people normally observe about things; and whether they are useful from a practical point of view in providing relevant frameworks to assist in investigating, thinking, and making decisions in ways that take everything needed into account.

These concepts aim to be fundamental enough that ideological and cultural biases and experiential limitations do not foreclose access to the full playing field needed for good assessments and decisions. I see these concepts as the way to mutually accommodate Whitehead's narrowness as the basis of all achievement and the vastness of things; and to reflect adequately Northrop Frye's view that authority does not rest in ownership, institutions, hierarchies, positions, achievements, status, or charismatic personality but, rather, in the subject matter itself (which by definition is bias-free, although it may not be bias-free in the particular way we see it).

The world we live in is all about transformations – of materials and activities into goods and services; of information and ideas into stories, images, meanings, and symbols. These transformations always have two dimensions – a practical or functional dimension in the so-called real world outside ourselves; and a symbolic dimension in the human world of the imagination inside ourselves. Both reveal and conceal always. You may aspire to getting it all, but you can never quite get there. That is why we should all be better listeners and better understanders of ourselves than we are; and why politics that is inflexible (too much either/or) and not sufficiently inclusive (both/and) can be so dangerous and costly.

The results of these transformations will always be more or less functional (what you get is more or less what you want and need to get) and more or less congruent (what you see is more or less what is there) in terms of what they reveal and conceal. The relationship between public and private transformations will probably rise in importance in the decades ahead. What then is required to shape the separateness and connectedness (discussed later as key fundamental concepts) in a functional manner? This question has become more complex, and it now risks unmanageable tensions and dysfunctional breakdown.

The English philosopher and mathematician Alfred North Whitehead, who spent most of his career at Cambridge University in England and his final years after age sixty-three at Harvard University in the United States, made four separate observations that, at one level, are or seem to be paradoxical (I have paired them into two offsetting ideas):

- the world is shot through and through with numbers, and all exactness is a fake; and
- the universe is vast, and narrowness is the basis of all achievement.

These observations are two huge "both/ands" that need to be mutually accommodated if big mistakes are to be avoided and big opportunities seized.

The fundamental concepts seek to provide a full framework for addressing the numbers and vastness dimensions of the full playing field while at the same time enabling the use of the full playing field to avoid the dangers of exactness fakery. They can also help determine the most appropriate full playing field – in a world that is both the inflexible either/or and the flexible both/and, and also functionally narrow and at the same time vast – in order to improve concrete outcomes in particular settings.

Paradox is far more at the heart of things than is generally explicitly recognized, although it is implicitly acted upon all the time. Paradox is the child of an either/or world. There is no paradox in a both/and world. What is inconsistent and thus paradoxical in the either/or world is not inconsistent or paradoxical in a both/and world. The primary power of Western thought and practice since the Renaissance, if not before in the Judaeo-Christian and Greco-Roman traditions, has been either/or. But either/or has also resulted in what Whitehead described as the fallacy of misplaced concreteness (it is not the whole story or as fully real as it seems to be when stated in the compelling black and white of either/or). The everyday world is full of the fallacy of misplaced connectedness. That does not matter, usually, because it normally makes no practical difference in most outcomes. The fallacy of misplaced concreteness is another version of all exactness is a fake. The either/or world is real, or it could not have produced the power of science and technology. So, to paraphrase Whitehead, the world is shot through and through with either/orness. But either/orness is a fake and reflects the fallacy of misplaced concreteness.

The fundamental concepts are descriptive rather than prescriptive. They do not seek to suggest what the world should look like or how any particular individual, organization, or country should go about its business or thinking. Whatever validity there may be in the fundamental concepts lies in their ability to capture the main elements of the full playing field – but from reality, not some underlying philosophical or scientific outlook. Their validity will come from conceptualizing them into usable frames and edible mental bites.

The largeness of the realms of religion, art, and entertainment is that they enable us to move beyond the constrained and limited world of Mother Nature and either/or to the unconstrained and unlimited world of the human imagination. Religion, art, and entertainment provide metaphors for the not yet freer and more human world of tomorrow. That is why the best of each is so magical. It is what each shares with all else that is magical in people's lives, like the worlds of words that is literature, interpersonal caring love, and the courage in everyday life. All these qualities bring together the inner and the outer, feeling and thinking, and the connectedness and separateness of things.

The three most important of the fundamental concepts are

- separateness and connectedness;
- inner (a world without limits) and outer (a world with limits); and
- both both/and and either/or.

These concepts may or may not help a philosopher or a scientist, but they can be used to analyze the nature of particular scientific and philosophic outlooks. In addition, I have found them practically useful in everyday work and life. They are also useful because they inhere in other less fundamental concepts that may be seen as more directly related and immediately usable to address particular practical issues.

Each of these separateness and connectedness/inner and outer sets of concepts can be viewed in a Western and in an Eastern (and Indigenous) manner. In the Western manner, they will generally be viewed in an either/or context – in both the everyday working world and the philosophical and scientific worlds. In the Eastern and Indigenous manner, they are each seen as inextricably linked – always both and never only one. This approach is a more complete and inclusive view that the Western way of thinking now urgently needs.

The Western manner unquestionably captures a huge part of the essential nature of these concepts. If this were not so, science and technology, and rights and freedoms, which have flowed from the Western manner would not have been so enormously powerful and influential in shaping the Western world since the Renaissance. The widespread success of the Western manner in the spread of technology, markets, rights, and democratic majorities has also driven the relative rise in the horizontal forces and structures. This success also eroded the vertical forces that foster identity and solidarity. It also, and in turn, often produced dysfunctional forms of those qualities because of the power of producer and military dominance in societies largely governed by vertical structures and forces.

The ideas of separateness and connectedness are far from original. They unavoidably (if often only unconsciously) underlie all serious thought. In Western thought, however, they almost always tend to slip into the dominant either/or category. In the natural world, the fundamental categories are space and time. It is impossible for us to conceive of the world of nature, or of any world, without both of these ideas. The simplest, while still the most comprehensive way, of describing space and time is that they are forms of both separateness and connectedness – that is, they are both either/or and both/and. This description does not tell us what physics and cosmology tell us about space and time, where the devil (or the god) is in the details. It does, however, provide a frame. If the frame is departed from, it means that we are looking at something less than a full playing field, so that, in any particular instance, something – maybe important, maybe not – is missing from the subject matter that is the ultimate source of authority. The consequences will be mistakes, mostly not very consequential, but sometimes huge and dangerous.

It is not easy to think of separateness always and unavoidably including connectedness, and of connectedness always and unavoidably including separateness (to do so runs counter to the dominant either/or Western way of thinking). Yet this is how we inevitably act (because it is the full reality). We may not choose to do so, but we have no choice. We are also always being pressed to act differently, on the assumption that we face this either/or choice. The pressure is to make false either/or choices, especially in the human realms of politics, religion, and personal relations. If it is always both both/and, and also always either/or, the real choice is not the false one about favouring separateness over connectedness or vice versa. It is over which forms of separateness and connectedness to choose in any particular instance. Life is essentially about the changing forms of separateness and connectedness (both inner and outer) and their mutual accommodation. It is also about humans always simultaneously living in a world that is both outer and inner. We live in a world of interpenetration (to use Whitehead's word), not of isolation.

There can never be an escape into either separateness or connectedness, or into inner or outer. On this basis, the more separate we aspire to, the more connectedness we will need to functionally balance and sustain it, and vice versa. For example, it would be possible to view the Jesus of the New Testament as among the most separate of men and to conclude that he was able to be separate safely and functionally only because he was at the same time among the most connected of men. Looked at another way, if both separateness and connectedness inhere at all times in the nature of things, neither can ever be said to be dominant. So, if one or the other seeks dominance, its growth toward dominance would have a cancerous quality. Such growth can never achieve its end and can only end up undermining what it sought to be dominant. Dominance is a sort of cancer that, if out of control, threatens the whole system.

The American psychiatrist/psychotherapist Erik Erikson once said that being adult (a consciously separate but connected individual) meant asserting oneself (separateness) in ways that enhance the ability of others to assert themselves (connectedness). That adult state is clearly both either/or and both/and, one that works to enhance not only individual identity, effectiveness, and meaning (separateness) but, simultaneously, solidarity and community (connectedness). In turn, there are forms of connectedness (family solidarity and community) that can work to enhance individuality and freedom (separateness). The more adult one wants to be, the more mutual accommodating of separateness and connectedness is needed. Perhaps the most sophisticated and advanced, yet simple and common, example is the good mother and the infant baby – both are separate yet deeply connected in a relationship of continuously changing separateness and connectedness. This relationship continues so long as the child's mother lives.

The distinction between reality and truth is not itself a fundamental concept as such, nor is it in itself directly useful in analyzing issues.

Rather, it is a red-flag reminder of the risk of slipping into the idea that any particular grasp of reality has captured the full truth about things. Put another way, this distinction, in the context of these fundamental concepts, enables us to make two useful assertions that can be related to assessment about any issue:

- no one thing is ever everything; and
- no one thing is ever only one thing.

So long as intransigent issues can be seen only as constituting the sole one-dimensional truth about them, significant chunks of reality, which may be critical to an acceptable outcome, will be ignored. Solutions will then be sought on something less than the full playing field – and so be destined to fail or to fall short at least to some significant degree.

We can also look at the characteristics of societies, organizations, and individuals on the basis of where they sit in the vertical/horizontal and feminine/masculine spectrums. In terms of the cultural forces shaping our new world and the cultural impact of new world forces, we can also use the same spectrum to determine where different societies, organizations, and individuals fall within it. The profound differentness of Japanese culture has long constituted a fundamental challenge to others and to itself. For a North American, that difference – especially opposite the culture of the United States at an opposite extreme – permits the construction of a Japanese mirror that can help us see ourselves better. Japan has been too vertical (too connected, not separate enough), while the United States is too horizontal (too separate, not connected enough).

The approach to framework-assisted decision-making at its broadest seeks, first, different frameworks at different levels, and, second, different areas of human affairs that can assist individuals with particular roles and particular knowledge to make better assessments and decisions. These frameworks can cover issues of politics, economics, policy, culture, and organizational structures and dynamics, both separately and as part of a larger system. As a result, they should, over time, lead to efforts to enhance the coherence between different frameworks by getting at underlying elements that are common to all. The idea is for individuals to seek to describe everything they can call upon to understand and on which to make decisions. It has led to three fundamental observations (the most basic and inclusive possible, not theories or any claims of scientific or other truth):

- we all live in two worlds at one and the same time – an outer and an inner world that interpenetrate each other;
- those worlds can be described exhaustively (nothing is excluded) in terms of their fundamentals as constituting different forms of separateness and connectedness within and between each of them; and
- there is nothing more fundamental we can say about those worlds that also encompasses everything we can say about them or about anything and everything.

These fundamentals assist thinking and decision-making by providing the needed context and perspective. They also facilitate and encourage the development of new perceptions and insights to place within that context and perspective. In addition, they are free of cultural bias and permit the assessment of the most sensitive subjects without the need to assert inferiority or superiority or to cast blame or claim praise. These qualities seem likely to be increasingly important in a global village of diverse cultures and stages of development.

The outer world of nature comprises space and time. Connectedness in the outer nature world is found in the processes of cause and effect, which are the domain of science. The massiveness of causation in the outer world can be seen in the overwhelming impact of science. But science does not reach the separateness of the outer world, nor does it reach very far into the inner world. It may even have bumped up against the separateness of the outer world in the realms of chaos theory and the uncertainty principle in physics. The inner human world is the existential world of meaning, will, death, and a sense of ultimate isolation or aloneness. In fact, isolation is perhaps more accurately a dysfunctionally excessive focus on the separateness of things and of oneself at the extreme end of possibility, but without the rebalancing dimension of connectedness. The latter is felt by most people in the normal course of their lives to be as much an existential reality as separateness. Death is the ultimate challenge, because it seems as if separateness wins a final victory over connectedness.

In the absence of *both* separateness and connectedness, death would seem to lead necessarily to nothingness. It is this line of reasoning that haunts most humans through history and to which most of the great religions seek to respond. The Indigenous peoples, in contrast, with their natural both/and perspective, do not see human life (history) as ending in isolated nothingness.

We can also usefully look at human development in these same terms: children, as they grow through adolescence to adulthood, encounter the need for changing forms of separateness and connectedness. This need extends first to their parents, then to other members of their family, and ultimately to others. Their developmental task, as changes take place in the outer world around them and also in their own inner world, is to constantly shift the forms of their separateness and connectedness in as functional a manner as possible. As they become more and more aware of both, they also become increasingly elusive and mysterious over time. Their parents have a similar developmental task. Similar ongoing shifts take place in the worlds of politics, society, and organizations.

All humans must address at the same time both the connectedness of the causal reality and the constraints of the outer world of time and space (the world of nature that cares not for humans) as well as the inner world of freedom and human concern and of narrative and metaphor (the human world of the imagination). Each culture and each individual in their own way seeks to restore to fallen man the Old Testament Garden of Eden (a world that actually cares for man). If successful, that would reverse the alienation of the freedom-seeking human from the uncaring limits of nature (a Northrop Frye idea) that ignores the deepest of human desires. This desire is the human need for a world where people are free to do what they would most deeply like to do, unrestrained by the alienating limits of uncaring nature. In this world, our human needs that arise out of our concern for a world that is also a better one than the one we live in can be met – one free from pain and loss.

We are at a very big moment in human history. We need to find ways to overcome the limits that have brought us to where we are today. We need better big decisions than we usually get at the end of the good eras in our alternating good and bad eras (e.g., the horror story of the bad era of 1914–45 after the good era of 1815–1914).

These better solutions are to be found in ever deeper understanding of each of the four better ways of going about things – freedom, science, mutual accommodation, and compassion – and in always working to achieve a better balance among them. What is most missing in action in today's world is mutual accommodation. Getting enough for a bearable world will require huge pivots by most of the countries of the world, and no major country will be exempt. It requires a much better understanding of the reality of choice.

Postscript

I thought the young Haida contributor to my Indigenous update (Chapter 9) would be interested in the paragraph in this chapter where I note that the Eastern/Indigenous manner of thinking was more inclusive than the Western. Here is her response: "I was very interested in Chapter 20's ideas of either/or, both/and, and the concepts of the inner and outer world in different contexts. It has quickly become something I have applied to my daily life in regard to my train of thought in order to empathize with and understand people better."

21

New Ways of Thinking Are
Essential in a New World

Every dimension of the Western World is changing – personal, societal, technological, political, economic, and geopolitical. Although we know there will be another recession, the discussion in Chapter 22, "The Post–Thatcher/Reagan Economy, 2008–09," sets out the post-2008 economic forces that stand to make the US and global economies different from what they were post-1945. It refers to an increasing number of books, primarily from the United States and the United Kingdom, that are looking at what is going on with fresh analytical eyes – much more so than I am aware of in Canada. It is beyond the scope of this book to explore the full range of what has recently been written. However, I discussed a few of these ideas in a talk at Trent University at the end of 2017 – and I repeat part of it here.

Adam Gopnik, a *New Yorker* staff writer who grew up in Montreal, had a long article in the magazine, May 15, 2017, titled "We could have been Canada. Was the American Revolution such a good idea?" His opening paragraph read:

> And what if it was a mistake from the start? The Declaration
> of Independence, the American Revolution, the creation of the
> United States of America – what if all this was a terrible idea, and
> what if the injustices and madness of American life since then
> have occurred not in spite of the virtues of the Founding Fathers

Drawn from a speech given at the symposium *The Canadian Difference: Dialogues in Diversity*, Trent University, December 9, 2017.

but because of them? The Revolution, this argument might run, was a needless and brutal bit of slaveholders' panic mixed with Enlightenment argle-bargle, producing a country that was always marked for violence and disruption and demagogy. Look north to Canada, or south to Australia, and you will see different possibilities of peaceful evolution away from Britain, toward sane and whole, more equitable and less sanguinary countries. No revolution, and slavery might have ended, as it did elsewhere in the British Empire, more peacefully and sooner. No "peculiar institution," no hideous Civil War and appalling aftermath. Instead, an orderly development of the interior – less violent, and less inclined to celebrate the desperado over the peaceful peasant. We could have ended with a social-democratic commonwealth that stretched from north to south, a near-continent-wide Canada. (Actually, you could not have been Canada, because Americans are not Canadians. They could not have thought that way, so the outcome could never have been politically achievable – then or now).

The Gopnik rumination about the founding of the United States is important. "Birth myths" are often too limiting and lead to lasting self-misunderstanding and self-limitation. A recent book from Kurt Andersen, *Fantasyland: How America Went Haywire: A 500-Year History* (2017), suggests that what is happening today in the United States – this strange, post truth, "fake news" moment – is not entirely new. Rather, it is the ultimate expression of a key part of America's national character and path. Andersen sees a United States formed by wishful dreamers – by hucksters and their suckers. He sees the "whatever-you-want" fantasy as deeply embedded in the American DNA. A world in which it is fake news, not reality, that gets in the way of what you want.

Identity and culture are the new driving forces of the twenty-first century. Canada has the strength of being able to live without a firm identity in a world when all identities are incomplete. It has a vast land that it can call home and still include a diversity of newcomers.

Leadership greatness in business and politics requires a rare combination of objectivity and empathy. My oldest friend – we were sometimes in the same baby carriage together in Montreal – became a leading child psychotherapist pioneer at the Hospital for Sick

Children in Toronto. He had that combination. So did Shakespeare and Jane Austen.

I was very interested to read that after four years into the job, the new head of Microsoft, Satya Nadella, in his book, *Hit Refresh: The Quest to Rediscover Microsoft's Soul and Imagine a Better Future for Everyone* (2017), put the need for empathy at the centre of his Microsoft reawakening challenge. Empathy is not just basic to his personal philosophy; it is what is working for him as he seemingly takes Microsoft successfully down its needed new path. Empathy from a hi-tech guy – an Indian-born engineer heading one of America's greatest technology companies – may be telling us something about how needed US movement beyond its current turmoil might take place. I have said the Western world has become unbalanced as the more dominant horizontal Western forces of freedom and science have prevailed. Empathy is a key element in making mutual accommodation work.

A second book that is hopeful for America's future is *Principles: Life & Work* (2017) by Ray Dalio. He is the founder and co-chairman of Bridgewater Associates, now the largest and best-performing hedge fund in the world with about $150 billion in global investments. Dalio would probably not realize that his radical transparency believ-ability weighting and idea meritocracy, integrated into algorithms for decision-making, is a specific and highly successful methodology for mutual accommodation decision-making. This one liner does not begin to capture what it takes to use people and algorithms to accommodate everything each has to offer in order to make superbly successful investments. It's necessary to read the whole book to see how much goes into that success.

There is not much immediate visible empathy at Bridgewater – the ability to start from where the other guy is, until you better understand what is really going on. Markets are a huge and largely effective but imperfect mutual accommodation way. Finance markets are for investors the other guy who must be listened to. Algorithms provide the base data to which disciplined ways of individual thinking are then applied to get to a decision.

Empathy is about listening in an objective way. I see the Dalio/ Bridgewater approach as a superb way of hearing what you need to hear before you invest. Investments are not about being empathetic. Financial markets capture where other investors are at a particular point in time. The best objective understanding in the Dalio world involves data and people-weighted belief. The challenge is finding out how to accommodate everything relevant – data and the best thinking – to future market outcomes. The method is to combine data with rules about how to get the best thinking out of the best people – a difficult mutual accommodation to achieve. It has proven itself as a successful way to invest in a tough world, but it can be hard on the participants.

I could mention many more of these kinds of books. They are likely only the beginning of a steady stream, and we should all be on the lookout for them. It is challenging to read Gopnik's suggestion that the United States was itself fundamentally misconceived. Even if it was, it remains one of the great countries of history, despite the number of significant things it has got wrong. New ideas will be needed for every aspect of American life – as they will for other Western countries too. Trump has disrupted American political life with his egocentric and bullying grasp of the world. The extreme left of the Democratic Party, by tackling "big ideas," are talking about another round of huge disruptions. After so much Trump disruption, this tack may not be what the American voters want or what the country needs.

22

The Post–Thatcher/Reagan Economy, 2008–09

The Thatcher/Reagan era was one of the greatest triumphs of mutual accommodation in history. It was achieved through a combination of free markets, globalization, and, in a time of economic crisis, global policy coordination. It rested on a foundation of the rule of law and freedom. The mutual accommodation was not, however, inclusive enough. Its primary focus on only one of the five stakeholders, the shareholders and shareholder value, has proved to be increasingly inadequate.

This chapter underlines how the post-war global macroeconomic policy environment has radically and importantly changed and provides a basis for exploring needed changes in policy and behaviour. In addition to fiscal/monetary policy imbalances, there are issues such as the general slowdown in productivity and the increase in global imbalances and in income and wealth inequality. Together, these issues are fostering extremism and populism. The world of economic policy prevalent under Thatcher/Reagan (and in previous decades, where demand persistently exceeded supply) has run its course. No "silver bullet" changes in policy will be able to bring about more economic dynamism. What must now be explored are five main areas of potential structural change beyond monetary and fiscal policy. To succeed, all five need to be mutually accommodated.

The Thatcher and Reagan era is behind us. The world has experienced a "regime shift" in economic conditions (as James Bullard, CEO and president of the St Louis Federal Reserve Bank, said at the "Challenge for Monetary Policy" symposium in Jackson Hole, Wyoming, in August 2019). Right now we need reduced expectations and better explanations from central bankers about the world they face. Central bankers seem to be slowly getting a better understanding of the new dimensions of the post-Thatcher/Reagan era. The public needs a greater understanding of monetary policy and the potential role of other policy, but the central bankers have not met this need. They find it difficult to explain the limits of what they are doing because it moves them away from their vital political independence and toward the dangerous world of the partisan politics of policy change. Nonetheless, they need to find a way to educate the public about the new monetary policy world.

Right now the global economy faces the consequences of a huge rise in savings at the same time that there are fewer available private-sector investment opportunities. I discuss later what I think are the four main factors that have brought this situation about. Unless and until some or all of them are adequately addressed, the current unsustainable underlying economic conditions will persist, and central banks will be largely powerless. Fiscal policy will be needed, but to be fully effective, sources of the current "savings glut" must be addressed.

Something new is definitely going on. Byron Wien, the veteran Morgan Stanley strategist, wrote a September 2019 piece headed "Plenty to worry about, not much to do." In its summary of the Jackson Hole symposium, the *Financial Times* concluded that "there was a sense that things will never be the same again." Bullard added that yes, "something is going on, and that is causing a total rethink of central banking and all our cherished notions about what we think we are doing" – something I have been saying for several years now. The blog ZeroHedge stated that "there has never been so much hostility to central bankers – even among other central bankers – in the past decade as over the past month. Something is about to snap." Ray Dalio, "in an ominous warning," compared the current period to the years 1935–45. He pointed to three big issues:

- the end of the long-term debt cycle (when central banks are no longer effective);
- the large (US) wealth gap and political polarity; and
- China as a rising world power, challenging the existing world power (the United States).

Mark Carney, the governor of the Bank of England, has also sent a warning "that extended periods of low interest rates effectively become self-reinforcing and lead to catastrophic results." Very low interest rates, he said, tend "to coincide with high risk events such as wars, financial crises, and breaks in the monetary regime."

What is significant is that all these comments are coming at the same time. The current US economic expansion is the longest ever. It likely still has enough strength to go another year – perhaps more. The Thatcher/Reagan era has ended, and no one knows what will happen when the inevitable recession comes. Monetary and fiscal policy can no longer do all the tasks needed to guide and support Western economies in a savings glut/low to flat interest-rate world.

This challenging situation will not change until there is an underlying shift in the structural imbalances among consumption, savings, and investment within and between countries. No country is addressing these issues – and none is likely to do so until after the US and global economic expansions come to an end. The reason is partly because they are politically challenging, and partly because the central banks and the policymakers failed to understand that different ills – cyclical or structural – require different cures. These structural challenges are likely to be addressed only when the political costs of not addressing them come to be seen by governments as greater than those of addressing them – and when voters accept that fact. Pain is often necessary to get needed change. Central banks and politicians are generally averse to pain.

So the big economic ideas floated during the era of Prime Minister Margaret Thatcher in Britain and President Ronald Reagan in the United States are no longer as effective in promoting economic growth. They did good work, and they still matter, but they are not enough for a balanced and sustainable future. The West now needs to move on from the world of Thatcher and Reagan. The initial thirty-five to fifty years of the post-Second World War period were a time when demand (which had been suppressed by a fifteen-year global depression and war) recovered and consistently moved above supply. When necessary to curb demand and/or wage and other inflation pressures, the central banks intervened with higher interest rates to counter them and bring the early post-war business cycles to an end. That, however, is no longer the central economic policy challenge.

The Thatcher/Reagan economic policy was based on several ideas which were mostly good, though limited: expanding free markets at home and abroad; making little distinction, mistakenly, between financial and goods-and-services markets; and regarding shareholder value as the underlying driver of fair and successful economies (which was true only to a certain point). Strong corporate profits are always essential: shareholders are not only wealthy individuals but include pension funds. It is true that shareholders are owners of the company, but ownership is not the sole story. Shareholders are only one of five corporate stakeholders, alongside employees, customers, suppliers, and communities. All of them matter, not just for business but for society too (as populism is teaching us).

Honda, whom I worked with closely for twenty years in Canada, the United States and the United Kingdom, is the company I know well that has best understood the importance of all five stakeholders right from its beginning in 1948 (as a motorcycle manufacturer, before it later became a top-of-the-class global motor vehicle manufacturer). It also knew something else: the need for respect for them all. That is why, as I explained in Chapter 1, when Brazil asked the company to locate its motor vehicle manufacturing assembly plant among illiterate workers in the Amazon Valley, the company found a way to get around that shortcoming.

US business leaders have recently started a "business rethink" by proposing to ditch the creed of shareholders first. The US Business Roundtable adopted, in its mid-August 2019 announcement, the same five stakeholders Honda has espoused from its very beginning. As Mohamed A. El-Erian explained, "it reflects an emerging consensus about the importance of more inclusive capitalism" (in my language, more both/and, less either/or).

Inequality, alongside fears arising from excessive threatening change in relation to culture and identity, are the fuel of populism and rising centrifugal forces. Globalization is not the primary reason for the rise in inequality. The main post-2000 economic management policy mistakes have been to rely excessively on monetary policy and insufficiently on fiscal policy; and to blur the differences between what structural and cyclical policy requires and how best to achieve the former. Since 1980, the policy focus has increasingly been on cyclical remedies for structural ills.

Central banks are not what they used to be, for two main reasons. First, the economic conditions between 1945 and 1990 no longer prevail. Second, cyclical economic management needs the right balance between monetary and fiscal policy in a better balanced consumption/savings/investment world. Mainly because of politically driven and ideology based fear of government deficits, monetary policy was asked to do too much. Today, central banks do not face the serious cyclical inflation pressures of the five decades after the end of the war. In fact, these pressures have largely gone. Monetary policy has failed to address the now post-2008–09 structural challenge of a savings glut alongside a lack of sufficient available good investment opportunities – simply because it does not have the right tools.

The post-war level of all forms of US debt (consumer, business, and government) as a percentage of GDP was flat from 1945 to 1980. It then took off under the so-called financially conservative Reagan Republicans. That first big "fake news" moment of post-war America is now being repeated by President Donald Trump on both the fiscal and the monetary fronts. President Barack Obama faced a global balance-sheet recession, which Reagan did not. Reagan, however, initially had his own challenges in a deep 1980–82 cyclical recession caused by Federal Reserve chair Paul Volcker pushing the federal funds rate to 20 percent in June 1981. That crisis passed, but the Reagan government economic policy, which expanded all forms of debt, continued – the opposite to the fiscal/financial conservatives they claimed to be.

The post-war era was inflation prone until the 1990s. Since then, inflation has not been the primary problem for the United States and other major Western economies. Nonetheless, central bank talk has continued to focus on an inflation threat that has not been seen in the West for some thirty years. Today, central banks are looking to get minimum inflation, not to counter it. We can only assume that is because all central banks have failed to understand two things: the nature of the post-1990 structural imbalances; and their own contribution to them as they wrongly used cyclical remedies to address the consequences of structural imbalances.

In the fall of 2019, some ten years after the beginning of the recovery/expansion that followed the global financial crisis in 2008, both real and nominal interest rates in G7 countries are very low throughout the West, and available private-sector investment opportunities are well below the level of savings. One important consequence is the rise in corporate share buybacks. If there were enough good investment opportunities, that would not be happening.

The working assumption of the Thatcher/Reagan era was that there would be a broad, automatic and ongoing structural balance among consumption, savings, and investment. Instead, there have been persistent and growing gaps between them. Between 1945 and 1980, supply shortages and rising real wages led to inflationary pressures and higher interest-rate interventions by central banks, followed by lower central bank interest-rate interventions. Today, there is a gap between the amount of global savings and the availability of good global private-sector investment opportunities – a situation that continues not to improve. With extremely low interest rates, alongside a lack of enough available private investment opportunities, savings are in effect being hoarded – largely used for private and public consumption, not investment. Persistent low rates mean that investors such as pension funds have actuarial assumptions that can't be met by current bond yields. This threat will bring pressure on them to continue to shift their asset mixes increasingly into riskier, higher yielding assets – Forced Buyers of Risk (FOBOR). The assets are also being used for high-risk, high-return investment in emerging markets – a reaching for return strategy that can be dangerous.

Ultra-low to negative interest rates, nominal and real, are likely to remain until private-sector investment demand, together with more new public-sector investment, better matches levels of savings. When rates finally increase, there will be major policy, marketplace, and asset price changes throughout the world.

There appear to be four main reasons for the persistent and growing gaps among consumption, savings, and investment over the last two or three decades. Ben Bernanke, the former chair of the Federal Reserve, called attention in 2005 to a global "savings glut" – which produced the pressures that brought today's ultra-low to negative interest-rate environment:

• the shift in income distribution away from the less well-off, who spend a high percentage of their income on consumption, to the better-off, who spend a lower percentage of their income on consumption;

- the shift from manufacturing to hi-tech and digital products and services, which require less physical investment;
- the fact that public infrastructure, education, and research – which have fallen behind needs in the United States, as well as in many other countries – will require more private-sector investment; and
- the trend in too many countries (the European Union [especially Germany], China, and Japan) to structure their economies so that they spend less than they earn (export-led economies) and to use the resulting excess savings to lend to countries (such as the United States, the United Kingdom, and Canada, who are running current account deficits) that persist in consuming more than they earn and borrowing from other countries that do the reverse.

These issues need to be addressed over time by policy changes (which means challenging political discussions) to get a more sustainable global economic and financial structural balance. Better economic performance, as well as a reduction in populism and other centrifugal political and societal forces, requires this attention. Free markets in goods and services are always subject to the limits of the real world. Not so financial markets. They can get too much central bank liquidity and provide so-called financial products removed from economic reality. Real limits exact pain, which is informative. Inadequate financial limits led by central banks are an effort (often at high cost) to escape the pain that comes from real world limits.

Central banks drive money and credit creation. The system goes wrong when the results cushion too much of the pain of real economy limits. Since 2000, the world has seen too much money/credit creation overall in attempts to avoid too much pain, alongside too tight fiscal policies since the financial crises almost everywhere (but, fortunately for the global economy, not in the United States under Obama). The numbers reported a while ago from Richard Koo make the post-2008–09 monetary overreach case:

- the US monetary base was expanded by the Federal Reserve by 357 percent from the end of 2008 to 2015; and
- credit to the private sector increased only 19 percent over seven and a half years.

In other words, an elephant effort for a mouse outcome.

In the 1980s, Paul Volcker at the Federal Reserve and the Bank of England ran very tight monetary policy to bring inflation down – the last decades of real inflation in G7 countries. Canada's moment came at the end of the 1980s under John Crow, governor of the Bank of Canada. Volcker raised the federal funds rate, which had averaged 11.2 percent in 1979, to a peak of 20 percent in June 1981. He switched Fed policy from targeting interest rates to targeting the money supply. He stood Wall Street down – a rare accomplishment. (The traders always want low interest rates and lots of liquidity – which are good for share prices until they are not.) He also killed US inflation (it has never really come back), for which, not surprisingly, the US economy paid an unavoidable real cost.

More productive public investment will undoubtedly be needed to sustain productivity growth. The United States still does not adequately understand the degree to which post-war US federal public-sector spending on the space program and the military provided the foundation for the huge post-war US private-sector innovation drive. That, not tax cuts largely unrelated to encouraging new risk private-sector investment, is what is needed now to get a more sustainable balance in the United States among consumption, savings, and investment.

The new world of consumer rather than producer dominance, alongside the new world of globalization, have together structurally altered the cost-price environment by putting consistent downward pressure on prices. First, the shift of a lot of lower-end manufacturing from advanced to low-wage newly emerging economies has also reduced prices for many manufactured goods, as has technology, including robots. Second, the shift from producer to consumer dominance led to price-based costing (getting your costs down below the price you can get) in place of cost-based pricing (adding up costs to get the price). That pushed consumer prices down, driven by the downward price pressures from the new consumer-dominant world. Together, these pressures for lower prices seem much more structural than cyclical. That could also mean more of the improvements in standard of living will now come from non-deflationary falling prices.

The private sector has reduced its investment borrowing for two main reasons: the persistent consumption, savings, and investment imbalances within and among countries; and the slow recovery from the global balance-sheet recession of 2007–08. The private sector will start serious levels of borrowing again only when the impact of the 2007–08 global balance-sheet recession is fully behind us and when the structural consumption, savings, and investment imbalances within and among countries are adequately addressed by policy. It could turn out that the next recession awaits an excess on the investment front (balance sheets/asset bubbles), not the earlier post-war excess of too much consumer demand for available supply (cyclical). Or the recession could come from interest rates suddenly increasing and the resulting downward impact on asset prices.

Since the 1990s, Western central banks have talked the inflation talk, but there has been no real inflation walk to walk. What central banks and fiscal authorities need to better understand is that structural imbalances (as opposed to cyclical ones) cannot be successfully addressed by monetary policy, and only partially by fiscal policy. Each can make the structural imbalances worse over time.

Monetary policy, in particular, does not work to fix structural trade imbalances, but it can be a big contributor to them. It did not work for Japan in the 1980s, and it will not work for China (or Japan or Germany) today. What sort of monetary policy is required at a time when private-sector demand for investment funds is relatively weak? The answer is that monetary policy cannot accomplish a structural change. To fix the problem, a different policy path will be needed.

The current Federal Reserve chair, Jerome Powell, said in a speech in June 2019 that the last two recessions were caused by financial imbalances (the Information Technology [IT] and the housing bubbles). They were not caused by rising real economy costs and prices or by Federal Reserve rate hikes aimed at curbing inflation. Households in developed nations continue to save for the future. In the absence of sufficient available opportunities for private-sector investment, those savings can only be used by consumers ready to borrow to increase consumption or for existing, not new, business investment assets – which, over time, can themselves foster asset bubbles.

Some new "out-of-the-box" policy thinking for a different world is needed from economists, governments, and central bankers. Each needs to move on from its post-1980 thinking, which seemed to suggest they have the tools for everything. Instead, they need to refocus what they say and take a much more limited and better disciplined role. They need to concentrate on the long overdue and harder political challenge of structural rebalancing through changes in government policy, and move away from the short-term focus and politically easier monetary or fiscal loosening.

It will primarily take events, along with leaders and followers who are willing to accept the needed economic and political adjustment pain, to get from here to there. The moment of truth will likely come after the end of the current US and global economic expansions. Cyclical remedies between now and then will only postpone the moment of structural truth. Unconventional monetary policy does not offset the economic drag from structural imbalances. Structural change in the consumption, savings, and investment imbalances is the only lasting and stable way forward. In the meantime, the end of the current expansion may come still later than many have expected. Recovery takes longer after an asset bubble gets out of hand. There are still no signs the post 2008–09 US expansion will end – or that rising inflation will need to be cut back by higher central bank interest rates. Nor is there any sign that negative interest rates are a sustainable way forward.

The cyclical economic policy management tools – fiscal and monetary – are not suited to address the structural imbalances outlined above. The lack of attention to the rising structural imbalances is part of why all Western economies are being held hostage to the centrifugal/populist forces that have been rising so strongly. This also partly underlies the rising trade wars. Too tight fiscal policy after 2008–09 in the European Union (unlike the United States) contributed to higher EU unemployment, and probably contributed to Brexit and rising EU and UK populism too.

Structural policy change (with its potential political divisiveness) will now be needed in five areas, but the required political consensus will not be easy to get, especially in a polarized/divided United States.

- The big current-account surplus countries will have to implement policy change that leads to a structurally sustainable increase in domestic demand and a reduction in their excessive reliance on export demand.
- The massive shift of wealth within many Western countries from

the spenders (the less well-off) to the non-spenders/savers (the better-off) needs to be reversed through balanced, more progressive, structural policy.

- American public infrastructure increasingly needs major new investment.
- Just as post-war America benefited from the influx of the publicly supported education of GIs, so a stronger US educational performance is again needed. In particular, the United States needs post-secondary vocational education, which will require more public funding.
- Renewed US government publicly funded support for research/innovation is needed. The Pentagon-financed innovation research after 1945 not only built the world's strongest military but also laid the groundwork for the superior post-war US private-sector innovation strengths.

The first forty-five post-war years addressed cyclical challenges with cyclical cures (monetary and fiscal). That strategy worked, though not always smoothly, because it suited the prevailing economic conditions. Since then, the structural ills brought by the end of the Thatcher/Reagan era have almost solely been addressed by cyclical cures. That has not worked well. Instead, we now have a world with ultra-low interest rates and too much debt. The growing amount of low-interest debt has become a hostage to the future. This debt has been brought on by persistent consumption, savings and investment structural imbalances that are the accumulated fallout from the misguided cyclical cures for the structural imbalances that first emerged in the 1980s.

This situation will not change until there is an underlying shift by less structural imbalance among consumption, savings, and investment within and between countries. No country is addressing these structural challenges. No country is likely to do so until after the current US and global economic expansions come to an end. The reason they have not been addressed is partly because they are politically challenging, and partly because the central banks seem to have failed to understand that different ills – cyclical or structural – require different cures. These structural challenges are likely to be addressed only when the political costs of not addressing them come to be seen by governments as greater than those of addressing them and voters accept it.

Today's unsustainable low to flat interest rates are for a different world, and they will not be sustainable until they return to more realistic higher levels. Institutions are mostly more about the past than prescient about the future. Central banks are no exception. Western central banks still publicly frame events primarily in inflation terms, although there has been no inflation for some thirty years. They are now even seeking (promoting?) inflation – as something to be wanted, not cured. Milton Friedman, the great American economist, wrote in 1966 that "inflation is always and everywhere a monetary phenomenon." Today's non-inflationary environment suggests it is well to keep in mind that no one thing is ever everything. Understanding that can avoid lot of wrong turns.

The economies in the West have seen several big changes. So far, we have no well-thought-out policy approach to address them. The period from 1930 to 1980 was primarily about demand management: seeking to expand demand in the 30s, and to expand or contain demand (as required) from 1945 to 1980. Then came the US supply-side economics from 1980 to 2007–08. Now we are looking at savings/private-sector investment structural imbalances that cannot be successfully addressed by cyclical loosening or tightening of monetary or fiscal policy.

These issues need to be addressed if the immediate and unsustainable negative (flat/low) real and nominal interest-rate environment is to be overcome. Central banks are on the wrong track looking for (wanting) inflation – a response more akin to looking at symptoms rather than real causes. The central banks will find it hard to get what they will need in a world of consistently too much savings and not enough investment. Today, these two issues – excessive savings and not enough investment opportunities – are the biggest structural challenges.

The most significant changes since the arrival of the Thatcher/Reagan economic policy era of globalization, free markets, and supply-side tax cuts are as follows. They have driven us to where we are today:

• Before the Thatcher/Reagan era (1980), there was never in all
  recorded history more "savings" than available investment opportunities for any length of time. The result of this massive change
  is the growing structural imbalances today among consumption,

savings, and investment. They are undoubtedly a factor – possibly the biggest single one – in the current low to negative normal and real interest rates and in the socio-political rise of centrifugal (populist) forces in the West.

- We cannot properly evaluate the consumption/savings/investment structure of any economy, and how it is affecting the economy, unless we see the total level of savings (both domestic and foreign) and where the savings are used (both consumption and investment). Savings used for investment and savings used for domestic consumption have a fundamentally different long-term economic impact. For this discussion, we need to see the total of savings before it is reduced by borrowers for consumption or investment. At some point there will be a limit to how much borrowing can be done for consumption. Recent Canadian data suggest that in Canada, given its very high household-sector debt, this limit may soon be reached.
- The relative shift from manufacturing to hi-tech economic growth has required less physical investment, thereby reducing investment demand relative to the level of available savings.
- Income distribution has shifted in favour of higher rates of personal savings and the overall share of national income going to investment relative to wages. This trend has shifted income away from spenders to savers. The spenders may then feel they have to borrow to maintain their level of consumption.
- Globalization has enabled countries such as Germany, China, and Japan to structure their domestic economies so that they can arrange to export more than they import – forcing the net importers to borrow from the net exporters to finance their consumption. This imbalance has become one of the major contributors to populism.
- Around the beginning of the Thatcher/Reagan era, another never-before-in-history event took place. Until then, the economic world had always been producer dominant. In the years since, it has become increasingly consumer dominant for more and more people. That has put downward pressure on consumer prices, and thus on inflation (and interest rates), resulting in rising excess savings being used increasingly for consumption. At some point, consumers will not be able to manage more and more consumption beyond what they have earned – even at very low interest rates.

- Low interest rates, because of excessive savings, are not good for the overall economy and, moreover, cannot last. Banks cannot stay safe or remain able to lend without adequate earnings from interest; and pension funds cannot pay adequate pensions in a flat or negative interest-rate world. Low interest rates can result from the different factors that reflect a deep structural imbalance in the consumption/savings/investment system – and that is happening now. It is unlike any previous world, and it could bring stagnation (low interest rates, low inflation, low investment, low productivity gains, and weakened financial institutions). Larry Summers, the former president of Harvard and former secretary of the US Treasury, has recently expressed his fears that a stagnation era could be at hand. Today's low interest rates are not sending the same message as low interest rates did during years 1930–80. It could be that an inverted yield curve may not be enough in today's changed environment to bring a recession, as it has done for the last forty years. Time will now tell.

The current state of economic policy thinking is that it is too narrow and over-focused on the short term. It is too often about what to do now to minimize short-term political and economic pain, and not enough about what has gone wrong and how best to address the problems. In economics, as in medicine, you never get the right cure if you don't have the right diagnosis of what is wrong. I know of no credible policymakers anywhere who really seem to know how we got here or have any diagnosis helpful to a cure. It is hard not to conclude that Western policymakers have for some time now been conducting macroeconomic policy management from an out-of-date diagnosis. Wrong or incomplete diagnosis unavoidably leads to mistakes – sometimes very serious ones – especially if they become cumulative.

The savings and investment structural imbalances are both an effect and a cause. Yesterday's cause becomes today's effect and tomorrow's cause – and so on. The world is more complicated than Reagonomics understood. It is easier said than done for both current and capital flows between countries to fit in with each other comfortably. In his book *The Other Half of Macroeconomics and the Fate of Globalization* (2018), Richard Koo has delved deeply into the related issues of exchange-rates misalignment and what he calls the "pursued phase" of economic development (where manufacturing in advanced economies loses competitiveness to emerging economies that pursue them). Exchange rates determined by capital flows and those determined by current flows will often differ substantially, making macroeconomic policy far less simple than is presumed by the Thatcher/Reagan model.

Three striking developments have taken place since this chapter was initially drafted. First, the acknowledgment at the Jackson Hole meeting of central bankers in August 2019 of how much more limited the reach of monetary policy has been than they thought. Monetary policy needs a deeper, more thoughtful look than the anti-inflation simplicities of the last thirty years. Second, the acknowledgment at the US Business Roundtable that if capitalism is to work, all five corporate stakeholders must be taken into account. Third, the launch by the *Financial Times* in early September 2019 of The New Agenda with Martin Wolf's article on saving capitalism; there he made the point that for the economy to work, it has to work for everybody. I can sum all this new thinking up by asking one simple question: "Where has Henry Ford been when we needed him?" Ford understood from the beginning that he needed his workers to earn enough in order to afford his cars. So, today, capitalism needs to work for all five stakeholders. It is good news that central bankers, the US Business Roundtable, and the *Financial Times* are starting to get that.

Finally, there are two overarching themes that should be mentioned. First, there is a demographic dimension to the savings glut. People are living longer and need savings for a longer period when they are not working. Second, populism, alongside monetary policy that is less effective in the post-Thatcher/Reagan era low/no interest, savings glut world, leaves monetary policy facing a world where what it can do is not enough. Together, they risk loss of central bank political independence. Governments and central bankers will have to find a way to engage in publis discussion of monetary policy limits and direct public discussion to where politically fragile policy changes need to be thought about – not easy in today's populist world.

Further Reading

Mohamed A. El-Erian, *The Only Game in Town* (2016).*

Richard C. Koo, *Escape from Balance Sheet Recession and the* QE *Trap* (2014).

Richard C. Koo, *The Other Half of Macroeconomics and the Fate of Globalization* (2018), especially Chapters 3 and 4.

Richard Koo, "Time for a Plaza II," *The International Economy Magazine*, Summer 2019.

Gillian Tett, "Does Capitalism Need Saving from Itself," *Financial Times*, August 31/September 1, 2019.

Martin Wolf, "Big Read, Global Economy," *Financial Times*, September 18, 2019.

Martin Wolf, *Escaping the Trap: Secular Stagnation, Monetary Policy and Financial Fragility* (SUERF Policy Note, Issue No. 94, September 2019).

* El-Erian identifies central bank overreach as the primary source of current instability. He sees another big collapse within the next three years if reliance on central banks is not reduced. I agree that the central banks overreached. While they did, their monetary policies helped structural imbalances to grow. See my essays in Chapter 10.

A Second Sir John A. Macdonald Moment

Great countries get the shoulders to stand on that they need. They can also fail to respond to what they need. Quebec – and later Canada – did not stand on the shoulders of Champlain (who had the needed inclusion vision) to establish the equality relationships he foresaw between French settlers and First Nations. Fortunately, Canada later had the shoulders to stand on to create a coast-to-coast country despite pressures from a United States bent on manifest destiny and from French/English and Catholic/Protestant divisions. Since then, it has mostly had the shoulders it needed. Business and policymaker shoulders are now urgently needed for a moment of high danger for everything the last six centuries of Western civilization has achieved. In response, we must enlarge our imagination about what is required and what is possible. In a very real sense, this book is an effort to provide one more set of shoulders for the future.

The fall 2019 Canadian federal election is behind us. We have recently elected a government that is likely to face the potentially hardest-to-get-over recession since the 1930s. Canada faces a global economic order that is not very friendly to it, primarily because of disruptive politics in almost every significant country. The federal government needs to start thinking and acting quickly if it is to get some positive anti-recession policy underway before the inevitable recession finally arrives.

Now is the time for a no- or low-carbon national energy corridor; ahead-of-the-curve agricultural product opportunities to respond to the negative impact of climate change on global agricultural supply; and a capital pool tax approach to investment and new businesses.

These policy changes are urgent and they are possible, but they will require shared leadership from both government and business leaders.

Missing in Action

These changes are something for business leaders and policymakers to think about right now, even if action is not yet timely for political reasons. Action may not come until the combination of a global recession, an eroding inclusive global order, and unaddressed made-in-Canada economic challenges (including household-sector and global indebtedness) force it to happen. Canada has borrowed some $750 billion from the rest of the world for consumption since 2006. If action on what Canada's future will need is not yet possible, thinking and discussion are necessary and possible.

Canada's biggest post-election challenges are two – the economy and national unity. (This current unity crisis derives from conflicting views about oil pipelines and is particularly intense in oil-rich, land-locked Alberta, which now appears to be in recession.) There will almost certainly be a US and global recession by the mid-term of the next government. It will likely be severe, though not as severe as in 2008–09. However, it will probably be harder to get out of for both the United States and Canada. In addition, Canada is exposed from a weak current account deficit and its high household-sector debt (higher as a percentage of GDP than similar debt was in the United States in 2008, though less burdensome because of today's much lower interest rates). It has little ammunition to fight a recession. Once the recession hits, it will intensify the Alberta oil sands-based disaffection and anger. The coming economic downturns around the globe will be serious and hard to manage politically, and they will once again put Canada's mutual accommodation to the test.

There are three positive ways forward for Canada: a no- or low-carbon national energy corridor that works for the oil sands and for Quebec's need for Canadian markets to the west for its hydro power; a national policy focus on stronger and broader agriculture supply capacity; and a capital pool incentive in capital gains taxation to enhance Canada's strengthening hi-tech competitiveness.

Canada will need a strong mutually supportive effort by policymakers and business leaders to get the needed new policy framework. For the last decade and a half, both groups have been missing in action. Canada is not well prepared for either the disruptive world Trump has brought or for the unavoidable hard path for it to reverse the past fifteen years of living beyond its means: foreign debt borrowing; household-sector debt; and the loss of global goods competitiveness.

Canada's business leaders and policymakers cannot afford to be missing in action any longer. Canada's transformational economic achievements during the post-war era happened when both groups were working well together over extended periods of time.

Canada's Sir John A. Macdonald Moment

Confederation got underway at the Charlottetown Conference of 1864, and it was completed when the railway reached Vancouver in 1886. Together, against many odds, these two accomplishments created a coast-to-coast country. One hundred and fifty years later Canada has become a different kind of great country for a different kind of world. Canada is at least as well able to prosper in this different world as are other countries – and more so than most.

Those twenty-two years from 1864 to 1886 were Canada's "Sir John A. Macdonald moment." Canada now needs a second such moment. Confederation and a coast-to-coast Canada were the response of British North America to two life-threatening dangers from its US neighbour: a United States sure of its manifest destiny to occupy the whole North American continent; and the political turmoil of the Civil War. Today, Canada has new life-threatening dangers on its own national unity and economic fronts and from a destabilizing world. It will need everyone on deck to get through to the other side.

Different Dangers and Opportunities

Canada today faces comparable external dangers to those in 1867: a go-it-alone United States in political turmoil; a world in the midst of centrifugal (populist) forces within and between countries; and multiple global geopolitical stresses (especially from the United States and China). Canada now has the possibility of, and necessity for, its own second transformational moment. It comes from the potential outcomes of three initiatives: overcoming growing climate change negatives for the oil sands; introducing new agricultural opportunities to get ahead of the negative climate change impact on agricultural supply (see the August 2019 United Nations scientific report); and a capital pool approach to capital gains taxation to boost Canada's increasing hi-tech opportunities in a world where the United States and the United Kingdom are now losing competitive ground for the best people who work in this area.

Canada can no longer rely as much on the integrity of the global trading system for goods and natural resources. It needs an edge to add to its mutual accommodation ways to increase both savings and hi-tech entrepreneurship. Hi-tech and other services are less vulnerable to punitive unilateral trade actions.

A No- or Low-Carbon National Energy Corridor

No matter your scientific views of climate change, the political and societal pressures to do something about it are real; and finding the right political responses to these pressures, and their negatives for Canada's economic and national unity consequences, are essential and urgent. Alberta's current political anger against Ottawa may not be balanced or entirely fair, but it exists. It needs to be heard and acted upon. Canada must avoid not taking Alberta seriously enough, or it may repeat the kind of careless, massively consequential mistake David Cameron, the former UK prime minister, made over calling the Brexit referendum – a mistake that need not have happened. It came about because of a huge misjudgment based on complacency. It would be a mistake for Alberta to separate, as well as for all of Canada. But Alberta could still make that mistake if everyone is not careful and appropriately responsive.

Alberta's disaffection with Canada needs far more attention than many people think it does. But Alberta itself also needs more honest self-assessing. For example, a recent Fraser Institute report finds that Alberta's high-deficit situation is the result of excessive government spending – 18.5 percent more than in British Columbia, it seems. Canada got through its Quebec referendum crisis by the early foresight of three men in particular: Prime Minister Lester Pearson and Ontario and Quebec premiers John Robarts and Daniel Johnson. That same kind of foresight is now needed for Alberta.

A few weeks before the fall federal election, an advertisement in the *Globe and Mail* (August 1, 2019) headed "We have big decisions to make as a country" from Canadian Natural Resources Limited (CNRL), Cenovus Energy Inc., and MEG Energy Corp. sought to put responsible energy decisions at the centre of the upcoming election. The CBC reported just a few days before (July 24, 2019) that CNRL has adopted a long-term aspirational goal of achieving zero net greenhouse gas emissions from its oil sands operations. It includes a statement from Steve Laut, the CNRL executive vice-chairman, which shows the policy path forward. "Instead of relying on planting trees or purchasing carbon offsets to reach the net-zero goal, innovation will be the key. We're trying to get there just using technology and Canadian ingenuity."

Canada's overall response to the CNRL challenge and aspiration should be to create a no- or low-carbon national energy corridor with the support of Ottawa, all the provinces, First Nations, non-ideological environmentalists, and the energy industry. The needed discussions could be launched in 2020. If it were to take as long to get to net zero emissions from the oil sands as it took to get a coast-to-coast Canada, the no- or low-carbon goal could be reached by 2042. It is worth taking the time to get all the way there in the name of national unity. Slightly too high greenhouse gas (GHG) emissions from the oil sands are not fundamental to addressing climate change. Endangering Canadian unity would be a larger global and Canada negative.

While hugely ambitious, this plan is realistic. In 2012, the GHG intensity of CNRL's oil sands oil production was about 100 kilograms per barrel; in 2018, it had declined to 37 kilograms per barrel. Further improvement from one already proven technology and one very likely soon-to-be-proven technology could well bring it down from 100 to zero (or close to) in approximately twenty-two years (2042), and to around 20 GHG intensity within five years (already better than the average GHG intensity for US-produced oil). Laut expects continuous, significant additional GHG reductions through innovation, citing carbon capture and storage, carbon capture and conversion, transformational production technologies, and hundreds of individually small optimizations that cumulatively will be meaningful. "It won't be easy, but there is a lot of technology out there," he said. "It's impressive."

There are two other reasons to see CNRL's no- or low-carbon project as believable. First, CNRL has put its name behind it. It is not a company that would position itself to be humiliated on such a big promise. Second, CNRL is a deeply serious oil sands player (at a time when many are abandoning the oil sands). It has made two large oil sands acquisitions (Shell's oil sands mining assets and Devon Energy's oil sands and heavy oil assets) to become Canada's largest oil sands producer. It is also moving other large capital investments into potential future oil sands projects. CNRL has decided to lead and has put its money where its mouth is.

There are multiple benefits to a no- or low-carbon energy corridor:

- Preserve national unity: No- or low-carbon crudes from the oil sands would see the "both/and" achievement of economic growth and real climate change action, tempering rising separatist sentiment in Alberta without triggering negative sentiment elsewhere.
- Diminish regional tensions:
  o a Quebec/Alberta team effort, with Quebec Hydro exporting green electricity to the rest of Canada, and Alberta exporting lower carbon than most other oil across Canada and to the world; and
  o a BC/Alberta team effort, with green electricity exports from British Columbia to Alberta (displacing higher GHG energy) and market access through British Columbia for Alberta no- or low-carbon oil sands crudes and natural gas.
- Enhanced opportunity for First Nations: No- or low-carbon crudes would support a "both/and" achievement of increased economic opportunity and jobs for First Nations in the oil sands sector while also addressing climate change and other environmental performance issues (e.g., tailings, water, land).
- Achieve a better economic balance: No- or low-carbon oil sands would support a long-term, revitalized energy industry alongside a forward-looking agricultural policy and a strong, globally competitive Canadian hi-tech sector. This hi-tech sector is located primarily in Toronto, Montreal, and Vancouver, and Calgary (Edmonton) would be able to join in as Alberta's energy-based economy stabilized. Canada's future hi-tech and agriculture political/policy story is for the new government to develop.

- Meet Paris Accord commitments: Because the oil sands represent the single largest source of GHG emissions growth in Canada, progress toward no- or low-carbon oil sands crudes would make a huge contribution to meeting or exceeding Canada's Paris commitment (which as things stand right now, Canada would not meet).
- Reduce emissions outside Canada: No- or low-carbon Canadian products could displace higher GHG-intensity products outside Canada, thereby reducing emissions globally. Global carbon emissions from non-Canadian oil range from 20 to 100 kilograms per barrel.
- Strengthen short-term economic growth: A no- or low-carbon energy corridor would enable Canada to achieve the normal recovery/expansion rotation from consumer to export to business investment – something it failed to do after the 2008–09 recession (primarily a failure of Canadian policy). Recently, Canada finally rotated to the current late-in-the-cycle uptick in exports, but it has not yet achieved increased business investment.
- Strengthen long-term economic growth: No- or low-carbon oil sands crudes, by opening markets, improving product pricing, and allowing full recovery of reserves (reducing stranded asset risks for capital and credit providers), would reinvigorate investment and long-term economic growth in Canada.
- Preserve middle-class jobs: Global populism is the result in part of reduced opportunities for less-educated or less-skilled workers to support their families with adequate wages. Canada's natural resource sector jobs are high paying and cannot be outsourced, so they provide a unique strength in minimizing the number of those "left behind."
- Safeguard social programs: No- or low-carbon oil sands provide outsized royalty and tax revenues to Alberta and Canada which help to sustain valued social programs.
- As part of making the no/low carbon national energy work, the federal, Alberta and Saskatchewan governments need to start a huge joint research program aimed at removing more and more carbon from oilsands CO_2 emissions and finding more and more environmentally responsible ways of putting that carbon to good use (see The Guardian's Sunday, October 13, 2019 issue "Firms

ignoring climate crisis will go bankrupt" say Mark Carney,
Governor of the Bank of England (https://www.theguardian.
com/environment/2019/oct/13/firms-ignoring-climate-crisis-
bankrupt-mark-carney-bank-england-governor).

Canada's Opportunities to Expand Its Agricultural Supply Capacity

Canada also urgently needs to begin an aggressive increase in environmentally responsible agricultural supply capacity. The recent
United Nations scientific report states that all countries must rethink
global agricultural supply in response to the dramatic degrading of
land as it interacts with climate change.

Canada will also suffer from this same impact. If we begin now,
however, we can get ahead of the curve and develop more competitive
agricultural products. Moreover, we can seize the advantage climate
change seems likely to have for Canada in expanding our usable
agricultural land. The new government must prioritize research and
development on this critical issue.

A Powerful Capital Pool Tax Boost to Global Competitiveness

Trade in goods has become vulnerable to unilateral actions by the
big trading countries – especially the United States and China. That
danger seems unlikely to lessen anytime soon. Hi tech services are
less vulnerable than goods to arbitrary trade action. Also, the loss of
relative US and UK competitiveness in hi-tech jobs for the best people
gives Canada a new advantage.

Canada can become a serious place from which the United States
can access those best people who are kept out of the country or
who choose not to go there because of current US identity politics.
A capital pool tax approach to capital gains would be a powerful
cumulative boost to Canada's competitive ability to attract the best
people. Every kind of capital gain in financial and business assets
could be treated as part of a pool, the gains in which would be taxed
only if they were withdrawn from the pool or when the taxpayer died
or left Canada (see Chapter 10, essay 3).

The Challenge and the Opportunity

As the new government takes the reins, Canada has the opportunity of a second Sir John A. Macdonald moment, with hugely positive long-term outcomes. In a world that is now not as friendly to Canada as it was only five years ago, we must work together to meet the challenges before us – and succeed. We have the resources, a history of mutual accommodation, and an inclusive society – three huge assets in today's disruptive, every country for itself, world. All we need is the will and the determination to make it happen.

Canada After the October 2019 Federal Election

The Campaign to Nowhere

The October 21, 2019, federal election campaign was weird by normal standards and, by election day, became the campaign to nowhere. The result is a stable minority government, though also a canary-in-the coal mine message on national unity and the economy. Federal governments elected in Canada for the first time with strong majorities usually win a second reduced majority. In this election the previous winner did not get a majority. The last occasion on which that happened was in 1972 (forty-seven years ago), when Pierre Trudeau got only two seats more than the Progressive Conservative leader, Robert Stanfield. Moreover, this federal election is the only one that started in a near dead heat between the two leading parties and saw them each lose ground over the campaign, as third parties gained.

In the next three or four years, Canada could face both a unity crisis originating in Alberta and a hard-to-get-out-of recession. At some point, these challenges will force the Liberals or the Conservatives, or both parties, to find leaders who, through learning or replacement, do better and find more realistic paths forward. Right now, neither party nor their leaders look up to the task. They desperately need two sources of help on the policy front – from the civil service in Ottawa and from business leaders. Time is not on Canada's side to get from where it is to where it needs to be. The divisive nature of the election outcome will likely make these changes even more urgent, and, for this reason, perhaps also more possible. The way forward cannot come without a broad-based public discussion on the country's key substantive challenges. Narrow ideology or party partisanship will not help.

The Voters Always Get It Right

Two parties lost both seats and votes from the last election – the Liberals and the NDP. Nonetheless, the Liberals won what should turn out to be a politically stable minority. The NDP saw its leader achieve a modest personal brand win, as the party brand continued its decline from its 2011 high. The winning Liberals lost ground over the course of their campaign, and the Conservatives ended flat. No party in Canada has ever formed a government before with only 33.1 percent of the vote. The Liberals should have done better, given how weak the Conservative Party and its leader proved to be. The Conservatives should have done better too, given how weak the Liberals and their leader were during the campaign.

The Conservatives needed to move beyond their small shift to a moderated Harper party that remained stuck with tax cuts as the way forward. They lacked an environmental policy in a country where two-thirds of the population believes there is a serious environmental problem to address. They need to find a path to expand beyond their reliable base, and that will require broader political and policy perspectives.

The Liberals began to lose their majority eighteen months into their mandate. Trudeau needed to move beyond the PMO team at the top who won the 2015 federal election and open himself to wider thinking and broader sources of governing advice. He did neither. The Liberals needed to move beyond their misguided, narrow, progressive voter/social advance political theme, which was right for 2015 but wrong for 2019. The backroom Liberals in Ottawa were also too Ontario-centric. Canadians tired of juvenile stunts such as those surrounding the visit to India, as well as the Liberals' self-appointment as post-Obama progressive leaders in a world of rising populism and centrifugal forces – a role that did not fit those emerging forces.

Overall, the election outcome confirmed one long-standing Canadian political reality: it is difficult to change the federal government if the election remains regional and fails to become nationalized.

Canada Has Two Primary Immediate Problems

Canada has emerged from the election with two key immediate problems – the economic challenges ahead and the unity challenge posed by Alberta/Saskatchewan voters who form the base of intensifying Western alienation. These angry voters must be taken seriously. Fortunately for Canada, no significant anti-immigrant voting emerged, thanks to Canadians in general and to Stephen Harper's earlier policies – most of the anti-immigrant sentiment was in his party, and he shut it down. However, increasing care will be necessary. Quebec has recently shown that the economic need for immigrants is not yet by itself enough to change attitudes.

The resurgence of Quebec's Bloc Québécois did not take the form of a dangerous populism or a return to separatism or sovereignty. Rather, it reflects a long-standing, though reduced, Quebec identity/survival anxiety challenge in the context of a federal election campaign where neither of the two main parties or their leaders offered enough in the eyes of many Quebeckers. The last unity crisis came out of Quebec, when Canada faced the double challenge of Quebec separatism and Western alienation. As of now, the rise of the Bloc Québécois is not existentially threatening. It may best be seen as a moderate – almost comfortable – Quebec form of identity populism, without much populism and with more "look out for Quebec" nationalism. Looking ahead from 2019, the Bloc will continue to be important until Quebec decides it wants to have a stronger voice within the federal government.

Do the Parties and Their Leaders Get It?

Only the Bloc Québécois and its leader, Yves-François Blanchet, gained real substantive ground over the campaign. Blanchet is also the only leader who seems to understand what the election outcome means for him and his party. He had the easiest task of any leader, needing only to align himself with the popular Quebec premier, who has recently won the provincial election and has inherited the strongest Quebec economy and provincial fiscal position in some fifty years. It is far from clear, however, whether the Liberals or the Conservatives comprehend what the voters have just told them or whether their leaders and parties have what it takes to change themselves to meet the difficult demands of the coming decade.

NDP leader Jagmeet Singh did well for reasons not relevant to the policies Canada needs. During the campaign he turned out to be a more empathetic leader than either of his two main opponents. But he was not judged by the standards applicable to a potential prime minister, which was not his role. If he had held serious prospects, his calls for the impeachment of President Donald Trump and for a provincial veto of national projects would have totally disqualified him. In a campaign where, outside Quebec, there was so little cause for joy, he was a small bright spot.

In the rest of Canada, the future lies with the Liberals and Conservatives, depending on which one figures out first how to address the two emerging big worries Canada is about to face: a hard-to-get-out-of recession in a hard-to-navigate global economy; and how to respond to the economics and federal politics of the resurgence of strong Western Canadian alienation.

What Canada Needs

Canada must move immediately to initiate the wide discourse it needs to face the regional and economic problems of a seriously, but not yet deeply, divided country. Broad-based public discussion on the issues of the future is the first order of business, followed by partisan action. The government should start with energy, agricultural, and hi-tech entrepreneurship (see Epilogue); then move on to Canada's economic prospects in the current global order – one that is the least favourable to Canada since 1945; and gradually introduce a more globally competitive and domestically fair tax system. Right now, action on oil and on Alberta are both urgent. Agriculture is also critical, to get out of range of Chinese hostage-taking and the arbitrary restrictions that are now badly hurting this sector.

The Alberta and Saskatchewan disaffection with the rest of Canada needs to be taken seriously by all Canadians. These two provinces can also help their cause by reflecting on the contribution of past energy company and Alberta government failures to their current discontent. Anger can be a good goad to action, but it is nearly always a bad guide to action. This reflection should take into account the two big global forces that have nothing to do with Canada's shortcomings. First, the market forces that may drive down the level of new oil investment and, at some point, the price of oil. Second, the widespread political and public belief that climate change is, over time, bringing big risks to the planet and that it has human causes.

Alberta and the oil industry have problems with Canadian energy policy. But Canada is not the only problem country. No substantial new pipeline has yet been approved in the United States under the Trump administration. There will also be problems for Alberta and oil beyond Canada's shortcomings, as the Paris Climate Accord interacts with oil investment and other market forces. Inevitably, social and political pressure to implement policies that forcefully address the threat of climate change will become more intense globally. Policies will be implemented at national, regional, and local levels around the world as politicians find they need to be part of the perceived solution.

At the same time, technological advances will both enable and force emissions reductions by changing the relative economics of old fossil-fuel systems vs new energy systems to favour the latter. Together, these forces will likely produce a tipping point in the demand for oil that requires higher cost/higher greenhouse gas (GHG) production abilities – one that chills new investment at the same time as volumes and prices decline. A similar tale is now playing out for coal.

The fact that central banks, financial supervisors, securities regulators, and institutional investors are now focused on addressing this risk speaks to how real it is. In addition, oil sands executives are setting much more ambitious environmental goals. Clearly, this change will happen regardless of the policies adopted in Canada. Climate change is a global problem, and oil is a global commodity, so there will be no escaping decarbonization when it comes. Alberta urgently needs an economic transition strategy that balances progressive decarbonization with new economic ways forward. That means driving innovation in the oil sands to reduce costs and GHG emissions and to develop non-combustion uses for its bitumen. In other words, Alberta needs to effectively extend the sector's runway while investing progressively to diversify and replace oil and gas as the bedrock of its economy. This transition will be hard and slow. With 2050 as the consensus target date for achieving net zero global

GHG emissions, aggressive early action is the safest course. Canada as a whole needs to help.

The Good News

The election brought some good news. First, Canadians have a healthy political realism. They lacked confidence in both major parties contending for government, so they sent the messages those parties needed even as they also got a stable minority government. In summing up his election documentary on the CBC, Peter Mansbridge said that the voters were less concerned with their own immediate needs than with how best to cope with the larger dangerous threats to the world and to the country. Later, he told me privately that Canadians have a knack for moving on. The federal election is over and Canadian voters, he says, are now looking forward and expecting their politicians to do the same. Canada remains more reality and less ideology based than the United States.

The Harper/Justin Trudeau way of doing politics has not delivered the shared vision, ideas, and projects that are the only way to move beyond today's politically divided country. Only more broad discussions around shared ways forward can hope to work. Harper took progressive out of progressive Conservatives, and Justin Trudeau took conservative out of conservative Liberals. Whichever party first takes on this task successfully will become the dominant one in the years ahead. As one example, according to a recent Environics Research report in the *Globe and Mail*, Canadian public opinion is ready for both the Trans-Mountain Pipeline and an energy corridor.

Paul Volcker on Canada's
Mutual Accommodation

Over a span of seventy-five years or so, from childhood vacations through years of official relationships and intellectual debate, I can reasonably claim acquaintance with Canada. One thing I know is that our countries are quite different in size, in geopolitical aspirations, and in some cultural instincts.

I also know that the idea instilled in my youth of a unique and constructive American role in the larger world underlay all my education and years in public service.

Now, I regret to say, internal divisiveness, angry ideological differences, huge and growing disparities in wealth, and more visibly eroding infrastructure are undercutting our presumption of a society to be emulated – what has been termed our "soft power."

For all of our vaunted capacity for innovation, the outlook for strong economic growth and financial order has come into question. We spend enormous amounts on the military and on intelligence, but it's really hard to know how to bring those resources constructively to bear.

I confess, I look toward Canada with a certain envy these days. Take my own specialty. As you know, I have had for decades a certain responsibility for, and a continuing interest in, American financial performance and regulatory policies. Unfortunately, the truth is that our vaunted system let us down badly, to the point a

Paul Volcker was chair of the Federal Reserve from 1979 to 1987. This extract is from a talk he gave at the University of Toronto, May 2015. He died in December 2019. He was the greatest man I have known.

few years ago of requiring massive public support to fend off deep-seated recession.

From my observation, the Canadian financial world seems to have weathered the international financial crisis with relative equanimity. That hasn't gone unnoticed – the very idea of a Canadian central banker being invited to take over the Bank of England, the storied mother of all central banks, is eloquent evidence of recognition and respect.

A good Canadian friend of mine (I still have some, despite hearing complaints here about the so-called Volcker rule) makes a point of extolling what he sees as the essential point of Canadian history and its governance; he calls it a capacity for "mutual accommodation."

Those are not exactly thrilling words, stirring the blood, inspiring fervent patriotic hymns, or hailing military victories. You haven't found it necessary to fight a war of independence or a civil war. When tensions arose, your leaders didn't need to claim manifest destiny or foster delusions that the American way of life was somehow not only pre-eminent but a model for the world. For you, the vast expanse of Canada has been challenge enough.

The point is that what has happened here is truly remarkable and has lessons for others. The Canadian nation, built out of different national instincts and cultural traditions, whether Indigenous or from abroad, has in the end held together. The narrow band of population stretched over 3,000 miles of difficult landscape no longer seems so subject to centrifugal forces. Remarkably, a large influx of immigrants has not only been absorbed, but they seem to have added life and vitality. My own observation is that this city of Toronto has itself become a true international city, in more than size, with all the cultural variety, energy, and outlook that implies.

Now, I didn't come here simply to praise you. I'm not about to give up my American citizenship. I don't doubt the inherent vigour and potential of either the American economy or our constitutional system. I don't see any alternative capacity to provide a needed element of constructive leadership in a troubled world. But I am also very aware that the world of 2015 is not the world in which I grew up, a world in which the capacity of the great democracies to work together with American leadership in a common cause seemed to be well understood.

Today we need some of the Canadian genius of mutual accommodation, of a shared order. The ability of North America – Mexico included – to work together in the common interest has been well demonstrated.

Now, a critically important thought: Can we not extend that degree of harmony and stretch it across the Pacific? Can we reason together to deal with the common concerns about climate change? And, at the same time, can we work together to make sure that a radicalized Middle East does not become a destructive force economically or politically?

I stand here before a large Faculty of Law. These days, eight centuries after signing the Magna Carta, we are reminded that it is indeed dedication to the Rule of Law that provides the basis for strong and open democratic societies.

And the Law School is joined here by the much newer Munk School of Global Affairs. Its presence is a simple recognition of the fact that, these days, lasting success must be global success.

Welcome to the challenge, graduates. We need your energy, your professional commitment, and that good sense of mutual accommodation.

I add only one bit of special pleading. Some of you graduating here today, I feel certain, are from the United States. Come home! We need your perspective, we need your commitment, we need some of that sense of accommodation that has marked Canadian life.

Appendices

Four Mutual Accommodation Overviews

1. MUTUAL ACCOMMODATION AS SEEN IN 2019[*]

As Alfred North Whitehead put it, narrowness is the basis of all achievement. But it also helps to stand back from things to get a better and fuller look. The whole world is in the midst of vast, interconnected changes; the West is in its biggest transition since the Middle Ages, and China post-Deng Xiaoping is also entering a new era.

I have for a long time used the idea of eras, which start a new direction with strong momentum and override everything in their way. The momentum finally begins to weaken as the counterforces it provokes strengthen. This dynamic is coming to a head in the West (simultaneously and separately in the United Kingdom, the European Union, and the United States). It is coming to a different head in China, which has been on its own separate era tracks over the last one hundred years. Each of the four is coming out of what have been good eras. For the first time in history, each will have to accommodate the new momentum and direction eras of the others as well their own. Managing the combination of the unprecedented separateness and interconnectedness of everything makes what is going on unique in the scale and complexity of the emerging challenges.

---

* Extract from the *Might Nature Be Canadian?* booklet, 2019, by W.A. Macdonald.

The biggest questions for the future remain the same as they have since the Brexit referendum and the election of Donald Trump as US president. The postwar global order was built and led by the United States – by broadening the inclusive order at home and abroad, and by containing what could not yet be included. The broadening has now stalled within and between countries, and the containing is weakening. Will a new order be shaped under some form of co-leadership by the United States and China? Or will the centrifugal forces within the West and between the West and the rest of the world continue to gain ground, undermining the stability on which relative global peace and prosperity have rested since 1945? The heart of the challenge can be seen in the deepening and spreading controversies about Huawei Technologies Co. Ltd. China wants for Huawei in the West what it will never grant to Western companies in China.

The geopolitical world has grown scarier. In May 2018 Paul Volcker, discussing his upcoming memoir in the *New York Times*, saw "a hell of a mess in every direction." The primary financial and economic questions are two: How and when the current US and global expansions will end (likely 2020–22), and how can the United States and the world act to recover. A good global economic future needs better politics and policy management than it now has from both the West and other major powers. It will also need stronger technological advances and the timely spread of a capacity for mutual accommodation.

The two – technology and mutual accommodation – must increasingly go hand in hand. Public expectations of economic expansion in both the West and the non-West have been set by strong rates of past productivity growth and a relatively peaceful, stable world. Both are under threat from within and beyond the West. The best way forward will be long, slow, and stressful. But it will be better than the alternative.

The world will face several other great challenges over the next decade:

- We must avoid war with North Korea, in the Middle East, and in Eastern Europe.
- We need to find minimum mutual accommodation among the four great powers: the United States, China, Europe, and Russia (to which India may soon be added).

- We must use and manage sanctions and higher tariffs as the new economic and political disciplines. Collaboration is the key to their effectiveness. Because of greater underlying Western economic strengths, US-led collective action could be a major advantage for the West.
- We must rebalance demand and supply among our economies for the longer term in a way that avoids trade wars. China, the European Union (especially Germany), and Japan are the biggest "imbalance" culprits today. The world's central economic challenge is to find a better structural economic balance between economies and among consumption, savings, and investment. Changing structure is painful and politically difficult; but better balance between the big economies has become essential.
- We must find a solution to the growing economic and political inequality within countries.
- We must realize that technology (especially artificial intelligence) and workplace changes driven by globalization will reinforce the identity challenges from rising anxieties around language and cultural differences.

Overall, the next five years will likely look dramatically different from the past five years. The new visions, ideas, and projects needed are as yet nowhere in sight.

Here's my view of where Canada stands right now. For the first time in history, we have come to a moment of global transition. It began when the West moved on from the Middle Ages to the Renaissance. It has only recently become fully global with the rise of China. The past six centuries have seen four better ways for humans to go about doing things: freedom, science, mutual accommodation, and compassion. But the first two have overwhelmed the second two, even though mutual accommodation and compassion represent a better approach for containing the overreach of freedom and science. Their relative weakness has resulted in the dangerous centrifugal imbalances that have emerged in the Western world of the twenty-first century.

A better balance of the four better ways of going about things has become urgent, if the world of the future is to be bearable. Otherwise, it will be dominated again by force and violence, and the achievements of civilization we have seen since the end of the Middle Ages will recede or disappear.

Three big changes are happening in Canada amid the vast transformational forces that are affecting the world right now. First, Canada is emerging as a different kind of great country for a different kind of world. Second, Toronto is on a path to becoming one of the great global cities of the next fifty years. Third, Canada has always been dependent on others – first, the United Kingdom and then the United States. Canada remains intertwined with the rest of the world, but it has never been more on its own. It is challenged by both the United States and China at the same time in ways that will bring real costs and challenges to the Canadian economy. If Canada is to remain Canada, it will have no choice but to stand up for who it is and incur the costs. It has done so before. We know from history that Canadians can and will do what they have to, once they realize that they must choose. The next five years will provide Canada's next big test.

A longtime friend, wise and broadly experienced in government and policy, looked at my two essays on Indigenous peoples and on Toronto. We have shared views on a broad range of subjects over some forty years. He asked if I was being too optimistic. I don't think so. You can be realistically optimistic about hard challenges. His question, however, made me realize that both these positive Canada stories – central to its future – need to be viewed in the broader context of what is currently going on in the world.

Yes, I am optimistic about the improving approach to seeing and co-operating with Indigenous peoples, just as I am about the path Toronto is forging toward a transformed competitive global future. Montreal and Vancouver are also changing along similar positive lines in terms of inclusiveness and technology. None of these transformations will be easy or assured. Still, they are happening today after a long fifty-five-year period during which Canada confronted and overcame strong existential and identity threats – threats that Europe and the United States are beginning to face and that they may or may not overcome.

If the rest of the world goes badly wrong, things will also become much harder for Canada. This is so despite its array of unmatched strengths: water, vast land, three oceans, mineral and energy resources, agriculture, and a still relatively safe (if no longer so good) neighbourhood. Climate change will bring with it more usable land for Canada. The continued rise in global population will make these multiple positives a magnet for immigration – an influx of people that could be extremely challenging in its scale and from the accompanying pressures from outside and within the country. Canada has the strengths needed for the future. Right now, it is not using many of those strengths well enough.

Global economic stresses intensified in the 1980s as President Ronald Reagan launched the United States on an economy-wide debt spree that included not only government but the business and household sectors as well. The US economic, financial, and geopolitical overreach that started with Reagan was followed more than two decades later by the overreach of China's global economic surge in 2005. Together, they created the worldwide global and domestic economic, financial, and political imbalances that led, first, to the post–Lehman Brothers crises and then to today's populism and centrifugal forces in the West: Brexit, followed by the election of Donald Trump, and resurgent nationalisms across Europe. Under Trump, the United States is again headed into high levels of debt, largely limited so far to the federal government but also growing elsewhere.

The United States got an excessive and unsustainable fiscal stimulus boost from the Trump tax cuts and spending increases. It is now getting a fuller boost from low-priced commodities and oil. It may be about to get a China-US trade-deal boost on the export front. Inflation is under control, and the US dollar is stronger. Together, these benefits may further extend the current, already long economic expansion. But when the expansion ends, the resulting contraction could prove harder to get out of than in 2008–9.

––––––––––––––––––

The driving forces of freedom and science in the six centuries since the Middle Ages have now reached the whole world, leading to a new moment of huge transformation akin, perhaps, to the Renaissance. The last huge transformative moment was Western (European). Today's huge moment is global. This scale of change creates unavoidable risks for everyone, but it is also a time of great opportunity. The counterforces to extreme bad outcomes are three: an intertwined world; stronger economic underpinnings; and the fact that half the global population is now middle class, with a big stake in outcomes. The world has a lot to work with. Will it have the will and the skill to use it well?

Canada is arguably the best place to be today, despite the pressing challenges of competitiveness and living within its means. Fortunately, Canada's net country and household-sector debt may just be starting to improve somewhat (its apparently strong economic numbers may not be as sustainably strong as they look). The slight decline in Canadian consumption is likely the result of an expected Bank of Canada path toward higher interest rates, reinforced by ongoing, mostly Trump-driven anxiety about the future of the Canadian economy. This may well get worse with the combined impact of lower oil prices and the growing oil price gap, along with the shutdown of the General Motors plant in Oshawa, Ont. Canada's current account deficit should also begin to decline as domestic consumption moderates (a good thing) and a long-awaited pickup in US-bound export volumes finally arrives. The improvement in the current account deficit last summer was deceptive, because it reflected a big drop in imports – one that could soon be reversed.

Canada's mutual accommodation ways are desperately needed by the world – most urgently by the United States and China. Canada has a limited but still useful international role to play in its own self-interest. Two things are needed. First, a better balance can be achieved by spreading mutual accommodation and compassion to contain the imbalances caused by the dominance of freedom and science/technology that could threaten our civilization. Second, countries that are normally attached to force at home and abroad need to discover the practical benefits for them of mutual accommodation, the rule of law, and rules-based relationships.

The immediate economic challenges are more likely to flow not from trade wars but from new financial and/or economic crises in 2020–22. These may prove difficult to overcome because of the current US federal debt surge and too-much-for-too-long US monetary stimulus. Belatedly, US monetary stimulus appeared to be on a steady reduction path, first stalled and now being reversed. The Federal

Reserve always leans away from hurting the stock market too much. It has yet, however, to reach positive interest rates after inflation. If this rising trade protectionism continues, it will become more detrimental over time for both the global economy and global peace. It is not too late to manage it better.

The looming struggles between China and the United States and other Western nations will be more and more over global leadership in the technologies of the future. A better structurally balanced global economy is needed to get bearable outcomes for everyone. The world needs the United States and China to see that the way forward is twofold. Job one is to work together for a stable global economic and geopolitical order. Job two is to compete against each other within that order for whatever relative economic ascendancy they can achieve. A balanced outcome over time would threaten neither country. Imbalances that persist could become dangerous for both. It is vital for the whole world – including the two superpowers themselves – that such a rivalry take place within a mutually achieved global order that is fundamentally stable and minimally contained. China faces middle-income and demographic growth challenges that the West has largely moved beyond. These issues could prove to be China's deepest and most long lasting economic challenges.

The West, led by the United States, retains substantial advantages over China in terms of military prowess, technology, economic freedom, and mutual accommodation ways and alliances. These advantages are weakening in the post-Trump, post-Brexit world. Their decline is due more to what the United States and Europe are doing to themselves than to increasing Chinese strengths, though these strengths are large and real. Until now, China's rise has been largely on its own terms. Now its feet are being held more to the fire. China is in self-weakening overreach, just as the United States under Trump is in self-weakening underreach. Overreach led to the collapse of the Soviet Union. US overreach led to the post-2008 economic and financial crisis. China is overreaching much earlier in its ascendancy than the United States did.

Will it be China or the United States that finally gets its reach closer to the demands and limits of reality? Or will they get there more or less at the same time? Or will they both fail? China overdid it in 2005, with its huge global export surge. It was predictable that this surge, unless moderated, would negatively affect US politics for longer-term Chinese interests. On my visit to China in 2010, I predicted this outcome in both Shanghai and Beijing. At an earlier 2009 post–Lehman Brothers symposium in Toronto, I also said there was a real risk that the postwar inclusive global economic and financial order would not be sustainable, in part because China's export surge was bad for both the United States and China. With the benefits of hindsight, both predictions have since had a considerable measure of validation.

Before President Xi Jinping, China was primarily seen by most in the West as a market or a low-cost production opportunity. It was regarded by many as a candidate over time for a Western-style naively global political and economic order. The West saw its own ways as the global wave of the future. Now China is seen by ever more countries as using its growing economic clout coercively and going too far in stealing Western technology. A US-China mutual accommodation, what the world needs most, looks less probable than it seemed two or three years ago, before Brexit, Trump, and Xi. But it is not impossible. It is not helping, however, that the same economic imbalances – excessive demand in the United States and insufficient demand in China – which led to the post–Lehman crises are growing again as the current economic expansion moves toward its end.

Both China and the United States face huge challenges in domestic economic management and in related domestic political evolution and stability. The United States already faces an identity challenge. It could also face an existential political challenge in its unresolved gender and patriarchy issues. Canadian pollster and author Michael Adams says that only 23 percent of Canadians think men should dominate the family, but 50 percent of Americans hold that belief; a century ago, the statistic for both countries was 95 per cent. The challenge of US patriarchy could become today's equivalent of the existential crisis brought on by slavery and the Civil War – still far from likely but also far from impossible. The US DNA has a lot of extremism in it.

China has no such existential or identity problems. It must nonetheless find a political way of dealing with its vastly changed post-Mao political reality at home and its internal structural economic growth challenges. Both China and the United States require a minimum level of global economic and political stability to best address their domestic political challenges. They cannot get there by themselves. Each will have to coexist with the other – and that will be best done with a large measure of co-operation.

The recent important book by Harvard Kennedy School professor Graham Allison, *Destined for War: Can America and China Escape Thucydides's Trap?* (2017), investigates the failure of the established power, Sparta, to cope with the rising power, Athens. Two huge differences between today's world and the worlds in which Sparta (in the fifth century BC) and Germany (1914–45) were new rising powers provide grounds for hope. First, the United States, despite its Trump-inflicted self-harm, is on the whole still relatively stronger than China, though that advantage cannot be guaranteed forever. Second, the world is simply too intertwined for either the United States or China to separate from it at an acceptable cost. The late Quebec premier Robert Bourassa privately told a small group some thirty years ago, at the height of Canada's separatist crisis: "Even if Quebec voted to separate, it could not do so, because we are too intertwined." One-country separatism is no more viable today than Quebec separatism was then.

Accepting the reality of "intertwined" is the path forward for both China and the United States. Whoever most accepts that reality in practice will do best over both the short and the long haul. As never before in its history, Canada will have to fit its own challenges into the much greater ones facing the external world. No country will prove big or strong enough to avoid doing the same to varying degrees. Countries that are disunited politically and socio-culturally will almost certainly fail.

The world that emerged from the multiple horrors of the 1914–45 era introduced new ideas, visions, and projects that led to a much more prosperous and peaceful era. The direction and momentum of that era are no longer as strong as they once were. The centrifugal counterforces have become stronger. You cannot fight something with nothing. The world – and Canada – once again needs new visions, ideas, and projects.

But the time to make them happen is rapidly shortening, and as many countries as possible need to act decisively and quickly. Unfortunately, in human history, big foresight-based action is rarely forthcoming when it is needed. Too often, it takes ultimately unbearable horror stories to force the new ways forward – as in the 1914–45 years and in the pre-1815 Napoleonic era. The task of the post-2018 world is to find a less costly way forward to a better world. Great power dominance that works solely for the great powers should no longer be conceivable as the best way forward to even the most super of superpowers. The world has a lot to work with. How well it will do remains uncertain.

2. MUTUAL ACCOMMODATION AS SEEN IN 2018 *

It is not only timely for Canadians to discuss and understand the Canadian difference in relation to diversity and identity but it is important for others to understand. My pilgrimage on the "Canadian difference" path started in early 2011 – not quite seven years ago. It began with the idea of "Canada, the Unknown Country," whose only shared story seemed to be its drive and capacity for mutual accommodation. Bill Innes and I launched the Canadian Difference project with Trent University around the time of the November 2014 special meeting of Canadian history academics in Charlottetown, PEI, in November 2014. Tom Symons and later Chris Dummitt were indispensable in putting Trent University at the heart of the project.

---

* Extract from a speech by W.A. Macdonald delivered at the symposium *The Canadian Difference: Dialogues in Diversity* at Trent University, Peterborough, Ontario, December 9, 2017.

My first essays for the *Globe and Mail* on mutual accommodation started in June 2015 and now total some 90,000 words – more than John Stuart Mill used in his celebrated 50,000-word essay *On Liberty*. The Canadian difference most relevant to the future of Canada and the world is the mutual accommodation foundation of its identity and diversity.

The diversity of today's world is inescapable. It requires never-ending ongoing accommodations on a scale without historical precedent. The big question is whether the needed accommodations will be mutual or forced. Mutual accommodation strength is best alongside the strengths from the other three better ways humans have found for going about things – freedom, science and knowledge, and compassion. Each of these better ways is inexhaustible. They each rest more on persuasion than force. How do people feel safe and know who they are and should be in a world that is no longer narrowly bounded as it once was?

My first mutual accommodation line of thought came from two ideas in the early nineties. Idea one was a response to the feelings of some English Canadians at the time of the second Quebec independence referendum that Canada needed a stronger sense of identity. My response was that, in a world in which all identities are partial, if one could live without a firm identity, that made one stronger. I think this description is starting to play out.

Idea two came around the same time, when some Canadians used to pride themselves on our greater tolerance. I do not favour intolerance, but I do not like the implications of a tolerance that puts oneself in a higher position than others by tolerating something about them. Also, I was far from sure that Canadians were more tolerant than others. Still, I did believe that Canada had a stronger drive toward mutual accommodation than any other country. Indeed, I saw a key difference between Canadians and Americans: a Canada with the strongest drive toward mutual accommodation of any country, and a United States with one of the strongest drives toward division.

One of the ways we better understand ourselves is to better understand others by comparison, and vice versa. Ken Dryden's 2000 Charles R. Bronfman lecture, "Finding a Way: Legacy for the Past; Recipe for the Future," compared Canada's number one sport, hockey, with America's number one sport, football, and its earlier

number one, baseball. The bottom line was that the shift from baseball to football required stronger central control. It was the opposite
of hockey. Once the puck is dropped in hockey, there is chaos – the
opposite of control. The only choice is to do what it takes. Dryden
believes Canada's choice to do that has shaped today's country.
Canadians have mostly done what it takes for diverse people to live
together in mutual accommodation.

Canada has found the more one can include others' identity
strengths, the stronger one's own can become. A country like the
United States, driven more and more by ideology – sometimes mas-
querading for a narrow identity – finds compromise and mutual
accommodation very difficult. Ideology has two fatal problems –
it excludes too much reality, and it divides people. Ideas are good
because they are open to other ones. Ideology is more closed.

Identity and culture are the new driving forces of the twenty-first
century. Canada has the strength of being able to live without a firm
identity in a world when all identities are incomplete. It has a vast
land that it can call home and still include a diversity of newcomers.

Context mattered less when things were stable and changed slowly.
Twenty years ago I told a Japan Society conference in Toronto that
we had been witnessing the emergence of a New World brought by
globalization, growing consumer dominance, and rapid technological change – a prediction even more true today. We have moved from
many different separate worlds into a single global world and from a
producer-dominant society to an increasingly consumer-dominant one.

Culture and identity are today's emerging driving forces. Culture
affects how we go about things – how we face birth and death, personal conflict and business and political challenges, and the way we
live and dream. Confidence in our own culture and identity makes
moving forward easier. Identity gives us the sense of who we are: of
borders, places, and feelings that separate us from others. Difference
is central to identity, but it can lead to fearfulness of others' differences. The challenge is to see different identities as potential sources
of strength, not threats. Strong identity needs a culture that can live
and work with others who are different.

Right now, a strong sense of identity is giving Canada an advantage
compared with both the United States and Europe. Canada used to
look to Europe and the United States for its way forward, but now

each of them needs to look to Canada as part of their way forward. For some reason, Canada often goes through things before others do. Most recently, Canada has gone through existential and identity crises which, to different degrees, the United States, the United Kingdom, and Europe are now going through.

Culture and identity always matter. They change slowly, for better and for worse. Culture and identity aspirations and anxieties affect the dominant military, political, and economic forces. The choice between inclusive and exclusive identities – and the possibility of having both – has become central to all our futures.

We live in two worlds at the same time – inner and outer. Sometimes one dominates but, over time, they are best balanced. Humans are always in search of a home. The Old Testament story about Adam and Eve being pushed out of their Garden of Eden home by God can be seen as making refugees of us all. Today, the world is dominated by the growing number of desperate people looking for safe places to go. The Australian TV drama *A Place to Call Home* is about searching for every kind of home where the characters can feel safe – both their outer physical space and their inner space where people can be most themselves.

The emergence of a single, inclusive global order means people must now get along as never before. Not all societal or organizational cultures have been equal in terms of finding mutual accommodation ways to successfully pursue both individual and group goals. Cultures with this ability have an advantage. Lasting strength will increasingly come less from winning and putting oneself first, and more from making things work for everyone involved. The New World requires identity strengths that are enhanced by room for other identities. Those who use their own strengths to get others to follow them will be the best leaders for the kind of new world we are entering.

Since the Renaissance, the main Western driving forces have been centrifugal – horizontal rather than vertical, more separate than connected. Horizontal forces – the United States is the best example – are indifferent to individuals. They respond to the need for equal treatment for everyone. Vertical structures like Japan, even overly restrictive ones, can give individuals a sense of having a place – a home and of being cared for by others. Politics, societies, and cultures each need the right balance between horizontal and vertical forces.

Canada today may well have a lot of that balance – a balance that is dynamic and can be lost.

Canada's culture and identity strengths are Western. Canada is competitive on freedom, science and knowledge, and compassion. It has the advantage on mutual accommodation, where it also has unfinished business with its Indigenous people from the past and its Muslims looking ahead. All sides will have to help. It is hard to think of anything the post-2017 world would benefit from more than the steady spread of mutual accommodation strengths and skills throughout the world.

It is difficult to feel hopeful about our US neighbour, whose leader does not stand against the serial sexual abuse of women or white supremacists and is actively stoking anti-Muslim fears in similar ways to what Hitler did with the Jews. It is hard to feel optimistic, but not impossible, because strong resistance is starting to come from within the US system. The Trump United States of 2017 has been on a global separatist kick whose outcomes and potential damage remain uncertain. On the Muslim front, it is playing with genocide fire.

The world has changed and our closest neighbour is not who it has been for most of the last one hundred years. The United States is still a good neighbour, but is becoming less and less reliable and an increasing threat to continental and global stability. The question for Canada – and for a too self-absorbed world – is whether Canada can become the kind of great country the new emerging world needs.

No one thing is ever everything. Nothing is ever only one thing. Canada's first great moment came 150 years ago. Words – persuasion, not force – and a railway created a coast-to-coast country that has become a different kind of great country for an emerging very different kind of world. Canada has also found an "asymmetrical equivalence" way of holding a huge and diverse country together. Over time the total Canadian societal system delivers what most people want. Canada today is basically a largely sane and balanced country in which economic and social advance go hand in hand.

This is the post-1945 Canada that most Canadians have come to love. The US-led post-war global order will no longer work if the United States is not able to move with China – a vastly different kind of country – to a less centralized, more asymmetrical leadership approach. The United States has more of the right kind of leaders for the new world. But too big a gap is still to be bridged between them and too many everyday fellow-Americans who do not understand how important it is to the United States to work together with other countries.

Three noted Canadian historians took a look at an early version of my initial paper on mutual accommodation. One dismissed the mutual accommodation perspective out of hand. Another helped me a lot, but was worried that a mutual accommodation narrative for Canada would run against his idea – which I share – that it is better for countries not to have a single story. Indeed, the genius of a mutual accommodation narrative is its open-ended nature, so there can never be only one story. Mutual accommodation leaves more than enough room for separate narratives. Its inherent nature is inexhaustibility. The third historian was cryptic and not given to ready praise. So I loved his comment, "I think you are onto something."

Historians matter. So do business leaders. Even if no historians liked "mutual accommodation" (many in fact do), I would still like it because, over a long business and professional life, I have often seen its power in getting the truly big and hard things done. Two Canadian CEOs of two different global professional organizations in Canada are today not only the Canadian heads of their firms but responsible for the whole Western hemisphere other than the United States. Another Canadian senior business leader (who got his start in Canada, and subsequently served as the Japan CEO of his US-headquartered multinational and became the director of its global research and development arm located in the United States), says that he got his job because of his Canadian mutual accommodation skills. It can help to be a Canadian in business where working successfully with different cultures is more and more valuable in a globalized business world.

I saw mutual accommodation most powerfully at work in the business world at the Honda Motor Company. It never bought into the Ronald Reagan/Margaret Thatcher era, when "shareholder value" was the primary driver of a company. Honda believed a broader set of standards were needed to include all stakeholders, not just investors. That meant not just shareholders, but suppliers, consumers, workers, and communities.

I have two stories to illustrate this point. Mr. Kawamoto, the CEO of Honda in Tokyo, spoke at the Canadian Club of Toronto at the time of Honda's opening of its second assembly plant in Alliston, Ontario. He told the story of Honda wanting to establish a plant in Brazil and how the Brazilian government wanted Honda to put the factory in the Amazon valley. Honda found that the workers would be their first assembly-plant workforce anywhere that could not read an operator's manual. The company found a way to go forward, without diminishing a single standard necessary for the highest performance for all its stakeholders. Honda started from where the Amazon workforce were and found a way to enable them to meet what Honda required – the highest and best kind of win-win mutual accommodation.

A second story came out of a small dinner in Tokyo on my way from Singapore back to Toronto. All the top global Honda management was present, except the newly elected president and CEO. They apologized for his absence. He was away showing Japan's Crown Prince and Princess an assembly plant in Kyushu province. I remarked they had no doubt seen all the assembly plants they would ever want to see. Not like this one, I was told. It was a plant initiated by Mr. Honda so that 70 percent of the workers who ran it could be handicapped.

Canada has two big jobs. First, to broaden its role in the world (a much harder challenge since the Trump/US-China struggle has gone viral). Second, to strengthen its economy for an unsettled world in the future where neither the United States nor China will be easy to work with. Canada should think about deploying more diplomats for a world that is in desperate need of them and has too few to do what will be needed. Moreover, Canada has one of the best special forces in the world for tackling specific high-risk military challenges. It should increase this force because the world needs more of them.

The biggest issue for the next twenty to thirty years is how much internationalism, how much nationalism there will be, and how many will co-exist. That will largely depend on what the United States and China choose to do. If they can find a way to work together for mutual advantage, it will make them the leaders of a new, shared stable order.

It will likely be some time before Trump, a Brexit Europe, and a China feeling stronger than ever externally, and more vulnerable internally than it has been for some two decades, are able to come together. China will do best if it seizes the opportunity US withdrawal from global overreach affords it in ways that work globally and do not risk its internal stability. For several decades, the United States has overreached externally and underreached domestically. This imbalance is now being changed by US domestic politics.

Canada is a different kind of country. Its mutual accommodation – albeit flawed, as all great nations and all great national qualities always are – makes it a great country. In the sixteenth century and beyond, small England took liberty to the world. In the twenty-first century, small Canada must take mutual accommodation to today's changing world. Mutual accommodation need not use force or occupy territory. Force and occupation, like vaudeville, ain't what they used to be – and that is making everything different. There are three big sets of changes from the world we knew in 1945–2000. First, centrifugal forces are rising in a world too intertwined for separatists to succeed. Second, the US withdrawal from overreach to ground it can hold is going off the rails under Trump. Third, there is no replacement for the United States, with the broad strengths it displayed from the 1940s to the 1960s.

In 1900 the global population was 1.4 billion. By 2000 it was 6.0 billion. It could reach 9.0 billion by 2100. Amid this huge increase, three factors have become globally very important: resources, technology, and successful internal and external governance of the diversity of the world. Canada now has an unmatched combination of positive elements for addressing these features of the world ahead. It has spent the last 150 years navigating its own domestic mutual accommodation challenges. Whether it wants to or not, it will spend the rest of this century navigating its own and the world's mutual accommodation and containment challenges. The outcome will be either a new great country called Canada or a failed Canada.

I have called this twenty-first-century challenge a second Sir John A. Macdonald moment. To succeed, Canada will have to move forward on more than one front with the same kind of boldness Macdonald brought to Confederation and the transcontinental railway. One such front has recently been proposed by the biggest Canadian oil sands producer – to push hard on the technology front to produce no- low-carbon oil sands oil.

Canada will have to manage the opportunities and pressures from its great resources of food, water, energy, and minerals, as well as its vast land mass (which may be made more valuable by global warming). It could also have a second key set of strengths: a high level of IT and quantum innovation capability in a century where innovation will match, if not exceed, resources in importance. Canada could have a head-start of information and quantum technology from the institutional and cluster critical mass in the Greater Toronto region (including Waterloo, Ontario) – a region that is now in third place in North America after Silicon Valley and New York.

Could it be that Canadian federalism and its mutual accommodation way of governing diversity will provide the fundamental long-term stable path forward beyond traditional nationalism and the nation state? The United States, China, and Russia are all powerful nation states with powerful nationalisms. Each also has nuclear weapons. State-based nationalism will be a powerful force in these three countries for years to come. They are the big three either/or force-based powers in the world. Canada's role will always be different because of its lack of competitive either/or and force-based strengths. Canada's advantage is that there is no good way forward for the world without the spread of mutual accommodation.

Stability is essential for mutual accommodation to succeed. Each promotes and reinforces the other. The combination of stability, balance, trusted institutions, asymmetry, and the accommodation of equal and special treatment are the central elements that have made the mutual accommodation ways of Canada possible. Canadians need to recognize and use them to their and the world's benefit.

Canada and the world must each become bold. Only mutual accommodation can provide the firm base needed for bold to work. Dialogues in diversity and identity are the indispensable place to start what will be a very long and very hard journey for Canada – and for the world. We are only at the beginning of the journey. It will require new vision, new ideas, and new projects. If the world fails, it could lead to a new Dark Age that spreads to most, if not all, of the world.

3. MUTUAL ACCOMMODATION AS SEEN IN 2017[*]

There were three great mutual accommodation achievements in the twenty-first century. Two of these – Canada's mutual accommodation story and Gandhi's non-violent resistance achievements in India – are discussed here. The third was the post-war initiative led by the United States to broaden the inclusive global order and contain what could not be included at any given moment. When I told a prominent American psychotherapist about this achievement, he responded that his profession used that same method: they tried to broaden the inclusive order in the psyche and contain what was not yet includable. It is a way of looking at things that has wide application – and it works.

I first got the idea of mutual accommodation some thirty-five years ago – not as a big idea or the only shared Canada story, but as a better way than its much self-touted "special tolerance" to distinguish Canada. I saw two different driving forces in Canada and the United States: Canada's drive was toward mutual accommodation; and the American drive was toward division. Then two things happened. The great Canadian goaltender Ken Dryden told me in 2011 that "Canada needs a shared story to help reduce the Ottawa political fractiousness" he was experiencing as an MP at the time. A week later, one of the world's leading authorities on resilience in children told me that the normal way forward in treating children at risk was to look for sources of strength rather than weakness. Nonetheless, she said, every once in a while a child with no visible sources of strength of any kind would succeed. They found it was because the child created stories about itself – in a sense, out of nothing. That example showed how profound stories can be, and how the power we have as individuals comes from the stories we have that tell us who we really are.

In the early 1980s, I was on the board, along with Bill Innes, of Imperial Oil – a partly owned Canadian subsidiary of Exxon-Mobil. Bill then left for Japan, where he headed Esso Japan for ten years before

---

[*] Extract from a speech delivered by W.A. Macdonald at the symposium *Gathering on Common Ground* at Queen's University, Kingston, Ontario, June 25, 2017.

becoming director of one of the largest industrial research and engineering organizations on the planet – Exxon Mobil Research in New Jersey. We reconnected when he returned to Canada and, together, we explored the idea of mutual accommodation as the shared narrative of Canada. In 2014 we launched the Canadian Difference project with Trent University and, in November of that year, distributed a booklet on that theme at a special meeting of Canadian historians in Charlottetown, PEI.

When David Walmsley, editor of the *Globe and Mail*, saw that booklet, he suggested that I write a series of essays on different aspects of mutual accommodation for his newspaper. His goal was to launch a national conversation. Since then, I have written some 65,000 words for the newspaper – more than any outside writer in its history – and have come to see how big and inexhaustible the idea of mutual accommodation can be.

Shawn Atleo, a former chief of the Assembly of First Nations, read one of my early articles on mutual accommodation. There I wrote that the First Nations are Canada's biggest piece of unfinished mutual accommodation business. We both now believe Canada and our Indigenous people have found a way forward and, while the journey will be long and hard for both sides, both will stick to the Truth and Reconciliation path until, together, we finish the unfinished mutual accommodation business.

Canada was fortunate to realize that it is necessary to put "what works" ahead of nationalism, ethnic difference, religion, class, and ideology. This understanding has made Canada not just a good country but a great country. Great countries (like great leaders) make many mistakes, including big ones, but they get the most important things right. As examples, I refer to three occasions in Canada's history when both our leaders and their followers entrenched the mutual accommodation story in our national psyche: first, the alliance between Louis-Hippolyte LaFontaine and Robert Baldwin in 1848, twenty years before Confederation; second, the election and re-election of Sir Wilfrid Laurier between 1896 and 1908; and three, the way Pierre Trudeau's unilateral instincts were contained when he patriated the Constitution in 1982 and achieved the Charter of Rights by accepting the "notwithstanding clause" (the temporary override power by legislatures) demanded by the western premiers. What a different country the United States would be if its Constitution had a notwithstanding clause!

The alliance between LaFontaine and Baldwin resulted in the only reform movement from 1848 in the Western world to prevail as a responsible government and never lose its democracy. The francophone Catholic LaFontaine in Lower Canada needed the strength of the anglophone Protestant Baldwin from Upper Canada to overcome the anti-reform position of the Quebec clergy. Baldwin, in turn, needed the strength of LaFontaine to combat the anti-reform power of the Family Compact. Both were able to work together successfully at a time when differences of religion and nationality were intense everywhere. When LaFontaine lost his Quebec seat, and Baldwin lost his in Ontario, each ran successfully in the other's province – despite Ontario English Protestants who did not much like French Catholics, and Quebec French Catholics who did not much like English Protestants. This accommodation showed, twenty years before Confederation, that a shared public purpose pursued through compromise could trump nationality and religion with Canadian voters.

The idea of restraint is also a striking element in this story. LaFontaine stood down the anti-reform mob outside the Legislature in Montreal by asserting that reform would prevail without recourse to violence. A century later, Mahatma Gandhi, Nelson Mandela, and Martin Luther King championed much larger and more consequential non-violence movements, respectively, in India, South Africa, and the United States.

The second example of successful Canadian mutual accommodation is Wilfrid Laurier. His vision was political – to achieve peace, prosperity, and public purpose through compromise and accommodation. Laurier said that the twentieth century would belong to Canada. In many ways, that proved true, in the relative goodness of life available in Canada to ordinary people (never forgetting that Indigenous people were largely left out). It became true primarily because Canada followed the Laurier vision of public achievements through compromise and restraint. The very election of Laurier, a francophone Catholic from Quebec, as prime minister only thirty years after Confederation, is but one example. This approach was so powerful and suited to Canada that it kept the federal Liberal Party in office three out of every four years over the following century. This is completely opposite to the American approach, which is to use inflexible stands of no compromise to counter public purpose.

The third example deals with Pierre Trudeau's unilateral constitutional patriation effort. This issue is still not politically resolved in Quebec because the Constitution was brought to Canada without Quebec's inclusion – something I said publicly at the time was wrong. It still remains so and will likely remain that way for a very long time. Canada's two most ideologically driven and uncompromising either/ or prime ministers of the last century, Pierre Trudeau and Stephen Harper, were each forced by Canadian voters to live within Canada's overriding mutual accommodation reality.

It will be vitally important for Canadians to understand what these stories mean for the country, so they can draw upon them when they are needed. Americans have never really grasped their role in the foundation of the peaceful and prosperous post-war global order. That is a key reason why Trump could so easily start abandoning it.

Trump and the Tea Party were spurred on by voter divisiveness, not held back by American voter moderation. Trudeau was forced by Canada's mutual accommodation ways to abandon unilateral constitutional patriation and accept the "notwithstanding clause" override to his Charter of Rights and Freedoms. This clause simultaneously made a Quebec language bill possible (something Trudeau opposed), which in turn helped to keep Quebec in Canada (an outcome René Lévesque did not want). It needed the intervention of Western premiers, who would not accept the courts as the final word in every situation. It was a very Canadian outcome: Quebec stays but gets its language bill.

Much of American politics is driven more by loathing of the other party and its leaders than by anything positive. Both federal Liberals and Harper made the same mistake. Harper thought voters hated the Liberals more than they did. Liberals thought voters disliked Harper more than they did.

Mackenzie King called the CCF (socialists) of eighty years ago "Liberals in a hurry." Justin Trudeau in 2015 referred to Conservatives as our neighbours, not our enemies. By contrast, Hillary Clinton in the 2016 US presidential election called Trump voters "the deplorables." American voters are spurred on by the extremes of their leaders. Canadian leaders are contained by Canadian voter rejection of extremism.

Canada's defining narrative began early, with the reliance, amid a difficult geography, of European traders and settlers on Aboriginal people. Over the centuries, the nation that has emerged has continued – in fact, extended – this tradition of mutual shaping and accommodation. Canada has not been entirely free of violence, but its primary markers have been a blend of vision and of what works on the ground. In this way, it has become a great country unlike any other in history. It is a different kind of great country for a very different kind of world.

Canada's three greatest visionary leaders – Samuel de Champlain, John A. Macdonald, and Wilfrid Laurier – each combined vision, practical boldness, and an ability to work and get along with a wide range of diverse people. Baldwin and LaFontaine, in 1848, showed that political and social reform could be achieved by non-violent means in an era when that did not happen elsewhere. All these leaders would see much of their visions embedded in the fabric of modern Canada.

Champlain wanted a new kind of society – one in which Aboriginals and Europeans could live together in amity and with mutual respect. Individualism underlies the American dream – the right to "life, liberty and the pursuit of happiness" for every citizen that is reflected in the Declaration of Independence and the Constitution. The still unrealized Canadian dream comes from someone best remembered as an explorer, but who arrived here as a soldier familiar with the horrors of war in Europe.

Champlain had many dreams – one was the colonization of New France, which he did; the other, finding a passage to China, which he did not. The greatest of his dreams was humanity and peace. In North America, Champlain became a political leader and statesman who, through his ability to get along with different people, was able to convert dreams into reality. One of Canada's greatest remaining challenges is to complete Champlain's great societal vision. If Canada had stuck with the Champlain vision, we would not still have the unfinished business of a traumatized Indigenous people.

Canada had to accommodate people of French and English heritage and of Catholic and Protestant faith. It had to be ready to stand up to the United States and to build a sound economy. Sir John A. Macdonald remains the country's greatest builder, striving for a nation of "one people, great in territory, great in enterprise, great in credit, great in capital." He got three big things right: Confederation, a transcontinental railway, and containment of American expansionism. He also got English-French politics mostly right. Finally, when the country needed a looser federation than Macdonald sought, his Confederation later allowed it. But he got a very big thing wrong – the failure to extend inclusiveness to Canada's Indigenous people.

Macdonald found, in his partnership with George-Étienne Cartier, a way forward on the Quebec political front. And he recognized how fundamental mutual respect was to mutual accommodation: "Treat them as a nation, and they will act as a free people generally do – generously," he said of French-speaking Canadians. Canada would be very different today if, instead of advancing residential schools, Macdonald had, as Champlain did, extended this inclusiveness to Indigenous people.

Confederation was a first. No previous colonials had written their own constitution. It set in motion a coast-to-coast country that has survived and mostly thrived. Canada also has emerged as one of the better places for most to live. Because of its achievements in mutual accommodation, it is one of history's truly remarkable countries. Moreover, because of the potential importance of this idea to the world right now, Canada has vastly more runway ahead than it has used so far.

The belief of Baldwin and LaFontaine in reform through non-violent means has become the Canadian way. Macdonald's vision of a coast-to-coast three-ocean country has led to the quality of life that Canadians enjoy. And Laurier's political model of accommodation has, for the most part, been followed. Together these visions have made Canada great and a country of unexpected magic – but because of its unfinished mutual accommodation business, still a flawed one.

Mutual accommodation involves two fundamentals. One is effective two-way communication – careful listening and careful speaking. The other requires a belief that a shared and meaningful order exists at the heart of things. Geography creates one kind of communication problem – it helps to explain why western Canadians feel alienated from Ottawa and Toronto, and why midwestern and southern Americans disdain Washington and New York. But breaking away from history can result in much bigger and deeper challenges than holding onto and moving forward within it. The US Civil War lasted for just four years, but its aftermath persists and contributes to our neighbour's current political turmoil.

Canada did have its own break in history, but it was not abrupt. Rather, it was more a slow moving on while also holding on. Its English and French connections have remained, though they have gradually become less relevant. The American rupture between North and South was sudden, violent, and destructive. Canada's recent Quebec existential crisis was peaceful and lasted for decades. Words prevailed over force. These differences have produced very distinctive communication, institutional, and socio-cultural results in each country.

Champlain's vision was societal; Macdonald's was national; and Laurier's was for a different way of doing politics. All three visions survive and thrive. The visions of its founders have shaped Canadian society in ways that have become mutually reinforcing. Champlain's desire for a diverse and peaceable society remains a dominant, if not yet fully realized, aspiration. Much remains to be done in mutual accommodation with the Indigenous people. Today, too, we must find a way to cope with anxieties about extreme Muslim groups, fed in part by a fearful neighbour and its hyped-up media.

No one thing is ever everything. I first saw mutual accommodation simply as the distinctive drive Canadians have developed. I have come to see it as much more – as a better way for humans to go about things everywhere and at all times. And a way the world urgently needs to adopt and promote. I have come to see mutual accommodation as one of the four better ways humans have found to go about things. The other three are freedom, science, and compassion. The West over the last five centuries has been dominated by freedom and science. The world has become increasingly hard to manage because of the resulting imbalances. The West, to be manageable, needs more mutual accommodation and compassion – for reasons of basic survival and thrival. Canadians have exhibited a stronger drive toward mutual accommodation than any other country – especially in

comparison with a United States driven by division. Mutual accommodation – the shared Canadian story (possibly the only story shared
by all Canadians) – is crucial to Canada today and to all the world.
The world needs a global conversation about mutual accommodation. This puts Canada and mutual accommodation at the centre of
the next stage in world history.

The United States has been great in freedom and science – the two
most transformative forces for doing things in a better way since the
Renaissance. There is still more to do in the areas of science and freedom, but they need to be better balanced by mutual accommodation
and compassion.

Since its beginnings – first Quebec in 1608 and then Confederation
in 1867 – Canada has had three very big achievements. First, it has
survived – not just as a nation but as one that includes the distinctive province of Quebec – and it has thrived. Second, it made itself
a coast-to-coast country. Finally, despite its divisions of nationality,
culture, language, religion, and class, it has developed a political
and socio-cultural outlook that works. The one big failure with its
Indigenous people it is starting to address.

Use words, not force. Make railways, not war. These overly simple
ideas capture a Canadian story that differs from those of most countries. Canada's story has increasingly been driven by persuasion. The
American story has more often been shaped by war and violence: the
Revolutionary War, Civil War, Indian Wars, Mexican Wars, lynching,
and 300 million guns in private hands. As one of the great American
historians put it over twenty-five years ago at a private meeting I
attended in Boston, the United States was created by force and preserved by force. He told us, there was nothing – and he repeated,
"I mean nothing" – the United States would not do to preserve the
Union. Canada accepted, unlike the Americans, that Quebec could
choose to leave. After several decades, Quebec has decided not to do
so. Both Quebec and Canada are the stronger for it.

In the past, Canada's main mutual accommodation challenges have
revolved around religion and language. Today they revolve more
around identity and differences. Our sense of being different – as
individuals and groups – is what gives us strength in, and meaning for,
our world. What we need to talk more about is the possibility that the
differences on which our sense of identity rests can be strengthened,

not threatened or weakened, by making room for the differences of others. Our anxieties in Western countries revolve around our identities and also underlie today's populism. We cannot simply tell others not to be anxious or call them names. We have to talk about anxieties and find ways to work our way through them together.

An American journalist friend, Bill Hessler, once the foreign affairs editor of the *Cincinnati Enquirer*, told me many years ago (in the sixties) that he had decided the big difference between Canada and the United States was that, in his country, you had to shout to be heard – in Canada you did not. Today, in the small world of Canada, Canadians still do not need to shout to be heard. That is a huge strength and blessing for coping with the world that lies ahead.

That comment made me realize that "celebrity" is a form of shouting – one of the explanations why there are so many celebrities in the United States and so few in Canada. Mutual accommodation is a long and hard path. Freedom has taken centuries to take hold. Shouting is a harder way forward. The Canadian difference – the Canadian advantage – may be that we can hear each other without having to shout.

4. CELEBRATE MAGIC CANADA*

The last time Jeff McBride was here, I said, "You've probably already thought this, but magic would not be magic if it really was magic." He agreed, but said he had not thought that before. He then said that real magic comes from limits that force creativity.

Canada's magic is the kind of mystery and miracle that comes from having the right leaders and the right followers at the right time – people who have the required creativity to do what it takes.

Canada shares with the United States the New World of North America. It differs from the United States in three fundamental ways. The United States has a drive toward division; Canada has a drive toward mutual accommodation. The United States sees the world as a never-ending struggle between good and evil – a world

---

* Remarks by W.A. Macdonald at the Celebrate Magic Canada dinner, Toronto, April 17, 2019.

of winners and losers, without mutual accommodation. Canadians, by contrast, lean to the idea that there is an underlying order at the heart of things. Canada has always faced strong limits that it had to overcome creatively: a difficult geography; French-English divisions; and a very large neighbour sure of its manifest destiny to occupy the entire North American continent. By contrast, the United States sees itself as a country with virtually no limits.

Here are just some of the many amazing events that shaped a magic Canada that is worth celebrating:

· The year 1848 was one of revolutionary reform in the Western world. The French Catholic Louis-Hippolyte Lafontaine from Quebec and the English Protestant Robert Baldwin from Ontario led the only non-violent reform movement of that year which never lost its democracy. When Lafontaine was defeated in his Quebec seat, he won a by-election in Ontario. When Baldwin was defeated in his Ontario seat, he won a by-election in Québec – an amazing feat for a country where the French did not much like the English, and the Catholics did not much like the Protestants, and vice versa.
· Only twenty-nine years after Canada was formed, this same dynamic saw a majority English Protestant national electorate elect Wilfrid Laurier as its first French Catholic prime minister.
· Following the Quiet Revolution in Quebec in 1960, the country's leadership showed rare political foresight. Prime Minister Lester Pearson launched the Bilingualism and Biculturalism Commission and recruited three progressive leaders from Quebec to his government: the academic Pierre Trudeau, labour leader Jean Marchand, and the journalist Gérard Pelletier, the editor of *La Presse*, the largest French-language newspaper in North America. Around the same time, Progressive Conservative Ontario premier John Robarts and Union Nationale Quebec premier Daniel Johnson launched the Confederation of Tomorrow Conference.
· Finally, during the great Quebec separatism battles of the Pierre Trudeau, René Lévesque, Bill Davis, and Peter Loughheed era, Trudeau wanted two things: no French-language primacy in Quebec, and for Quebec to remain inside Canada; and Lévesque wanted the opposite – French-language primacy, and Quebec

outside Canada. Then the Western premiers came along and forced the "notwithstanding" clause as part of the Charter of Rights and Freedoms. That gave Lévesque a route to French-language primacy, which kept Quebec in Canada. It also did something more. By giving politics the final word over the Charter, Canada does not have the highly politicized Supreme Court that the United States has today.

This small part of our history reveals some of the magic that is solidly rooted in its miracle/mystery story. The late Quebec premier Robert Bourassa captured Canada in a single unmatched sentence: "One of the world's rare and privileged countries in terms of peace, justice, liberty, and standard of living."

Now a quick word on where we are heading. We are at the very early stages of exploring the possibility of multiple academic and mutual accommodation study centres: on Canada and global issues at the University of Toronto; on Canada's Indigenous mutual accommodation failures and successes at Trent University; on Canada and Quebec at McGill University; mutual accommodation on a global scale at Harvard and Cambridge (Whitehead's two universities); and, ideally, two universities with a majority black population in Africa – a continent whose future depends largely on the world's ability to spread mutual accommodation.

Mutual accommodation has become to the twenty-first century what freedom became to the world following the Renaissance. Success will depend primarily on getting the right scholars – experts who can see this study area as good for their own academic careers.

Peter Howard wrote a book in 1945 called *Ideas Have Legs*. Mutual accommodation is an idea that needs legs right now if the new and different world that is upon us is to be bearable.

Inclusive Ways of Seeing and Living

I. REMARKS AT MY GRANDDAUGHTER'S FUNERAL

Everything we do and write contains implicit, unexpressed views about the world. I have written about a lot of different topics in this book. For some unknown-to-me reason, at the very end of this long process, I remembered what I said at the funeral of our second granddaughter. I am a believer in crying (Winston Churchill did a lot of it), and I had to read my remarks some twenty-five times before I could say them at her funeral service without crying. Many people told me afterwards that before I spoke, they were unbearably sad, but what I said had changed that and lifted their spirits.

I think my words at her funeral underlie everything I have written in the book. When General Charles de Gaulle's daughter with disabilities, Anne, was buried, he told his wife, "Now she is like everybody else." I repeated that about our Alex, and I added, "While she lived, she was like nobody else." The deep bottom-line aspiration underlying the book is to help us all to find the inclusive (both/and) path of seeing, to realize that each of us, simultaneously, is always like everybody else and always like nobody else – that everybody is and can be a "best" somebody.

My father never looked down on anyone except those who looked down on others. This single idea, which he lived every day, is one of the many blessings of my life. Without it, I would probably never have written the book. Although he probably never heard the phrase, mutual accommodation was his way of conducting his life.

My Words at the Funeral
of Alexandra Elizabeth Anne Macdonald

Alexandra came to us seven and a half years ago. She broke our hearts because she was not the baby we had all hoped for. Alexandra left us two days ago. She broke our hearts again because we loved the darling girl for who she was and for what she meant to us.

Molly Anne and I were in England when Alex was born, and we were warned that she might not be alive by the time we got back. The fact she lived for more than seven years tells us something of her own special strengths and of the special loving and caring strengths of her mother and father and of Ludy.

We were lucky enough to be with Barbara and Dougal and Barbara's mother a few days after Alex's birth when the pediatrician came to explain the hard facts of her diagnosis. Because Alex's condition was so rare, he could not tell us much about her future. What he did say, however, I will never forget: "Love her while you have her. Never do anything to hurt her. When her time comes, let her go."

Barbara, with the help and support of Dougal, achieved two wonderful things in the months after Alex was born:

- Within the limits of the heavy demands a child like Alex makes, Barbara made and kept her home a normal home. There were stresses in their lives, but their lives were never distorted.
- Barbara saw that Alex must be seen quite simply as Alex.

One of the books I read in the weeks after Alex's birth was a biography of de Gaulle. I learned that this great man of destiny and his wife also had a daughter – Anne – not unlike Alex, and like her, with no hope of real improvement. One of his closest friends said after she died that "Anne was to be one of those children without whom there would be less love in the world." I have no doubt our Alex was another one of those children.

At the end of his life, this hardened man of war and politics said, "Without Anne, perhaps I should not have done all that I have done. She made me understand many things. She gave me so much heart and spirit." I think that whatever life holds and however long they live, Barbara and Dougal will feel as Charles de Gaulle felt about his

Anne – that Alex made them understand so many things and gave them so much heart and spirit.

Alex's life also makes clear that we cannot live as isolated persons. She never ceased to be almost completely helpless and dependent on others. Yet help and care and love were always forthcoming – from her parents, from Ludy, from her younger sister, Katrina, from family, friends, and the community, and from special institutions with special people in both Toronto and Hong Kong.

In the days before Alex died, but after we knew that her time with us had become very limited, I happened to read a comment about the future made by the late French scientist and philosopher Pierre Teilhard de Chardin. "The day will come," he said, "when, after harnessing the winds, the tides and gravitation, we shall harness for God the energies of love."

I thought then that this is what Alex did. In her special way, because she was a special person, she harnessed energies of love for God and for us – and most especially for her mother, her father, her sister, and Ludy.

We do not mourn Alex because her death cut short possibilities never to be realized. She was fully herself throughout her life. We mourn her because we have lost a special, darling presence, a small, helpless girl who still mysteriously was able to give more than she received to those who gave of their time and care to her.

Alex was for the most part a very happy little girl. She loved what most of us love: music, companionship, eating, drinking, being stroked, and yes, being loved. Her personality was distinctive. She had her very own likes and dislikes; she had a will, which included a mighty will to live. She had a sister, Katrina, who loved her and who was very good with her.

A week ago this morning, I was privileged to have Alex all to myself for just twenty minutes at the Sick Children's Hospital. I was able to look into the deep blue eyes her father loved so much. Her skin, her face, her lovely brushed hair seemed more beautiful than ever. She was peaceful and self-possessed. I do not know if I have ever experienced anything more wholly beautiful than being alone with her in that way. Two things came to me:

The first was that she not only had a distinctive personality but she also had something strong and rooted deep in the core of her being

– something I could only feel was character. The second was that in our time together, looking, talking, and touching, I was able to do nothing for her, yet she, by her presence and simply being who she was, was doing so much for me. In some sense I cannot explain, I felt something of the mysteries of life and of love, and of how they are connected one to the other.

These have been a grandfather's words about his second grand-daughter. Each of you who knew Alex would have said something different if you had been here. My hope is that I have captured at least something of what you think and feel about Alex and her life.

After Anne de Gaulle was buried, the general took his wife and led her away, saying, "Come. Now she is like everybody else." And so I believe for Alex. But I would also add that during her time with us, she was like nobody else, and that is what we will miss. That is the loss we mourn.

2. GOD KNOWS BECAUSE GOD IS GOD

Extract from the sermon by Dr Charlotte Stuart,
August 18, 2019, drawn from Isaiah 5: 1–7

I began to think a little differently after reading and re-reading the passage from the prophet Isaiah. It seems that we have here an instance when God does not know. It seems almost as if God is baffled.

God's bewilderment is cast in the story of a vineyard owner who does everything right. He has cleared the land on a fertile hill and selected choice vines to plant. No shortcuts, no skimping on costs, nothing but the best.

In addition to this excellent soil and plants, the owner has spared no effort in constructing some nice features. A watchtower is built, a wine vat made. Everything about the vineyard is perfect it would seem – good land, good soil, good vines, good accessories. In a real sense the vineyard has become an object of devotion and affection for the owner.

It is the love of his life, the passion of his soul. Having invested much of himself and many of his resources into it, the vineyard owner sits back and waits for the expected harvest, naturally expecting a healthy return on his investment.

God knows he deserves it. God knows he's done all that he can. Amazingly, astoundingly, the vineyard owner's expectations are unfulfilled. In place of fine grapes, the vines produce only wild, unmanageable grapes. He can't believe it. He did his best for that vineyard, yet it failed to produce. How could it be? How could all this be? Only God knows.

But in this story, this Old Testament parable, not even God knows because the baffled owner of the vineyard is God, and the vines that failed to meet expectations are the people of God.

God gave them much, sparing no cost, no effort, no love. God gave them the best of everything. Yet God's beloved vineyard could produce only wild grapes, not good for much of anything. God's beloved people could not live up to their lover's expectation.

Here Is a Vulnerable God

A God who loves what he has made, a God who has invested his all in creation, who longs for love to be returned and aches for the potential to be realized, and yearns for righteousness and justice from those whom he has created.

Yes, God has expectations – like any lover, God has expectations. And when those expectations are not realized, God is not free from pain and disappointment.

Capitalism at a Crossroads:
Reform or Revolution

1. THE PROBLEM

a) "Capitalism ... is not working well for the majority of Americans because it's producing self-reinforcing spirals up for the haves and down for the have nots ... Not reforming capitalism would be an existential threat to the US." (Ray Dalio, April 5, 2019)

b) "We have managed to recreate both the economics and the politics of a century ago – the first Gilded Age – and remain in grave danger of repeating more of the signature errors of the twentieth century ... The road to fascism and dictatorship is paved with failures of economic policy to serve the needs of the general public." (Tim Wu, *The Curse of Bigness*, 2018)

c) "There's class warfare, all right, but it's my class, the rich class, that's making war, and we're winning." (Warren Buffett, *New York Times*, November 26, 2006)

2. SYMPTOMS THAT CAPITALISM IS FAILING ORDINARY PEOPLE

a) Inequality is way up (Dalio, Collier, Cass, Yang, others)
  i. Income growth
    1. Bottom 60% have seen no real income growth since 1980
    2. Top 10% up 100% since 1980
    3. Top 1% up 200% – now match peak income share from 1920s

Notes for a business presentation, May 8, 2019.

    ii. Wealth distribution
- 1. Wealth share of top 1% is higher (>40%) than bottom 90% (<30%)
- 2. Top 0.1% own 20% of wealth (up from ~10% in 1960s)

    iii. Economic mobility now among worst in OECD
- 1. 1970: 90% of kids grow up to earn more than their parents
- 2. 2018: 50% of kids grow up to earn more than their parents

    iv. Labour income share down, profits share up
- 1. Labour share has fallen from peak of 64% to low of 56% since 2000
  - a. At today's GDP of ~US$20T, that represents a decline in labour income share of ~US$1.6T or twice the Trump stimulus
- 2. Profit share near long-term high (see below)

b) Widening geographic, economic and social divide, measured in incomes, job growth, house prices, and skill levels between leading cities (the metropoles) and the hinterland, particularly since 1980 (Collier, Yang)

    i. Reflects scale and specialization advantages, particularly in services (tech, law, consulting, finance, medicine, academia), that facilitate clusters and productivity growth in large, dense cities connected to national/global markets ("gains from agglomeration")

    ii. Higher productivity drives higher incomes, attracting more internal migration and weakening of talent/skill base in smaller cities and towns (the "left behind")

    iii. Globalization extends comparative advantage reach of leading cities, while undermining that of smaller centres, reinforcing the gap with the left behind

    iv. Automation replaces workers in sectors with high levels of repetition – manufacturing, food service, transportation, retail and administration, further undermining prospects for smaller centres and weaker sectors. As this process is consciously prosecuted by the highly skilled in metropoles, Yang characterizes it as "The War on Normal People"

    v. Gains from agglomeration are shared among city dwelling,

highly skilled, and city landlords as real estate values and
rents rise, creating class of city dwelling left-behind people

c) Middle- and lower-class health and life outcomes are deteriorating
(Dalio, Collier, Yang, Cass)

    i. Life expectancy for white working-class males is declining

        1. Death by alcohol/drugs increasing (up over 100%
since 2000)

           a. Opioid epidemic reveals both the struggles of the left
behind and the harsher capitalism, given the corporate
role in the crisis (Purdue, etc.)

        2. Suicides up by over 50% since 2000 ("Deaths
of Despair" Case and Deaton)

    ii. Family life for working class is now more precarious

        1. Divorce rates for non-college grads are now twice that of
college grads (up from being the same in 1980)

    iii. Bottom 20% live ~10 years less than top 20%

d) Poor children are malnourished and badly educated (Dalio)

    i. Low incomes, poorly funded schools, weak family support,
high incarceration rates for parents are major barriers to
developing skills for life and work

    ii. Leads to poor academic achievement, low productivity, low
incomes, social/emotional problems, high incarceration,
lower life expectancy and high societal burden

    iii. Big lost opportunity for economy and large cost for society

e) Investment and productivity declining (Barclays)

    i. Net capital investment has halved in past 20 years
(Barclays), falling from 3.5–4.0% to ~2.0% of GDP today

    ii. Biggest declines is in sectors with highest concentration
(Barclays)

    iii. Productivity growth declines reflect lower investment levels
(Barclays)

    iv. Reflects increased corporate market power and lower
demand growth

f) Dynamism declining (*Economist*, Barclays)

    i. Lower new business formation

    ii. Fewer initial public offerings (IPOs)

    iii. Reduced geographic mobility (dual income earners,
occupational licensing partly to blame?)

    iv. Lower employee churn as job switching falls (15% in
1990s to 12% today)

g) Innovation slowing (Barclays)

h) Profits are high and unusually durable (*Economist*)
  i. Profits are 76% above 50-year average in US
  ii. Abnormal profits (above cost of capital) are concentrated
in the US (72% of global total), with Europe (26%) and the
Rest of World (2) trailing
  iii. Good for wealthy shareowners
  iv. Suggests diminishing effectiveness of competition, rising
market power, higher barriers to entry, and rise of
monopoly/oligopoly in the US

i) Capitalism is losing public support
(Gallup, Realclearpolitics.com, others)
  i. Public support for capitalism has declined from 80% to
60% over past decade
  ii. Millennials now favour socialism over capitalism (but
unclear how defined)
  iii. General support for Medicare, Medicaid, and other "socialist"
programs is now well into majority territory (~65%)
  iv. Support for unions at 62% – highest since 2003 (Gallup)
  v. 63% of public believe US is on "the wrong track" vs 28%
in the right direction (Realclearpolitics.com)

3. REASONS CAPITALISM IS WORKING BADLY FOR MOST PEOPLE

a) Changing social, moral, political, and financial norms (Collier,
Pearlstein, Autor, others)
  i. Post-WW2 to early 1970s: shared purpose, sacrifice, and
success in WW2 made shared prosperity a consensus goal
for all – reflected in stable labour income share, rising with
productivity, muted executive salaries, high marginal tax
rates, and rise of government-funded social programs
  ii. 1970s: cost and wage-push inflation and oil crises led to
stagflation – beginning of productivity/pay gap and
declining labour income share
  iii. 1980s until recently: business culture shift to "maximizing

shareholder value" (online sources under McKinsey, Bain, BCG, Stern Stewart) and "greed is good" (e.g., Gordon Gekko in *Wall Street*), political shift to deregulation and privatization, emergence of raiders, private equity, hedge funds and economic financialization, executive salaries explode. As rich and non-rich live increasingly separate lives in separate geographies, bonds between them decline – ordinary Americans become abstract "muppets" to be exploited, as labour or consumers

b) Technology (Yang, Dalio, Autor, others)

   i. Replaces workers in many repetitive functions, undermining demand side for labour, weakening labour bargaining power, raising worker anxiety and insecurity

   ii. High skills gap reduces scope for easy redeployment of displaced labour from old to new economy and from hinterland to metropoles

c) Globalization (Cass, Dalio, Autor, others)

   i. Outsourcing by multinationals and domestic firms reduces demand for labour at home, while increasing total globally accessible labour supply for US employers

   ii. Tempers wage gains at home while raising overall margins

   iii. US regions most open to China competition have the greatest challenge regenerating jobs, with adverse social consequences (lower marriage rates, higher divorce, more single mothers, etc.) as loss of work undermines male status, identity in family and community

d) Central Bank monetary policy (Dalio, others)

   i. Quantitative easing (QE) enriched wealthy financial asset owners as asset prices rose by design

   ii. QE inefficient in delivering aggregate demand to reverse macro-economic weakness

     1. Asset sellers (the wealthy) have lower marginal propensity to consume

     2. Asset sellers reinvested gains in riskier financial assets, not consumption, getting richer as QE floated all assets

e) Budgetary myopia (Dalio)

   i. Focus on annual budget cycle, not lifetime returns on investment, results in under-investment in education, healthcare, and infrastructure

f) Rising corporate concentration and market power (Barclays, *Economist*, Tepper, Wu)
  i.   75% of non-financial sectors have seen concentration rise of 60%+ since 2000
  ii. Driven by merger and acquisition (M&A) boom, mostly horizontal in old economy, leaving top 3–4 firms in many sectors highly dominant, and mix of organic growth and M&A in tech
       1. In tech, many acquisitions are to kill potential future competitors early
  iii. Clear link to rising profits (Goldman Sachs, Barclays, Buffett)
       1. Pricing power in product markets (pharmaceuticals is extreme example)
       2. Monopsony power in input markets (labour, suppliers)
  iv. Declining labour incomes (Barclays, Tepper)
       1. Lower wage gains in concentrated industries
          a. One-factory towns
          b. Rise of non-competes (fast food, tech) – now >20%, up from 3-5% 20 years ago
          c. Rise of arbitration clauses – now >20% up from 3–5%
          d. Rise of "no poach" agreements
          e. Rise in "occupational licensing" – now ~25% vs 15% in 1980
       2. Decline of unions (from ~30% in 1960s to ~10% today); rise of "right to work" laws (prohibit mandatory union dues now in 26 states)
       3. Decline of real minimum wage (from ~$10.75 in 1968 to ~$10.00 in 1980 to $7.25 in 2017 in real terms)
       4. Rise of temporary work and the "gig economy"
       5. Rise of "independent contractors" (no benefits) vs employees (with benefits)
g) Regulatory capture
  i.   Dominant firms compete to tilt legislation and regulation in their favour, often to strengthen their market power
       1. Increase pricing power in product markets (patents, copyright, regulation as barrier to entry)
       2. Increase monopsony pricing power in input markets (labour, suppliers)
       3. Increase barriers to entry

ii. Pharmaceutical industry is extreme example
(Reich, Tepper)

1. Spent $90 million in mid-2000s lobbying to get incremental $90 billion pa in revenue by convincing Congress to prohibit Medicare from using its bargaining power to get lower drug prices
   a. Same drugs in Canada cost ~1/3 as much
2. Lobbied to make "Pay to Delay" legal (illegal elsewhere)
   b. Allows incumbent makers of off-patent drugs to pay generic makers to delay production – clearly anti-competitive (but legal)
3. Lobbied successfully to bar imports of generic prescription drugs from Canada on "health and safety" grounds (risk that Canadian drugs are really from Third World!)
4. Lobbied to get "evergreening" of certain patents (top 12 drugs got 38 years vs allowed 20 years of patent protection)

h) Money in politics and lobbying

1. While the effect of money in politics is inconclusive at best and buys influence at worst, its scale suggests it has real effects
   a. In 1976, in *Buckley vs Valeo*, the Supreme Court decided that limits on independently funded ads were unconstitutional as contrary to free speech protections under the First Amendment
   b. In 2010, Citizens United confirmed that corporations are "persons" entitled to free speech protection, including right to make unlimited contributions to independent political vehicles (Super PACs). Kept ban on direct donations by corporations or unions to candidates
2. Lobbying may be a bigger problem, supporting the view that the "system is rigged"
   a. Corporations spend about $3 billion a year lobbying
   b. Lobbyists are often ex-Congress members – 10–20% of departing lawmakers join lobbyist firms in what is known as the revolving door between Capital Hill and K Street

3. Studies suggest that "average citizens" get what they want only when their desires are aligned with those of elites or special interests (Vox, January 28, 2015)
4. Regulation is fiercely contested by special interests, again leaving the impression or creating the reality that the elites are tilting the playing field in their favour, undermining fairness, open opportunity and competition

GENERAL CONCLUSION
(COLLIER, DALIO, TEPPER, REICH, WU, YANG)

a) Today's version of US capitalism, while good for shareholders, is not delivering for ordinary people who are responding to populist offerings on the left (Sanders, Warren) and the right (Trump)
b) It is unsustainable, and the question is whether it can be reformed collaboratively from within or whether changes will be imposed by populists empowered by disaffected people who are left behind
c) Declining competitiveness and rising elements of "crony capitalism" are at the heart of much that ails current capitalism. Restoring real economic competition is the best way to rebalance the position of labour and capital, to reduce inequality, to increase consumption demand and in turn investment, which will drive productivity growth and innovation
d) Targeted investments in education, healthcare, and infrastructure offering high returns (see Dalio) will release more resources to support faster economic growth

POTENTIAL POLICY RESPONSES

a) Strengthened anti-trust law
  i. Redefine objectives for mergers (Wu)
    1. Brandeis (decentralize economic and political power, reduce inequality, anti-monopoly, favour small firms, maintain competition dynamics) vs Bork ("consumer welfare" test only)
  ii. Redefine analytical framework
    1. Focus on competitiveness impacts, static and dynamic

      2. The "moats" framework set out in the *Economist* is intriguing – level and durability of profitability, innovation, ease of new entry, power to claw back current subsidies, market share, and concentration all considered

  iii. Horizontal mergers face higher standard

      1. Wu proposes outright bar for mergers over $6 billion; Tepper would bar mergers in sectors with fewer than six players

      2. Outright bar big tech firms buying start-ups

  iv. Vertical mergers face higher scrutiny

      1. No vertical mergers were contested from 1979 to 2018

  v. Reintroduce "break-ups" to anti-trust tool-kit

      1. Standard Oil, US Steel, AT&T, etc.

  vi. European-style "market investigation" law to reduce concentration/improve competition in non-merging sectors (attack existing concentration, not just new mergers that create more of it)

b) Enhanced regulation (or deregulation) to prevent abuses of dominant market positions

  i. Predatory pricing

  ii. Price discrimination

  iii. Tied selling

c) Data ownership (Barclays)

  i. Make data portable by consumers to ease switching costs – break hold of large tech

d) "Common Carriers" rules developed in utilities and telecoms could be applied to natural monopolies in tech (Facebook, Alphabet, Uber), dramatically reducing barriers to entry and increasing effective competition

e) Pro-competition macro-economic policies

  i. Tax breaks for small business (already high)

  ii. Higher investment tax credits (already high post-Trump budget)

  iii. Improve portability of employer health insurance, pensions, etc., to enhance labour mobility

  iv. Invest in basic education, particularly for disadvantaged

  v. Invest in retraining of old economy or technology displaced workers

f) Labour market reforms
    i. Limits on non-competes
    ii. Limits on arbitration clauses
    iii. Limits on unnecessary occupational licensing

g) Tax economic rents (Collier)
    i. "rents" are returns in excess of what the market requires to fund an activity, so taxing rents raises revenue and reduces profits without reducing investment
    ii. Big Tech, real estate in big cities, and certain socially valueless financial and legal activities are prime targets
    iii. Taxes on rents could be used to fund investments in education, healthcare, and public infrastructure

h) Wealth tax (Elizabeth Warren)
    i. Proposing a tax of 2% on wealth above $50 million with an additional surcharge of 1% on wealth above $1 billion, in addition to existing taxes on income, interest, dividends, and capital gains
    ii. Would slow wealth gains of super-wealthy, reduce inequality, and stimulate the economy (by having unspent capital spent on investment or consumption), and fund social investments

i) Universal Basic Income (Yang)
    i. Yang proposes a Universal Basic Income (UBI) of US$1,000 per month to every US citizen funded by a 10% VAT on all goods and service purchases
    ii. UBI support widely shared by tech/libertarian circles (the winners from the current system)
    iii. Would ensure minimum level of individual consumption and a sustained boost to aggregate demand by effectively redistributing income from low to high marginal propensity to consume spenders, but does not address the identity, status, and personal fulfilment and meaning roles that actual productive work can provide

POLITICAL PROSPECTS

a) Dalio proposes
    i. "Leadership from the top" to proclaim a national emergency

   ii. A "bipartisan commission" of "skilled sharpers of policy" to redesign the system

  iii. Clear metrics to judge performance and defined accountability

  iv. Redistribution of resources to improve well-beings and productivity

b) In 2019, there is no clear "leadership from the top" or "bipartisan" support for skilled redesign. Dalio notes that "ideological polarity is greater ... and the willingness to compromise is less than it's ever been"

c) To Dalio, the key question is whether populists of left or right or "sensible and skilled people" reform the system

d) In politics, enormous change can happen quickly – a week is a long time!

e) Happily, from Ray Dalio and Jamie Dimon to Elizabeth Warren and Andrew Yang and in many think tank and academic corners, a national discussion on the future of capitalism seems to be well underway.

Selected Source Materials

Autor, David, and others, "The China Shock," National Bureau of Economic Research (NBER), 2016

Barclays, "Increased Corporate Concentration and the Influence of Market Power," March 26, 2019

Berman, Russell, "An Exodus from Congress Tests Lure of Lobbying," Atlantic, May 1, 2018

Case, Anne, and Angus Deaton, "Deaths of Despair," Tanner Lecture, April 2019

Cass, Oren, The Once and Future Worker, Encounter Books, 2018

Collier, Paul, The Future of Capitalism, Harper, 2018

Dalio, Ray, "Why and How Capitalism needs to Be Reformed," Linked in, April 5, 2019

Economist, The, "The Next Capitalist Revolution," November 17, 2018

Fivethirtyeight.com, various

Gallup, "Labour Union Approval at 15-Year High," August 20, 2018

Goldman Sachs, "Does Consolidation Create Value,"
    February 12, 2014
Illing, Sean, "Is Capitalism Worth Saving?" *Vox*, February 26, 2019
Pearlstein, Steven, *Can American Capitalism Survive?*
    St Martin's Press, 2018
Realclearpolitics.com, various
Reich, Robert, "Why We Allow Big Pharma to Rip Us Off,"
    robertreich.org, October 5, 2014
Tepper, Jonathan, *The Myth of Capitalism*, Wiley, 2019
Wu, Tim, *The Curse of Bigness: Antitrust in the New Global Age*,
    Columbia Business Reports, 2018
Yang, Andrew, *The War on Normal People*, Hachette, 2018

Index

IGNITE
THE SPIRIT OF EDUCATION FOUNDATION INC.®

CULTURE AUTOCHTONE
INDIGENOUS CULTURE

Indigenous
Education Resource

WELCOME TO **IGNITE** – THE SPIRIT OF EDUCATION FOUNDATION INC.®

The **IGNITE Indigenous Education Resource** is an initiative led by the Spirit of Education Foundation, borne out of the recognition that too few Indigenous communities across Canada see themselves, their culture and their stories reflected in their schools and libraries.

The Foundation set about raising the Indigenous profile in learning centres, libraries, public and professional offices by launching the **IGNITE Indigenous Education Resource**, a portable book module stocked with Indigenous literature, largely by Indigenous authors, on culture, history, language and tradition.

Designed in accordance with many of the Calls to Action from the Truth and Reconciliation Commission, the Spirit of Education Foundation has placed 68 **IGNITE Indigenous Education Resource** bookshelves in 52 libraries, offices and community centres, to date.

Over 30% of our shipments are donated by individuals and corporations, going to the community recipient of their choice or where the greatest need exists.

The **IGNITE Indigenous Education Resource** has had a very positive impact in Indigenous communities and we welcome your participation in this initiative. Please contact us for details and personalization options with a minimum order of 10 units.

"If we don't have truth, we can never have reconciliation."
Rick McLean

FEATURES

- Sturdy and attractive, constructed of stained and sealed particle board
- Compact size, fits almost anywhere (5 ft H x 3 ft W x 2 ft D)
- Stands on 4 heavy duty casters for easy movement and storage
- Easily holds 25 books on each side
- Includes 25 "Indigenous Collection" spine labels and bookmarks

How powerful is the
IGNITE
Indigenous Education Resource?

"We welcomed the Ignite: The Spirit of Education Foundation portable bookshelves to the classrooms and common areas of our new facility. We also added a number of these to our other campuses and classrooms in communities in the Treaty #3 area. The ability to have our company logo and Anishinaabe name on the headboard of the shelving units is a great feature. Needless to say, the resources are relevant to our students, communities and staff and a great addition to our organization. Miigwech."

Brent Tookenay, CEO, Seven Generations Education Institute

"Our First Nations, Metis & Inuit collection is an important part of our commitment to making the promise of Truth and Reconciliation real in our community. The Indigenous bookshelf showcases the collection and has raised its profile with library users, catching people's attention and drawing them in to browse. The two-sided feature doubles its capacity and allows it to be placed in open areas instead of just up against a wall. We're very pleased with the look and function of this bookshelf."

Cathy Simpson, Chief Librarian & CEO, NOTL Public Library

"Education (in the form of residential schools) created many of the historic problems endured by Indigenous peoples, BUT education about their many contributions can help lead to a better future for all Canadians. The wonderful little bookshelf units filled with Indigenous titles provide large and small organizations an excellent opportunity to advance Reconciliation across Canada in a meaningful and modestly-priced way."

Maurice Switzer, Mississaugas of Alderville First Nation

GET INVOLVED!
CONTACT US TO LEARN HOW COMMUNITIES CAN BENEFIT
FROM THE **IGNITE** INDIGENOUS EDUCATION RESOURCE

IGNITE
THE SPIRIT OF EDUCATION
FOUNDATION INC.®

5418 Yonge Street, Suite 912, Toronto, Ontario M2N 6X4
Telephone: 416-488-7187   Email: ignitesef@gmail.com
Charitable Registration Number: 79396 8496 RR0001